Ritual Meanings in the Fifteenth-Century Motet

...h study of how motets were used and performed in
...his book dispels the mystery surrounding these
...al polyphony. It covers four areas of intense
...nd, the Veneto, Bruges, and Cambrai,
...Dunstaple, Forest, Ciconia, Grenon,
...ance, motets functioned as cere-
...sion through the streets of a
...l of a parish church or at
...irely vocal genre that
...Nosow outlines
...rporation of
...melodic
...and

Ritual Meanings in the Fifteenth-Century Motet

ROBERT NOSOW

 CAMBRIDGE
UNIVERSITY PRESS

CAMBRIDGE UNIVERSITY PRESS
Cambridge, New York, Melbourne, Madrid, Cape Town,
Singapore, São Paulo, Delhi, Tokyo, Mexico City

Cambridge University Press
The Edinburgh Building, Cambridge CB2 8RU, UK

Published in the United States of America by Cambridge University Press, New York

www.cambridge.org
Information on this title: www.cambridge.org/9780521193474

First published 2012

Printed in the United Kingdom at the University Press, Cambridge

A catalogue record for this publication is available from the British Library

Library of Congress Cataloguing in Publication data
Nosow, Robert Michael.
Ritual meanings in the fifteenth-century motet / Robert Nosow.
p.   cm.
Includes bibliographical references and index.
ISBN 978-0-521-19347-4 (hardback)
1. Motets – 15th century – History and criticism.   2. Music – Social aspects.   I. Title.
ML3275.N65   2012
782.2′609024 – dc23   2011041128

ISBN 978-0-521-19347-4 Hardback

For Cindy
Exultet celum laudibus aer ponthus et terra
musicorum nobilium societas preclara
psallentes

Contents

Illustrations

Figures

Music examples

Tables

Acknowledgments

When an individual scholar reaches the end of a long research project, he becomes acutely aware of the extent to which he forms part of a larger scholarly community. It is with great pleasure that I acknowledge the assistance and support of numerous scholars who contributed their expertise in the process of writing and research. I particularly wish to thank my readers, Patrick Macey, Janine Riveire, and Kathleen Sewright, as well as two anonymous reviewers for Cambridge University Press. Several scholars read or commented on portions of the work as I presented it in individual papers: J. Michael Allsen, Margaret Bent, Lyn A. Blanchfield, David Fallows, David Fiala, Paul F. Gehl, Michael Long, John Nádas, Sigmund Nosow, and Anne Walters Robertson. For work on Cambrai Cathedral, I benefitted greatly from the generosity of Barbara Haggh-Huglo, Alejandro Enrique Planchart, and Craig Wright. Nello Barbieri consulted on the Latin transcriptions and translations. Andrew Brown shared his broad knowledge and research in the archives in Bruges.

The project began in 1993–94 at Villa I Tatti, the Harvard University Center for Italian Renaissance Studies in Florence. Research at Villa I Tatti was supported by the National Endowment for the Humanities, the Francesco E. De Dombrowski Bequest, and the Robert Lehman Endowment Fund. Assunta Pisani, Librarian of the Biblioteca Berenson at Villa I Tatti, first sparked my interest in the motet as a communicative art form. Work in Bruges was undertaken in part thanks to a Janet Levy Research Grant in 2008 from the American Musicological Society. I wish to thank the Rev. Kurt Priem, Director of the Bisschoppelijk Archief in Bruges, and Hilde de Bruyne, Archivist of the Archief OCMW in Bruges. I am also grateful to the staff of the Music Library at the University of North Carolina at Chapel Hill for their manifold and kind assistance.

Introduction

As a dynamic force in the musical development of the fifteenth century, the motet has long been studied for the beauty of its polyphony and its prominent place in the manuscripts of the period. The genre has been associated with important churches, cathedrals, and princely courts across Western Europe. Motets rank among the most celebrated works of John Dunstaple, Guillaume Du Fay, Jacob Obrecht, and a host of other brilliant composers. Yet the motet also appears as a mysterious genre, both because of the multiplicity of forms it takes and because of the intractability of several related, unanswered questions. The investigation that follows addresses one central question: why did people write motets?

In the last two decades, scholarly explications of individual motets have aimed to elucidate their potential significance for the late medieval period. Working from the texts and music outward has yielded new insights into the relationships between motets and fifteenth-century culture.[1] Scholars inevitably have focused their attention on the few motets with overt ceremonial associations, the *Staatsmotetten*. At the same time, the ability to ground interpretive or theoretical approaches in a concrete understanding of how motets were used in performance has proven elusive. Chroniclers of the fifteenth century, despite their keen interest in matters of ritual, did not consider it important enough to describe in detail the music at events of high state, or at imposing ecclesiastical ceremonies. They rarely mention the performance of motets, expressing more interest in the personages who

---

[1] Among such studies for the first three quarters of the fifteenth century are J. E. Cumming, "Music for the Doge in Early Renaissance Venice," *Speculum* 67 (1992): 324–64; C. Wright, "Dufay's *Nuper rosarum flores*, King Solomon's Temple, and the Veneration of the Virgin," *Journal of the American Musicological Society* 47 (1994): 395–441; R. C. Wegman, "From Maker to Composer: Improvisation and Musical Authorship in the Low Countries, 1450–1500," *Journal of the American Musicological Society* 49 (1996): 471–77, on Loyset Compère's *Omnium bonorum plenum*; R. Nosow, "Du Fay and the Cultures of Renaissance Florence," in *Hearing the Motet*, ed. D. Pesce (New York and Oxford: Oxford University Press, 1997), 104–21; R. C. Wegman, "For Whom the Bell Tolls: Reading and Hearing in Busnoy's *Anthoni usque limina*," in *Hearing the Motet*, 122–41; P. Weller, "Rites of Passage: *Nove cantum melodie*, the Burgundian Court, and Binchois's Early Career," in *Binchois Studies*, ed. A. Kirkman and D. Slavin (Oxford and New York: Oxford University Press, 2000), 49–83; and C. Saucier, "Acclaiming Advent and *Adventus* in Johannes Brassart's Motet for Frederick III," *Early Music History* 27 (2008): 137–80.

1

attended and the number of horsemen they brought with them. Pay records, charters, and liturgical books that offer specific evidence concerning motets are few and far between. Moreover, the types of record that yield information vary broadly across geographies. These circumstances have made the social aspects of motet performance difficult to study and characterize.[2] Given the thick ties of community that were normal in the fifteenth century, however, an assessment of the social environment of the motet becomes crucial to realizing its latent meanings. Indeed, all motets of the fifteenth century originated as ceremonial vehicles, and cannot easily be separated from the rituals of which they formed part.

The present volume is organized in four double chapters. Each double chapter comprises one chapter devoted to historical evidence for motet performance, followed by a theoretical discussion based on the same material. The odd-numbered chapters offer case studies from four different geographical areas: England, the Veneto, Bruges, and Cambrai. They focus on the basic context for motets, addressing journalistic questions of who, when, where, and for what audience. In many instances, the use of a motet can be securely documented, but the work itself does not survive. In other cases, a specific work fits clearly within a given context, but not all the details of performance are known. The discussion of individual motets necessarily makes connections of varying strength between music and the larger ceremony. But in most instances, the ceremony itself can be reconstructed in considerable detail. To the extent possible, the documentary chapters also address questions of performance practice, particularly the specific forces denoted in the records and their physical placement within ritual space.

Each of the even-numbered chapters takes up a different interpretive point of view. "The motet as ritual" draws on anthropological and sociological definitions of ritual actions, which set a foundation for the rest of the volume. "The motet as ritual embassy" treats motets with newly composed texts that display ambassadorial language or rhetorical organization. "Contemplation," on the other hand, primarily treats motets with pre-existent texts that lend themselves to meditative purposes. "Choir and community" addresses the heterogeneous nature of the genre and the dynamics of style transference and change in response to complex social environments,

---

[2] L. Lütteken, *Guillaume Dufay und die isorhythmische Motette: Gattungstradition und Werkcharakter an der Schwelle zur Neuzeit*, Schriften zur Musikwissenschaft aus Münster 4 (Hamburg and Eisenach: K. D. Wagner, 1993), 306, concludes "dafür ist der historische Beweggrund ihrer Entstehung nur aüßerst selten faßbar."

together with questions of reception and audience. The study as a whole does not attempt to explain the broader changes in motet style during the fifteenth century, but rather to relate individual motets to these larger currents. Each of the double chapters rests on the interdependence of contrasting methodologies, which approach the central question of the study from different directions. The final chapter serves as a coda to the whole.

The study covers the first three quarters of the fifteenth century, 1400–75. The oldest document discussed here dates to 1367 in Cambrai, and the latest to 1489 in Bruges. The first two decades of the fifteenth century saw an increase in the numbers of motets that were composed and copied into manuscripts. The earliest motet treated here, *Albane misse celitus/Albane doctor maxime* by Johannes Ciconia, dates from 1406. All but one of Ciconia's motets were composed in Padua between 1401 and 1412; in some ways they mark the end of an era in Italy. New motet styles, including the song motet, began to appear in the 1420s, leading to the wide variety of styles, or subgenres, characteristic of the period. The terminus of the study coincides with the death of Guillaume Du Fay in 1474, marked by the performance of his last motet, *Ave regina celorum III*. The musical scene began to change rapidly just at this time, as a new generation of composers from northern France and the Low Countries – Loyset Compère, Gaspar van Weerbecke, Josquin des Prez, Jacob Obrecht, Heinrich Isaac – came into maturity. They brought Latin vocal polyphony to an unprecedented level of intensity. Around 1475, the motet began to take on forms typical of the late fifteenth and early sixteenth centuries, heralded by Du Fay's late motet. The social background of the motet changed, as well, as witnessed by the increasing number and similarity of foundations in the churches of Bruges.[3] As polyphonic music became more widespread, so did attacks on it increase.[4] Rather than extending the investigation to the late fifteenth century, clarity and concision call for a natural terminus coinciding with these historical trends.

Theoretical definitions of the motet from the fifteenth century tend to be relatively sparse and unhelpful, occasioning considerable debate with respect to the boundaries of the genre. Scholars have sought guidance from

[3] D. Salokar, "*Ad augmentationem divini cultus*: Pious Foundations and Vespers Motets in the Church of Our Lady in Bruges," in *Musicologie en Archiefonderzoek*, ed. B. Haggh (Brussels: Archives et Bibliothèques de Belgique, 1994), 316–17.
[4] R. C. Wegman, *The Crisis of Music in Early Modern Europe 1470–1530*, chapter 2, "Polyphony and Its Enemies: Before and After the 1470s." Wegman, ibid., 39, also points out that, in some cases, war and famine led to a decrease in support during the last two decades of the century.

manuscript sources, which often group motets together in distinct sections.[5] It will not be necessary to rehearse the dimensions of the problem here, since it has been treated at length elsewhere.[6] One theoretical definition that has been largely overlooked, however, is that of Paulus Paulirinus de Praga, in the *Liber viginti artium*, a treatise devoted to the twenty liberal arts. Paulus is an original thinker and observer when it comes to music, as witness his elegant description of the motet:[7]

Mutetus est cantus mensuralis per triplum vadens, in quo discantus habet textum proprium et medium eciam (non) habet textum proprium diversificatum a discanto, sed tamen uterque textus una cum suis notis ita bene concordat, quod haec difformitas uniformitatem videtur parere; tenor autem nullum textum habet, sed occurit utrique suaviter se inmiscendo.

A motet is a mensural song proceeding in three voices, in which the discant has its own text and the middle voice even has a characteristic text differentiated from the discant. But nevertheless, the text of each concords so well together with its own notes, that this lack of conformity seems to appear as uniformity. The tenor, however, has no text, but it replies to both, sweetly intertwined with each.

Paulus describes a double-texted motet in which each of the three voices occupies a different vocal range – high, middle, low. He further conveys an image in which text and melody are closely united. The word *difformitas* could also be translated as "double form," in contrast to *uniformitatem*. Paulus wrote the *Liber viginti artium* in Bohemia circa 1459–63, but his definition appears to be older;[8] the word *non* added to the sentence, either by Paulus himself or by the scribe, changes the entire meaning. It disrupts

---

[5] Among the manuscripts with significant motet sections are: Turin, Biblioteca nazionale universitaria, MS J.II.9; Bologna, Museo internazionale e biblioteca della musica, MS Q15; Cambridge, University Library, MS Add. 4435 and Oxford, Bodleian Library, MS Don b. 32, "Royal English Choirbook"; Bologna, Biblioteca universitaria, MS 2216; Modena, Biblioteca Estense universitaria, MS α.X.1.11; Lucca, Archivio di Stato, MS 238, Pisa, Biblioteca arcivescovile "Cardinale Pietro Maffi," Cartella 11/III, and Lucca, Archivio arcivescovile, MS 97, "Lucca Choirbook"; Prague, Památník Národního Písemnictví, Strahovská Knihovna, D.G.IV.47, "Strahov Codex."

[6] See R. M. Nosow, "The Florid and Equal-Discantus Motet Styles of Fifteenth-Century Italy" (Ph.D. diss., University of North Carolina at Chapel Hill, 1992), chapter 2, "Genre and Style"; Lütteken, *Guillaume Dufay und die isorhythmische Motette*; J. E. Cumming, *The Motet in the Age of Du Fay* (Cambridge University Press, 1999), 7–62; A. Kirkman, "The Invention of the Cyclic Mass," *Journal of the American Musicological Society* 54 (2001): 5–12.

[7] Ed. and trans. in C. E. Brewer, "The Introduction of the Ars Nova into East Central Europe: A Study of Late Medieval Polish Sources" (Ph.D. diss., City University of New York, 1984), 431–37, at 435.

[8] Ibid., 218–19.

the parallel phrases, "discantus habet textum proprium et medium eciam habet textum proprium." The definition now refers to a single-texted work in which the discantus and *medius*, but not the tenor, carry the same words. The text of each "concords...well together with its own notes." With the addition of a single word, the description of the motet is brought up to date with respect to the stylistic currents of the mid-fifteenth century. It matches in many respects the widely distributed song motets of Johannes Touront, who was active in Bohemia at just this time.

The four case studies take an inclusive approach toward motet performance. For periods of weak – and evolving – genre definition, it proves helpful not to become too doctrinaire. Motet composers deliberately borrowed from other genres or blurred the divisions between them, for both social and artistic reasons (see Chapter 8). As a result, some of the most interesting works occur on the peripheries of the genre. The English motet was an exception, for it maintained its traditional identity through the first four decades of the century. It featured two or more texts sung simultaneously, a *cantus firmus* tenor fashioned from plainchant, and organization in proportions, or ratios of time. English antiphon settings, or cantilenas, constituted a separate genre, typically in three voices with a single text. They often carried the *cantus firmus* in a single voice, but ornamented in such a way as to create a flowing melody. English scribes copied motets and antiphons separately, confirming their generic distinction.[9] But in continental manuscripts, English antiphons appear side by side with motets, denoting a different reception history, one that that allies them with the new types of motet that were created in the early and mid-fifteenth century.

Motets were performed for a fascinating array of ceremonies during the fifteenth century, ceremonies that place them at the enactments of royal and ducal power, civic identity, or ecclesiastical rites. These works speak of an age in which church and polity were inextricably intertwined, for both were subject to divine favor. As Paulus Paulirinus de Praga writes, "with praises of God, the cantilena connects the earth-born with the heaven dwellers, gladdens the mournful, and . . . calls forth with harmonious sweetness to the heaven, earth, seas, and turning stars."[10] Our hearing and understanding of

---

[9] G. Curtis and A. Wathey, "Fifteenth-Century English Liturgical Music: A List of the Surviving Repertory," *Royal Musical Association Research Chronicle* 27 (1994): 1–69.

[10] Brewer, "The Introduction of the Ars Nova," 431: "Deum tum protunc laudibus terrigenas nectit celicolis, tristes exhilarat et celum, terram, mara et sidera volventes . . . armoniata provocat suavitate."

these splendid sonic remnants of the past can only be enriched by a stronger knowledge of their actual use, whether at a baptismal font, in the streets of a town, or at the high altar of a cathedral. We then place ourselves in a position to ask the questions that puzzle us most, and to ponder their possible answers.

1 | Motets in the chronicles of Henry V

When Henry V of England was crowned at the age of twenty-five, on March 21, 1413, he had already taken an active part in consolidating royal power against rebels in Wales. A shrewd, capable ruler and military commander, he quickly undertook to strengthen the crown and to plan a military campaign in defense of his hereditary rights in France. The overwhelming English victory over a superior French force at the Battle of Agincourt in October 1415, with Henry V at the head of the army, ranks as the most heralded British victory prior to the defeat of the Spanish Armada in 1588. As part of his overall policy, he worked internally with Parliament to secure his position vis-à-vis opposition forces, and externally via foreign diplomacy. Most notably, he collaborated with Sigismund, King of the Romans, both in negotiating with the French and in efforts to end the Great Schism at the Council of Constance (1414–18).

The historical chronicles characteristic of the period relate directly or indirectly to these diplomatic efforts. The central historical source, the *Gesta Henrici Quinti*, written by an unknown chaplain of the Chapel Royal, follows in remarkable detail the first years of Henry V's reign, from March 1413 to July 1417. It was composed with the clear intent to persuade other authorities, both domestic and foreign, of the righteousness of the king's cause. It pays particular attention to the liturgy, including chant, and its role in the life of the king. Henry V himself knew how to sing and how to compose, leaving Mass movements in the royal choirbook, Old Hall, attributed to "Roy Henry."[1] Other chronicles, in Latin or English, similarly extol the virtues and exploits of the young king. The most important of these, the *Liber metricus de Henrico Quinto*, written by Thomas of Elmham, is particularly helpful for understanding the liturgy of the Chapel Royal. Through them, we gain an unusually strong view of the role that polyphonic music played within the overall policy of Henry V.

---

[1] London, British Library, MS Add. 57950, "Old Hall": Sanctus, fols. 12v–13r; Gloria, fol. 80v.

The daily procession in the Chapel Royal

Although the king's household chapel, or Chapel Royal, often accompanied English sovereigns in their travels and even their military campaigns, its normal seat was the private chapel of the king, St. Stephen's Chapel at Westminster Palace.[2] Each day, the royal chaplains were charged with observing High Mass and the four principal canonical offices – Matins, Lauds, Vespers, and Compline. Mass was preceded by a daily procession that began in the choir and circled the chapel before re-entering the choir at the west door. A three-voice motet in the Old Hall manuscript, *Alma proles/Christi miles/Ab inimicis nostris* by John Cooke, may have been composed for that procession.[3] Cooke was a member of the Chapel Royal between mid-1413 and July 1419, and accompanied the king to Agincourt.[4] He and Leonel Power are the only two composers to appear in both the first and second layers of Old Hall, which in its later stage was employed in the Chapel Royal.[5] The first layer originated in the chapel of Henry V's brother Thomas, Duke of Clarence, but the book moved to the Chapel Royal at least by the time of Clarence's death in March 1421.

The indirect evidence for the performance of *Alma proles/Christi miles/Ab inimicis nostris* stems from the chapel of the king's son, Henry VI. In 1448–49, William Say, Dean of the Chapel Royal, wrote the *Liber regie capelle* for the benefit of a Portuguese knight of the Order of the Garter, Count Alvaro Vaz d'Almada.[6] The resulting book is as much a description of royal ceremony as a manual for the Chapel Royal. According to the *Liber regie capelle*, a special procession and litany were made every Wednesday and Friday "for the state of the king and queen and the peace of the realm."[7] This parallels the daily procession and litany before Mass in the chapel of

---

[2] F. Ll. Harrison, *Music in Medieval Britain*, 4th edn. (Buren, the Netherlands: Frits Knuf, 1980), 19, cautions that St. Stephen's Chapel also had its own college, consisting of "a dean, twelve canons, thirteen priest-vicars, four clerks and six choristers."

[3] Fols. 90v–91r. See the inventory in A. Hughes and M. Bent, "The Old Hall Manuscript," *Musica Disciplina* 21 (1967): 97–147.

[4] M. Bent, "Cooke, John," in *The New Grove Dictionary of Music and Musicians*, 2nd edn. (London: Macmillan, 2000).

[5] M. Bent, "Old Hall Manuscript," in *The New Grove Dictionary of Music and Musicians*, 2nd edn. (London: Macmillan, 2000).

[6] *Liber regie capelle: A Manuscript in the Biblioteca Publica, Evora*, ed. W. Ullmann, Henry Bradshaw Society 92 (London: Henry Bradshaw Society, 1961), 9–11.

[7] Ibid., 59: "pro statu Regis ac Regine et pace Regni." In the Sarum rite, Wednesdays and Fridays in Lent were the prescribed days for the procession and litany before Mass.

Henry V, which the *Gesta Henrici Quinti* calls "the customary procession and litany with which he had long been wont to invoke divine aid."[8]

The twice-weekly procession described in the *Liber regie capelle*, led by a cross and two candlebearers, begins:

cum antiphona, precibus, genuflexionibus et psalmis precedentibus, ut in processionali continentur, ac cum communi letania subsequente, presente aliquando rege in processione, et raro deficiente Regina, magna parte domus regie comitante, sicque processione ad Capellam redeunte, ac percantata per Capellam solenniter antiphona *Ab inimicis*, et cetera, ut habetur in processionali, et dicta oracione de omnibus sanctis, statim per rectores chori incipitur missa de die, quam chorus prosequitur

in the first place with antiphon, prayers, genuflexions, and psalms, as are contained in the processional books, and with the common litany following. Sometimes the king is present in the procession, and rarely is the queen absent, the majority of the royal household taking part. Thus, with the procession returned to the chapel, the chapel also solemnly sings through the antiphon *Ab inimicis*, et cetera, as is found in the processional book, and a prayer is said of All Saints. Immediately the rulers of the choir begin the Mass of the day, which is continued by the choir.[9]

Since the work of Manfred Bukofzer in 1950, the tenor of Cooke's motet has been identified as a verse from the litany, said in time of war.[10] *Ab inimicis nostris* is the first of eight verses, all with the same melody. An anonymous three-voice setting of the odd-numbered verses appears in Cambridge, Magdalene College, MS Pepys 1236 (fols. 46v–47r). The contratenor ornaments, or paraphrases, the chant differently each time, most likely in alternation with the unadorned plainchant in the even-numbered verses. Since the manuscript dates to circa 1460–65, the setting shows that the conclusion of the litany could be elaborated as a separate musical item.[11] Moreover, that same chant, *Ab inimicis nostris*, also served as a processional antiphon in the Chapel Royal.[12] The *Liber regie capelle* demonstrates that *Ab inimicis nostris* was appropriate to accompany the procession on a regular basis, not just in time of war. The specific liturgical elements cited correspond,

---

[8]　*Gesta Henrici Quinti: The Deeds of Henry V*, ed. and trans. F. Taylor and J. S. Roskell (Oxford: Clarendon Press, 1975), 150–51: "solitas processionem et letaniam quibus usus est diu ante pro invocando divino auxilio."

[9]　*Liber regie capelle*, 59–60.

[10]　M. Bukofzer, *Studies in Medieval & Renaissance Music* (New York: Norton, 1950), 68.

[11]　S. R. Charles, "The Provenance and Date of the Pepys Ms 1236," *Musica Disciplina* 16 (1962): 57–71.

[12]　M. Williamson, "Royal Image-Making and Textual Interplay in Gilbert Banaster's *O Maria et Elizabeth*," *Early Music History* 19 (2000): 247 n. 36.

in abbreviated form, to those prescribed for Rogation Days in the Sarum Processional.[13] The litany is said as the procession moves through the nave of the church and re-enters the choir. The *Liber regie capelle* then adds the antiphon *Ab inimicis*, finishing with a versicle and the requisite prayer to All Saints, *Presta quesumus*, said by the priest at the choir steps.

Cooke's motet fulfills the same objects as those specified in the *Liber regie capelle*, namely to entreat divine protection for the sovereign and realm. Both motetus and triplum have ten rhymed stanzas, with twenty-one syllables per stanza in the motetus and twenty-six syllables per stanza in the triplum (Figure 1.1). Scholars have had difficulty in associating the work with a specific time or event because of the nature of the texts.[14] The triplum, *Alma proles*, in the first place petitions the Virgin Mary for compassion, drawing on the iconography of the fountain of grace, centering on the phrase "Open the course of the font." The fountain of grace appears in the *Madonna of the Fountain* from the workshop of Jan van Eyck, where Virgin and Child are surrounded by a paradisiacal garden (see Illustration 6.2).[15] In the last two stanzas, the triplum invokes Christ, with reference to the Father. The allusions to the Madonna's majesty and splendor make a fitting conclusion to a prayer on behalf of the Chapel Royal.

In contrast, the motetus incipit, *Christi miles*, hails St. George as the type of the warrior saint. A leaf from the Bedford Missal illustrates the devotion of the royal house (Illustration 1.1). The brother of the king, John, Duke of Bedford, kneels before St. George with his hands clasped in prayer. He wears a black tunic surrounded by a heavily embroidered silk cloak. A prayer book or psalter lies open before him, on a blue, white, and red banner with the ducal motto *A vous entier*. The saint is arrayed as a knight of the Order of

---

[13] *Liber regie capelle*, 59. The Use of Sarum, prevalent across much of England, pertains to Salisbury Cathedral. In its normal position, *Ab inimicis nostris* represents an addition to the third litany in Rogationtide, for Wednesday on the eve of Ascension Day. See the *Processionale ad usum Sarum*, ed. R. Pynson (London, 1502; facsimile reprint, Clarabricken, Clifden, County Kilkenny: Boethius Press, 1980), fols. 108r–111r, with an illustration at fol. 95v. The texts are transcribed in *Processionale ad usum insignis ac praeclarae ecclesiae Sarum*, ed. W. G. Henderson (Leeds: M'Corquodale, 1882; facsimile reprint, Farnborough, Hants.: Gregg International, 1969).

[14] R. Bowers, "Cooke, John," in *Die Musik in Geschichte und Gegenwart*, 2nd edn. (Kassel and New York: Bärenreiter, 1998–), comments, "Offentsichtlich entstand die Motette im Kontext des Wiederaufflammen des Krieges mit Frankreich in den Jahren 1414 bis 1415 und 1417 bis 1421, obgleich der Text in keinem notwendigen Zusammenhang mit bestimmten Ereignissen zu stehen scheint." Bent, "Sources of the Old Hall Music," *Proceedings of the Royal Musical Association* 94 (1967–68): 23, suggests that the motet could have been composed for "the rogation days in 1415, 6–8 May."

[15] On the iconography of the fountain of grace, see G. Kipling, *Enter the King: Theatre, Liturgy, and Ritual in the Medieval Civic Triumph* (Oxford: Clarendon Press, 1998), 163–67.

Triplum

Alma proles regia	Bountiful, regal daughter,
celi imperatrix,	empress of heaven,
omni plena gracia	full of every grace,
mundi dominatrix.	mistress of the world,
Que misericordie	Who hast given birth
fontem geniusti,	to the fount of pity,
ac tocius gracie	and hast brought forth
rivum peperisti.	the channel of complete grace;
Venam fontis aperi	Open the course of the font,
mater pietatis,	mother of piety,
ut qui sumus miseri	so that we wretched ones,
mersi in peccatis.	immersed in sin,
Consequamur veniam	May attain forgiveness;
et da prece pia,	and by thy holy entreaty
veram penitenciam	grant us true penitence
dum sumus in via.	while we are on the journey.
Quid agemus miseri	What shall we sinners do
opem si negabis?	if thou deniest us help?
Heu, perimus perditi	Alas! We shall perish,
te dum elongabis.	lost while you are aloof.
Nescit tua pietas	Your compassion
succursum negare,	could not deny succor
illis quos humilitas	to those compelled by their humility
cogit postulare.	to request it.
O immensa bonitas	O boundless charity
matris salvatoris,	of the Savior's mother,
o magna securitas	O profound reassurance
pii petitoris.	for the pious petitioner;
Hec vota petencium	She is accustomed
solet prevenire,	to anticipate our prayers
atque penitencium	and to soothe the grief
luctus delinire.	of penitents.
Jhesu serva servulos	O Jesus, save the servants
tue pie matris,	of thy holy mother,
quos a labe liberos	those servants, freed from stain
in conspectu Patris.	in the sight of the Father,

Figure 1.1. John Cooke, *Alma proles/Christi miles/Ab inimicis nostris*

Dones frui gloria	Whom mayst thou grant to enjoy
tante majestatis,	the glory of such majesty,
quo regnas in secula	by which thou reignest forever
regno claritatis.	in the kingdom of the splendor.

Motetus

Christi miles inclite	Renowned soldier of Christ,
Georgi sanctissime	most holy George,
qui es decus militum.	who art the glory of warriors,

Celum nunc inhabitas	Who now dwellest in heaven
ubi tua sanctitas,	where in the choir of martyrs
choro fulget martirum.	thy holiness shines;

Quicquid tu oraveris,	Whatever thou prayest,
impetrare poteris,	thou wilt, by thy worthiness,
propter tua merita.	be able to accomplish.

Regnum serves Anglie	Guardest thou the realm of England,
que non ruat misere	that it may not wretchedly collapse
nostra per demerita.	because of our unworthiness.

Matris tocius gracie	Entreat mercy of the mother
instes tu clemencie	of all grace,
ferat ut auxilium.	that she may bring help,

Terram suam protegat,	May protect her country,
regemque custodiat	and guard the king
ab incursu hostium.	from the invasion of enemies.

Virgo decus virginum	O virgin, glory of virgins,
regi sis refugium,	be a refuge to the king,
quem serves ab hostibus.	whom thou protectest from his enemies.

Quicquid vis ut faciat	Whatever thou desirest that he do,
semper tibi placeat	may he always be pleasing to thee
in ipsius actibus.	in his deeds.

O columpne auree,	O golden pillars,
pacem veram poscite,	urgently request true peace
nostris in temporibus.	in our times,

Date seu victoriam,	And give us victory,
et post mortem gloriam	and after death glory
regnis in celestibus.	in the heavenly kingdom.

Tenor

| Ab inimicis nostris | Defend us, Christ, |
| defende nos, Christe. | from our enemies. |

Figure 1.1. (*cont.*)

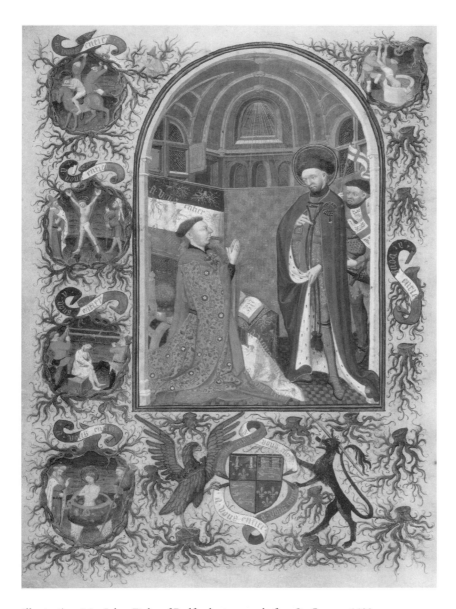

Illustration 1.1. John, Duke of Bedford, at prayer before St. George, 1423

the Garter, with the badge of the order on his chest. A squire attends him, bearing his helmet, his shield, and a pennant with St. George's cross, red on a field of white. A sheathed sword hangs from the squire's belt. The miniature clearly demonstrates the patterning of the duke's knightly virtues on those of the heavenly saint, who almost frowns as he inclines his head forward.

In a similar attitude of supplication, the motetus voice addresses St. George as the "Renowned soldier of Christ / . . . / who art the glory of warriors." It asks that he "Entreat mercy of the mother / of all grace, / that she may bring help, / May protect her country / and guard the king / from the invasion of enemies." Turning to the Virgin Mary, it continues, "glory of virgins, / be a refuge to the king, / whom thou protectest from his enemies." These lines explicate or gloss the tenor, which reads, "Defend us, Christ, from our enemies." The cogent imagery reflects the charged atmosphere during the wars with France. The motetus moves beyond the ideas of the tenor, however, when it requests, "Whatever thou desirest that he do, / may he always be pleasing to thee / in his deeds." Addressing both St. George and St. Mary in the final two stanzas, it goes on to "urgently request true peace / in our times." The confluence of these appeals, to the Virgin Mary, St. George, and Christ, fulfills the stated goals of the procession and litany.

Henry VI was less than nine months old when he inherited the crown in September 1422, and his father's chaplains continued in the service of the infant monarch. The Dean of the Chapel Royal, Robert Gilbert, remained in office between 1417 and 1432.[16] Given the inherent stability of the liturgy and the medieval tendency toward institutional stasis, if one assumes that liturgical elements persisted from the chapel of Henry V to that of Henry VI, then that same antiphon, *Ab inimicis nostris*, may have concluded the procession before Mass at the time of Henry V.[17] Cooke's *Alma proles/Christi miles/Ab inimicis nostris* combines the antiphon with two poems that entreat divine favor for the king and realm, addressed to the saints most often invoked by Henry V (Figure 1.1). The motet could well have been sung in the procession before Mass in the chapel of Henry V, particularly on

---

[16] A. Wathey, *Music in the Royal and Noble Households in Late Medieval England: Studies of Sources and Patronage* (New York and London: Garland, 1989), 284.

[17] The Chapel Royal of Henry VI also preserved three of the six memorials after Compline, listed in Table 1.1: those to the Trinity, St. George, and St. Mary. On the schedule of the daily Mass and offices under Henry VI, see the *Liber regie capelle*, 58. Compline directly followed Vespers: "Deinde circa decimam horam altam missam, circa horam vero quartam post nonam vesperas cum completorio immediate sequente . . . Preterea omni nocte per annum nisi in tribus noctibus ante Pascha, fiunt in Capella Regis post completorium dictum immediate tres memorie solennes, prima de Trinitate, de qua est specialiter Capella supradicta, secunda de sancto Georgio, et tercia de gloriosa ac beata Virgine, cum versiculis et collectis sive oracionibus pertinentibus." ("Thereupon, High Mass about the tenth hour [past sunrise]; Vespers four hours past None, with Compline immediately following . . . Moreover, every night of the year, except the three nights before Easter, in the chapel of the King, immediately after Compline were said three solemn memorials, first of the Trinity, of which the aforesaid chapel is especially, second of St. George, and third of the glorious and Blessed Virgin, with the pertinent versicles and collects or prayers.")

Sundays. It would have been performed at the steps of the choir, followed by the daily psalm and respond at the high altar.

Alma proles/Christi miles/Ab inimicis nostris is an accomplished work that incorporates typical elements of English motet style (Example 1.1). It projects a sharply defined external structure, within which exists a certain freedom of sonority and rhythm. The structure begins with the tenor, which borrows its pitches from the unmeasured plainchant. Cooke endows the first ten notes of the chant with a precise rhythm in note values of longs and breves; this rhythm is then repeated for the next ten notes, a technique known as *talea*, which dates to the thirteenth century. All twenty notes are then repeated, including rests, but in diminished note values worth only two-thirds as much as in the first section. The twenty-note *cantus firmus* (or "fixed song") is then sung once more, again with the notes diminished to two-thirds of their prior value. Cooke needed to notate the tenor only once; the three mensuration signs that follow dictate how it should be sung each time. The first long G, which originally was worth eighteen minims (the smallest note value), diminishes to twelve minims in the second section and only eight in the third. The overall proportions of the motet thus incorporate six *taleae* in the unusual ratio $9 : 9 : 6 : 6 : 4 : 4$. In Pythagorean terms, 6 represents the geometric mean of 9 and 4. The first and second sections total 540 minims, while the second and third sections total 360 minims, each of which represents a Trinitarian number, a matter returned to below. These mathematical ratios govern the precise length of time required to sing each section of the motet.

The rhythmic structure of the motetus and triplum voices is designed to fit neatly into the parameters outlined by the tenor, in a way that illustrates the uses of rhythmic notation in the period (Figure 1.2). In order to declaim the texts properly, the upper voices employ smaller note values in breves, semibreves, and minims.[18] The two *taleae* in each statement of the tenor coincide with two *taleae* in the motetus and triplum. The first two *taleae* are in perfect time, major prolation (⊙), with the breve worth three semibreves and the semibreve three minims (3×3), the smallest nominal note value. The mensuration then changes in the next two *taleae*, mandating different relationships among the note values. The motetus and triplum change to imperfect time, minor prolation (C), with the breve divided into two semibreves and the semibreve into two minims (2×2). The tenor, however,

---

[18] *Quatuor principalia*, in *Scriptorum de musica medii aevi nova series a Gerbertina altera*, ed. E. de Coussemaker, 4 vols. (Paris: Durand, 1864–76), vol. IV, 263. In Figure 1.2, the breves are square-shaped, the semibreves diamond-shaped, and the minims have stems.

Example 1.1. Cooke, *Alma proles/Christi miles/Ab inimicis nostris*, third *talea*

BREVIS IMPERFECTA DE MINORI PROLATIONE

BREVIS PERFECTA DE MINORI PROLATIONE

BREVIS IMPERFECTA DE MAJORI PROLATIONE

BREVIS PERFECTA DE MAJORI PROLATIONE

Figure 1.2. Anonymous, *Quatuor principalia*. The four divisions of the breve:
(1) imperfect time, minor prolation: C; (2) Perfect time, minor prolation: O;
(3) imperfect time, major prolation: C; (4) perfect time, major prolation: ⊙

has a different mensuration, perfect time, minor prolation (O), with the
breve worth three semibreves and the semibreve two minims (3 × 2). In the
last two *taleae*, the mensurations change again, with the motetus and triplum
now in imperfect time, major prolation (C), where the breve is worth two
semibreves and the semibreve three minims (2 × 3). The tenor meanwhile
changes to imperfect time, minor prolation (C), again contrasting with the
other voices. The rhythmic changes in the upper voices are clearly audible

to the listener during the tenor rests at the beginning of each *talea* (Example 1.1). Further, because the tenor statements become proportionally shorter and the note values smaller, the rhythmic velocity of the motet increases toward the end. As its speed increases, the *cantus firmus* itself becomes more recognizable, emerging from the sonic background into sharper focus.

While the tenor is sung at the pitch of the original plainchant, covering a mere sixth, the motetus extends upward a tenth, spanning f–a'. The triplum, or highest voice, lies a fifth higher than does the motetus, c'–d''. The music reinforces the G final that begins and ends the *cantus firmus*, which itself is sung three times; every cadence falls on G or A. The long notes of the *cantus firmus* allow for a variety of rhythms and sonorities to be sung against it, including passing dissonance, with the motetus singing both above and below the tenor. Neither motetus nor triplum projects a strong lyrical character; instead, sonic interest inheres in the shifting sonorities and contrasting word-sounds. In comparison to unadorned plainchant, which moves freely through time in unison voices, the motet reconciles the conflicting mensurations between the tenor on the one hand and the motetus and triplum on the other, in strict obedience to mathematical principles. The perfect, geometric proportions and interlocking mensurations frame simultaneous messages of penitence and supplication to higher powers.

The daily memorials of Henry V

On August 21, 1416, shortly after the signing of the Treaty of Canterbury with Sigismund, King of the Romans, word of another English victory against the French reached Henry V at the seacoast in Kent. John, Duke of Bedford, brother of the king, had captained the English navy in the Battle of the Seine, the triumph coming less than a year after the Battle of Agincourt. According to the *Gesta Henrici Quinti*, the king "did not dismount from his horse until he had brought this news to the emperor at Canterbury."[19] A Mass of thanksgiving followed at Canterbury Cathedral.

A manuscript source of the Latin *Brut* relates how the king augmented the daily services in his chapel in response to the naval triumph:

---

[19] *Gesta*, 150–51. There is no solid justification for the supposition that any motets were sung at the Mass of Thanksgiving in Canterbury Cathedral, however, for which the only music specified is the *Te Deum*.

Et quia ea fuerat optenta victoria feriis Assumpcionis beate Marie virginis mandauit vt singulis diebus vite sue in eius sacrario Antiphona cum versiculo et collecta in commemoriacione beate virginis semel a capellanis et sacerdotibus eius decantaretur.

And because the victory was gained on the day of the Assumption of the Blessed Virgin Mary, [the king] ordered that on each day of his own life an antiphon with versicle and collect ever be sung by the chaplains and sacerdotes in his chapel, in commemoration of the Blessed Virgin.[20]

The *Gesta Henrici Quinti* offers a detailed description of the regimen of daily liturgies mandated by Henry V, shown in Table 1.1: first, after the procession and litany, and preceding Mass, a psalm with respond, different for each day of the week; second, directly after Mass, three memorials, to the Trinity, to the Assumption of the Virgin, "on whose feast the naval victory had been yielded to the English," and to St. George, "our champion and protector"; third, following Vespers and Compline, a set of six pre-existing memorials, to the Trinity, the Holy Spirit, St. Edward the Confessor, St. John the Baptist, St. George, and St. Mary. These liturgies were "ordained from that time forward, to God's praise and in glorification of His marvellous doings."[21] Their elaborateness indicates that Henry V took some pains to promulgate them in consultation with his chaplains and the ecclesiastical establishment at Canterbury.

The Holy Trinity, to which the Chapel of St. Stephen is dedicated, receives first position in all three sets of memorials established by Henry V.[22] The weekly cycle of psalms with responds was probably sung in plainsong, beginning on Sunday with the psalm *Cantemus* and respond *Summe Trinitati*, and ending on Saturday with the psalm *Exultavit cor meum in Domino* and respond *Benedicamus* (Table 1.1). Settings of such responsory texts are

---

[20] C. L. Kingsford, ed., *English Historical Literature in the Fifteenth Century* (Oxford: Clarendon Press, 1913), 329. Almost exactly the same wording appears in T. L. de Foro-Juliensis, *Vita Henrici Quinti* (Oxford: Theatro Sheldoniano, 1716), 26: "Postera die cum jam omnia regia sententia perfecisset, dux navim ascendit, & cum captis rostratis & captivis navalibus militibus in Angliam optatissimo vento tranquillissimoque mari proficiscitur. Rex autem ut fratrem cum tanta victoria vidit redeuntem, cognito prius quo fuerat ordine pugnatum, & quid in omnibus gestum erat, gratias agens immortali Deo, quoniam ea fuerat obtenta victoria feriis assumptionis beatae Mariae Virginis, mandavit ut singulis diebus vitae suae in sacrario suo Antiphona cum versiculo et collecta in commemoratione prefatae Virginis semel a capellanis & sacerdotibus suis decantaretur."

[21] *Gesta*, 150–53.

[22] The *Liber regie capelle*, 61–62, explicitly confirms the dedication of the chapel in its reference to the feast of "Sancte Trinitatis, que est festum loci in Capella Regis Anglie" ("the Holy Trinity, that is the feast of the site of the Chapel of the King of England").

Table 1.1. Daily services in the Chapel Royal of Henry V

Gesta Henrici Quinti	*Liber metricus*	Motet or anthem
[Matins]		
[Lauds]		
Procession and litany		Cooke, *Alma Proles/Christi miles/Ab inimicis*
Memorial to the Trinity:	**Memorial to the Trinity:**	
Sunday: Psalm *Cantemus*	(Same weekly order)	
Respond *Summe Trinitati*		
Monday: Psalm *Jubilate*		
Respond *Benedictus*		
Tuesday: Psalm *Confitemini*		
Respond *Quis Deus*		
Wednesday: Psalm *Laudate nomen Domini*		
Respond *Gloria Patri*		
Thursday: Psalm *Benedicite omnia*		
Respond *Honor virtus*		
Friday: Psalm *Laudate Dominum de celis*		
Respond *Tibi laus*		
Saturday: Psalm *Exultavit cor meum*		
Respond *Benedicamus [Patrem]*		
High Mass	**High Mass**	
Three memorials at high altar:	**Three memorials:**	
Trinity: Antiphon *O beata et benedicta*	(Same daily order)	
Versicle *Tibi laus*		
Collect		
Assumption: Antiphon *Ascendit Christus*		Forest, *Ascendit Christus*
Versicle [*V. Exaltata es, sancta*		
Dei genetrix. R. Super choros		
angelorum ad celestia regna.]		
Collect [*Veneranda nobis*]		
St. George: Antiphon *Hic vir despiciens*		
Versicle [*Gloria et honore*]		
Collect [*Deus qui nos beati*]		
[Vespers]	**[Vespers]**	
Compline	**Compline**	
Six memorials:	**Six memorials:**	
Trinity: Antiphon *Libera nos*	**Trinity:** *Libera nos*	
Versicle *Benedicamus Patrem*		
Collect *Omnipotens*		

Table 1.1. (*cont.*)

Gesta Henrici Quinti	Liber metricus	Motet or anthem
Holy Spirit: Antiphon *Veni Sancte Spiritus* Versicle *Emitte spiritum* Collect *Deus qui corda*	**Holy Spirit:** *Veni Sancte Spiritus*	Dunstable, *Veni Sancte Spiritus/ Veni Sancte Spiritus et infunde/Veni Creator/Mentes tuorum*
St. Edward: Antiphon *Ave sancte Rex Edwarde inter celi lilia* Versicle *Ora pro nobis* Collect *Deus qui nos beati*	**St. Edward:** *Confer ave rex gentis etc.*	
St. John: Antiphon *Inter natos* Versicle *Fuit homo* Collect *Perpetuis nos*	**St. John:** *Preco/Inter natos*	Dunstable, *Preco prehemi-nencie/Precursor premittitur/Inter natos*
St. George: Antiphon *Hic est vere martyr* Versicle *Ora pro nobis* Collect *Deus qui nos beati*	**St. George:** *Miles/Hic est vere martyr*	
St. Mary: Antiphon *"Ad placitum chori"* Versicle *Ave Maria* Collect *In omni tribulacione*	**St. Mary:** *Regina· Beata*	*"Placet hec ad placitum chori"*

uncommon in the early fifteenth century, and none survive for these seven chants.

The ordering of memorials at the high altar after Mass follows common usage. Each suffrage employs the formula of antiphon, versicle with response, and collect or common prayer. Frank Ll. Harrison observes that "The special interest of memorials is that, like processions, they provided a liturgical situation in which an antiphon was sung without a psalm, thus establishing iself as a separate item of ritual."[23] The second memorial called for the antiphon *Ascendit Christus super celos* in commemoration of the Assumption of the Virgin. The Latin *Brut* employs the word *decantaretur* in reference to this antiphon, which may denote performance in discant.[24] In fact, a setting of *Ascendit Christus* by Forest, with a tenor that paraphrases the Marian antiphon *Alma redemptoris mater*, appears in the second layer of

[23] Harrison, *Music in Medieval Britain*, 76–77. See also J. Harper, *The Forms and Orders of Western Liturgy from the Tenth to the Eighteenth Century* (Oxford: Clarendon Press, 1991), 127, 130–31.
[24] Harrison, *Music in Medieval Britain*, 109–11, demonstrates how, from the early fourteenth century, "plainsong and polyphony should be employed (*cantent et discantent*) according to the rank of the festival and the nature of the chant."

the Old Hall manuscript.[25] Forest's work represents what the later fifteenth century referred to as "anthemes" (the parallel French term was "anthi-ennes"). No other English setting of the text from the early fifteenth century survives. In the Sarum rite, *Ascendit Christus* served as the processional antiphon before Mass on the feast of the Assumption of the Virgin and as the Magnificat antiphon at first Vespers the evening before.[26] *Alma redemp-toris mater* was sung as one of the processional antiphons at Vespers on Saturdays or before Mass on Sundays for the extended period between the Octave of Trinity Sunday and Advent. Yet it was not so employed between the feasts of the Assumption (August 15) and the Nativity of the Virgin (September 8). One effect of combining the text of one antiphon with the melody of another was to broaden the frame of reference for the work, making it suitable not just for the feast of the Assumption, but for use throughout the year. Forest's *Ascendit Christus* was likely written for the Chapel Royal and would have been sung on Saturdays, called Our Lady's Day in honor of the Virgin Mary, but may also have been performed on a daily basis.[27]

The six memorials after Compline employ well-known office antiphons and collects (Table 1.1). The memorials are described in a verse chronicle, the *Liber metricus de Henrico Quinto*, that relies on the *Gesta Henrici Quinti*, but provides significantly different details.[28] The *Liber metricus* survives in three fifteenth-century manuscripts in the British Library: Cotton Vespasian

[25] Margaret Bent makes the connection between chronicle and anthem in *Dunstaple* (London and New York: Oxford University Press, 1981), 8 n. 17. In Old Hall, *Ascendit Christus* appears on fol. 57v (incomplete). The work is attributed to Dunstaple in Modena, Biblioteca Estense universitaria, MS α.X.1.11, "Modena B," fols. 96v–97r. The attribution to Forest in Old Hall is both more authoritative and two decades earlier.

[26] The "versicle and collect of the feast" that completed the memorial have been reconstructed in Table 1.1, according to Sarum use. See the *Processionale ad usum Sarum*, fols. 150v–151r.

[27] The statutes of Middleham College in Yorkshire, dated 1478, mandate that each day, "after high messe be said, the antheme of *Stella celi* . . . be song priked song," meaning in written polyphony. *Stella celi* was a popular Marian antiphon in England, for which several settings survive. Middleham College was established by Richard, Duke of Gloucester, who later acceded to the throne as Richard III. Even though the Wars of the Roses prevented full funding for the college, the statutes clearly demonstrate Richard of Gloucester's expectations for a well-founded institution, which included daily performance of the choral anthem by four clerks and six choirboys. For the document, see J. Raine, "The Statutes Ordained by Richard Duke of Gloucester for the College of Middleham, dated July 4, 18 Edw. IV. [1478]," *Archaeological Journal* 14 (1857): 160–70.

[28] *Elmhami liber metricus de Henrico Quinto*, ed. C. A. Cole in *Memorials of Henry the Fifth, King of England*, Rerum Britannicarum medii aevi scriptores, or Chronicles and Memorials of Great Britain and Ireland during the Middle Ages 11 (London: Longman, Brown, Green, Longmans and Roberts, 1858), 140–41.

D. XIII; Harley 861; and Cotton Julius E. IV.[29] The first two redactions differ in certain respects, as shown in Table 1.2. There are two rows of text, each with superscript above in very small handwriting. The six memorials are separated from one another by means of lines, drawn freehand through the rows of text. For the Trinity, the memorial corresponds exactly to the *Gesta Henrici Quinti*: the object of devotion, *Trinitas*, appears in the first line, with the antiphon text, *Libera nos*, in the second. For the second memorial, to the Holy Spirit, the antiphon *Veni Sancte Spiritus* likewise appears in the second line. For the fourth memorial, to St. John the Baptist, the first line presents the text *Preco*, with the name of the saint now in superscript. Margaret Bent states that since the manuscripts join together the texts *Preco* and *Inter natos*, they undoubtedly refer to the motet *Preco preheminencie/Precursor premittitur/Inter natos* by John Dunstaple, with the antiphon *Inter natos* in the tenor.[30] Both the triplum text, *Preco preheminencie*, and the motetus text, *Precursor premittitur*, are otherwise unknown.[31]

Dunstaple also composed two settings of the text *Veni Sancte Spiritus*, which both the *Gesta Henrici Quinti* and the *Liber metricus* specify for the second memorial after Compline (Tables 1.1 and 1.2). While the memorial calls for an antiphon, however, Dunstaple sets a sequence with the same incipit. As Bent comments, "the text is common enough to discourage speculation."[32] But the case may be put in a more positive light when we consider the intimate structural relationships between *Preco preheminencie/Precursor premittitur/Inter natos* and *Veni Sancte Spiritus/Veni Sancte Spiritus et infunde/Veni Creator Spiritus/Mentes tuorum*. As in several Dunstaple motets, they divide into three *colores* of two *taleae* each, in the ratio 3 : 2 : 1. The relationship does not end there, however. The two works are in four voices, lasting 540 imperfect semibreves (Table 1.3). Alone among Dunstaple's motets, the tenors make use of *modus major perfectus*, in which not only breves and longs are perfect, but the maxima as well: one maxima lasts nine breves altogether (Examples 1.2 and 1.3).[33] The tenor changes to imperfect time (C) in the second *color*, and must be read in diminution in the third.

---

[29] A fourth manuscript copy, London, British Library, Royal 13A XVI, dates from the eighteenth century.
[30] Bent, *Dunstaple*, 8.   [31] *Ibid.*, 65.
[32] *Ibid.*, 8. The second Dunstaple motet to employ the sequence is the three-voice *Veni Sancte Spiritus/Consolator optime/Sancte Spiritus assit*.
[33] *John Dunstaple: Complete Works*, ed. M. Bukofzer, Musica Britannica 8, 2nd edn., rev. M. Bent, I. Bent, and B. Trowell (London: Stainer & Bell, 1970), 78–81, 88–90, 191–92.

Table 1.2. *Liber metricus*: Memorials after Compline in the Chapel Royal of Henry V

British Library, MS Cotton Vesp. D. XIII, fol. 171v

nitas	ritus sanctus	edwardus	Johannes baptista	georgius	sancta Maria	
Tri	Spi	Rex	Preco	Miles	Regina	beata
bera nos	ni sancte	rex sancte edwarde	ter natos	e[st] vere martir		ad placitum chori
li	Ve	confer Ave iungis	In	Hic		placet hec

British Library, MS Harley 861, fol. 183r

initas	ritus sanctus	Edwardus	Johannes baptista	Sanctus georgius	Sancta Maria	
Tr	Spi	Rex	Preco	Miles	Regina·Beata	
bera nos	ni sancte spiritus	Rex gentis etc.	ter natos	e[st] vere		ad placitum chori
li	Ve	confer ave iungis	In	Hic		Placet hec

Table 1.3. *Talea* structure in two Dunstaple motets

	Preco preheminencie			*Veni Sancte Spiritus*	
	Breves	Semibreves		Breves	Semibreves
○	6 + 39	135	○	9 + 36	135
	6 + 39	135		9 + 36	135
C	6 + 39	90	C	9 + 36	90
	6 + 39	90		9 + 36	90
○	2 + 13	45	○	3 + 12	45
	2 + 13	45		3 + 12	45
Total		540	Total		540

The first two *taleae* of the motets begin with a duet between the upper voices, lasting eighteen and twenty-seven semibreves respectively, and proportionally reduced thereafter (Examples 1.2 and 1.3). In the opening duet of *Preco preheminencie*, the triplum paraphrases the first twelve notes – the first *talea* – of the antiphon *Inter natos*. Dunstaple embeds the notes within the syncopated melodic line, although the initial long on c″ must be counted twice (Example 1.2).[34] This treatment would normally be found only in a polyphonic anthem or hymn. Dunstaple expands the scheme to the entire work in *Veni Sancte Spiritus*, but at a greater level of complexity. In the introduction to each of the six *taleae*, the triplum ornaments the four phrases of the hymn tune, *Veni Creator Spiritus*, in consecutive order, alternating with long-note statements of phrases two and three of the hymn in the tenor (Table 1.4).[35] Edgar H. Sparks remarks that "Dunstaple has . . . achieved a union of the two common methods of treating the *cantus firmus* in one composition."[36]

Looking to the manuscript sources, *Veni Sancte Spiritus* and *Preco preheminencie* are copied adjacent to each other in Trent, Castello del Buonconsiglio, MS 92.[37] *Veni Sancte Spiritus* also appears in the royal manuscript, Old Hall, the only Dunstaple work to be so included. It appears in the same gathering

---

[34] Charles Atkinson notes a parallel procedure in chant: "In the settings of proses to melismas in the monophonic repertoire there can certainly be one note extra, or a repeated note will receive only one syllable in the prose" (personal communication). Following common editorial practice, Examples 1.2 and 1.3 mark the notes corresponding to the *cantus firmus* with a "+."

[35] Compare E. H. Sparks, *Cantus Firmus in Mass and Motet, 1420–1520* (Berkeley and Los Angeles: University of California Press, 1963), 106–07.

[36] Ibid., 107.

[37] Trent, Castello del Buonconsiglio, MS 92, fols. 182v–184r and 184v–186r, respectively. I am grateful to J. Michael Allsen for pointing out the significance of the motets' transmission. *Preco preheminencie* also appears in a manuscript associated with Canterbury Cathedral: Canterbury, Cathedral Library, MS 128/13. See N. Sandon, "Fragments of Medieval Polyphony at Canterbury Cathedral," *Musica Disciplina* 30 (1976): 37–53.

Example 1.2. Dunstaple, *Preco preheminencie,* first *talea*

Example 1.2. (*cont.*)

Example 1.2. (*cont.*)

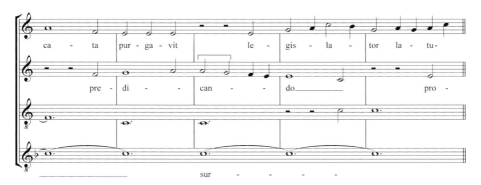

Table 1.4. Use of the four melodic phrases of the hymn *Veni Creator Spiritus* in John Dunstaple, *Veni Sancte Spiritus/Veni Sancte Spiritus et infunde/Veni Creator Spiritus/Mentes tuorum*

	Triplum	Tenor
Talea 1	Paraphrase 1	Phrase 2
Talea 2	Paraphrase 2	Phrase 3
Talea 3	Paraphrase 3	Phrase 2
Talea 4	Paraphrase 4	Phrase 3
Talea 5	Paraphrase 1	Phrase 2
Talea 6	Paraphrase 2	Phrase 3

as *Ascendit Christus*, separated only by Forest's *Qualis est dilectus*, a unique situation in which anthems and a motet are copied together in an English source.[38] Given the close structural, numerical, and source relationships between *Preco preheminencie* and *Veni Sancte Spiritus*, they were probably conceived and performed as a pair for the daily memorials of Henry V. The introduction of *cantus firmus* paraphrase into both motets allows them to sound, at least initially, like polyphonic anthems, comparable to the memorials for the Virgin Mary. The opportunity to hear the two motets repeatedly would have rendered their several texts and structural interrelationships both more familiar and more intelligible to members of the royal court and chapel.

[38] *Veni Sancte Spiritus*, fols. 55v–56r (anonymous); *Qualis est dilectus*, fols. 56v–57r; *Ascendit Christus*, fol. 57v (beginning of triplum only).

Example 1.3. Dunstaple, *Veni Sancte Spiritus*, first *talea*

Example 1.3. (*cont.*)

Example 1.3. (*cont.*)

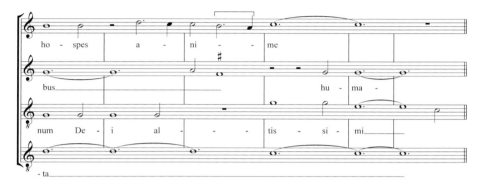

Table 1.5. Mathematical structures in four works for the Chapel Royal

Cooke, *Alma proles/Christi miles/Ab inimicis nostris*	
Sections 1 + 2	540 minims = 27 × 20
Sections 2 + 3	360 minims = 18 × 20
Dunstaple, *Preco preheminencie/Precursor premittitur/Inter natos*	
Section 1	540 minims = 27 × 20
Section 2	360 minims = 18 × 20
Section 3	180 minims = 9 × 20
Dunstaple, *Veni Sancte Spiritus/Veni Sancte Spiritus et infunde/Veni Creator Spiritus/Mentes tuorum*	
Section 1	540 minims = 27 × 20
Section 2	360 minims = 18 × 20
Section 3	180 minims = 9 × 20
Forest, *Ascendit Christus*	
Total length	660 minims = 33 × 20

Moreover, an underlying numerical symbolism ties *Preco preheminencie* and *Veni Sancte Spiritus* to both Cooke's *Alma proles/Christi miles/Ab inimicis nostris* and Forest's *Ascendit Christus*. The first section of *Preco preheminencie*, comprising two introductions and two *taleae*, totals 540 minims, where two minims equal one imperfect semibreve (Table 1.5). The second section totals 360 minims, and the third 180 minims, a 3 : 2 : 1 proportion. *Veni Sancte Spiritus* takes on the same precise dimensions. The first two sections of *Alma proles*, employing the additive method common in the medieval period, also total 540 minims. The second and third sections together total 360 minims. When divided by 20, these totals yield consecutive Trinitarian numbers, 9, 18, 27, where 9 represents the square of 3, 18 represents twice the square of 3, and 27 the cube of 3. In addition, *Ascendit Christus* has a total length of 660 minims, which yields thirty-three when divided by twenty.

Number symbolism was a common and accepted way of viewing the cosmos in the fifteenth century. In medieval number symbolism, 33 is a familiar term, for it denoted the lifespan of Christ. An attractive interpretation of the number 20 sees it as a symbol of kingship, the product of 4 and 5. The number 4, associated with the four elements, the four winds, and the four points of the compass, symbolizes dominion, while 5 represents the king, Henry V. The "nuptial" numbers 4 and 5 are joined together in the person of the king.[39] Further, the appearance of the squares and cubes of 3 in the Cooke and Dunstaple motets ties them to St. Stephen's Chapel in Westminster, dedicated to the Trinity. The use of twenty as the common denominator in the structure of all four works not only ties them strongly to the daily liturgies of the Chapel Royal, but indicates that the composers knew each other's work.

The relationship is strengthened further by the poetic construction of the triplum and motetus texts in Cooke's *Alma proles/Christi miles/Ab inimicis nostris*. The triplum consists of ten four-line stanzas in the pattern $A^7B^6A^7B^6$ $C^7D^6C^7D^6$ and so on (Figure 1.1).[40] This yields a total of twenty-six syllables per stanza and 260 for the entire work, or 13×20. It also precisely matches the rhyme scheme and syllable count for the triplum of *Preco preheminencie*, which also yields 260 syllables, with a play on the royal number, 20.[41] The motetus of *Alma proles/Christi miles/Ab inimicis nostris*, on the other hand, comprises five double stanzas in the pattern $A^7A^7B^7$ $A^7A^7B^7$. The total comes to 210 syllables, or 7×30. It exactly matches the rhyme scheme and syllable count for the triplum of *Veni Sancte Spiritus*.[42] Since the latter text is a sequence for Pentecost Sunday, it is entirely possible that Cooke patterned his motet texts on the triplum voices of the two Dunstaple motets. Cooke must have written *Alma proles/Christi miles/Ab inimicis nostris* before his departure from the Chapel Royal in July 1419.

---

[39] M. J. B. Allen, *Nuptial Arithmetic: Marsilio Ficino's Commentary on the Fatal Number in Book VIII of Plato's "Republic"* (Berkeley and Los Angeles: University of California Press, 1994), 52.

[40] J. M. Allsen, "Style and Intertextuality in the Isorhythmic Motet, 1400–1440" (Ph.D. diss., University of Wisconsin-Madison, 1992), 452.

[41] Ibid., 494.   [42] Ibid., 452, 502.

To return now to the chronicles, the *Liber metricus* further differs from the *Gesta Henrici Quinti* in its description of the texts for St. Edward the Confessor, St. George, and the Virgin Mary, the three patron saints of the Order of the Garter. For St. Edward the Confessor, all three sources present the name of the saint as "Rex Edwardus," which does not appear to denote a motet, despite the confused and contradictory presentation of the antiphon incipits (Table 1.2). For St. George, the *Liber metricus* specifies the texts *Miles* and *Hic est vere martyr*, now presenting the name of the saint in superscript. The first incipit may allude to the image of the *Miles Christi*, the "Soldier of Christ," associated with Henry V and already encountered in Cooke's *Alma proles/Christi miles/Ab inimicis nostris*. As with *Preco preheminencie*, the coupling of the two texts suggests a motet, with the antiphon *Hic est vere martyr* as the tenor, but none so far has been identified.

The graphic presentation of the texts given for St. Mary in the *Liber metricus* differs among the manuscript sources (Table 1.2). Reflecting the original situation in the *Gesta Henrici Quinti*, they do not provide an antiphon text in the lower line, but instead read "Placet hec / ad placitum chori." The direction parallels the Sarum Processional between the Octave of Trinity Sunday and Advent, where the cantor has the choice of antiphon:

In introitu chori dicatur una istarum antiphonarum sequentium per ordinem, tam in processione in sabbatis, quam ad processionem ante Missam in dominicis pro dispositione cantoris.

At the entrance to the choir one of the following antiphons is said in order, both in the procession on Saturday and in the procession before Mass on Sunday, according to the disposition of the cantor.[43]

The antiphons that follow are *Beata Dei genetrix*, *Ave regina celorum*, *Alma redemptoris mater*, *Speciosa facta es*, *Ibo michi ad montem*, and *O quam pulchra es*.[44] These were sung as the procession re-entered the choir on the west side.

---

[43] *Processionale ad usum Sarum*, fols. 119v–121v.

[44] Ibid., fols. 121v–123v. The *Ordinale Exon.: Exeter Chapter Ms. 3502 Collated with Parker Ms. 93*, ed. J. N. Dalton, 4 vols, Henry Bradshaw Society 37, 38, 63, 79 (London: Henry Bradshaw Society, 1909–40), vol. I, 177, presents the antiphons in the following order: *Ave regina celorum, Alma redemptoris mater, Beata Dei genetrix, Speciosa facta es, Ibo michi ad montem, Quam pulchra es*. Oxford, Bodleian Library, MS Rawlinson liturg. e. 46, fols. 86v–89r, lists the same antiphons, "per ordinem secundum disposicionem cantoris": *Alma redemptoris mater, Beata Dei genetrix, Ave regina celorum, Speciosa facta es, Ibo michi ad montem, Quam pulchra es*.

Unlike the memorial after Mass, the suffrage for St. Mary does not pertain specifically to the Annunciation. Cotton Vespasian D. XIII lists the texts for the Virgin Mary as *Regina* and *beata*, separated by a red line (Table 1.2). Harley 861 gives a similar reading, with *Regina* and *Beata*, both capitalized and separated by a period. The graphic appearance, whereby the texts are collated horizontally rather than vertically, the familiarity of the incipits, and the direction *ad placitum chori* ("at the pleasure of the choir"), point to two different musical settings, rather than two texts combined in a single work. The direction itself was an open invitation to polyphony. The first text, *Regina*, most likely refers to a setting of *Regina celi*. The second incipit, *Beata*, could refer to any of three different antiphon texts: *Beata progenies*, *Beata Dei genetrix*, or *Beata mater*. Settings of *Beata progenies* by Leonel Power and *Beata Dei genetrix* by Thomas Damett, a singer in the Chapel Royal, appear in gathering 7 of Old Hall, while an anonymous *Regina celi* appears in gathering 6, all written in score format.[45] Since the music for St. Mary was variable, other works could be sung, such as Forest's *Qualis est dilectus*, setting a Vespers antiphon for the Assumption of the Virgin. Overall, at least three of the six daily memorials established after Compline – to the Holy Spirit, St. John the Baptist, and the Virgin Mary – were sung to motets or anthems composed for the royal chapels.

The genesis of Dunstaple's *Preco preheminencie* and *Veni Sancte Spiritus* is illuminated by another chronicle, the *Vita & gesta Henrici Quinti, Anglorum regis*, which relates how the Duke of Bedford (Illustration 1.1) was received by the court in joyous state not long after the Battle of the Seine in 1416. The writer ties together the homecoming of the duke with the establishment of a new memorial:

Princeps vero, assumptis secum conquisitis navibus & captivis, cum universa classe sua, aura, nautarum opinionibus congrua, insufflante, versus regem rediens, post pauca in partes Angliae feliciter applicabat. Regia quoque discreta & devota nobilitas, de tanta victoria gracias reddens Deo, nobilem fratrem suum applausu jocundo recepit, & de cetero quondam antiphonam cum versiculo & collecta de festo Assumpcionis beatae Mariae, in quo tantus triumphus collatus fuerat, omnibus diebus vitae suae in capella sua propria cantari constituit & decrevit.

In fact, the prince, having taken the defeated ships and captives with him, along with his entire fleet, the breeze blowing fair, in the agreed opinion of the sailors,

---

[45] Anonymous, *Regina celi*, fol. 36v; Power, *Beata progenies*, fol. 38; Damett, *Beata Dei genetrix*, fols. 39v–40r.

steered in the direction of the king, and after a short while landed in England. The court, and the distinguished and devoted nobility, rendering thanks to God for such a victory, received his noble brother with joyous applause; and moreover a certain antiphon with versicle and collect of the feast of the Assumption of the blessed Mary, on which day so great a triumph was conferred, he decreed and constituted to be sung in his own chapel every day of his life.[46]

Alone among Dunstaple's motets, the texts of *Preco preheminencie/ Precursor premittitur/Inter natos* refer to contemporary events. The opening of the triplum, while describing the advent of St. John the Baptist, at the same time alludes to the arrival of the naval fleet to lift the seige of English forces at the town of Harfleur:

Preco preheminencie
principi precessit;
Salus sapiencie
subito successit.

The herald of the preeminent
prince went out before;
soon after, salvation
succeeded knowledge.[47]

The motetus begins in a similar way:

Precursor premittitur
populum parare
nebulosis nititur
nova nunciare.

The forerunner is sent ahead
to prepare the people;
he struggles through the mists
to announce the news.[48]

---

[46] *Thomae de Elmham Vita & gesta Henrici Quinti, Anglorum regis*, ed. T. Hearne (Oxford: Theatro Sheldoniano, 1727), 83. Hearne's attribution of the chronicle to Thomas of Elmham is discounted by modern scholarship.

[47] Allusion appears in the technical sense, as a product of the choice of words, their connotations, and the parallelism of action.

[48] The translation of these four lines is indebted to D. Howlett in the notes to Orlando Consort, *Dunstaple*, CD sound recording (Metronome MET CD 1009, 1995).

These texts make use of a standard trope for the *adventus* or joyous entry of a prince in the late Middle Ages, one that identifies him with St. John the Baptist.[49] In the Gospels, the saint proclaims the words of Isaiah 40:3: "Prepare ye the way of the Lord, make straight in the wilderness the paths of our God." The untexted tenor refers to this prophecy, stating:

Inter natos mulierum non surrexit major Joanne Baptista qui viam domino preparavit in heremo.

Among men born of women, none greater arose than John the Baptist, who prepared a way for the Lord in the desert.

In a parallel register, John, Duke of Bedford, prepares a way for the warrior king in France, Henry V. The triplum employs political imagery in the words *princeps* ("prince"), *pax* ("peace"), *legislator* ("lawgiver"), and others. The motetus, on the other hand, uses a military vocabulary in words such as *precursor* ("scout" or "forerunner"), *captus* ("prisoner"), *presidium* ("garrison"), and *subsidium* ("relief forces"). The connotations of this language, unusual for Dunstaple, serve to augment the topical references. The conclusion of the motetus reinforces the martial imagery:

prestent per presidium
preces precursoris
sequentis subsidium
sancti Salvatoris.

May the prayers of the precursor
secure through intercession
the protection of the holy
Savior coming after.

The end of the triplum characterizes the return of the royal prince on or after September 8, 1416.[50] Poetically, the subject remains St. John the Baptist, but a topical allusion to his namesake, John, Duke of Bedford, nonetheless emerges:

Premebatur patria
primitus penalis;
Renatos ne regia
recipit regalis.

[49]   E. H. Kantorowicz, "The 'King's Advent' and the Enigmatic Panels in the Doors of Santa Sabina," *Art Bulletin* 26 (1944): 217–19.
[50]   E. C. Williams, *My Lord of Bedford, 1389–1435* (London: Longmans, 1963), 38.

At first, the suffering homeland
was hard pressed;
verily, the royal court
receives the ones restored.

Since Henry V had already departed for Calais on September 4, 1416, the Duke of Bedford's return to Westminster Palace on or after September 8 was celebrated by his own chapel and the royal court.[51] Dunstaple's *Preco preheminencie* alludes to the homecoming, but its ultimate destination was the daily memorials of Henry V. Within that context, the performance of *Preco preheminencie* allowed for the commemoration of St. John the Baptist to recall also the virtues and courage of the royal patron, John, Duke of Bedford. Since the *Gesta Henrici Quinti* was written between November 1416 and July 1417, and the *Liber metricus* in 1417–18, only one year later, the verse chronicle reflects a later state of affairs than does the *Gesta*, one that allows for polyphony to replace the chant.[52] Consequently, *Preco preheminencie* dates to between September 1416 and December 1418. Since Dunstaple modeled *Veni Sancte Spiritus* directly on *Preco preheminencie*, it likely was written second in order during the same period. While *Veni Sancte Spiritus* lacks the topical references of the earlier motet, it carries out the patterned alternation of chant paraphrase and tenor *taleae* to a logical conclusion (Table 1.4).

The Agincourt celebrations

One of the best-documented civic celebrations of the late Middle Ages is the welcome given to Henry V in London following his decisive victory over the French at the Battle of Agincourt on October 24, 1415. Three weeks later, King Henry returned to England via Dover and Canterbury, pausing at his castle at Eltham, southeast of London.[53] The entrance into the city of London took place on November 23, affording ample time for preparation by the civic and royal authorities. The celebrations incorporated musical,

---

[51] *Gesta*, 156–57. None of the chronicles, in fact, states that the king received his brother in person.

[52] *Gesta*, xxi, xxiv, xlix. The *Liber metricus* covers the first five years of Henry V's reign to March 21, 1418.

[53] *Gesta*, 101.

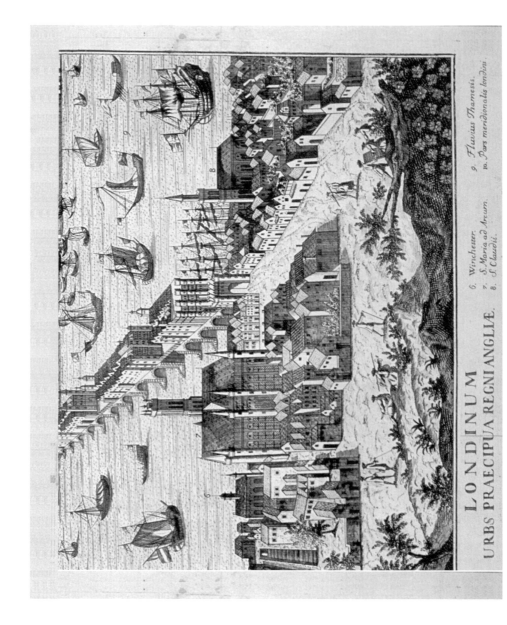

Illustration 1.2. Panorama of London with view of London Bridge, etching, circa 1660

architectural, pictorial, literary, and liturgical elements;[54] consequently, they provide a civic and processional context for motet performance.

According to the *Gesta Henrici Quinti*, a procession of twenty thousand citizens, led by the mayor and aldermen, left London at daybreak and proceeded four miles southeast to Blackheath.[55] The civic leaders were clothed in scarlet, while the citizens wore "red gowns with parti-colored hoods of red and white."[56] All the main trade guilds of the city were represented, for they each "wore some particular richly fashioned badge which conspicuously distinguished one craft from another." Around ten o'clock, the mayor and aldermen ceremonially greeted the king, and the procession returned to London Bridge, while the king and his retinue, including noble French prisoners, followed.[57] The procession was met by the monks of Bermondsey Abbey, singing in plainchant.[58]

London Bridge, covered with buildings in the manner of the Florentine Ponte Vecchio, was adorned in three places (Illustration 1.2): at the south entrance tower, at the small drawbridge in the middle, and at the northern end.[59] "And, all around them, projecting from the ramparts, staffs bearing the royal arms and trumpets, clarions, and horns ringing out in multiple harmony embellished the tower, and the face of it bore this choice and appropriate legend inscribed on the wall: *Civitas Regis Iusticie.*"[60] According to the English *Brut*, as the procession stopped on Southwark High Street and gathered round the king at the entrance to London Bridge, he was greeted by a Latin "song":

And so rode he forth to London on Saint Clement day, where as he was riolly receyvet with precession and song *ave anglorum, flos mundi, miles Christi*, and when he come to Londonn brigge where as were ij turrettes on the drawbrige, & a great Geaunt and

---

54 Kipling, *Enter the King*, discusses the constituent elements and symbolism for a great number of *adventus* ceremonies of the fifteenth and sixteenth centuries; for the Agincourt celebrations, see 205–09. See also A. M. Cummings, *The Politicized Muse: Music for the Medici Festivals, 1512–1537* (Princeton University Press, 1992), chapters 5 and 8.

55 R. C. Trexler, *Public Life in Renaissance Florence* (New York: Academic Press, 1980), 308, observes that "For the welcoming party to travel any significant distance from the city was a signal honor, carefully recorded by chroniclers."

56 *Gesta*, 102–03. According to *The Chronicle of Adam of Usk*, ed. and trans. C. Given-Wilson (Oxford: Clarendon Press, 1997), 260–61, there were "ten thousand people, nobles and citizens mounted on horses and dressed in red, wearing parti-colored hoods of black and white, their hearts leaping with joy."

57 *Gesta*, 102–03, 112–13.

58 *Elmhami liber metricus*, 125: "De Bermondseya conventu prodiit Abbas; / Concordes cleri voce dedere sonos."

59 *Gesta*, 104–05; *Chronicle of Adam of Usk*, 260–61.   60 *Gesta*, 102–03.

on the turrettes stonding a lyon and a antelope with many angels synging *Benedictus qui venit in nomine domini.* And so rode he forth in to london.[61]

The chronicle is very specific concerning the music sung for King Henry upon his arrival at London Bridge. Three texts, given as *Ave Anglorum/Flos mundi/Miles Christi*, represent the incipits of a three-voice motet, with two fully texted voices – motetus and triplum – declaimed simultaneously over a tenor. The *Benedictus*, on the other hand, belonged to the second stage of the progress. According to the *Gesta Henrici Quinti*, a crowd of boys dressed as angels, singing in counterpoint, were located in a house "next to and behind the tower" that had been erected at the north side of London Bridge.[62] The *Benedictus* constituted a musical element distinct from the motet, one that accompanied the procession as it passed over the elaborately decorated bridge into the city of London.[63]

A second, verse chronicle advances a similar report, but because the fourth line of the stanza must rhyme with "ryght," the poet substitutes the English "goddes knyght" for the Latin *miles Christi*, yielding *Ave rex Anglorum/Flos mundi/Goddes knyght*:

To londonn Brigge thanne rood oure Kyng
The processions there they mette hym ryght
Ave Rex anglorum thei gan syng
Flos mundi thei seide *goddys knyght.*
To londonn Brigge whan he com right
Up on the gate there stode on hy
A gyaunt that was full grym of syght
To teche the frensshemen curtesy.
And at the drawe brigge that is faste by
To toures there were up pight

---

61   *The Brut or The Chronicles of England*, ed. F. W. D. Brie, 2 vols. (London: Kegan Paul, Trench, Trübner, 1908), vol. II, 558. The text is corrected by Margaret Bent, who first drew attention to the chronicles, in "Sources," 23.

62   *Gesta*, 104–05: "qui concinebant in adventu regio suavi vocis modulacione et organis, litteram prosequentes, hanc angelicam cantilenam: [*Benedictus qui venit in nomine Domini*]."

63   Bent, "Sources," 22–26, connects the performance of the *Benedictus* at London Bridge to two related motets by Thomas Damett and Nicholas Sturgeon: *Salvatoris mater pia/O Georgi Deo care/Benedictus Marie Filius qui ve–* and *Salve mater Domini/Salve emplum gratie/ –nit in nomine Domini.* The two works are copied close together in the Old Hall manuscript, fols. 89v–90r and 91v–92r. They split between them the *cantus firmus, Benedictus Marie filius qui venit in nomine Domini.* Bent acknowledges, however, that "The texts of the upper parts of these motets do not correspond directly to anything in the chronicles of Henry's homecoming." The *Benedictus* text itself is so common that, absent reference to the *Marie filius* trope, a specific connection is difficult to maintain.

An Antelope and a Lyon stondyng hym by
Above hem seynt George oure lady knyght;
Besyde hym an angell bright,
Benedictus thei gan synge
Qui venit in nomine domini goddes knyght
Gracia dei with yow doth sprynge.[64]

The motetus incipit, *Ave rex Anglorum* ("Hail, King of the English"), greets the triumphant monarch. The text alludes to the antiphon *Ave rex gentis Anglorum*, and was likely addressed to St. Edward the Confessor, a special patron and predecessor of British kings.[65] Henry V made an offering to St. Edward at the last stage of his royal entry, in Westminster Abbey, before retiring to the royal palace.[66] The triplum text, *Flos mundi* ("Flower of the world"), appears to be unique, written especially for the occasion. The motet tenor may have derived from *Miles Christi*, a processional chant for the common of a confessor: "Miles Christi gloriose [Sancte Edwarde] sanctissime tuo pio interventu culpas nostras ablue" ("Glorious soldier of Christ, most holy Saint Edward, through your pious intervention cleanse our sins").[67] The motet again relies on the image of the holy knight, as seen in the Bedford Missal (Illustration 1.1). As in Cooke's *Alma proles/Christi miles/Ab inimicis nostris*, the notes of the tenor would be taken from the chant, in whole or in part, and rhythmicized. These texts represented King Henry as the living model of the virtuous monarch, a theme that resonated throughout the daylong progress through the city of London, with particular reference to King David.[68] The combination of new and pre-existent texts, in two chronicles that complement the official program, strongly points toward a motet performance.

---

[64] Bent, "Sources," 23. The entire poem is published in *A Chronicle of London, from 1089 to 1483; Written in the Fifteenth Century* (London: Longman, Rees, Orme, Brown and Green, 1827; facsimile reprint, Felinfach: Llanerch, 1995).

[65] The text was originally for St. Edmund, king and martyr. See G. M. Dreves *et al.*, eds., *Analecta hymnica medii aevi*, 55 vols. (Leipzig: O. R. Reisland, 1886–1922), vol. XVIII, 292.

[66] T. Walsingham, *The St. Albans Chronicle, 1406–1420, Edited from Bodley MS. 462*, ed. V. H. Galbraith (Oxford: Clarendon Press, 1937), 98: "Votis ergo sancto Edwardo persolutis adijt regale palacium ubi per dies aliquot perhendinavit." St. Edward the Confessor founded Westminster Abbey and was buried there in his own chapel in 1066.

[67] *Processionale ad usum Sarum*, fol. 160r.

[68] On the strong Old Testament typology in the pageant, see S. Tolmie, "*Quia hic homo multa signa facet*: Henry V's Royal Entry into London, November 23, 1415," in *The Propagation of Power in the Medieval West: Selected Proceedings of the International Conference, Groningen 20–23 November 1996*, ed. M. Gosman, A. Vanderjat, and J. Veenstra (Groningen: Egbert Forsten, 1997), 363–79. Kipling, *Enter the King*, 205–09, views the typology of the *adventus* as based on the liturgy for the dead, with the devout king entering a New Jerusalem.

The chronicles of Henry V do not inform us who sang the motet *Ave rex Anglorum/Flos mundi/Miles Christi*, but they are quite specific as to the location, just before the gates of London Bridge. An anonymous etching from circa 1660, prior to the Great Fire of London in 1666, shows a panorama of the city from the south bank (Illustration 1.2). The etching shows that the south bank of the River Thames remained fairly rural into the seventeenth century, with clusters of houses along the river. To the left of the bridge stands Southwark Cathedral, named St. Mary Overy, which was completed in 1420. The large square before the cathedral, together with the main street running up to the bridge, were large enough to accommodate the crowds of people gathered to see the king and hear the voices of the choir, with the gate itself as an acoustical backdrop.[69] The arrival of Henry V was heralded by trumpet calls from the top of the gate tower. Despite the specificity of the motet incipits, the music has not survived, or at least not in recognizable form. Nevertheless, it created an important diplomatic gesture as the first musical item, apart from fanfares, at the ceremonial entrance into London, sung before an audience of thousands. It acted both as a celebratory greeting and as a full, formal expression of the joy felt by the people of the city toward their king.

The motets in the chronicles for Henry V, those extant and those irrecoverable, fall into three different categories of use. Cooke's *Alma proles/Christi miles/Ab inimicis nostris* represents a motet for an ecclesiastical procession, specifically the procession before High Mass in the Chapel Royal. Second are motets and anthems written for memorials, or suffrages, which took the traditional form of antiphon, versicle, and collect, in which a motet or anthem replaced the plainchant antiphon. In the Chapel Royal, motets and anthems still voiced the liturgical text or carried the chant in the tenor. Forest's *Ascendit Christus* was probably composed for a set of three memorials directly following daily Mass. Dunstaple's *Preco preheminencie/Precursor premittitur/Inter natos* and *Veni Sancte Spiritus/Veni Sancte Spiritus et infunde/Veni Creator Spiritus/Mentes tuorum* were sung at two of the six memorials after Compline, a traditional place for the addition of memorials to the liturgy. Forest's *Qualis est dilectus*, Leonel Power's *Beata progenies*, or Thomas Damett's *Beata Dei genetrix*, in the Old Hall manuscript, may have been heard within the same series of six memorials, in commemoration of the Virgin Mary. On Sundays, principal feasts, and occasions of state, a dazzling series of polyphonic works could be

---

[69]   The original gate tower fell into the river in 1437; see W. Rendle, *Old Southwark and Its People* (London: Drewett, 1878), 15.

marshalled by the singers of the Chapel Royal. Lastly, *Ave rex Anglorum/Flos mundi/Miles Christi* was performed for a civic procession, the Agincourt celebrations of November 1415. The motet marks a joyous entry to the city for Henry V, being sung outdoors before the heavy gates of London Bridge. Each of the three categories of motet finds complements elsewhere in Western Europe during the fifteenth century.

2 | The motet as ritual

The motets and anthems in the chronicles of Henry V demonstrate a remarkable specificity of use. The wealth of historical detail affords an opportunity to examine how motets operated within particular social contexts. Processions, whether civic or ecclesiastical, made up a natural environment for the motet, for the aesthetic intensity of polyphonic voices contributed a drama that might otherwise be lacking. Processions, in fact, had provided an opportunity for polyphony since the organum of Chartres in the eleventh century.[1] The growth of memorials as accretions to the liturgy in the fifteenth century also prompted the composition of motets. The usefulness of motets within different social contexts favored their performance before audiences as diverse as the royal household or the amassed citizens at the Agincourt celebrations.

Ritual performance

Each of the motets and anthems functioned as a ceremonial performance, demonstrating a number of the characteristics of formal ritual. The definitions of ritual advanced by Eric Rothenbuhler offer a concise model for comparison. While the theory of ritual has a long and complex history, Rothenbuhler synthesizes the research of both sociologists and anthropologists, but without reference to music.[2] To begin with, the performance of a motet constituted a ritual action.[3] The polyphonic choir, made up of chaplains, clerks in minor orders, or choirboys, occupied a privileged social position by virtue of its ecclesiastical character. The clergy were considered

---

[1] C. Wright, "The Palm Sunday Procession in Medieval Chartres," in *The Divine Office in the Latin Middle Ages: Methodology and Source Studies, Regional Developments, Hagiography, Written in Honor of Professor Ruth Steiner*, ed. M. E. Fassler and R. Balzer (Oxford and New York: Oxford University Press, 2000), 344–72.

[2] E. W. Rothenbuhler, *Ritual Communication: From Everyday Conversation to Mediated Ceremony* (Thousand Oaks: Sage, 2000), chapter 2, "Definitions." See also C. M. Bell, *Ritual: Perspectives and Dimensions* (New York and Oxford: Oxford University Press, 1997), chapter 4, "Basic Genres of Ritual Action."

[3] Rothenbuhler, *Ritual Communication*, 7–8.

the representatives of Christ on earth. When the choir sang, it could "speak in tongues of men or of angels."[4] A motet potentially communicated with both celestial and terrestrial audiences.

Moreover, it was embedded in a ritual situation. *Ave rex Anglorum/Flos mundi/Miles Christi* functioned as the welcome given to King Henry V by the people of London, the first stage of a lavish royal entry. The historian Sarah Tolmie, working from the *Gesta Henrici Quinti*, notes that the ceremony before London Bridge "is sharply attenuated."[5] It is the motet, however, that furnishes the drama otherwise lacking at this moment. Not mentioned in the *Gesta*, but only in secondary chronicles composed in English, rather than Latin, it represents a civic addition to the royal program, the point of greatest participation of the city of London in the celebrations.[6] Similarly, the choir singing Dunstaple's *Veni Sancte Spiritus/Veni Sancte Spiritus et infunde/Veni Creator spiritus/Mentes tuorum* addresses the Holy Spirit within a cycle of memorials, as an established addition to the daily liturgy. Far more elaborate than even the most complex responsory chant, the motet carries multiple prayers on behalf of the royal house and all those present.

Two aspects of ritual that might be taken for granted are its regular recurrence and conformity to custom.[7] The extensive daily cycle of offices, memorials, and Mass that Henry V required of his chaplains was ritualistic in this traditional sense. If performed each Sunday, the motets composed for the cycle would fall into the category of periodic rites; if performed occasionally, whether on double feasts or occasions of state, they functioned as augmentations of the daily liturgy. Whether they were fixed or occasional elements, however, the important point is not that the motets themselves recurred, but that the ceremony of which they formed part was both recurrent and customary. Motets contributed to calendrical rites that sacralized the passage of time.

As its incipits suggest, the motet for the Agincourt celebrations, *Ave rex Anglorum/Flos mundi/Miles Christi*, reflected more the exigencies of the moment. Catherine Bell explains that "*Periodic* rites, such as those for life

---

[4] I Corinthians 13:1.

[5] S. Tolmie, "*Quia hic homo multa signa facet*: Henry V's Royal Entry into London, November 23, 1415," in *The Propagation of Power in the Medieval West: Selected Proceedings of the International Conference, Groningen 20–23 November 1996*, ed. M. Gosman, A. Vanderjagt, and J. Veenstra (Groningen: Egbert Forsten, 1997), 369.

[6] K. Schnith, "Musik, Liturgie, Prozession als Ausdrucksmittel der Politik Heinrichs V. von England," in *Festschrift Rudolf Bockholdt zum 60. Geburtstag* (Pfaffenhofen: Ludwig, 1990), 41–52, emphasizes a pageantry that was directed toward the London burghers and common folk, rather than toward the king.

[7] Rothenbuler, *Ritual Communication*, 20–21.

crises and calendrical holidays, are balanced by *occasional* rites that respond to specific situations, such as rites of affliction or political enthronements."[8] The royal entry itself followed a relatively common pattern, however, which ensured its conformity to ritual expectations. Several features of the Agincourt celebration, including banners, *tableaux vivants*, and music, duplicated the entry of Richard II into London on August 21, 1392.[9] These in turn characterized the entry of Margaret of Anjou into London on May 28, 1445, following her marriage by proxy to Henry VI. One chronicle describes "devises and storyes, angeles and oþer thinges, with songe and melody in dyuers places."[10] The route itself was similar: Margaret was met by a procession of aldermen and guildsmen at Blackheath, stopping at the foot of London Bridge, where the song given in her honor was in English, rather than Latin.[11] Such royal entries were an expected and customary feature of life in England, Burgundy, and France, and continued through the sixteenth century.[12]

English motets share another important characteristic of ritual: they express a connection to the sacred.[13] The connection is all the more natural in motets because they were created by the men or boys of the ecclesiastical choir. The works we have considered all incorporate at least one text or plainchant of ecclesiastical origin; they may also set freely written prayers directed to the saints. Whereas motets composed in the Italian city-states often project a limited or merely implied connection to the divine, in English works the appeal to celestial powers remains prominent and direct. The poems of Dunstaple's *Preco preheminencie/Precursor premittitur/Inter natos* deal primarily with the relationship between John the Baptist and Christ, and their sacrifices on behalf of mankind. The tenor *cantus firmus, Inter natos,*

---

[8] Bell, *Ritual*, 175.

[9] G. Kipling, *Enter the King: Theatre, Liturgy, and Ritual in the Medieval Civic Triumph* (Oxford: Clarendon Press, 1998), 12–21; L. Staley, *Languages of Power in the Age of Richard II* (University Park: Pennsylvania State University Press, 2005), 169. Kipling, *Enter the King*, 12, remarks of the 1392 progress that "It uses many of the pageants, symbols, and ceremonies that characterize these shows throughout northern Europe for the next 150 years." See also the chronological table at ibid., 373–74.

[10] *The Brut or The Chronicles of England*, 2 vols., ed. F. W. D. Brie (London: Kegan Paul, Trench, Trübner, 1908), vol. II, 489.

[11] C. Brown, "Lydgate's Verses on Queen Margaret's Entry into London," *The Modern Language Review* 7 (1912): 225–34.

[12] Kipling, *Enter the King*; L. M. Bryant, *The King and the City in the Parisian Royal Entry Ceremony: Politics, Ritual, and Art in the Renaissance* (Geneva: Droz, 1986), 69–87; Tolmie, "Henry V's Royal Entry," 367–68.

[13] Rothenbuhler, *Ritual Communication*, 23–24. Bell, *Ritual*, 164, writes that "The most clear-cut examples of ritual . . . tend to be a matter of communal ceremonies closely connected to formally institutionalized religions or clearly invoking divine beings."

comes from an antiphon for the feast of St. John the Baptist, celebrated on June 24th. Even though the motet served to honor John, Duke of Bedford (see Illustration 1.1), and to commemorate English victory at sea, it worked above all as a musico-poetic retelling of the story of the duke's Biblical namesake.

Motets thus are special works that set apart ceremonial occasions from ordinary life. On days that required greater ceremonial intensity, including Sundays, double feasts, and occasions of state, as many as five motets or anthems could have been sung in the Chapel Royal, including three at the memorials after Compline, the last office of the day. The audience on such occasions would have included noble visitors, both secular and ecclesiastical, as well as high officials of the royal court.

In a real sense, the daily liturgy in the Chapel Royal, studded at intervals with intricate polyphony, constituted a form of political theater. The procession before Mass might incorporate candles, incense, liturgical vestments, chant, and a motet. As a heavily sensory experience for those participating or merely present in the nave, the flow of the procession and its daily repetition served as an expression of political power: this was not merely the chapel of a collegiate church, but the king's own Chapel Royal. In addition, as Bell relates, "the more participants in a ritual conform to the canonical structure of the liturgical order by minimizing self-referentiality, the more authority is located within the liturgy itself."[14] Here, the structure of the liturgy has been modulated by command of the sovereign; its formulation and the elaborateness of ceremony speak to his pious nature. At the same time, the impersonality of the motet texts, with praises of the saints and the glory of Christ, endows the liturgy with greater scope and power. The lack of direct reference to the king is maintained except in Cooke's *Alma proles/Christi miles/Ab inimicis nostris*, which occurs, appropriately, at the end of the litany, with a prayer to the Virgin Mary to "be a refuge to the king, / whom thou protectest from his enemies." The theatrical aspect of the liturgy was calculated to impress all comers with the majesty of the Chapel Royal and with the devout character of the *verus electus Dei*.[15]

As the polyphonic creation of an ecclesiastical choir, in sound if not in words, the motet demonstrated an inherently social orientation.[16] In anthems with pre-existent texts, such as Forest's *Qualis est dilectus*, the text

---

[14] Bell, *Ritual*, 176.

[15] *Gesta Henrici Quinti: The Deeds of Henry the Fifth*, ed. and trans. F. Taylor and J. S. Roskell (Oxford: Clarendon Press, 1975), 2. On the utility of the liturgy for Henry V's royal image, see Schnith, "Musik, Liturgie, Prozession," 47–48.

[16] Rothenbuhler, *Ritual Communication*, 13–15.

reverberates with a history of shared meanings. Not only does the work set a Vespers antiphon for the feast of the Assumption of the Virgin, but the text itself derives from the Song of Songs, a traditional font of Marian imagery. Motets with newly composed texts, in contrast, express important social relationships. Cooke's *Alma proles/Christi miles/Ab inimicis nostris* reflects the hierarchical view of late medieval society, in which each person held a closely defined role in the social order, reflected in every aspect of life, including one's clothes. The king ruled by divine favor, and the motet asks for protection not just for the larger realm which he governs and adjudicates, but for his personal protection.[17] The standard salutation at the beginning of royal letters, "Henri by the grace of God Kyng of Englande and of Fraunce and lorde of Irlande," was more than a formula; it expressed a relationship between the sovereign, heaven, and the realm. *Alma proles/Christi miles/Ab inimicis nostris* accordingly portrays the king as the locus of social order, whose ability to uphold justice mediates between the divine and mundane:[18] "whatever thou desirest that he may do, / may he always be pleasing to thee / in his deeds."

By the same token, the ritual use of motets helps to explain their lack of realism.[19] While a motet such as Thomas Damett's *Salvatoris mater pia/O Georgi Deo care/Benedictus* may refer to the bows and shields of war, it nevertheless points to an ideal state, in which the safety and success of King Henry are vouchsafed by heaven.[20] Such works proclaim the world not as it is, but as it might be. One must admit that our contemporary culture is inimical to ritual, undervalues it, and overlooks its power.[21] Part of that power resides in the ability of ritual to acknowledge conflict and at the same time to mediate or override it. Cooke's *Alma proles* recognizes that enemies

---

[17] Henry V's attitude toward his subjects is illustrated by an anecdote in the *The Brut or The Chronicles of England*, vol. II, 537, which describes his arrival in England after the Battle of Agincourt: "And when þe Kynge come to Caleys, he rested hym þere awhile, and after shippit, and come into Englond, and landet at Dovir, and passit so forth to Berehamdoune, where-as mette with hym þe v portes, with x M men clenly harnesshit and arrayet. And þen said þe Duyk of Orlyaunce: 'What! shal we now go ageyne to bataile?' and þe Kyng hym ansuard and said: 'Nay: thes ben childer of my cuntre come to welcome me home.'"

[18] Schnith, "Musik, Liturgie, Prozession," 47–48.

[19] Rothenbuhler, *Ritual Communication*, 15–16.

[20] The motetus, addressed to St. George, entreats, "Strong soldier, guardian of the people, be present at the deliberations of Henry our king; warn against enemies, offer arms – the shield, the bow; bring help to him." See *The Old Hall Manuscript*, ed. Andrew Hughes and Margaret Bent, Corpus mensurabilis musicae 46, 3 vols. (Rome: American Institute of Musicology, 1969–73), vol. II, 110–13.

[21] E. Muir, *Ritual in Early Modern Europe*, 2nd edn. (Cambridge University Press, 2005), 2, remarks that "Rituals give access to emotional states that resist expression in language, which is why they have become so desired and yet so distrusted in our logo-centric culture."

press in all around, yet expresses a belief in intercessory prayer that will safeguard and guide the sovereign. Likewise, the performance of Forest's *Ascendit Christus* as a commemoration of the naval victory of John, Duke of Bedford, in the Battle of the Seine represents more than a gesture of thanks; it represents faith in the righteousness of the English cause.

The ritual functions of the motet and anthem demonstrate direct connections to the creation of political power in the reign of Henry V. While the surviving records allow for a reconstruction of the daily memorials of the king, other royal and ecclesiastical establishments undoubtedly echoed the pattern set by the Chapel Royal. The Old Hall manuscript, which originated in the chapel of Thomas, Duke of Clarence, before passing to the Chapel Royal, underscores the importance of elaborate music in the invocation of God's grace. Dunstaple wrote his motets and anthems for the royal patrons whom he served in succession: John, Duke of Bedford (before 1428), Joan of Navarre, queen consort of Henry IV (1428–37), and Humphrey, Duke of Gloucester, youngest brother of Henry V (1437–47).[22] Processions, highlighted by chant and polyphony, also served as important means of symbolic communication between the royal house and different entities of the body politic. The expression of piety characteristic of the motet and anthem thereby served to strengthen the policy and position of the House of Lancaster, at least until its dissolution in the Wars of the Roses.

Motets and anthems fit the characteristics of ritual in two further senses that may be considered together: they are aesthetic creations, by virtue of which they manifest a density of symbolic meanings.[23] The first characteristic may seem self-evident, given the Western history of absolute music. But to understand the aesthetic import of an anthem such as Forest's *Ascendit Christus*, we need to contrast it with the performance of plainsong. Chant may also carry aesthetic value, but by the later Middle Ages had long since been seen more as a sacred object, a natural condition of the liturgy. Both words and tone were subject to manipulation in English motets and anthems, which could greatly elevate their aesthetic value. In *Ascendit Christus*, the triplum and contratenor carry the words of the antiphon,

---

[22] For a detailed summary of Dunstaple's biography, see P. M. Lefferts, "Dunstaple," in *Die Musik in Geschichte und Gegenwart*, 2nd edn. (Kassel and New York: Bärenreiter, 1998–). See also A. Wathey, "Dunstaple in France," *Music and Letters* 67 (1986): 1–36. In the surviving manuscripts, Forest's five anthems and lone motet overwhelmingly appear alongside the works of Dunstaple, regardless of whether they are attributed to Forest or not, suggesting comparable service to the royal family. See G. Curtis and A. Wathey, "Fifteenth-Century English Liturgical Music: A List of the Surviving Repertory," *Royal Musical Association Research Chronicle* 27 (1994): 1–69.

[23] Rothenbuhler, *Ritual Communication*, 16–20.

Example 2.1. Forest, *Ascendit Christus*, interior duet

sometimes beginning phrases together, other times delivering them separately (Example 2.1). Each half of the work begins with a long, wreath-like
duet for triplum and contratenor alone. The first six notes of the contratenor quote the beginning of the plainsong, as an allusive gesture. When
the tenor finally enters, it introduces a completely different Marian melody,
Alma redemptoris mater. In Modena, Biblioteca Estense universitaria, MS
α.X.1.11, the scribe labels the tenor *Alma redemptoris*, but otherwise sets
it to text phrases from *Ascendit Christus*, allowing for the melodic elaboration of one antiphon to be heard with the words of another. Although
Forest creates a phrase structure appropriate to the new text, there is no
mistaking the origin of the melody, which is complete except for the final
phrases. The overall balance of the work between two halves contributes to
its aesthetic effect. The work incorporates English anthem style in strikingly
euphonious harmonies and intricate, overlapping rhythms, akin to the patterning of embroidered silk.[24] While daily performance of *Ascendit Christus*
in plainchant fulfilled the basic requirements of the liturgy in the Chapel

---

[24] On the English anthem or "cantilena," see J. E. Cumming, *The Motet in the Age of Du Fay*
(Cambridge University Press, 1999), 90–95, 190–92, with an analysis of Forest's *Alma
redemptoris mater*; and R. Strohm, *The Rise of European Music, 1380–1500* (Cambridge
University Press, 1993), 211–21, with a discussion of Forest's *Ascendit Christus*.

Royal, the aesthetic heightening achieved by Forest's anthem would have lifted the ritual to a higher level of effective intensity.

To witness the depth of symbolic condensation possible in the motet, one need look no further than John Dunstaple's *Veni Sancte Spiritus/Veni Sancte Spiritus et infunde/Veni Creator Spiritus/Mentes tuorum* (see Example 1.3). The combination of two well-known texts in honor of the Holy Spirit – the sequence *Veni Sancte Spiritus* in the triplum and the hymn *Veni Creator Spiritus* in the contratenor – barely begins to describe the "supersaturation" of symbolic effects in this work.[25] The motetus carries yet another text, *Veni Sancte Spiritus et infunde*, which effectively expands upon, or glosses, the sequence in the triplum, but in a different tone of voice. At the same time, the triplum paraphrases the melody of *Veni Creator Spiritus* in the duet at the beginning of each *talea*. It incorporates one of four melodic phrases in the hymn in each of the six successive *taleae* (see Table 1.4). The paraphrase serves to introduce the tenor *cantus firmus*, *Mentes tuorum*, which quotes the second and third phrases of the hymn in alternation. Simultaneous expression of three texts creates, on a very fundamental level, a superfluity of meaning, a verbal polyphony very difficult for modern ears to absorb. At the same time, the heterogeneity of the musico-poetic structure enables different layers of symbolism to emerge in response to the interests of different auditors. Dunstaple multiplies the symbolic interplay of music and words and their potential relationships within the proportional, mathematical construction of the whole. In the ritual of commemoration, the symbolism of texts and music moves outward, connecting to the audience, to the architecture of the chapel, to the vestments of the choir and chaplains, and to the Proper liturgy of the day.[26]

Processional anthems

Despite the lack of topical references in most English motets and anthems, it is a fair conclusion that nearly all were composed for specific ritual situations, including the numerous free settings of antiphon texts without *cantus firmus*. The form of the procession after Vespers on Saturday between the

[25] Rothenbuhler, *Ritual Communication*, 18.
[26] L. Lütteken, *Guillaume Dufay und die isorhythmische Motette: Gattungstradition und Werkcharakter an der Schwelle zur Neuzeit*, Schriften zur Musikwissenschaft aus Münster 4 (Hamburg and Eisenach: K. D. Wagner, 1993), 331, writes "Die Motetten sind Teil des zeremonialen Textkontinuums, sind also Text im Text, Zeichen in einer Folge von symbolische Zeichen."

Octave of Trinity Sunday and Advent, as prescribed in the Sarum Processional, accords on a fundamental level with the rite of separation, known
in many different cultures.[27] The clergy leave the choir through the north
door, singing a responsory chant. The movement behind the main altar
(presbytery), into the south aisle, around the baptismal font, and through
the nave corresponds to the act of transition. The priest sprinkles each of
the side altars with holy water along the way.[28] The goal of the procession,
called a station, may be located at an altar or chapel within the church.
On ordinary Saturdays, the procession halts at the rood (crucifix) on the
west side of the choir for a brief memorial. The procession then re-enters
through the west door of the choir, singing an antiphon.[29] The act of transition acknowledges and symbolically recognizes the laity in the nave of the
church, while the sprinkling of altars acts as a symbol of renewal. The return
to the choir corresponds to the act of incorporation, where the participants
are returned to the body of the clerical community. The basic action of the
procession thus serves to bring the clergy into the nave of the church, in
contact with and in sight of the common people, before retreating behind
the choir screen for Compline.

The station of the cross consists of an antiphon, the censing of the rood, a
versicle and response, and the prayer *Deus qui unigeniti*. The censing of the
rood belongs to the act of transition.[30] One of three antiphons, chosen by the
cantor, could be sung: *O crux gloriosa*, *O crux splendidior*, or *Crux fidelis*.[31]
The procession then began one of six Marian antiphons as it moved into
the choir: *Beata Dei gentrix*, *Alma redemptoris mater*, *Ave regina celorum*,
Speciosa facta es, *Ibo michi ad montem*, or *Quam pulchra es*.[32] At the steps

[27] A. van Gennep, *The Rites of Passage*, trans. M. B. Vizedom and G. L. Caffee (University of
Chicago Press, 1960), chapter 2, "The Territorial Passage"; Bell, *Ritual*, 36–37.
[28] T. Bailey, *The Processions of Sarum and the Western Church*, Studies and Texts 21 (Toronto:
Pontifical Institute of Mediaeval Studies, 1971), 13–14. Bailey describes only the procession
before Mass, which shares its basic characteristics with the procession after Vespers.
[29] Ibid., 14–15; F. Ll. Harrison, *Music in Medieval Britain*, 4th edn. (Buren, the Netherlands: Fritz
Knuf, 1980), 88–90, 95–96.
[30] Van Gennep, *Rites of Passage*, 20, notes that "rites carried out on the threshold itself are
transition rites."
[31] *Processionale ad usum Sarum*, ed. R. Pynson (London, 1502; facsimile reprint Clarabricken,
Clifden, County Kilkenny: Boethius Press, 1980): *O crux gloriosa*, fol. 120v; *O crux splendidior*,
fols. 120v–121r; *Crux fidelis*, fols. 121r–121v. See also the fourteenth-century *Ordinale Exon.:
Exeter Chapter Ms. 3502 Collated with Parker Ms. 93*, ed. J. N. Dalton, 4 vols., Henry Bradshaw
Society 37, 38, 63, 79 (London: Henry Bradshaw Society, 1909–40), vol. I, 177.
[32] It is no coincidence that Dunstaple set all these texts save *Ibo michi ad montem*. They appear in
Modena, Biblioteca Estense universitaria, MS α.X.1.11, called "Modena B": *Quam pulcra es*,
fols. 81v–82r; *Crux fidelis*, fols. 97v–98r; *Speciosa facta es*, fol. 100Av; *O crux gloriosa/O crux
splendidior*, fols. 119v–120r; *Beata Dei genetrix*, fols. 133v–134r; *Alma redemptoris mater*, fols.
134v–135r. The stylistic heterogeneity of the works, however, indicates that they were written
at different periods in the composer's career, not as a single set.

Example 2.2. Dunstaple, *O crux gloriosa*, interior phrase

within the choir itself, the procession closed with a versicle and prayer said by the priest. Dunstaple's *O crux gloriosa/O crux splendidior* sets two of the antiphons for the Holy Cross consecutively, the first section ending on F, the second on B-flat. The setting forms a natural pair with *Beata Dei genetrix*, also sung by low voices with a final on B-flat (Examples 2.2 and 2.3). Both works have two flats (e♭ and b♭) in the lower voices; *Beata Dei genetrix* also has two flats in the triplum, while *O crux gloriosa/O crux splendidior* has only one.

The two works are stylistically similar, juxtaposing an active contratenor voice against an unusually slow tenor in the same range. Dunstaple places a premium on flowing melodic lines in the triplum, with constantly shifting rhythmic shapes and cadential goals. As in most anthems, the text delivery is highly melismatic. The tenor in *O crux gloriosa/O crux splendidior* begins with the pitches f – B♭ – c – f, which keep reappearing in leaps of a fourth or fifth (Example 2.2). The same three pitches inform the tenor of *Beata Dei genetrix*. At one point, Dunstaple creates an unusual ostinato between f and B♭ in the tenor of *Beata Dei genetrix*, to which the triplum responds

Example 2.3. Dunstaple, *Beata Dei genetrix*, end of first section

in kind (Example 2.3). The low ranges for men's voices often result in close, three-part harmonies. Each work begins with perfect time (○), changes to imperfect time (C), and then concludes with a short passage in the original mensuration (○). The free, yet carefully structured character of the paired works reflects the requirements of the Saturday processions during roughly half the year. Since complex polyphony could not be sung while in motion, they pertained to two different stations, at the rood and at the steps of the choir. In contrast to the plainsong that was sung and echoed as the procession moved through the church, the performance of ornate polyphonic antiphons accentuated the acts of transition and incorporation for the benefit of participants and onlookers alike, extending their musical and ceremonial breadth.

The ritual function of motet and anthem inhered in the recurrent nature of such ceremonies, whether calendrical or occasional. The special character of the performance influenced its social orientation on the one hand and the aesthetic density of both ritual and work on the other. Signal occasions required the kind of symbolic compression that only a motet could provide. These symbolic meanings, in turn, were shaped by the rituals of which the motet formed part. Because these ceremonies were set apart from daily life, motets expressed an ideal state rather than a realistic one. As celebratory works of often immense complexity and sophistication, they had the power to lift those present out of the ordinary and into the presence of the sacred.

3 | Processions in the Veneto

Unlike their English counterparts, Italian chroniclers and diarists of the fifteenth century rarely mention music; if they do, the description is commonly phrased in the most general terms.[1] What the Italians did keep were excellent financial and notarial records, whether ecclesiastical, governmental, mercantile, or confraternal. The Italians, indeed, were the leading financiers in Europe, owing both to the mastery of double-entry bookkeeping and to their superior economic organization. Financial records, combined with such sources as capitular acts and papal letters of supplication, allow us in many instances to trace the careers of musicians as they moved from cathedral to ducal chapel and back. In the Veneto, the sources are particularly rich for Padua, Vicenza, and Treviso, but less so for Venice itself.

The cities of Padua, Vicenza, and Verona all fell to Venice during the war of 1404–05 between Venice and the *signore* of Padua, Francesco Novello da Carrara. The territory acquired by Venice, the *terra ferma*, added greatly to her means of self-defense and to her economic and political power. Padua, Vicenza, and Verona all became integral parts of the *terra ferma*, remaining so until the fall of the Venetian Republic to Napoleon in 1797. Treviso had been aligned with Venice, with one brief intermission, since 1339, when Venice wrested it from the della Scala dynasty of Verona. Padua, home to one of the great universities of Europe, continued as a center of intellectual and musical activity. The broad, fertile plain of northern Italy allowed for a great deal of economic and cultural exchange among the cities of the Veneto, each ruled by a Venetian bishop and *podestà*.

The Veneto represents the main center for the cultivation of the fourteenth-century Italian motet.[2] The tradition continued for the first forty years of the fifteenth century in the Veneto, as well as in Florence and Rome; it was practiced by native Italians and northern composers

---

[1] For an illuminating Italian musical correspondence of the later fifteenth century, see B. Wilson, "Heinrich Isaac among the Florentines," *Journal of Musicology* 23 (2006): 97–152.

[2] M. Bent, "The Fourteenth-Century Italian Motet," in *L'Ars nova italiana del Trecento VI: Atti del congresso internazionale "L'Europa e la musica del Trecento," Certaldo, Palazzo Pretorio, 19–21 luglio 1984*, ed. G. Cattin (Certaldo: Polis, 1990), 85–125.

alike.[3] In the course of the fifteenth century, generations of skilled singers from the Low Countries and northern France traveled south to seek their fortune in the Italian ecclesiastical and secular courts. Their impact was felt on the development of the traditional Italian motet during the early fifteenth century.[4] They also cultivated tenor motets written with the French *Ars nova* techniques of *talea, color,* and proportional construction, as well as new styles that incorporated stylistic accents and dialects from sacred and secular genres, including improvised song. Many of the motets of the period have been connected to political or ecclesiastical occasions, although the specific ceremonial positions they occupied have proven exceedingly difficult to pinpoint. After about 1440, the role of the Veneto in the cultivation of the motet began to fade from view, not to be revived until the next century.

The reception of the Venetian bishops of Padua

Johannes Ciconia numbers among the first composers to migrate to Italy from the Low Countries and northern France. The illegitimate son of a priest, he was trained in Liège, a bishopric in the Low Countries. Ciconia came to Rome in 1391 in the household retinue of Cardinal Philippe d'Alançon. An extended period of residence in Rome helps to explain Ciconia's ready mastery of Italian styles upon his first arrival in Padua in July 1401.[5] The motet *Albane misse celitus/Albane doctor maxime* is one of nine Ciconia motets, all but one composed in Padua in the short period before the composer's death in July 1412.[6] It demonstrates a strongly individual musical style that nevertheless assimilates features of the traditional, fourteenth-century Italian motet.[7] The motet employs two equal discantus

---

[3] R. Nosow, "The Equal-Discantus Motet Style after Ciconia," *Musica Disciplina* 40 (1991): 221–75.

[4] J. E. Cumming, *The Motet in the Age of Du Fay* (Cambridge University Press, 1999), 71–82; R. M. Nosow, "The Florid and Equal-Discantus Motet Styles of Fifteenth-Century Italy" (Ph.D. diss., University of North Carolina at Chapel Hill, 1992), chapters 3 and 4.

[5] G. Di Bacco and J. Nádas, "Verso uno 'stile internazionale' della musica nelle cappelle papale e cardinalizie durante il Grande Scisma (1378–1417): Il caso di Johannes Ciconia da Liège," in *Collectanea I*, ed. A. Roth (Città di Vaticano: Biblioteca apostolica Vaticana, 1994), 7–74; G. Di Bacco and J. Nádas, "Papal Chapels and Italian Sources of Polyphony during the Great Schism," in *Papal Music and Musicians in Late Medieval and Renaissance Rome*, ed. R. Sherr (Oxford: Clarendon Press; Washington, DC: The Library of Congress, 1998), 50–56.

[6] A. Hallmark, "Gratiosus, Ciconia, and Other Musicians at Padua Cathedral: Some Footnotes to Present Knowledge," in *L'Ars nova italiana del Trecento VI*, 75–76.

[7] Bent, "The Fourteenth-Century Italian Motet," 94–95.

Example 3.1. Ciconia, *Albane misse celitus/Albane doctor maxime,* conclusion

voices over a free tenor, without *cantus firmus* (Example 3.1).[8] Ciconia divides the motet into two halves, of which the second precisely replicates the rhythms of the first. The rhythmic patterns themselves are quite complex, despite the use of imperfect time, minor prolation (C). The discantus parts declaim two separate texts of equal length (Figure 3.1); each begins with a direct address to Albano Michiel, Bishop of Padua in 1406–09.[9]

The performance context for which *Albane misse celitus/Albane doctor maxime* was composed may be reconstructed thanks to unusual historical circumstances that are clearly reflected in the texts. The first discantus begins:

Albane misse celitus
presul date divinitus
veni pater Padue;
Cui desolate penitus
confer medellam protinus
duce dudum vidue.

Albano, heaven-sent bishop,
come, father,
divinely given to Padua;
To whom, utterly bereft of a leader,
a short while ago a widow,
grant at once a remedy.

In 1404–05, the Carrara family, which had ruled Padua for much of the fourteenth century, engaged in a protracted, losing battle with powerful Venice. Verona, held by the Carrara, fell to Venice on June 22, 1405. Francesco Novello da Carrara, *signore* of Padua, finally surrendered to Venetian forces outside the walls of the city on November 18, 1405. He was arrested and put to death in a Venetian prison on January 17, 1406, together with his two eldest sons, Francesco III and Giacomo. Stefano Carrara, acting Bishop of Padua and an illegitimate son of Francesco Novello da Carrara, had fled to Florence before the defeat, and essentially was removed from

---

[8] The contratenor appearing in Bologna, Museo internazionale e biblioteca della musica, MS Q15, fols. 271v–272r, no. 273, is probably inauthentic and a later addition. The insufficiency of the additional voice becomes especially noticeable during numerous passages in syncopation between the upper voices.

[9] See *The Works of Johannes Ciconia*, ed. M. Bent and A. Hallmark, Polyphonic Music of the Fourteenth Century 24 (Monaco: L'Oiseau-Lyre, 1985), 85–88, 222–23. The translations herein follow those of M. J. Connolly at 222–23, but rendered more literally.

Discantus I:

Albane misse celitus
presul date divinitus
veni pater Padue,
Cui desolate penitus
confer medellam protinus
duce dudum vidue.

Veni pastor animarum
sparge lumen sidus clarum
cuncta solve debita.
Auffer quitquid est *amarum*
nichil sinas esse [varum]
queque prudens unita.

Justus pius et severus
*qui*a totus es sincerus
quis rimetur cetera
Constans lenis dominaris
vera laude predicaris
qua pertingis ethera.

Leteris urbs Anthenoris
adventu tanti decoris
plausu tota concine.
Michael, O stirpe clarus
tibi antistes datur gnarus
cantu numquam desine.

Discantus II:

Albane doctor maxime
virtute celo proxime
gradu nitens gemino:
Nam decretorum insula
et presulatus ferula
flores sine termino.

Vire celestis emulus
in omni bono sedulus
te Jhesu dedicasti.
Illustri domo genitus
humilitati deditus
sublima comparasti.

O Venetina civitas
in qua perfecta bonitas
virtus tanta nascitur;
Hoc alumpno iocunderis
tibi fulget instar veris
de quo mundus loquitur.

Viri tanti data cure
qui te reget equo iure
Paduana ecclesia,
Christo grates laudes pange
celum edis hymnis tange
cum tuo Ciconia.

Discantus I:

Petrum Marcello Venetum
Romano cretum sanguine
pastorem nostrum car[m]ine
laudemus bene meritum

Exultet urbs Euganee
adventu tanti presulis
exultet plausu jubilis
voces sonent etheree.

Stirps *lete*ris Marcellina
tali alumno decorata
cujus gradu sublimata
illi tota te declina.

Plaudat Patavinus chorus
laudes Jovi summo pangant
voce leta celum tangant
venit enim pastor verus.

Discantus II:

O Petre antistes inclite
vere virtutis speculum
quo nostrum inter seculum
nos mina recto limite

O pater amantissime
nos oves tuas dirige
et aberrantes corrige
judex cunctis justissime.

O cleri primas Padue
nos tuos rite regula
peccantes coge ferula
sordida cuncta dilue.

Sint laudes Regi glorie
qui nos te dignos red*i*dit
qui melon istud edidit
adesto tuo Cyconie.

Figure 3.1. Johannes Ciconia, *Albane misse celitus/Albane doctor maxime* and *Petrum Marcello Venetum/O Petre antistes inclite*, compared

office.[10] Venice wasted no time in publishing the Golden Bull on January 30, 1406, extending legal dominion over the city of Padua and the surrounding countryside, under authority of a Venetian *podestà*.[11] It further claimed the right to name the Bishop of Padua, Albano Michiel, who entered into the city on March 8, 1406.

Albane misse celitus/Albane doctor maxime employs a standard trope for the first entry of a bishop into his cathedral city, in which the relationship between bishop and town is symbolized as a wedding. When a bishop dies, he leaves the city "widowed," as cited in Ciconia's motet.[12] The phrase "desolate penitus" unexpectedly intensifies the tone (Figure 3.1). The true feelings of the populace and the singers of the cathedral are graphically expressed by the miniature that adorns the motet in its unique source, Bologna, Museo internazionale e biblioteca della musica, MS Q15. The illustration, which had been cut out from pages discarded in the remaking of the book between its first and second layers, then pasted in place above Ciconia's motet, shows a soldier, sword uplifted, ready to strike the head off St. Christopher, who is kneeling before him.[13] The motet as a whole, however, expresses a more conciliatory or optimistic view.[14] The fourth stanza of the first discantus refers directly to the advent of Albano Michiel:

Leteris urbs Anthenoris
adventu tanti decoris
plausu tota concine.

Rejoice, Antenor's city
at the arrival of such an honor;
celebrate fully with applause.

---

[10] B. G. Kohl, *Padua under the Carrara, 1318–1405* (Baltimore and London: Johns Hopkins Press, 1998), 332–35.

[11] B. G. Kohl, "Government and Society in Renaissance Padua," *Journal of Medieval and Renaissance Studies* 2 (1972): 215.

[12] D. Rando, "Ceremonial Episcopal Entrances in Fifteenth-Century North-Central Italy: Images, Symbols, Allegories," in *Religious Ceremonials and Images: Power and Social Meaning (1400–1750)*, ed. J. P. Paiva (Coimbra: Palimage Editores, 2002), 41–42. See also M. C. Miller, "Why the Bishop of Florence Had to Get Married," *Speculum* 81 (October 2006): 1055–91.

[13] For a color photograph, see M. Bent, ed., *Bologna Q15: The Making and Remaking of a Musical Manuscript: Introductory Study and Facsimile Edition*, 2 vols. (Lucca: Libreria musicale italiana, 2009), vol. I, 310. Bent discusses and catalogues the reuse of initials in the second layer of the manuscript in vol. I, 116–38, 243–92. See also S. Clercx, *Johannes Ciconia: Un musicien liégeois et son temps*, 2 vols. (Brussels: Académie Royale de Belgique, 1960), I, 68; and M. Bent, "A Contemporary Perception of Early Fifteenth-Century Style: Bologna Q15 as a Document of Scribal Editorial Initiative," *Musica Disciplina* 41 (1987): 185–86.

[14] The transcriptions in Figure 3.1 are original; words and letters in brackets represent emendations. Letters in italics are emendations offered by M. J. Connolly in *The Works of Johannes Ciconia*, ed. Bent and Hallmark, 222–24.

The first discantus addresses the city at large by reference to Antenor, the mythical Trojan founder of Padua, in a direct appeal to the city's heritage. Similarly, the fourth stanza of the second discantus engages the Paduan clergy:

Viri tanti data cure
qui te reget equo iure
Paduana ecclesia,
Christo grates laudes pange
celum edis hymnis tange
cum tuo Ciconia.

Entrusted to the care of such a man
who will rule thee with impartial justice,
O church of Padua,
Compose thanks and praises unto Christ;
touch the vault of the temple with hymns,
with thy Ciconia.

Three details in the passage help identify the occasion with the first reception of a bishop, as proposed by Margaret Bent and Anne Hallmark.[15] First, the text addresses the church of Padua, as the entity most concerned with the bishop's judgment, fairness, and constancy. Second, the motet is sung within Padua Cathedral itself, resounding in the *celum edis*. Third, the word *reget* in the second discantus – the only use of the future tense in either voice – places the work at or before the formal installation of the bishop. It concurs with the direct appeal in the first discantus, *veni pater Padue* ("come, father, to Padua"). The address to Venice in the third stanza, beginning *O Venetina civitas*, confirms that both the Venetian secular authorities and the representatives of the *urbs Anthenore* were in attendance. All the named audiences were present before the main altar of the cathedral.

Ciconia wrote motets for three successive bishops of Padua: *O felix templum jubila* for Stefano da Carrara, *Albane misse celitus/Albane doctor maxime* for Albano Michiel, and *Petrum Marcello Venetum/O Petre antistes inclite* for Pietro Marcello. Ciconia likely composed the last-named work for the first reception of the bishop at Padua Cathedral on July 28, 1409.[16] The musical structure of *Petrum Marcello Venetum/O Petre antistes inclite* is more complex than that of *Albane misse celitus/Albane doctor maxime*,

---

[15] Ibid., xii.

[16] The date often given for the entry of Pietro Marcello, November 16, 1409, traces back to an article by N. Pirrotta, "Il codice di Lucca, III. Il repertorio musicale," *Musica Disciplina* 5 (1951): 123.

Example 3.2. Ciconia, *Petrum Marcello Venetum/O Petre antistes inclite*, salutation

since Ciconia incorporates four voices disposed in two *taleae*, each repeated in diminution, a characteristic of French motets (Example 3.2).[17] Nevertheless, the motet again falls into two rhythmically identical halves. The texts, while less specific than in the motet for Albano Michiel, address many of the same topics, underlined in Figure 3.1: the *adventus* of the bishop,

---

17 See *The Works of Johannes Ciconia*, ed. Bent and Hallmark, 94–102, 224. The translations herein follow those of M. J. Connolly, ibid., 224.

or *antistes*; the *gradu*, in reference to his office; the *ferula*, or bishop's staff; *justus/judex*, justice or judge; and the *celum* or vault of the cathedral, which resounds with praises, *laudes*. The audiences implied are very similar, as well, beginning with the bishop himself and continuing with the Paduan church. Rather than the city of Venice, *Petrum Marcello Venetum/O Petre antistes inclite* addresses the family of Pietro Marcello, in the line "Stirps leteris Marcellina," which compares to "Michael O stirpe clarus" in the earlier motet. Particularly the reference, on two occasions, to the advent of the bishop, especially in the line "venit enim pastor verus" ("for a true pastor comes"), pertains to the first reception of Pietro Marcello.

Moreover, as shown in Figure 3.1, the author of the texts for *Petrum Marcello Venetum/O Petre antistes inclite* took those of *Albane misse celitus/Albane doctor maxime* as a starting-point. Both texts have four stanzas in each discantus voice, which Ciconia distributes evenly between first and second halves of the motet; there is some overlap in *Petrum Marcello Venetum*.[18] The first discantus, especially, employs numerous words closely related to those of *Albane misse celitus*. In two places, whole lines have been transformed, as at the end of the first discantus in *Albane misse celitus*:

Leteris urbs Anthenoris	Exultet urbs Euganee
adventu tanti decoris	adventu tanti presulis
plausu tota concine.	exultet plausu jubilis
Rejoice, Antenor's city	Let the Euganean city rejoice
at the arrival of such an honor;	at the arrival of such a bishop,
celebrate fully with applause.	rejoice with jubilation and applause.

The reference to the nearby Euganean hills, inhabited with wood-nymphs according to Roman mythology, makes for a more literary allusion than does the heavy-handed reference to Antenor in *Albane misse celitus*. The end of the second discantus likewise has been reused for the later motet:

Christo grates laudes pange	laudes Jovi summo pangant
celum edis hymnis tange	voce leta celum tangant
Compose thanks and praises to Christ,	let them compose praises to mighty Jove,
touch the temple vault with thy hymns	touch the vault with cheerful voice

[18] J. M. Allsen, "Style and Intertextuality in the Isorhythmic Motet, 1400–1440" (Ph.D. diss., University of Wisconsin-Madison, 1992), 107–08.

The employment of one motet as a starting-point (rather than as a model) makes sense particularly if the ceremony for which they were written is the same. Clearly, the names, metrical structure, and tone of *Petrum Marcello Venetum* differ from those of *Albane misse celitus*, but much of the same vocabulary and imagery remains. Since the reception ceremony was both recurrent and customary, the reuse of textual elements strongly suggests that the two Ciconia motets were sung at identical places in the first reception of the Venetian bishops of Padua.

The first reception of a bishop in his cathedral church became codified in the late fifteenth century as a special case under the general heading "Ordo ad recipiendum processionaliter prelatum vel legatum" ("Order for the processional reception of prelates or legates"). It should be distinguished from the consecration of the bishop, a prior ceremony that often took place in another city.[19] The essential elements of the procession appear in the *Pontificale Romanum* of 1485, a handbook for bishops, and subsequent liturgical books published prior to the Council of Trent.[20] While the basic elements according to the Roman rite were widely shared in the later Middle Ages, each cathedral had its own variants and ceremonial details.[21] Documents for the *adventus* for two bishops of Padua survive from our period: Raimondo di Provenza in 1374, and Pietro Marcello in 1409.[22] The first document, generated by the court of Francesco il Vecchio da Carrara, traces the procession to the door of the *duomo*, or cathedral. The second originates with the capitular acts of the cathedral, and describes the ceremony within the church. The two descriptions complement each other in that their central concerns are quite different.

[19] On the consecration of bishops in the late Middle Ages, see S. L. MacMillan, *Episcopal Ordination and Ecclesial Consensus* (Collegeville: Liturgical Press, 2005).

[20] *Pontificale Romanum* (Rome: Stephan Plannck, 1497), fols. 198r–199r; *Pontificale noviter impressum: Pro pulchrisque characteribus diligentissime annotatum* (Lyons, 1511), fols. 182r–183r. The Plannck edition was first published in 1485. The *Liber sacerdotalis* (Venice, 1537), fols. 295r–297r, transmits the same text, but also provides music for important processional chants, including *Ecce sacerdos magnus* and *Sacerdos et pontifex*.

[21] M. C. Miller, "The Florentine Bishop's Ritual Entry and the Origins of the Medieval Episcopal Adventus," *Revue d'histoire ecclésiastique* 96 (2002): 5–28, demonstrates that the bishop's *adventus* became standard in Rome in the late twelfth century.

[22] F. S. Dondi Orologio, *Dissertazione ottava sopra l'istoria ecclesiastica padovana*, 2 vols. (Padua: Tipografia del Seminario, 1815), vol. II, 241–44, document CXXIV, dated March 24, 1374; F. S. Dondi Orologio, *Dissertazione nona sopra l'istoria ecclesiastica padovana*, 2 vols. (Padua: Tipografia del Seminario, 1817) vol. II, 17–18, document VI, dated July 28, 1409. Dondi Orologio was himself Bishop of Padua at the time the histories were published. I am most grateful to Antonio Rigon for these references.

Illustration 3.1. First entry of a bishop into his cathedral city

The entry of Raimondo di Provenza took place on March 24, 1374. Unlike his predecessor, Raimondo had the trust of the *signore* of Padua, Francesco il Vecchio da Carrara, who sent two emissaries to greet him before the Ognissanti gate, in the eastern wall of the city. The procession of citizens and clerics met the new bishop at the ancient Benedictine monastery of Santa Maria di Fistomba. In Roman use, the bishop typically sojourned at a major Benedictine abbey or convent, where he dismounted and was formally received.[23] The two emissaries of the *signore*, Boscarino di Boscarini and Negro di Negri, brought the bishop a large palfrey, covered in white cloth, signifying his triumphant entry into the city.[24] The bishop himself would have worn a white cope and surplice, as shown in Illustration 3.1.[25] According to the *Pontificale Romanum*, the clergy and archpresbyter of the cathedral met the bishop, singing the antiphon *Sacerdos et pontifex* or the responsory *Ecce sacerdos magnus*. Boscarino and Negro then took the bishop's reins, walking alongside, as the entire clergy of Padua preceded them through the gates, over the Ognissanti bridge, and through the town. Before the doors of the cathedral, Bishop Raimondo dismounted and gave the palfrey back to Boscarino and Negro, in a typical symbolic exchange of authority.

A description of the Corpus Christi procession of 1441 in Padua gives an idea of the order of the main participants, beginning with the trade guilds, followed by the monastics:

Fratrum Servorum	Servites
Fratrum Carmelitarum	Carmelites
Fratrum Heremitarum de Observantia	Observant Eremites
Fratrum Minorum de Observantia	Observant Franciscans
Fratrum Minorum	Franciscans
Fratrum Praedicatorum	Dominicans

[23] In Bologna, the bishop arrived at the Benedictine church of Santo Stephani; see G. Belvederi, "Cerimonie nel solenne ingresso dei Vescovi in Bologna durante il Medio Evo," *Rassegna Gregoriana* 2 (1913): cols. 169–86. In Parma, the bishop repaired to the abbey of St. John the Evangelist; see G. Zarotti, "Codici e corali della cattedrale di Parma," *Archivio storico per le province parmensi*, series IV, 20 (1968): 215, with a transcription of Parma, Archivio Capitolare, MS 04. In Florence, the bishop remained overnight at the Benedictine convent of San Pietro Maggiore; see R. C. Trexler, *Public Life in Renaissance Florence* (New York: Academic Press, 1980), 273–74; and Miller, "Why the Bishop of Florence Had to Get Married." In both Bologna and Florence, the bishop was made to continue to the cathedral church barefoot.

[24] Rando, "Ceremonial Episcopal Entrances," 34–40.

[25] Illustration 3.1 shows the customary scene from the *Caeremoniale episcoporum* (Rome, 1600) and subsequent editions, retouched in the eighteenth century, but retaining late sixteenth-century dress and all relevant details.

Canonicorum Regularium	Canons Regular
Monacorum S. Benedicti	Benedictines
Praesbiterorum	Priests
Scolares utriusque; Univers.	Scholars of the University of Padua
D.D. Iuristarum Collegium	Doctors of the College of Law
[Sacratiss. Corpus Christi]	[Holy Sacrament]
D. Episcopus	Bishop
D.D. Rectores	Civil authorities
D.D. Milites	Knights of the city
Collegium D.D. Medicor.	Doctors of Medicine
Honorandi Cives	Honored citizens[26]

The document for the entry of Pietro Marcello, dated July 28, 1409, corroborates and substantiates the participants in the procession as it gathered within the cathedral. The Venetian *capitano*, Marino Caravello, stood in place of the *podestà*. Three Venetian representatives met the bishop, along with three representatives of the Paduan churches, three knights of the city, and three notaries, including the author, Andreas de Campanis. In addition, all the clergy of the city participated, as well as a multitude of laity. The archpresbyter of the cathedral, Francesco Zabarella, led the Paduan delegation. A native Paduan, a doctor of both civil and canon law, he had been elected to the episcopal seat by the cathedral chapter, only to see his election overruled by Pope Gregory XII.[27]

The first order of business for Zabarella was to receive the papal bull appointing Pietro Marcello as bishop. The notary duly observes that the bull was neither cancelled nor abraded. Zabarella then led the bishop to the eastern end of the church, where he was first seated upon the marble throne by the altar of St. Daniel, in the lower quadrant, then upon the marble throne behind the main altar, in the upper quadrant. Before proceeding to the high throne, according to the *Pontificale Romanum*, the bishop knelt on a faldstool on the lowest step of the main altar, while the archpresbyter said over him the prayer *Deus omnium fidelium*, employed until recent times as a prayer for the installation of a bishop.[28] The bishop then arose, said

---

[26] P. Saviolo, *Thesaurus urbis Paduanae* (Padua: Frombotti, 1682), 26–30.

[27] T. E. Morrissey, "*Ecce sacerdos magnus*: On Welcoming a New Bishop. Three Addresses for Bishops of Padua by Franciscus Zabarella," in *Nicholas of Cusa on Christ and the Church: Essays in Memory of Chandler McCuskey Brooks*, ed. G. Christianson and T. M. Izbicki (Leiden and New York: Brill, 1996), 61.

[28] *Liber usualis: Missae et officii* (Tournai: Desclée, 1953), 1842. The *Pontificale Romanum* states: "Deinde procedunt ad altare maius ecclesie: et ibi super faldistorio ante infimum gradum altaris parato procumbit et orat prelatus seu legatus."

a prayer to the patron saint of the church, did reverence at the altar, and blessed the people. Once the new bishop was seated upon his throne, as the 1374 document narrates, he and the cathedral chapter made an oath to uphold the rights and emoluments of the civil authorities, which oath was returned in kind to the bishop and chapter. Pietro Marcello then recognized the clergy and accepted their vows of obedience. The entire ceremony ended with all the clergy united in singing the *Te Deum*, "according to most ancient custom."[29]

The archpresbyter of the cathedral, the learned Francesco Zabarella, was Ciconia's patron, for whom he composed two of his motets, *Doctorem principem/Melodia suavissima* and *Ut te per omnes/Ingens alumnus Padue*. Not only would Zabarella have officiated at the installation of Albano Michiel and Pietro Marcello, but he had previously led the Paduan delegation to Venice, on January 4, 1406, when "the scepter, keys, and the silver seal of the Commune" were presented to the Doge, in token of the surrender of the city.[30] Zabarella made an oration to the Doge and council as part of the formal presentation. Later in the spring, on June 6, Zabarella welcomed the new bishop with a Latin oration in the presence of the Doge of Venice, Michele Steno, the *podestà*, Marino Caravello, the captain, Zaccharia Trevisano, and the cathedral chapter.[31]

Ciconia's *Albane misse celitus/Albane doctor maxime* and *Petrum Marcello Venetum/O Petre antistes inclite*, in their references to the *adventus* of the bishop, the vaults of the cathedral, the presence of clergy, the citizens of Padua, and the Venetian authorities, closely fit the ceremonial and historical situation at the reception and installation of the Venetian bishops of Padua. The "signature" of Ciconia at the end of the motets confirms that they were performed by the cathedral singers. None of the historical sources, however, specifies where during the installation ceremony the motets were sung. Andreas de Campanis issues a blanket statement concerning the ceremonies, with Zabarella "doing, effecting, and observing all and severally the attendant orders, as necessary, opportune, and customary."[32] The key word is *opportuna*, which hints at elements beyond the traditional in conformity

[29] Dondi Orologio, *Dissertazione nona*, vol. II, 18: "secundum morem antiquissimum in talibus consuetum."
[30] W. C. Hazlitt, *The Venetian Republic: Its Rise, Its Growth, and Its Fall*, 2 vols. (London: Adam and Charles Black, 1900), vol. I, 768–69.
[31] Morrissey, "On Welcoming a New Bishop," 60. Morrissey, ibid., 65–66, concludes that Zabarella also composed the address delivered by Albano Michiel on the same occasion. Zabarella's response to the bishop was "brief and to the point."
[32] Dondi Orologio, *Dissertazione nona*, vol. II, 18: "ac omnia alia et singula circa predicta necessaria opportuna ac consueta faciendo operando et observando."

with the exigencies of the moment. As the bishop knelt at the high altar, and after the prayer *Deus omnium fidelium*, said by the archpresbyter, the *Pontificale Romanum* of 1485 directs: "His dictis, cantores cantant aliquam antiphonam eis magis placentem, de sancto patrono ecclesie, cum versicolo de eodem sancto" ("This said, the singers sing some antiphon pleasing to these leaders, of the patron saint of the church, with a versicle of the same saint"). A motet honoring the bishop could easily have followed the antiphon and versicle, as occurs in the procession from the city gates: "cantantur post dictas antiphonas seu responsoris alia cantica vel hymni prout magis placebit" ("after the stated antiphons or reponsories, other songs or hymns are sung so far as it will please the leaders").[33] Consequently, the two works may have been performed at the central moment of the ceremony, before the bishop arose to give the benediction to the cathedral chapter and assembled dignitaries. That moment represented the rite of incorporation, when the bishop humbled himself before the city, cathedral, and archpriest, Francesco Zabarella, to assume his new identity in their midst. Regardless of their exact position, the placement of the Ciconia motets within the ceremony would have been the same. In many ways, they acted as a rhetorical summing-up of the diverse meanings of the ritual for those in attendance.

The Easter procession at Vicenza Cathedral

The composer Johannes de Lymburgia, like Ciconia, hailed from the diocese of Liège. He has been identified by Margaret Bent as the Johannes de Francia who was granted a benefice at Padua Cathedral in October 1424.[34] When Pietro Emiliani, Bishop of Vicenza, moved his residency from Padua to Vicenza in 1427, he brought Johannes de Francia with him. The composer is named "presbiter Iohannes Cantor de Limburgia q[uondam] Iohannis Vinandi" in November 1431, a beneficed singer at Vicenza Cathedral.[35] He may have filled a newly created position as teacher of polyphony to three choirboys in Vicenza Cathedral.[36] He also is called "mansionarius et

---

[33] *Pontificale Romanum*, fols. 198r–199r.

[34] M. Bent, "Johannes de Lymburgia," in *The New Grove Dictionary of Music and Musicians*, 2nd edn. (London: Macmillan, 2000). The request is contained in Padua, Archivio capitolare del Duomo, MS *Acta capitulorum* III, fols. 90r, 92r, 93v, 99v, 103v, 104v, under the heading "Giovanni di Francia Cantore la custodia vacante per morte del R. Bartolomeo Capolito."

[35] G. Mantese, *Movimento di riforma ecclesiastica pretridentina nel Quattrocento Vicentino* (Vicenza: Istituto S. Gaetano, 1990), 26–27.

[36] F. A. Gallo and G. Mantese, *Ricerche sulle origini della cappella musicale del duomo di Vicenza* (Venice and Rome: Istituto per la collaborazione culturale, 1964), 28–30.

tenorista" in a document of 1432, and was present in Vicenza as late as April 1435.[37] A *tenorista* in the early fifteenth century typically acted as leader of the choir in plainchant and polyphony. The position corresponds to the practical and theoretical primacy of the tenor in polyphonic music.

Johannes de Lymburgia is a leading figure in the manuscript Bologna, Museo internazionale e biblioteca della musica, Q15, compiled in Padua and Vicenza at the chapels of two Bishops of Vicenza, Pietro Emiliani (1409–33) and Francesco Malipiero (1433–51).[38] The manuscript is the single most important source for Latin polyphony in the first half of the fifteenth century, containing no fewer than a hundred motets copied into ten of the twenty-nine gatherings. Other sections of the manuscript contain Mass Ordinaries, hymns, and Magnificats. Although the single scribe of the codex has not been identified, Lymburgia may have had an editorial hand in its compilation, particularly in the second and third layers, which contain his music. His *Surexit Christus* appears in gathering 19, belonging to the second layer of compilation, dated circa 1430–33.[39]

Surexit Christus is unique among early fifteenth-century motets in that it combines mensural polyphony with a monophonic refrain, which sets the word *Alleluya* (Examples 3.3 and 3.4).[40] One other motet, Nicholas Grenon's *Nova vobis gaudia*, contains a polyphonic refrain, setting the word *Noel*. As the refrain suggests, the latter work is intended for the Christmas season (see Chapter 7). *Nova vobis gaudia* lacks bar lines to delineate poetic strophes, although because of the employment of *taleae* in all three voices, the refrain is sung to the same rhythms each time. It directly follows *Surexit Christus* in Bologna Q15. The simplified rhythms and short phrases of *Surexit Christus*, each one followed by a rest, betray the influence of the Italian *lauda*, or song of praise.[41] But the work lacks

---

[37] Mantese, *Movimento di riforma*, 27, 28 n. 22.

[38] Bent, "A Contemporary Perception of Fifteenth-Century Style," 184–89; M. Bent, "Pietro Emiliani's Chaplain Bartolomeo Rossi da Carpi and the Lamentations of Johannes de Quadris in Vicenza," *Il saggiatore musicale* 2 (1995): 5–15.

[39] Bent, ed., *Bologna Q15*, vol. I, 204.

[40] Bologna Q15, fols. 197v–198r, no. 175. The *Alleluya* is placed incorrectly in the edition in J. H. Etheridge, "The Works of Johannes de Lymburgia," 2 vols. (Ph.D. diss., Indiana University, 1972), vol. II, 240–49.

[41] Bent, ed., *Bologna Q15*, vol. I, 204, calls the work a "Hymn set as a motet." T. Schmidt-Beste, *Textdeklamation in der Motette des 15. Jahrhunderts* (Turnhout: Brepols, 2003), 66, categorizes the work as a *lauda*. Two considerations argue against such a classification: first, *Surexit Christus* is not strophic in its musical organization, despite the monophonic refrain; and second, it appears in the motet section of the manuscript, both preceded and followed by motets.

Example 3.3. Lymburgia, *Surexit Christus*, first two strophes and refrain

the melodic interest of the *lauda*, concentrating attention more on the contrast of the three-part harmonies with the unison refrain. The most rhythmically complex passage occurs for two soloists alone, in rhythmic imitation, illustrating the command *pergite* ("go on ahead").

Example 3.3. (*cont.*)

Example 3.4. Anonymous, *Surrexit Christus*

The precise performance context for *Surexit Christus* can be ascertained because a monophonic setting of the text appears in a Vicentine source containing the *Lamentations* of the composer Johannes de Quadris. The latter source, Vicenza, Seminario vescovile, MS U.VIII.11, has been discussed in articles by Giulio Cattin and Margaret Bent.[42] It contains two fascicles, the first with the *Lamentations of Jeremiah* and a series of six sequences, the second with chants and prayers for the *processione ad fontem* on the four days from Holy Saturday to Tuesday in Easter week. As Bent shows, the first fascicle was inscribed at the instigation of the episcopal chaplain Bartolomeo Rossi da Carpi in his testament of February 1453. The second, later fascicle, which contains the monophonic *Surrexit Cristus*, originated in the second half of the fifteenth century.[43] Despite the late date of the manuscript, performance of the monophonic *Surrexit Cristus* in Vicenza – and the ceremony of which it formed part – undoubtedly preceded Johannes de Lymburgia's polyphonic setting.

The Johannes de Quadris manuscript may be used in the first instance to reconstruct the motet *Surexit Christus*. It has not been pointed out heretofore that the monophonic melody, unknown outside of Vicenza, agrees note-for-note and syllable-for-syllable with the first strophe of the

[42] G. Cattin, "Uno sconosciuto codice quattrocentesco dell'Archivio capitolare di Vicenza e le Lamentazioni di Johannes de Quadris," in L'*Ars nova italiana del Trecento: Secondo convegno internazionale, 17–22 luglio 1969*, ed. F. A. Gallo (Certaldo: Centro di Studi sull'Ars Nova italiana del Trecento, 1970), 281–304; Bent, "Bartolomeo Rossi da Carpi."

[43] Bent, "Bartolomeo Rossi da Carpi," 10–14; Cattin, "Uno sconosciuto codice," 282–84. Bent comments that "Even if they were separately prepared, the intention to join the Lamentations and the Sequences is apparent from the will. That would leave the final fascicle of the volume, with later fifteenth-century additions of Easter rites and other liturgical items, as the true 'addition.'"

motet tenor. It comprises a single period, in the pattern *a a′ b a*. In the monophonic manuscript, each of the first three strophes, of which only the first is underlaid, is sung to this melody, followed by the *Alleluya* refrain.[44] The next three strophes are each sung to the same tune, again followed by the *Alleluya*. A comparison between Examples 3.3 and 3.4 suggests that despite the chant notation, the song was rhythmicized in strict accordance with the iambic meter of the text.[45]

Johannes de Lymburgia's setting in Bologna Q15 creates a more complicated pattern (Figure 3.2). A rubric, *chorus Alleluya*, occurs after the second strophe in the first discantus part, set off by a solid red bar line. The monophonic *Alleluya* itself is notated at the end of the first discantus, in F_3 clef, with the rubric *Corus semper respondens*. It uses only the first half of the tune, however, and contains four statements of the word *Alleluya*, as opposed to eight in the Johannes de Quadris manuscript; the latter setting most likely incorporates the entire melody. Hereafter, the red bar lines in the two discantus parts indicate the repetition of the refrain, which occurs symmetrically after the second, third, fifth, and sixth strophes.

The composer also varies the texture from one strophe to the next (Figure 3.3). Only the first strophe carries the *cantus firmus* in the tenor. According to the tenor rubric, the third strophe is sung as a duo between the upper voices. Each discantus is additionally marked *unus*, confirming performance by soloists; if reduced forces were required, the *unus* labels would be superfluous. The mensuration also changes to imperfect time, major prolation (₵). The fourth strophe, labeled *chorus*, with the tenor re-entering, returns to the initial mensuration of perfect time, minor prolation (○, unmarked). The fifth strophe has another duo, again with the upper voices marked *unus*, while the sixth has a *chorus*, followed by a final statement of the refrain in unison. In contrast to the *unus* passages, the *chorus* sections must have been performed with a minimum of five singers, two per part in the upper voices and one in the tenor. Moreover, the rubric for

---

[44] Fols. 16v–17r; facsimile in Cattin, "Uno sconosciuto codice," 287.

[45] The iambic rhythms of the motet *cantus firmus* and *Alleluya* suggest that the Easter sequences and prosa in Seminario vescovile U.VIII.11 were rhythmicized in a similar way, in accordance with metrical accent. On the question of rhythmicized plainchant, see J. Caldwell, "Plainsong and Polyphony 1250–1550," in *Plainsong in the Age of Polyphony*, ed. T. F. Kelly (Cambridge University Press, 1992), 6–31; and R. Sherr, "The Performance of Chant in the Renaissance and Its Interactions with Polyphony," in *Plainsong in the Age of Polyphony*, ed. Kelly, 178–208.

Surexit Christus hodie humano pro solamine mortem qui passus corpore miserimo pro homine.	Surrexit Cristus hodie humano pro solamine mortem qui passus corpore miserimo pro homine.
Apparuit discipulis expoliatis inferis recuperatis gaudiis patrie quondam perditis.	Apparuit discipulis expoliatis inferis recuperatis gaudiis patrie quondam perditis.
Alleluya, alleluya, alleluya, alleluya.	
Nos ergo dulci modulo cunctis canentes proprio in hoc pascali gaudio benedicamus Domino.	Nos ergo dulci modulo cunctis canentes proprio in hoc pascali gaudio benedicamus Domino.
Alleluya, alleluya, alleluya, alleluya.	Alleluya, alleluya, alleluya, alleluya, Alleluya, alleluya, alleluya, alleluya.
Mulieres ad tumulum donum ferunt aromatum album videntes angelum annunciantes gaudium.	Mulieres ad tumulum donum ferunt aromatum album videntes angelum annunciantes gaudium.
O mulieres trepide in Galileam pergite discipuli[s] predicite quid surexit Rex glorie.	O mulieres trepide in Galileam pergite discipulis predicite quid surrexit Rex glorie.
Alleluya, alleluya, alleluya, alleluya.	
Eterno ad sit claritas divina et humanitas et pia Dei unitas Deo dicamus gracias.	Eterno ad sit claritas divina et humanitas et pia Dei unitas Deo dicamus gracias.
Alleluya, alleluya, alleluya, alleluya.	Alleluya, alleluya, alleluya, alleluya. Alleluya, alleluya, alleluya, alleluya.

Figure 3.2. Comparison of Johannes de Lymburgia, *Surexit Christus*, with monophonic setting in Vicenza, Seminario vescovile, MS U.VIII.11, fols. 16v–17r. Boldface indicates *cantus firmus*

the unison refrain, as well as the refrain itself in F$_3$ clef, occurs in the first discantus part. Consequently, the singers would all have been men, reaching c″ at the top of their range in both discantus voices. They would have then switched to their natural register to sing the refrain.

Text	Texture
Strophe 1	Full with *cantus firmus* in tenor – perfect time, minor prolation
Strophe 2	Full
Refrain	Monophonic, unison voices
Strophe 3	Duo between solo discantus voices – imperfect time, major prolation
Refrain	Monophonic, unison voices – perfect time, minor prolation
Strophe 4	Full
Strophe 5	Duo between solo discantus voices
Refrain	Monophonic, unison voices
Strophe 6	Full
Refrain	Monophonic, unison voices

Figure 3.3. Texture in Johannes de Lymburgia, *Surexit Christus*

Cattin adduces another source, the Venetian *Liber sacerdotalis* of 1523, which corresponds in many details to the rite at Vicenza Cathedral.[46] The *Liber sacerdotalis* prescribes that the strophes of *Surrexit Cristus* be sung by two soloists, and the *Alleluya* refrain by a choir of eight, to the same melody as the stanzas. This agrees precisely with the distinction in the motet between polyphonic stanzas and monophonic refrain, with the entire choir in unison. Johannes de Lymburgia follows the general outline of the monophonic sequence, but varies the texture from one strophe to the next, cuts the length of the refrain in half, and adds refrains after the second and fifth strophes.

The *processione ad fontem* prescribed in the Johannes de Quadris manuscript took place at second Vespers in Vicenza Cathedral (Illustration 3.2). The liturgical structure of the ceremony is unusual in that the procession begins in the middle of Vespers, not at the end. On Easter Sunday, the processional items commence with the antiphon *Vidi aquam* and Psalm 135, *Confitemini Domino*, for the aspersion of holy water on the high altar and side altars along the way.[47] The antiphon *Et respicientes viderunt* introduces the Magnificat, in mode 3 on E, which would have been sung as the choir processed through the nave toward the baptismal font, located near the entrance of the church. On Easter Monday, the Magnificat antiphon specified is *Qui sunt hii sermones*, and on Tuesday, *Videte manus meas*, both in mode 8 on G. The procession continues with the traditional Easter processional respond, *Christus resurgens*. At the station, the choir

---

[46] Cattin, "Uno sconosciuto codice," 290 n. 18, citing the *Liber sacerdotalis* (Venice: Merchiorem Sessam et Petrum de Ravanis, 1523), fols. 278v–279r. See also the 1537 edition of the *Liber sacerdotalis*, at fol. 294v.

[47] For a summary of the contents of the second fascicle, see Cattin, "Uno sconosciuto codice," 284–88. The incipit *Confitemini domino* is added in a later hand.

Illustration 3.2. Vicenza Cathedral, nave and high altar

sings *Surrexit Cristus*, although only the first strophe is underlaid in the manuscript (Example 3.4).

Surrexit Cristus functions as a *Benedicamus Domino* trope in which the familiar words appear at the end of the third strophe, and the response, *Deo dicamus gracias*, at the end of the sixth (Figure 3.2). Even though every Vespers concludes with the same formula, here they are nevertheless followed (rather than preceded) by a short prayer, proper to each day. Each of the three prayers has the rubric *Ad fontem*, which demonstrates that the procession made only one station, at the baptismal font. The *Liber sacerdotalis* states that the Marian antiphon *Regina celi* was sung "in many churches" upon the return of the procession to the choir:[48] a setting in fauxbourdon by Lymburgia appears in Bologna Q15.[49] As in *Surexit Christus* and other texts of Easter week, the antiphon setting emphasizes the joyous refrain, *Alleluya*.

Pietro Rosso and the procession of the Annunciation

In Treviso, the feast of the Annunciation of the Virgin, March 25, was marked by a spectacular procession through the city. For the procession in 1443, a number of dignitaries received the gift of a fine pair of gloves (see Appendix A). The recipients are listed in the accounts of the confraternity of Santa Maria dei Battuti, which underwrote the costs of the procession, as well as of the sacred play, or *sacra rappresentazione*, presented in the cathedral that day in conjunction with the cathedral chapter. Santa Maria dei Battuti was the leading religious brotherhood in Treviso in the fifteenth century, a source of civic pride and identity.[50] Those who received gloves "of chamois leather lined with silk" included the Venetian patrician Ludovico Barbo, Bishop of Treviso, and the Venetian *podestà*. Next listed are the officials of Santa Maria dei Battuti: the four *gastoldi* or directors, the *quattorvice*, and the *sindico* or comptroller.[51] Two *cavali mariani* or *chavalcanti*, no doubt with appropriate equestrian trappings, were used to pull the wagon bearing

---

[48] *Liber sacerdotalis nuperrime ex libris sancte Romane ecclesiae* (Venice, 1537), fol. 265r: "Postquam in plerisque ecclesijs dicitur antiphona de beata virgine pro gaudio resurrectionis. *Regina celi. Ora pro nobis.* Oratio. *Gratiam tuam quesumus Domine.*"

[49] Bologna Q15, no. 199, fol. 207r.

[50] D. M. D'Andrea, *Civic Christianity in Renaissance Italy: The Hospital of Treviso, 1400–1530* (University of Rochester Press, 2007), chapter 1, "The City of God."

[51] The term *quattorvice* appears to be otherwise unknown; it conceivably denotes the post of deputy to the four *gastoldi*.

the young protagonists of the sacred play, *Il canto dell'angnol e la Maria* (*The Song of the Angel and Mary*), to be presented at the cathedral later that day. High officials of the cathedral likewise received the silk-lined gloves in 1443: the treasurer, the master of the choirboys, the archdeacon, and a cathedral canon, Maestro Pietro Rosso. One dozen gloves "of double kid" went to the cathedral singers and other officials, and yet a third set of "small gloves" to the boys who played the angels in the *sacra rappresentazione*. The boys, dressed in white and with wings, probably came in a separate wagon. The number used in the play had varied from four to six in previous years before suddenly doubling to twelve in 1443. The members of Santa Maria dei Battuti also participated in the procession, since they were required to march through the city on several occasions during the year, including the feast of the Annunciation.[52]

The procession wound from the cathedral to the church of Santa Maria Maggiore and back. The route followed the present Camaggiore and Via Independenza, turning left at the Via Martiri della Libertà. According to the accounts of 1438, two sacristans were paid three *lire* to peal the cathedral bells, called "el Fontego" ("the Big One") and "i Porci" ("the Pigs"), as a sign of assembly. Specification of the bells may imply a particular pattern of tolling. The accounts also mention a hundred wild birds that were required for the festivities, presumably to be released during the procession.[53] Two trumpet players led the way, one of whom was Messer Zanuso, who appears regularly in the accounts from 1438 to 1446. In 1447, however, payment to a new group appears: "a piero macharon e compagni piffari e zaramelle et trombeta per haver sona ala dita festa" ("to Piero Macharon and his companions, winds, bagpipes, and trumpet, for having played at the said feast").[54] The latter group was capable of performing a variety of vernacular music, not merely the traditional fanfares. The confraternity regularly included payment to four lay singers to participate in the procession, as well.[55]

In 1438 and 1439, the *magister scholarum* of Treviso Cathedral, Pietro Rosso, received not only a pair of gloves, but three ducats in gold, "per

[52] L. Pesce, *La chiesa di Treviso nel primo Quattrocento*, 3 vols., Italia sacra 37–39 (Rome: Herder, 1987), vol. II, 385–86.
[53] Ibid., vol. II, 596–98, edits the entire accounts for 1438.
[54] Treviso, Archivio di Stato, Ospedale di Santa Maria dei Battuti, Busta 3, fol. 168r. The group was paid three *lire*, as opposed to two *lire* for Messer Zanuso.
[55] D. Bryant and M. Pozzobon, *Musica, devozione, città: La Scuola di Santa Maria dei Battuti (e uno suo manoscritto musicale) nella Treviso del Rinascimento* (Treviso: Fondazione Benetton and Editrice Canova, 1995), 49–51.

sua fatiga di insegnar a i puti va' a cantar p*er* la maria."[56] In other words, the master of the choirboys taught the art of singing to the boys playing the Angel Gabriel and the Virgin Mary, as well as to the other boys who played the angels. In 1443, a substitute from the cathedral, Giacomo da Mantua, was required, and he also was paid three ducats in gold, but of a slightly higher weight, and therefore worth more.[57] The two protagonists were paid five *lire* apiece, while the angels received two *lire*. The officials of the confraternity attended the dress rehearsal, "according to custom."[58] The expenses for the procession of the Annunciation were kept under a separate account in the confraternal books, which vary in detail from year to year (see Appendix A). In 1443, the *sindico* notes the gift of a pair of gloves under a special heading: "et a m*esser* p*re* piero rosso fé el canto se ca*n*ta in + di via / missus est ang*elus* gabriel etc. / paio .1." ("and to the master priest Piero Rosso, [who] made the song that is sung at the crossing of the way, *Missus est Angelus Gabriel*, one pair"). The *croce di via*, located at the corner of the present Via Independenza and Via Martiri della Libertà, is a well-known meeting spot that goes back to ancient Roman times. Hard by stands the Loggia de' Cavalieri, an open-air colonnade erected for the use of the nobility of Treviso in the late thirteenth century.

The following year, 1444, one of the seventeen pairs of silk-lined gloves was again presented under a special heading: "pai .1. a m*esser* prè piero rosso fexe el ca*n*to missus est gabriel ecc." ("one pair to master priest Piero Rosso, who made the song *Missus est Gabriel* etc."). As it happens, the incipit *Missus est Gabriel* corresponds exactly to a three-voice motet in the manuscript Bologna Q15, ascribed to Petrus Rubeus, the Latin name of the musician and canon at Treviso Cathedral.[59] The inverted wording of the incipit in 1443 derives from the well-known antiphon *Missus est Angelus*

---

[56] Treviso, Archivio di Stato, Ospedale di S. Maria dei Battuti, Busta 1, fols. 167r and 190v, respectively. On the career of Pietro Rosso, see R. Nosow, "Rubeus, Petrus," in *The New Grove Dictionary of Music and Musicians*, 2nd edn. (London: Macmillan, 2000). Rosso served the cathedral chapter as *magister scholarum* in 1424–25 and 1437–39; see L. Pesce, *Ludovico Barbo, vescovo di Treviso (1447–1443)*, 2 vols. (Padua: Antenore, 1969), vol. I, 94–95.

[57] The ducats paid to Piero Rosso weighed 112 grains, or 16 *lire*, 16 *soldi*, whereas the ducats paid to Giacomo da Mantua weighed 114 grains, worth 17 *lire*, 2 *soldi*.

[58] The detailed synopsis edited in Pesce, *La chiesa di Treviso*, vol. II, 470–75, dated 1442, barely mentions the Angel Gabriel, the assembled angels, or the Annunciation itself, presenting instead an elaborate series of Old Testament scenes. Its relationship to the *sacra rappresentazione* at Treviso Cathedral remains uncertain, but it appears to represent an amplification of the original play.

[59] Bologna Q15, no. 200, fols. 207v–208r; ed. in G. Reaney in *Early Fifteenth-Century Music*, Corpus mensurabilis musicae 11, 7 vols. (Neuhausen-Stuttgart: American Institute of Musicology, 1955–83), vol. V, 96–98.

Gabriel, which in turn quotes Luke 1:26–27 in the Vulgate Bible. In March 1447, Rosso was likewise listed among the dignitaries to receive the silk-lined gloves. The 1447 accounts cite him as "m*esser* p*re* piero rosso fexe el ca*n*to missus est angelus gabriel." Although the entry is dated 22 March, three days before the procession, it employs the past tense *fexe*, which must be interpreted accordingly not as "sang," but as "composed."

Since the "singers of the cathedral" were provided every year with *malvasia e brasadelli* – white wine and cookies in the shape of bracelets – for their repast on the feast day, they were no doubt customarily entrusted with performance of the motet, which requires forces sufficient to create contrasts between *chorus* and *unus*. In 1438, four singers were provided with gloves, in addition to Pietro Rosso, the *magister scholarum*, creating an ensemble of five singers, two each for the discantus parts, and one for the tenor.[60] This accords with the minimal ensemble required for Lymburgia's *Surexit Christus*. The accounts present no evidence that the boys trained for the *sacra rappresentazione* were employed in the performance of the motet.

Missus est Gabriel Angelus appears in the second layer of Bologna Q15, and can be dated before 1434.[61] Since Pietro Rosso was also *magister scholarum* of Treviso Cathedral in 1424–25, the motet may have been composed at that time, while he was intimately involved with music, and specifically with the *sacra rappresentazione* for the feast of the Annunciation. A date between 1424 and 1434 also fits the style of the piece, which takes two different responsory texts with their verses and distributes them between the two discantus voices in such a way as to create both double-texted and single-texted passages (see Figure 4.1). The work projects bold melodic lines with strong rhythms throughout, including appoggiaturas (see Example 4.1). It is shaped with elaborate textural devices and constantly shifting mensurations in a way typical of the period and fitting for a civic occasion. Since the motet was sung at the *croce di via*, it necessarily was heard in the open air, at a point of maximum exposure to the assembled citizens of Treviso.

But the salient point is that the existing financial accounts, which begin in 1436, note the special gift of gloves to Rosso in 1443, 1444, and 1447. The intervening years, 1445 and 1446, have less complete accounts.[62] Rosso was reported "gravely ill" in January 1448, and his testament is dated

---

[60] Pesce, *La chiesa di Treviso*, vol. II, 596–98: "per malvasia e brasadelli per far colation per i cantadori del domo, el agnol e Maria, lire 1, danari 1." Presentation of the gloves that same year was made "a 4 cantadori para 4" (March 26, 1438).

[61] Bent, ed., *Bologna Q15*, vol. I, 209–10.

[62] Treviso, Archivio di stato, Ospedale di Santa Maria dei Battuti, Busta 2, fols. 435, 599; Busta 3, fol. 82.

February 26, 1449.[63] Given the persistence of other major festive elements, the logical conclusion is that *Missus est Gabriel angelus* was sung in the procession of the Annunciation every year from circa 1434 to 1447. Rosso received the gloves because the motet had become a fixture in the life of the city, on the day of its most elaborate procession.

[63] Pesce, *Ludovico Barbo*, vol. I, 94–95.

4 | The motet as ritual embassy

Motets in the Veneto were written and performed for specific ceremonial occasions. Like English motets, they conform to the definitions of ritual and, in every case studied, constitute important elements of larger ceremonies. Scholarly literature has often referred to certain works of the fifteenth century as *Staatsmotetten* because of their overt references to individual states or political and ecclesiastical personages. Yet, if all motets had a ritual function, then the categorization of individual works as *Staatsmotetten* creates a dichotomy between the political and devotional that fails to appreciate the profound interconnectedness of religion and politics in the fifteenth century. One can cut across the dichotomy by reference to a further aspect shared by many motets, one that was strongly characteristic of fifteenth-century culture: they often acted as ritual embassies.[1]

In the fifteenth century, embassy was the art of presenting one's interests, party, and honor in the most positive way. It was integral to ceremonial life, not just to the requirements of foreign relations. There were two or more sides to any embassy, a fact acknowledged and implicit in the shape of the language chosen. In the words of the Florentine Lapo Mazzei, "There is no embassy so displeasing that it cannot be made pleasurable with the mode and form of speech and with reverence and love."[2] Moreover, motets were sung in Latin, the language of learning, ecclesiastical authority, and diplomacy. To the polyphonic choir, schooled in Latin grammar, Latin was the natural language of formal communication.

The rhetoric of motets corresponds in many respects to the prescriptions of the *ars dictaminis*, the late medieval art of letter writing, but with a more fluid form (Table 4.1).[3] The *ars dictaminis* places strong emphasis

---

[1] R. C. Trexler, *Public Life in Renaissance Florence* (New York: Academic Press, 1980), 152, 168, 170, 188, citing three primary sources that describe "embassy," and its attendant forms of language, as as an essential part of daily life.

[2] Ibid., 152.

[3] I am grateful to Michael Long for suggesting an investigation of the *ars dictaminis* in relation to motets. On the *ars dictaminis* or *ars dictandi*, see Anonymous of Bologna, "The Principles of Letter Writing," in *Three Medieval Rhetorical Arts*, ed. J. J. Murphy (Tempe: Arizona Center for

Table 4.1. Elements of the *Ars dictaminis*, thirteenth century

Salutatio	Formal salutation
Captatio benevolentiae	Securing of goodwill
Narratio	Narration of facts or circumstances
Petitio	Petition or request
Conclusio	Summary or conclusion

on gauging the level of address in the *salutatio*, a concern shared with the motet. The opening flourish is balanced by the *conclusio*, which acts as a rhetorical summary. The use of praise and request in the body of the motet corresponds to the *captatio benevolentiae* ("securing of goodwill") and *petitio* ("petition"), though rarely in the paradigmatic form forecast by the *ars dictaminis*. As an embassy, the task of the motet is not to argue or persuade, as in classical rhetoric, but to praise and request. More rarely, the motet includes the *narratio* ("narration") in the recounting of saints' lives. Rhetorical principles thus allowed one to calibrate the embassy to the precise level required by the audience and situation, while at the same time presenting a petition or prayer in compact and cogent terms.

Ciconia's *Albane misse celitus/Albane doctor maxime* not only summarizes the political situation at the reception of the first Venetian Bishop of Padua, but it does so in a diplomatic way that reconciles conflicting forces and interests (see Figure 3.1). It voices the embassy of the Cathedral of Padua, acted out in the procession and installation of its new bishop. Following the recent defeat of the city and its ceremonial surrender to the Doge of Venice, the moment was one of intense sensitivity. Ciconia's motet accomplishes the task by acknowledging the underlying conflicts, addressing each of the major interests in turn. In this regard, it achieves what Julie E. Cumming terms "concord out of discord."[4] It begins with a dual *salutatio* to honor the new bishop, announcing the subject at hand:

Medieval and Renaissance Studies, 2001), 1–26; R. Witt, "Medieval 'ars dictaminis' and the Beginnings of Humanism: A New Construction of the Problem," *Renaissance Quarterly* 35 (1982): 1–35; E. J. Polak, "Dictamen," in *Dictionary of the Middle Ages*, ed. J. R. Strayer (New York: Scribner's, 1989); J. J. Murphy, *Rhetoric in the Middle Ages: A History of the Rhetorical Theory from Saint Augustine to the Renaissance*, facsimile reprint, Medieval and Renaissance Texts and Studies 227 (Tempe: Arizona Center for Medieval and Renaissance Studies, 2001), chapter 5, "*Ars dictaminis*: The Art of Letter-Writing."

[4] J. E. Cumming, "Concord out of Discord: Occasional Motets of the Early Quattrocento" (Ph.D. diss., University of California, Berkeley, 1987).

Albane misse celitus   Albane doctor maxime
presul date divinitus   virtute celo proxime

Albano, heaven-sent bishop,   Albano, most excellent doctor,
divinely given   near to heaven in virtue[5]

The *salutatio* encompasses the initial duet between the upper voices, up to the entrance of the tenor. The central portions of the motet offer both praise and welcome to the new bishop, weaving in details of the political moment. It refers to the leaderless position of Padua and the need for unity, as well as the reputed benevolence of the Venetian polity. The rhetorical *conclusio*, comprising the last half of stanza 4 in both voices, speaks in the first discantus to the bishop and his family (see Example 3.1). The second discantus addresses a short prayer to Christ on behalf of the cathedral, then effectively signs the embassy with the name of the composer. The *conclusio* encompasses the final two phrases of the motet, beginning in syncopation and ending with hocket. Both voices refer reflexively to music:

Michael o stirpe clarus   Christo grates laudes pange
tibi antistes datur gnarus   celum edis hymnis tange
cantu numquam desine.   cum tuo Ciconia.

O Michiel, to you a skilled   Compose thanks and praises unto
                                    Christ,
and noble bishop is given;   touch the vault of the temple with
                                    hymns,
so never cease with song.   along with thy Ciconia.[6]

Ciconia's *Petrum Marcello Venetum/O Petre antistes inclite* likewise acts as a ritual embassy from the cathedral to the new Bishop of Padua. The *salutatio* extends only so far as the incipits, in the first phrase of the motet (see Example 3.2): "Pietro Marcello, Venetian/O Pietro, famous bishop." Since the political situation had stabilized by July 1409, the texts comprise a more straightforward reception of the bishop by the cathedral and city. The motet is accordingly more elaborate than its predecessor and projects a more celebratory tone. As in the earlier work, the two texts speak to important elements present at the ceremony, drawing them into relationship with the bishop: leaders of the city, the Marcello family, the Paduan clergy, the cathedral, and the chorus itself. Venice is mentioned only in the salutation.

---

[5] Translated after M. J. Connolly in *The Works of Johannes Ciconia*, ed. M. Bent and A. Hallmark, Polyphonic Music of the Fourteenth Century 24 (Monaco: L'Oiseau-Lyre, 1985), 222–23.
[6] Ibid.

The *conclusio* again appears in the second half of the fourth stanza, which here occupies the second diminished *talea* of the motet:

voce leta celum tangant	qui melon istud edidit
venit enim pastor verus.	adesto tuo Cyconie.
touch the vault with cheerful voice,	protect thy Ciconia,
for a true pastor comes.	who composed this very song.[7]

The embassy is signed and sung by the composer, *Magister* Johannes Ciconia, on behalf of Padua Cathedral. Ciconia's gesture underscores the oratorical nature of the motet in the Veneto as a means of ritual communication.

The ambassadorial character of processional motets also plays out externally, in the symbolic organization of space. The lost Agincourt motet *Ave rex Anglorum/Flos mundi/Miles Christi* serves to exemplify the process. When Henry V was welcomed at Blackheath, outside London, the assembled craft guilds of the city all wore the same scarlet gowns, distinguished only by their badges;[8] the mayor and aldermen wore red parti-colored hoods. In contrast, the king wore black armor and a purple cloak. The initial speeches were made at Blackheath. As the procession arrived at London Bridge, the motet marked an act of transition, before the king was received into the territory and community of the city of London; his entrance into the city across the bridge symbolically marked the unity of monarch and subjects.[9]

In Italy, new bishops were traditionally met at the city walls by the cathedral chapter, clergy, and citizens, then accompanied through town with processional chant (see Illustration 3.1).[10] Ciconia's motets marked not the rite of transition, but rather the act of incorporation, after the bishop had already entered into the cathedral and received the blessing from the archpresbyter, Francesco Zabarella. It was the bishop, wearing his black *cappa* and traversing the sacred space, escorted by the canons in their vestments, who knelt at the high altar. In the rite of incorporation, the

---

[7] Translation by the author.

[8] See Illustration 1.1 for an example of an English badge for the Order of the Garter, inscribed with the motto "Honi soit qui mal y pense."

[9] See K. Schnith, "Musik, Liturgie, Prozession als Ausdrucksmittel der Politik Heinrichs V. von England," in *Festschrift Rudolf Bockholdt zum 60. Geburtstag* (Pfaffenhofen: Ludwig, 1990), 41–52.

[10] A. M. Strozzi, *Lettere di una gentildonna fiorentina*, ed. C. Guasti (Florence: G. C. Sansoni, 1877), 168, 174–76, in a letter dated July 27, 1459, remarks, "L'Arcivescovo entrò una mattina a buon ora, e sanza onoranza niuna" ("The Archbishop entered one morning betimes, and without any honors"). The event was unusual enough to be worth noting, particularly since the Strozzi family customarily received the gift of the archbishop's saddle.

embassies voiced by the motets were directed not merely to the bishops, Albano Michiel and Pietro Marcello, but to all parties concerned. Hence the import of words such as *ferula* ("staff") and *justus* ("just") or *justissime* ("most just"), in reference to the bishop's role in ordering the clergy and adjudicating disputes. The crosier, of course, was a potent symbol of the bishop's new office. The motets, in effect, ratified the ceremony with the power of decorous words and music.

Missus est Gabriel Angelus by Pietro Rosso furnishes an illuminating example of ritual embassy in the motet. At the center of the procession of the Annunciation were the figures of the Angel Gabriel and the Virgin Mary, represented by two boys trained for the sacred play heard later that day at Treviso Cathedral. Because of their perceived spiritual innocence, the boys embodied "powerful ritual objects as they processed through the city."[11] The elaborately decorated cart in which they traveled, drawn by the *cavalli mariani* or "Marian horsemen," marked their importance as the cynosure of attention. The Angel and Mary were accompanied by six to twelve other boys, dressed as angels in symbolic white. The official participants in the procession were ordered hierarchically, with the most important dignitaries placed closest to the Angel and Mary. As Miri Rubin comments of processions on the feast of Corpus Christi, "The centre of the procession was the most ornate, the most densely decorated; and it included people whose rank was reflected and enhanced by proximity to the holiest of holies."[12]

The confraternal accounts of 1443 and 1447 (see Appendix A) divide the recipients of the silk-lined, chamois gloves into two groups, preceding and succeeding the Angel and Mary; within each group, the recipients are listed in order of importance, denoting their position of honor. Thus, the brotherhood of Santa Maria dei Battuti may have followed the trumpeters at the head of the procession, followed by the *sindico*, *quattorvice*, and four *gastaldi* of the confraternity.[13] The Venetian *podestà* and bishop would have

---

[11]   K. Ashley, "Introduction: The Moving Subjects of Processional Performance," in *Moving Subjects: Processional Performance in the Middle Ages and Renaissance*, ed. K. Ashley and W. Hüsken (Amsterdam and Atlanta: Rodopi, 2001), 19. See also T. Borgerding, "Imagining the Sacred Body: Choirboys, Their Voices, and Corpus Christi in Early Modern Seville," in *Musical Childhoods and the Cultures of Youth*, ed. S. Boynton and R.-M. Kok (Middletown: Wesleyan University Press, 2006), 29–32.

[12]   M. Rubin, *Corpus Christi: The Eucharist in Late Medieval Culture* (Cambridge University Press, 1991), 255. T. A. Boogaart II, "Our Saviour's Blood: Procession and Community in Late Medieval Bruges," in *Moving Subjects*, ed. Ashley and Hüsken, 88, observes, "Proximity to the relic conferred honour and such positions were monopolised by notables."

[13]   The 1447 accounts add a *coaiutor* to the list of confraternal officials (see Appendix A); he would have been first in order of procession, as least important of the officers. Following Pietro Rosso, the same accounts also add "messer pre Nicolò Patavini," who coached the boys in the *sacra rappresentazione* that year. In a painting by Bartolomeo Orioli, *Procession with the Relics of the*

directly preceded the two Marian horsemen, the *cavalli mariani*. Following the Angel and Mary were the cathedral officials – the treasurer, *magister scholarum*, archdeacon, and Maestro Pietro Rosso – followed by the cathedral canons and chaplains, including the four singers of the motet. Other clergy and monastics of the city, not mentioned in the accounts, may have continued the procession, arrayed in order by institution.

The course of the procession along the Camaggiore, from the cathedral and episcopal palace to the Palazzo Signoria and Palazzo del Trecento, took it from the center of ecclesiastical authority to the center of political authority, effectively linking the two.[14] The procession continued across the city to Santa Maria Maggiore and back, thereby uniting the cathedral with the principal Marian church of Treviso. *Missus est Gabriel Angelus*, sung at the *croce di via* ("crossing of the way"), brought the message of salvation to the geographic and mercantile heart of the city. It was also visible from the Loggia de' Cavalieri, the meeting place of the aristocracy of Treviso. The motet performed before the figures of the Angel and Mary brought, in essence, the ancient, powerful story into the here and now. It served as the embassy of the city of Treviso to the embodied angel and saint in a double sense – in honor and in narrative, the meeting of human and divine.

Without knowledge of the performance context for *Missus est Gabriel Angelus*, we would assume the work to be a sacred essay.[15] Rosso fashions the texts by combining two great responsories with their verses, as diagrammed in Figure 4.1. Rosso splits the *salutatio*, which belongs to the first responsory, between the two discantus voices, employing the same musical phrase in succession: "Missus est / Gabriel Angelus." The second portion of text, "ad Mariam virginem, desponsatam Joseph," is taken by the two upper voices together. The second responsory text, "Suscipe verbum, Virgo Maria," appears in the second discantus alone, while the first discantus continues with the first responsory. Double-texting continues for roughly one-third of the motet; the two voices declaim similar, but competing, versions of the annunciation narrative. Both discantus voices take up the verse of the first responsory, *Ave Maria*, marked *unus*, without the tenor

---

Cross, Treviso, Church of the Ospedale di Santa Maria dei Battuti, dated 1624–25, members of the confraternity, dressed in hooded white robes with badges, carry crosses and torches before the baldachin. They are succeeded by a group of men singers, in white cloaks, reading from parts. The painting is reproduced in D. Bryant and M. Pozzobon, *Musica, devozione, città: La scuola di Santa Maria dei Battuti (e uno suo manoscritto musicale) nella Treviso del Rinascimento* (Treviso: Fondazione Benetton and Editrice Canova, 1995), figure 1, 34–35; figure 2, 37.

14 Rubin, *Corpus Christi*, 267, writes that "Itineraries fall into two main categories, those *demarcating* territories, and those *linking* them."

15 For another analysis of the motet, see D. J. Rothenberg, "Marian Feasts, Seasons, and Songs in Medieval Polyphony: Studies in Musical Symbolism" (Ph.D. diss., Yale University, 2004), 115–21.

Discantus I	Discantus II
Missus est	
	Gabriel Angelus
ad Mariam virginem desponsatam Joseph,	ad Mariam virginem desponsatam Joseph,
Nuntians ei verbum et expavescit virgo de lumine. Ne timeas, Maria. Invenisti gratiam apud deum. Ecce concipies et paries filium et vocabitur altissimi filius.	Suscipe verbum, virgo Maria. A Domino transmissum est: concipies et paries filium, Deum et hominem ut benedicta dicaris inter omnes mulieres.
Unus Ave, Maria, gracia plena, Dominus tecum,	*Unus* Ave, Maria, gracia plena, Dominus tecum,
Chorus Paries quidem filium, et virginitatis non patieris detrimentum eficieris gravida et eris mater semper	*Chorus* Paries quidem filium, et virginitatis non patieris detrimentum eficieris gravida et eris mater semper
intacta.	intacta.

Figure 4.1. Text organization by voice in Pietro Rosso, *Missus est Gabriel Angelus*

Fist responsory: The Angel Gabriel was sent to the Virgin Mary, espoused to Joseph, announcing to her the Word; and she panicked at the light. "Do not be afraid, Mary. You have found grace before God. Behold, you shall conceive and give birth to a son, and he will be called son of the Most High."

Second responsory: Receive the word, Virgin Mary, conveyed from God: "You will conceive and give birth to a son, both God and man, and you shall be called blessed among all women."

First verse: "Hail, Mary, full in grace, the Lord is with thee."

Second verse: "Indeed, you will bear a son, and your virginity will not suffer loss; you will become pregnant and will be a mother, remaining inviolate."

(Example 4.1). These familiar words mark the point of coming together, in jubilant address to the Virgin Mary. The motet then proceeds to the verse of the second responsory, *Paries quidem*, now in full texture, with tenor (*chorus*). The *conclusio* encompasses only the last, extended word, *intacta* ("inviolate"), underscoring the miraculous nature of Christ's birth, as well as the holy purity of the Virgin Mary.

In contrast to *Missus est Gabriel Angelus*, motets with pre-existent texts did not necessarily serve as ritual embassies. The question depended both upon the character of the individual texts and the circumstances of performance. A case in point is Johannes de Lymburgia's *Surexit Christus*, for Vicenza Cathedral. The Vespers procession to the baptismal font in Easter week, for which the motet was composed, lacked ambassadorial connotations, but nevertheless carried strong communal significance. The procession included the Magnificat, sung in the nave of the church rather than in the choir

Example 4.1. Rosso, *Missus est Gabriel Angelus*, contrast of *unus* and *chorus*

and thus visible as well as audible to the laity. The station on Easter Day carried meaning in that the yearly baptism of infants took place there the night before, at the midnight vigil Mass, along with the yearly, ceremonial rekindling of fires.

The text of *Surexit Christus*, widely known across Western Europe, tells in briefest form the story of the three Marys at the tomb of Christ.[16] Musically, the work borrows from the style of the Italian *lauda*, in a manner accessible to the laity, incorporating the familiar tune in the first strophe of the tenor (see Example 3.3). At its station before the baptismal font, the motet drew upon the parallel ideas of baptism and resurrection. The sound of polyphonic voices in close harmony, alternating with rhythmicized monophony sung in unison, also figured as an aural demonstration of the relationship between *divina et humanitas*. By the same token, it drew together clergy

---

[16] In German-speaking lands, the text was known as *Christ ist erstanden.*

Example 4.2. Du Fay, *Flos florum*, interior phrase with word painting

and congregation in common celebration in the open space of the nave of the church. The ecclesiastical choir, mediating between heaven and earth, thus carried out its charge for the care of souls before an audience of laity at Vicenza Cathedral.

Ritual embassy characterizes a large number of motets composed in northern and central Italy in the first half of the fifteenth century. Guillaume Du Fay's early motet *Flos florum*, written in northern Italy in 1420–24, sets a pre-existent poem that addresses St. Mary. Du Fay, a new arrival trained at the Cathedral of Cambrai, captures the melodic flow of secular Italian song and fashions it into an ornate musical speech (Example 4.2). The composer pays close attention to the unity of word and tone.[17] Du Fay

[17]   R. M. Nosow, "The Florid and Equal-Discantus Motet Styles of Fifteenth-Century Italy" (Ph.D. diss., University of North Carolina at Chapel Hill, 1992), 159–61.

Flos florum,	Flower of flowers,
fons ortorum,	fountain of gardens,
regina polorum.	queen of the heavens.

Spes venie,	Hope of forgiveness,
lux leticie,	light of gladness,
medicina dolorum.	remedy for pains.

Virga recens,	Fresh bough
et virgo decens,	and comely virgin,
forma bonorum.	model of virtues.

Parce reis,	Grant mercy to the accused,
et opem fer eis,	and bring help to them
in pace piorum.	in the peace of the righteous.

Pasce tuos,	Cherish your people,
succure tuis,	succor your people,
miserere tuorum.	have mercy upon your people.

Figure 4.2. Guillaume Du Fay, *Flos florum*

concentrates the melodic interest in a single discantus voice, which plays off the harmonic and contrapuntal relations of the slower-moving tenor and contratenor pair. All three voices are fully texted. The *salutatio*, *Flos florum*, immediately honors the Virgin Mary as the "Flower of flowers"; the entire motet illustrates and carries out this conception. The importance of the *salutatio* in the motet shows in the poetic imagery and tone of address, appropriate not to a living person, but to the celestial being crowned as the Queen of Heaven (Figure 4.2).

The first four stanzas of *Flos florum* alternate praises with earthly concerns. The fourth stanza makes a petition to "Grant mercy to the accused," who are guilty of sin. Structurally, the second and fourth stanzas are followed by untexted passages, again reminiscent of secular song. The fifth stanza, however, constitutes a direct prayer: "Cherish your people / Succor your people / Have mercy upon your people." In stark contrast to the rest of the motet, each syllable is set to a fermata or *corona*, in strict homophony. The dramatic, harmonically inflected halt to the florid runs of the discantus voice emphasizes not just the prayer, but the repeated inflections of *tuo*, "your people." In this regard, the extended *conclusio* binds the Virgin Mary ever more tightly to the choir and to the people for whom it speaks.

Du Fay's *Vasilissa ergo gaude* of 1420 may be categorized as an epithalamion presented to Cleofe Malatesta, daughter of Malatesta di Pandolfo Malatesta da Pesaro. The motet celebrates her embarkation from Rimini for

Discantus I and II:

Vasilissa, ergo gaude,	Empress, therefore rejoice,
quia es digna omni laude,	for you are worthy of all praise,
Cleophe, clara gestis,	Cleofe, glorious from the deeds
a tuis de Malatestis,	of your Malatesta kin,
in Italia principus	leading men in all of Italy,
magnis et nobilibus,	great and noble,
Ex tuo viro clarior	More glorious from your husband,
quia cunctis est nobilior:	for he is nobler than all;
Romeorum est despotus	he is despot of the Rhōmaioi,
quem colit mundus totus;	he whom all the world reveres,
in porphyro est genitus,	he was born in the purple,
a Deo missus celitus.	sent by God from heaven.
Iuvenili etate	In youthful bloom
polles et formositate	you abound and in beauty,
[ingenio] multum fecunda	very fertile [in your wits]
et utraque lingua facunda	and eloquent in both tongues,
ac clarior es virtutibus	and you are more glorious
pre aliis hominibus.	for your virtues above other human beings.

Tenor:

Concupivit rex decorum tuum	The King hath conceived a desire
quoniam ipse est dominus tuus	for thy beauty; for he is thy Lord

Figure 4.3. Guillaume Du Fay, *Vasilissa ergo gaude*

Greece as fiancée of Theodore II Palaiologos, son of the Byzantine Emperor (Figure 4.3). The motet has a single text, of which the first and last groups of six lines address Cleofe, while the middle group of six lines praises Palaiologos.[18] The motet serves a straightforward, diplomatic function: it ratifies the contract between the Malatesta family and representatives of the emperor, bringing out essential elements of the ceremony that no legal document could contain. Hence, the fifth and sixth lines refer to the Malatesta as "leading men in Italy, great and noble" while the tenth line refers to the imperial family, "whom all the world reveres."

The salutation is begun by one voice in the first discantus, then repeated in canon by a second singer, reading from the same part at the space of three breves, prior to the entrance of the second discantus, tenor, and contratenor (Example 4.3). Du Fay sets off the first two lines of text as a self-contained section, labeled *introitus* ("prelude"), parallel to the classical

---

[18] For an incisive commentary on the text, see L. Holford-Strevens, "Du Fay the Poet? Problems in the Texts of His Motets," *Early Music History* 16 (1997): 102–07. Holford-Strevens, ibid., 105, comments that "even by the standard of texts set to music this specimen is of poor quality."

Example 4.3. Du Fay, *Vasilissa ergo gaude, introitus* and four-voice entry

term *exordium*, indicating his awareness of its rhetorical function. The use of an untexted melisma after each line in the *introitus* allows each word to be clearly declaimed, despite the canonic construction. The first word, *Vasilissa*, means "princess" in Greek, highlighting the diplomatic logic behind the marriage, in efforts to bring unity to the Western and Eastern churches. Carlo Malatesta, *signore* of Rimini and Du Fay's presumed patron, had been instrumental in the Council of Constance of 1414–18, which brought to an end the Great Schism in the Western Church.[19] Line 16, "and eloquent in both tongues," points to Cleofe's linguistic abilities, at a time when Italian humanists were first beginning to learn classical Greek. The sharply

---

[19] A. Falcioni, "Malatesta, Carlo," in *Dizionario biografico degli italiani* (Rome: Istituto della Enciclopedia italiana, 1960–).

Example 4.3. (*cont.*)

defined cadential structure, the frequent commencement of musical phrases together or in imitation, and the Italian flair of the melodic lines all conspire to enhance the rhetorical impact of the motet. Unusually, the text contains not even an implicit prayer. The *cantus firmus* does, however, add weight to the moment, in the text "The King hath conceived a desire for thy beauty; for he is thy Lord."[20]

---

[20] The chant is a responsory for the Common of a Virgin; the text derives from Psalm 44:12.

Example 4.4. Antonio da Cividale, *O felix flos Florencia/Gaude felix Dominice*, conclusion

The use of motets as ritual embassies thus extends to works for whose precise performance contexts we have little evidence. One such work is Antonio da Cividale's *O felix flos Florencia/Gaude felix Dominice* of 1414. The musical style, in which melodic fragments come into focus in the two upper voices in quick succession, shifting and crossing back and forth, allows the text to be declaimed largely in overlapping phrases (Example 4.4). While the first discantus addresses the city of Florence, the second praises Father Leonardo Dati, a native Florentine (Figure 4.4).[21] Dati gained successive posts of leadership within the Dominican Order in the same year, first as Vicar General on March 27, then as Master General on September 29, 1414. The latter occasion coincided with the meeting of the general chapter of the Dominicans at the Church of Santa Maria Novella, outside the walls of Florence; it forms the likely background to the motet.

The initial words in salutation of Florence are heard, exceptionally, in the tenor, then repeated in melodic imitation by the first discantus. Taking up the tenor melody, the second discantus addresses St. Dominic, founder and patron saint of the Dominican Order, but with reference to the *leo fortis*, Leonardo Dati. Next, it speaks to the Order of Preachers, in its election of a new Master General, and lastly petitions Dati on behalf of the composer, *Anthonij de Civitato*, who was himself a Dominican friar. The last item essentially signs the embassy in the manner advanced by Ciconia. The text places Dati in relationship to the saint and his order, with the choir balancing them in a process of mediation. As Rob C. Wegman points out, "patron saints were musical patrons in exactly the same sense as secular rulers, because they received music as a gift, and responded with return favors of their own."[22] The first discantus, on the other hand, concerns itself with praises of the city of Florence, closing with an allusion to the *summis pastor*, in reference to Christ, portrayed as Pollux, the one who died and was resurrected. Castor then represents his cousin, John the Baptist, patron saint of Florence. Finally, the motet asks God to defend the city against her enemies, moving to a concluding passage (*conclusio*) in rhythmic sequence among all three voices (Example 4.4). Each part sings a repeated rhythmic cell that interlocks with the others. For emphasis, the tenor takes up the text and rhythms of the first discantus, with a staggered delivery. Between its two texts, the motet addresses multiple audiences: each represents a different form of power, and each receives the honor due to it by the choir.

O felix flos Florencia/Gaude felix Dominice may be heard as an expression of gratitude to the city of Florence on behalf of the Dominicans. As in the Ciconia motets, it also fulfills a different function, that of ratification. By invoking the blessings of St. Dominic, the choir recognizes and confirms the election of Leonardo Dati as master general, *quem promovit gracia* ("whom grace promoted"). It brings in the government of Florence as witness to

---

[21] Figure 4.4 is indebted to a translation summary by Benito Rivera, whose help is gratefully acknowledged.

[22] R. C. Wegman, "Musical Offerings in the Renaissance," *Early Music* 33 (2005): 431.

Discantus I

O felix flos Florencia	O happy flower, Florence,
divo munita numine	protected by divine favor,
pacata pacis federe	made peaceful by treaty of peace,
potata celso flumine	watered by a noble river;
Si tu demo[n]straris	if one describes you,
circularis perfectio	a circular perfection
orbem totum cludit	closes the full circle:
et sors tua ita cudit	and just as your destiny is forged
sapienter dum sic ludit,	while it plays out so wisely;
ut summo concepcio	so from on high the greatest
te summa generositas	conception and nobility
decorant et capacitas	adorn you, vitality,
prudencie vivacitas.	and the understanding of prudence.
Extollit superencia	The highest authority exalts you:
ut tergit summis pastor	as the Shepherd in the heavens cleanses you,
et defendat fidus Castor:	so may the faithful Castor defend you;
sic te servet Deus actor	so also may God, the prime mover,
princeps milicie.	leader of armies, protect you.

Discantus II

Gaude felix Dominice	Rejoice, blessed Dominic,
dum te leo fortis	while through you the strong lion
tuetur contra mortis	is guarded against the alliances
federa dans sortis	of death, granting destinies;
eterne vite portis	in sooth, with the gates
apertis veridice.	of eternal life opened.
Exultet desiderio	May the Order of Preachers
ordo predicatorum	exult with longing,
dum lux et norma morum,	while the light and standard of righteousness,
nardus in te fons odorum	the balsam, a perfect font of fragrance,
perfectus vehitur misterio.	is borne to you in divine mystery.
Ergo pater Leonarde	Therefore, Father Leonardo,
quem promovit gracia	whom grace promoted,
et quo decoratur leticia	and whence, heretofore with private lauds,
hactenus privata laud[e],	you are honored with joyfulness,
memor sis Anthonij	be mindful of the servant
de Civitato servuli	Antonio da Cividale,
te precantis seduli	supplicating you diligently;
ut comprehensor sis bravij.	and so may you remember a reward.
Amen.	Amen.

Figure 4.4. Antonio da Cividale, *O felix flos Florencia/Gaude felix Dominice,* text and translation

Dati's promotion, praising the city as being *pacata pacis federe* ("made peaceful by treaty of peace"). In spring 1414, the armies of King Ladislao of Naples had moved north against Florence, only to see him fall ill and perish in August. The choir offers its praises and blessings to the city at a time of danger recently past. Soon after, Dati served as a Florentine ambassador to the Council of Constance.[23] As a native son and master of theology at the university, he was in a position to bring greater honor still to the Florentine republic.

Another Florentine motet that embodies a ritual embassy is the celebrated *Nuper rosarum flores* of Guillaume Du Fay. The work was written for the consecration of the high altar of Santa Maria del Fiore on March 25, 1436. The date marked not only Passion Sunday and the beginning of the New Year in the Florentine calendar, but also the feast of the Annunciation of the Virgin. That day celebrated the massive cathedral dome designed by Filippo Brunelleschi that still dominates the city of Florence. Accordingly, the double *cantus firmus* derives from the Introit of the Mass of Dedication, *Terribilis est locus iste* ("Awesome is this place"). The *color* is stated four times in each tenor, once per section, in four different mensurations. Since the *Amen* adds nine semibreves at the end, the entire motet lasts 429 semibreves, or 13 × 33, a Christological number.[24]

While several written accounts of the ceremonies survive, none specifically mention the motet or the related, newly composed plainchant sequence *Nuper alma rose flores*, which appears to have belonged to the Mass of Dedication.[25] In consequence, the placement of the motet in relation to the dedication ceremonies becomes problematic. The most detailed account is the *Oratio* by the Florentine humanist Giannozzo Manetti.[26] As Sabine Žak points out, the *Oratio* describes two places in the ceremony where vocal

---

[23] P. Viti, "Dati, Leonardo," in *Dizionario biografico degli italiani.*

[24] The number 13 is often associated with Christ and the twelve apostles, while 33 represents the total years of Jesus' life. The number count does not include the final cadence. On the dense symbolism of the motet, see C. Wright, "Dufay's *Nuper rosarum flores*, King Solomon's Temple, and the Veneration of the Virgin," *Journal of the American Musicological Society* 47 (1994): 395–441; M. Trachtenberg, "Architecture and Music Reunited: A New Reading of Dufay's *Nuper rosarum flores* and the Cathedral of Florence," *Renaissance Quarterly* 54 (2001): 740–75; and V. S. Ramalingam, "*Nuper rosarum flores*, Brunelleschi's Dome, and the Iconography of Mary," unpublished paper delivered at the Annual Meeting of the Renaissance Society of America, Florence, Italy, March 23, 2000.

[25] Wright, "King Solomon's Temple," 434–37, 440–41. Wright points out that the sequence may also have been composed by Du Fay, an opinion seconded in M. S. Tacconi, *Cathedral and Civic Ritual in Late Medieval and Renaissance Florence: The Service Books of Santa Maria del Fiore* (Cambridge University Press, 2005), 156–58.

[26] G. Manetti, "Oratio," ed. E. Battisti, *Archivio di filosofia* 105 (1960): 310–20.

polyphony was heard: at the consecration of the altar and at the elevation of the host during Mass.[27] As yet we have no direct evidence for the performance of motets at the elevation before 1481, the date of the earliest document in Bruges.[28] The consecration of the altar of Santa Maria del Fiore, on the other hand, culminated a great procession through the city to the cathedral that morning, described in all the chronicles.

Pope Eugenius IV, who had stayed for thirty-one months at the Dominican monastery of Santa Maria Novella, outside the walls of Florence, consented to emerge from his quarters for the first time to officiate at the dedication of Santa Maria del Fiore.[29] To this end, the Florentine government built a wooden bridge from Santa Maria Novella through the city to the baptistry of San Giovanni, terminating at the steps of the cathedral.[30] Since St. John was the patron saint of Florence, it is significant in a topographical sense that pope and curia were made to pass through the magnificent Ghiberti doors of the baptistry. The Florentine Chancellor, Leonardo Bruni, describes the bridge as four *braccia* (240 centimeters) in width and the columns as seven *braccia* (420 centimeters) in height.[31] The columns, wound with myrtle, supported an awning of white and azure, the colors of the papal arms.[32] The pope, his cardinals, the Roman curia, foreign ambassadors, and the government of Florence processed over the bridge, preceded, according to Manetti,

---

[27] S. Žak, "Die Quellenwert von Gianozzo Manettis Oratio über die Domweihe von Florenz 1436 für die Musikgeschichte," *Die Musikforschung* 40 (1987): 14. See also M. Phelps, "A Repertory in Exile: Pope Eugenius IV and the MS Modena, Biblioteca Estense universitaria, α.X.1.11" (Ph.D. diss., New York University, 2008), 125–29.

[28] Bruges, Bisschoppelijk Archief, MS Reeks G131¹, Accounts of the Obedientie, 1503–04 (unfoliated): "Ex legatis domini eligij beck Succentorj pro motetis alternatis diebus dominicis a festo Johanne baptiste *usque* dominicam Invocavit. iij L xij S. // Domino Johannis bollaret capellano extra chorum capellanie fundate per dominum eligium beck dictis diebus dominicis immediate post motetum elevationum pro qualibet missa iiij L viij S." The first entry records payment for a motet sung by the succentor and choirboys of the Church of St. Donatian every other Sunday, except in Lent. The second entry pays the officiant of the Mass itself, which payment takes place "immediately after the elevation motet" noted in the previous entry. Both entries, hence the ritual actions, date back to 1481–82 in Bisschoppelijk Archief, MS Reeks G131¹, but without the explanatory phrase "immediate post motetum elevationum." The chapter of St. Donatian accepted the chaplaincy founded by Beck on March 21, 1481, as shown in Bruges, Bisschoppelijk Archief, MS Reeks A 55, *Acta capitulorum*, fol. 113r.

[29] F. Belcari, "The Consecration of the Cathedral of Florence," in *Images of Quattrocento Florence*, trans. S. U. Baldassarri and A. Saiber (New Haven: Yale University Press, 2000), 239.

[30] G. Cambi, *Istorie di Giovanni Cambi cittadino fiorentino*, vols. XX–XXII of *Delizie degli eruditi toscani*, ed. I. di San Luigi, 25 vols. (Florence: Gaetano Cambiagi, 1770–89), vol. XX, 208.

[31] L. Bruni, *History of the Florentine People*, ed. and trans. J. Hankins, I Tatti Renaissance Library 27, 3 vols. (Cambridge, Mass.: Harvard University Press, 2001), vol. III, 380–83.

[32] V. da Bisticci, *Le vite*, ed. A. Greco (Florence: Istituto Nazionale di Studi sul Rinascimento, 1970–76), 14–15.

by instrumental musicians:[33] "Primum nanque tubicinum fidicinumque ac tibicinum ingens ordo erat singuli quidem tubas fides, tibias sua manibus instrumenta portantes" ("First came a great line in single file of trumpeters, lutenists, and *pifferi*; each carrying his own instrument in his hands; trumpets, string instruments, and winds").[34] The procession took place above and in full sight of the crowds that swirled along the processional route; the ceremony brought the pontiff and cardinals into the city, but yet allowed them to remain apart.[35]

Another witness to the procession, Giovanni di Cino Calzaiuolo, writes of the pontiff:

Po' giunto al magno Duomo, ove si piglia
sulle prime scalee l'entrar maggiore,
discese lui e suo santa famiglia.
Qui v'era di Firenze il grande onore
de' maggior cittadin inginocchiati;
reverenti, accettâr nostro Signore

Then having arrived at the great cathedral, where one takes
the first steps of the main entry,
he descended with his holy family.
Here were the most honorable men of Florence:
the leading citizens, kneeling
reverently, received our Lord.[36]

The pope was then greeted by the Cardinal of San Marcello inside the cathedral, went beneath the great dome to the altar, knelt, and prayed. At the moment when the pontiff took his throne to the right of the altar, surrounded by cardinals, Manetti recounts:

Unus deinde postea Romanae Ecclesiae cardinalis omnibus sacerdotalibus ornamentis de more praeparatus ad altare accessit ut divinum officium celebraret. Interea tantis tamque variis canoris vocibus quandoque concinebatur, tantis etiam symphoniis ad celum usque elatis interdum cantabatur, ut angelici ac divini cantus nimirum audientibus apparerent:

---

[33] Belcari, "The Consecration of the Cathedral of Florence," 239; Cambi, *Istorie*, vol. XX, 209.

[34] Manetti, "Oratio," 315. Žak, "Die Quellenwert von Gianozzo Manettis Oratio," 13, corrects the word *fidetibias* to *fides tibias*, as given here. In general, Žak gives a skeptical account of instrumental music both in the procession and within the cathedral.

[35] Belcari, "The Consecration of the Cathedral of Florence," 239, numbers the crowd at over 200,000, swelled by an influx of people from the surrounding countryside.

[36] "Nel tempo che Firenze era contenta," in A. Lanza, ed., *Lirici toscani del Quattrocento*, 2 vols. (Rome: Bulzone, 1973–75), vol. II, 683–87.

Then one of the cardinals of the Roman Church, already dressed with all the customary sacerdotal vestments, went to the altar to celebrate the divine service. Meanwhile,
from time to time, so many and such different singing voices harmonized; in fact, so
many symphonies were sung, reaching as far as the sky, that doubtless they seemed
to the listeners like angelic and divine songs.[37]

Nuper rosarum flores, sung at the start of the lengthy consecration ceremonies, would have supplied the proper embassy, otherwise lacking at the
dramatic reception of the pope. The motet, in its rhetorical form, addresses
the Virgin Mary in a single poem on behalf of the Florentine people (Figure
4.5). The *salutatio* refers to the golden rose, made of hammered gold, given
by Eugenius IV to the city of Florence one week before, on Rose Sunday, and
placed in full view on the high altar. The contrast of the golden rose with the
harsh winter past, both literal and figurative, underscores the significance
of the feast of the Annunciation as a calendrical rite devoted to the Virgin
Mary.[38] The first two stanzas constitute a *narratio*, telling the Virgin Mary
the story of the pontiff's actions in the immediate past and present. It creates a tacit embassy to the pope couched in the third person, with emphasis
on the honor that he confers on the city. The rhetorical approach seems
surprising until one realizes that it is the papal choir, with the master of
the chapel, Guillaume Du Fay, that mediates between the Florentines and
the Queen of Heaven, to whom the citizens dedicate their cathedral. The
choir was situated to the left of the high altar, opposite the pope.[39] The third
stanza begins with the *captatio benevolentiae*, showering the Virgin Mary
with praise, before leading directly into a *petitio* on behalf of the Florentine
people. Both third and fourth stanzas carefully explicate the relationship
of St. Mary to her son: the *petitio* specifically asks for remission of sins
for anyone present who brings "pure mind and body" into her presence,
as embodied by the new church, an admonition also to the Florentines.[40]
The line *grata beneficia* refers to the indulgences to be granted those inside
the church at the end of Mass. Du Fay accordingly sets the word *Oracione*
("prayer") to a long duet to begin the third section of music. The *conclusio*,

---

[37] Manetti, "Oratio," 317; trans. in Phelps, "A Repertory in Exile," 191–92, emended. Phelps,
      ibid., 94–124, places Du Fay's *Salve flos Tusce gentis/Vos nunc Etruscorum/Viri mendaces*, the
      structural counterpart to *Nuper rosarum flores*, within the same ceremonies.

[38] Wright, "King Solomon's Temple," 411–12.

[39] Bisticci, *Le vite*, 14–15.

[40] According to the chronicler Giovanni Cambi, "after said Mass the pope gave the benediction to
      the populace and granted indulgences to all in said church of seven years and seven forty days,"
      freeing them from that amount of time in Purgatory. See *Istorie*, vol. XX, 209; trans. in Wright,
      "King Solomon's Temple," 429.

Nuper rosarum flores	The rose blossoms
ex dono pontificis	recently given by the Pope,
hyeme licet horrida	during the winter's cold
tibi virgo celica	have continued to adorn this temple
pie et sancte deditum	with its great device,
grandis templum machine	piously and solemnly dedicated
condecorarunt perpetim.	to you, heavenly Virgin.
Hodie vicarius	Today the vicar of Jesus
Jesu Christi et Petri	Christ and the successor
successor Eugenius	of Peter, Eugenius,
hoc idem amplissimum	has deigned to consecrate
sacris templum manibus	this same most splendid
sanctisque liquoribus	temple with his sacred hands
consecrare dignatus est.	and holy oils.
Igitur, alma parens	Therefore, kindly parent
nati tui et filia,	and daughter of your Son,
Virgo decus virginum,	you, O Virgin, glory of virgins,
tuus te Florencie	your devoted inhabitants
devotus orat populus,	of Florence implore
ut qui mente et corpore	that he who with pure mind
mundo quicquam exorarit,	and body has made some entreaty,
Oracione tua	By your prayer,
cruciatus et meritis	and by the merits of the crucifixion
tui secumdum carnem	of your Son, his Lord
nati Domini sui	made flesh, will
grata beneficia	deserve to receive
veniamque reatum	welcome favors and
accipere mereatur.	the forgiveness of sins.
Amen.	Amen.

Figure 4.5. Guillaume Du Fay, *Nuper rosarum flores*

however, appears in the music, rather than the text, in the brief *Amen,* with all four voices moving quickly in semibreves and minims. *Nuper rosarum flores* thus elaborated multiple embassies to the Virgin Mary, the Florentines, and Pope Eugenius IV, before the papal curia, foreign ambassadors, and assembled citizens of Florence. The clarity of construction and ornate beauty of the counterpoint made the work accessible to all those present, even as it sought to incorporate the holy person and honor of the pope within the city and its cathedral.

5 | Motets for the citizens of Bruges

The city of Bruges was the most important economic center of Flanders in the fifteenth century. Like Venice, it was an international point of commerce, a meeting place for merchants of different places and cultures. Commercial houses from Florence, Milan, Venice, and Lucca in Italy, Castille and Aragon in Iberia, England, France, and the Hanseatic League all established representatives in the city of Bruges. While the city jealously guarded its privileges, governed by charter, sovereignty belonged to the Dukes of Burgundy, who struggled to maintain control over the rich Flemish towns and their independent-minded citizens. Even more than in Italy, individual and corporate wealth was directed not just to master painters such as Jan van Eyck, Rogier van der Weyden, and Petrus Christus, but to the support of sacred polyphonic music. The singers trained in Flanders and northern France were among the finest and most sought-after in Europe, while the chapels of the Dukes of Burgundy – John the Fearless (1404–19), Philip the Good (1419–67), and Charles the Bold (1467–77) – which drew on the best musicians of the Flemish towns, were justly renowned. The dukes were able to hear new singers personally in the course of their peripatetic movements from one city to another of the Burgundian state.

A great deal of documentary evidence for motets survives in Bruges, archival material that has been presented by Reinhard Strohm in his pathbreaking *Music in Late Medieval Bruges.*[1] Despite widespread support for musical activity in the city, however, only one music manuscript with motets survives from the first three quarters of the fifteenth century, the fragmentary Lucca Choirbook. The manuscript was originally purchased by a Lucchese merchant in Bruges, Giovanni di Arrigo Arnolfini, for use in the Cathedral of Lucca.[2] Of the nine, mostly fragmentary motets in the manuscript, at

---

[1] R. Strohm, *Music in Late Medieval Bruges*, 2nd edn. (Oxford: Clarendon Press, 1990).
[2] Ibid., 122–23. See the facsimile edition, *The Lucca Choirbook: Lucca, Archivio di Stato, Ms 238; Lucca, Archivio arcivescovile, Ms 97; Pisa, Archivio arcivescovile, Biblioteca Maffi, cartella 11/III*, ed. R. Strohm, Late Medieval and Early Renaissance Music in Facsimile 2 (University of Chicago Press, 2008).

least two are English. It is impossible to tie any of them securely to specific evidence for motet performance. Nevertheless, the impressive variety of documentation sheds considerable light on the genre in the region of its most intense cultivation.

The *Missa "Spiritus almus"* and its motet

In 1451, Duke Philip the Good of Burgundy founded a Mass at the Church of Our Lady in Bruges, with a yearly endowment of £18.[3] The foundation, discovered by Reinhard Strohm, details the services at the high altar of the church: "in crastino Assumptio*n*is B*e*atissime Virgin*is* Marie Missam S*a*nct*i* Sp*i*ritus ad maius altare... Item organista .iiij. S. eius famulo ij S. Item... Kyriel*eyson*, Et in terra, Patrem, Sanctus, Agnus cu*m* moteto post missam."[4]

The foundation may have come about through the good offices of Isabella of Portugal, Duchess of Burgundy, who stayed in Bruges during the autumn of 1450 and had dinner with the provost of the Church of Our Lady (Onze-Lieve-Vrouw) on September 8, 1450.[5] She was joined on New Year's Eve by Duke Philip, who remained until February 16.[6] The ducal charter, located by Andrew Brown in the Archives générales du royaume in Brussels, carries the date August 12, 1451. The charter, largely written in French but beginning and ending in Latin, establishes that:

tant que nous serons en vie, une haut messe du Saint Esprit qui s*e*ra chantèe cha*c*un an le lendemain du jour de l'assumpcion de n*ost*re dame / a dyacre, soulzdyacre et chantre, qui seront tous chanoines, quatre enfans revestu*s*, et tout le college / a orgues, deschant et grande et notable sonnent durant icelle messe.

so long as we shall live, a High Mass of the Holy Spirit will be sung each year on the morrow of the day of the Assumption of Our Lady; with deacon, subdeacon, and cantor, who will all be canons, four boys revested, and all of the college [of the

---

[3] Strohm, *Late Medieval Bruges*, 46.

[4] Bruges, Archief OCMW, Register 179, fol. 98v. The folio, which has been restored, remains in fragmentary condition. The total sum provided by Philip the Good was thirty Flemish pounds, for which an income of eighteen Parisian *livres* represents a five per cent annual interest.

[5] J. Finot, ed. *Inventaire sommaire des Archives départementales antérieures à 1790, Nord. Archives civiles. Série B.* (Lille: L. Daniel, 1895), vol. VIII, 24: "et cedit jour madicte dame disna à l'ostel du prèvost de Nostre-Dame de Bruges."

[6] H. vander Linden, *Itineraires de Philippe le Bon, duc de Bourgogne (1419–1467) et de Charles, comte de Charolais (1433–1467)* (Brussels: Palais des Académies, 1940), 278–79.

church]; with organs, discant, and great and notable sounding [of bells] during this Mass.[7]

The Mass was established for August 16, the day after the feast of the Assumption of the Virgin, a date with its own liturgy in many churches. The foundation calls for bell-ringing throughout, as well as organ, which may pertain to the Proper items of the Mass.[8] The citation of the five movements of the Mass Ordinary ensures that this was a cyclic, polyphonic Mass.

Philip the Good's foundation is highly unusual in that it requires a polyphonic Mass of the Holy Spirit, normally spoken or sung in plainchant. The liturgical calendars in Bruges record hundreds of Masses of the Holy Spirit from the fourteenth through sixteenth centuries, but only one that calls for a polyphonic Ordinary. At the same time, the placement on the morrow of the Assumption, in the Church of Our Lady, lends the foundation a Marian background. A Mass that closely fulfills the requirements of the foundation is the celebrated *Missa "Spiritus almus"* by Petrus de Domarto. Domarto's Mass is similarly rare in that its *cantus firmus* comes from the Marian responsory *Stirps Jesse*, but the phrase chosen, *Spiritus almus*, refers to the Holy Spirit. Moreover, the headmotive of the Mass, heard at the beginning of every movement, derives from an Introit trope for the Mass of the Holy Spirit, *Spiritus almus adest.*[9]

Little is known concerning the biography of Petrus de Domarto. He may be the singer Pietro Domarlla who appeared at Siena Cathedral between November 1447 and January 1448.[10] More definitely, a Petrus de Domaro sang for several weeks at the Church of Our Lady in Antwerp during the half-year from June 24 to December 24, 1448.[11] Three years later, in October 1451, we find Domarto established at Tournai Cathedral, where he was considered

[7] Brussels, Archives générales du royaume, trésor de Flandre, 1er série, Charter 1698. See A. Brown, *Civic Ceremony and Religion in Medieval Bruges c. 1300–1520* (Cambridge University Press, 2011), 277. I am indebted to Andrew Brown for sharing his photograph of the charter.

[8] The Buxheimer Orgelbuch, Munich, Bayerische Staatsbibliothek, Mus. MS 3725, contains three polyphonic Introits for organ. See also Appendix B5, charter of the guild of barber-surgeons, Church of St. James, where the organ plays during the sequence at Mass.

[9] Strohm, *Late Medieval Bruges*, 124.

[10] F. A. D'Accone, *The Civic Muse: Music and Musicians in Siena during the Middle Ages and the Renaissance* (University of Chicago Press, 1997), 173–75.

[11] J. van den Nieuwenhuizen, "De koralen, de zangers en de zangmeesters van de Antwerpse O. L.-Vrouwkerk tijdens de 15e eeuw," in *Gouden jubileum gedenkboek van de viering van 50 jaar heropgericht knapenkoor van de Onze-Lieve-Vrouwkatedraal te Antwerpen 1927–28/1977–78* (Antwerp: Choraelhuys, 1978), 38, cited in R. C. Wegman, "Petrus de Domarto's *Missa Spiritus almus* and the Early History of the Four-Voice Mass in the Fifteenth Century," *Early Music History* 10 (1991): 235–36 n. 1.

for the vacant position of succentor at the Cathedral of Cambrai.[12] The Cambrai directive states that "etiam famatus est bonus musicus" ("likewise he is famous as a good musician"). To date, no document has been found attesting to Domarto's presence in Bruges. Domarto could have received the commission through the influence of the Bishop of Tournai, Jean Chevrot, a native of Burgundy who was hand-picked as bishop by Philip the Good. Chevrot served as president of the ducal council in 1433–57, and as chief advisor to Isabella of Portugal during the 1440s.[13] Since Bruges lay within the diocese of Tournai, the Church of Our Lady fell under the bishop's purview.

The 1451 foundation at the Church of Our Lady provided that the Mass should be sung during the life of Philip the Good, after which it was replaced by a Requiem. Both Charles the Bold and Marie of Burgundy later confirmed the foundation.[14] As a result, the polyphonic Mass would have been performed annually for a period of sixteen years, 1451–66. In this respect, the foundation inaugurated a long association with the ducal court, by virtue of which the Church of Our Lady functioned like "a second court chapel."[15] By the same token, the Mass of the Holy Spirit would have attracted a broad attendance in the city. Philip the Good himself, who generally avoided Bruges in the summer months, never heard the Mass sung on August 16. The longevity of the Mass, however, in one of the leading centers of polyphony in Western Europe, could only have added to its fame.

The *Missa "Spiritus almus"* is widely distributed, having been copied in no fewer than five manuscript sources. In the Lucca Choirbook, compiled in Flanders by 1464, it was headed by an enormous initial, now cut off.[16] At least five English Mass cycles succeed it, beginning with the anonymous *Missa "Caput,"* with which Domarto's work is closely associated. The readings of the *Missa "Spiritus almus"* in the Lucca Choirbook, the sole extant source to be copied in the Low Countries, carry particular authority. Moreover,

[12] R. C. Wegman, "Mensural Intertextuality in the Sacred Music of Antoine Busnoys," in *Antoine Busnoys: Method, Meaning, and Context in Late Medieval Music*, ed. P. Higgins (Oxford: Clarendon Press, 1999), 190.

[13] M. Sommé, *Isabelle de Portugal, duchesse de Bourgogne: Une femme au pouvoir au XVe siècle* (Villeneuve d'Ascq: Presses Universitaires du Septentrion, 1998), 413, 420–21.

[14] Strohm, *Late Medieval Bruges*, 46.

[15] M. J. Bloxam, "A Survey of Late Medieval Service Books from the Low Countries: Implications for Sacred Polyphony, 1460–1520," 2 vols. (Ph.D. diss., Yale University, 1987), vol. I, 15.

[16] Strohm, in *The Lucca Choirbook*, 32, concludes that the *Missa "Spiritus almus"* was preceded by the *Missa de Beata Virgine* of Henricus Tyk, the first folio verso for which has a decorated border. While the *Missa de Beata Virgine* occupies a full gathering, the original foliation for the manuscript does not survive.

the scribe of the Lucca Choirbook has been tentatively identified as the singer Waghe Feustrier, who was active at Tournai Cathedral in 1457–62, and therefore would have had direct access to Domarto's Mass.[17] In 1457, Feustrier was paid three times in the accounts of Charles of Charolais, son of Philip the Good, where he is listed as "messire Waghe, chapelain de ladite église de Tournai."[18] The scribe of the codex signed the name "Waghe" or "Waghes" in four separate places, which accords with the reading of the accounts. This kind of ad hoc patronage typifies the Burgundian court. While the redaction in Trent, Castello del Buonconsiglio, MS 88 was entered before 1462, the Mass continued to be copied to the end of the fifteenth century. The music theorist Johannes Tinctoris, in his *Proportionale musices* of 1472–73, cites it with disapprobation for introducing several errors of mensural notation into common practice. He nonetheless acknowledges that the *Missa "Spiritus almus"* influenced even the composers Johannes Ockeghem and Antoine Busnoys. In sum, the prominence and influence of the *Missa "Spiritus almus"* may stem as much from its association with the court of Burgundy as from the novelty of its mensural usage.

In the *Missa "Spiritus almus"*, Domarto sets only the final phrase of the respond, *Spiritus almus* ("nourishing Spirit"), a fifth higher than the chant. It begins and ends on A, in the second mode. Domarto states the *cantus firmus* in the tenor no fewer than thirteen times across the length of the Mass, in a dizzying array of mensural combinations vis-à-vis the other voices.[19] It may well have been texted in performance, as suggested by the redaction in the Lucca Choirbook. While the chant books of the Church of Our Lady in Bruges have not survived, *Stirps Jesse* was sung in the Church of St. Donatian at second Vespers on the feast of the Annunciation and the Octave of the Assumption.[20] It was also heard in the annual Holy Blood procession on May 3, the most important civic procession of the year in Bruges.[21]

[17] D. Fiala, "Prosopography of Renaissance Singers: Waghe Feustrier," at http://ricercar.cesr.univ-tours.fr/3-programmes/PCR/ (accessed 14 March 2011). Feustrier sang in the Chapelle Royal of Louis XI of France in 1464–72. See the concise discussion in R. Strohm, "Alte Fragen und neue Überlegungen zum Chorbuch Lucca (Lucca, Archivio di Stato, Biblioteca Manoscritti 238 = I-Las 238)," in *Musikalische Quellen – Quellen zur Musikgeschichte: Festschrift für Martin Staehelin zum 65. Geburtstag*, ed. U. Konrad (Göttingen: Vandenhoeck & Ruprecht, 2002), 62–63.

[18] Finot, ed., *Inventaire sommaire*, vol. VIII, 409.

[19] Wegman, "Petrus de Domarto's *Missa Spiritus almus*," 248–52. The number thirteen in this instance may symbolize Christ and the twelve apostles.

[20] Bruges, Bisschoppelijk Archief, MS Reeks A 141, entries for March 23–26 and August 20–23.

[21] Strohm, *Late Medieval Bruges*, 5. See Brown, *Civic Ceremony and Religion*, Chapter 1, "The Holy Blood Procession."

Although the exact provenance of the *cantus firmus* remains uniden-
tified, a comparison of Domarto's tenor with five plainchant sources for
Stirps Jesse points to an origin in the Low Countries (Example 5.1). Codex
Smijers contains both plainchant and polyphony, and was compiled for
the Confraternity of Our Illustrious Lady at 's-Hertogenbosch in the sixteenth century.[22] Bruges, Bibliotheek Grootseminarie, MS 75-37 is a hitherto
unknown processional book of local provenance dated 1600.[23] In contrast
to these sources, two antiphoners – Ghent, Rijksuniversiteit Bibliotheek,
MS 15 (2), inscribed at the Church of St. Bavone in 1471–81, and Cambrai,
Médiathèque municipale, fonds ancien 38, compiled for Cambrai Cathedral in the thirteenth century – offer readings close to one another, but
more distant from Domarto's tenor. The variants become especially pro-
nounced towards the end of the *Spiritus almus* melisma. The plainchant in
a noted breviary, Paris, Bibliothèque nationale, fonds lat. 15182, copied for
the Cathedral of Notre Dame in Paris circa 1300, differs markedly from the
cantus firmus.

The image of the Tree of Jesse to which the responsory *Stirps Jesse* refers
appears in Isaiah 11:1–2. The first verse introduces the branch and flower:
"And there shall come forth a twig out of the root of Jesse, / And a flower
shall rise up out of his root." The second verse refers to the Holy Spirit:
"And the spirit of the Lord shall rest upon him, a spirit of wisdom and
understanding, / A spirit of counsel and strength, a spirit of knowledge
and piety."[24] These images reappear in the respond, which the verse then
explains in symbolic terms:

R. Stirps Jesse virgam produxit, virgaque florem: et super hunc florem requiescit
spiritus almus. V. Virga Dei genetrix virgo est, flos filius est eius.

R. The tree of Jesse brought forth a twig, and the twig a flower: and upon this flower
rests *the nourishing spirit*. V. The twig is the Virgin, the mother of God, the flower
her son.[25]

---

[22] Transcription in Wegman, "Petrus de Domarto's *Missa Spiritus almus*," 243. The plainsong
portion of the manuscript was copied in 1529–32.

[23] Fols. 16r–17r, with the text "Virga Jesse." The manuscript is signed on the inside cover,
"Bernardus van Thienen / ·1·6·0·0· / Bona nardus oratio." The incipit *Stirps Jesse* appears on
fol. 29v, first among the chants for the procession on the third Rogation Day, with the
continuation on fols. 16r–17r.

[24] Isaiah 11:1–2: "Et egredietur virga de radice Iesse et flos de radice eius ascendet / et requiescet
super eum spiritus Domini spiritus sapientiae et intellectus spiritus consilii et fortitudinis
spiritus scientiae et pietatis." Trans. from *Douay-Rheims Bible*: www.drbo.org (accessed April
15, 2011).

[25] Transcribed in Wegman, "Petrus de Domarto's *Missa Spiritus almus*," 240–41.

Example 5.1. Comparison of *cantus firmus* in Domarto, *Missa "Spiritus almus"*, with five plainchant sources: s'-Hertogenbosch, Rijksarchief in Noord-Brabant, Archief van de Illustre Lieve Vrouwe Broederschap, Codex Smijers; Bruges, Bibliotheek Grootseminarie, 75-37; Ghent, Rijksuniversiteit Bibliotheek, MS 15 (2); Cambrai, Médiathèque municipale, fonds ancien 38; Paris, Bibliothèque nationale, fonds lat. 15182

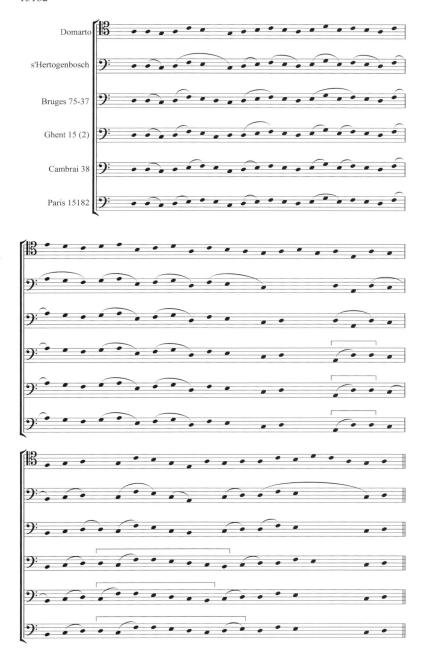

The *cantus firmus* naturally invokes both the responsory and the verses of Isaiah. In the iconography of the Tree of Jesse, the first figure in the tree is the son of Jesse, King David, the Psalmist, from whom St. Joseph is descended. By choosing only the phrase *Spiritus almus*, Domarto stresses the role of the Holy Spirit in fostering and upholding the princely qualities of wisdom, knowledge, strength, and piety implicitly associated with Philip the Good, Duke of Burgundy and Count of Flanders.

The foundation at the Church of Our Lady in Bruges specifies a motet "post missam," which may well refer to a Mass-motet cycle, current in the mid-fifteenth century.[26] Three such cycles are inscribed at the end of Trent 88: the *Missa "O rosa bella" I*, the *Missa "Esclave puist-il"*, and the *Missa "Spiritus almus"* by Petrus de Domarto. A motet in the Strahov Codex, *O pater eterne/O rosa bella*, matches the first cycle, while *Gaude Maria Virgo/Esclave puist-il* succeeds the second cycle in Trent 88.[27] Both motets are in four voices and carry the same, freely treated *cantus firmus* as appears in the Mass. A fourth cycle, the *Missa "So ys emprentid"* by Guillaume Le Rouge, appears in Trent 90, but its four-voice motet, *Stella celi/So ys emprentid*, is copied anonymously in the second gathering of Trent 88.[28]

The survival of a four-voice motet, *Salve mundi gloria*, to complete the implied Mass-motet cycle, supports the potential identification of the *Missa "Spiritus almus"* with the 1451 foundation at the Church of Our Lady in Bruges. Rob C. Wegman, in his erudite essay on the *Missa "Spiritus almus"*, points out that the motet shares its headmotive with the Mass.[29] Thus, while the text represents an elaboration of the *Salve regina*, the headmotive quotes the Introit trope *Spiritus almus adest*. The motet appears anonymously in an Austrian source, the Choirbook of Nicholas Leopold, in a layer dated to

---

[26] Strohm, *Late Medieval Bruges*, 46, 258.

[27] (1) Anonymous, *Missa 'O rosa bella' I*, Trent 88, fols. 363v–372r, and motet *O pater eterne/O rosa bella*, Prague, Památník Národního Písemnictví, Strahovská Knihovna, MS D. G. IV. 47, "Strahov Codex," fols. 160v–161r. (2) Anonymous, *Missa "Esclave puist-il"*, Trent 88, fols. 388v–399r, and motet *Gaude Maria Virgo/Esclave puist-il*, fols. 399v–400r. (3) Petrus de Domarto, *Missa "Spiritus almus"*, Trent 88, fols. 401v–410r. *Gaude mater miserorum*, the contrafact of a rondeau, *Quant ce viendra*, attributed to both Antoine Busnoys and Johannes Ockeghem, follows the *Missa "Spiritus almus"* in Trent 88, fol. 411r.

[28] *Missa "So ys emprentid"*, Trent, Castello del Buonconsiglio, MS 90, fols. 310v–318r, *Stella celi/So ys emprentid*, Trent 88, fols. 11v–13r. On the Mass-motet cycle, see R. Snow, "The Mass-Motet Cycle: A Mid-Fifteenth-Century Experiment," in *Essays in Musicology in Honor of Dragan Plamenac on His 70th Birthday*, ed. R. Snow (Pittsburgh University Press, 1969), 301–20; R. Strohm, *The Rise of European Music, 1380–1500* (Cambridge University Press, 1993), 428–29; and J. E. Cumming, *The Motet in the Age of Du Fay* (Cambridge University Press, 1999), 258–59, 263–65.

[29] Wegman, "Petrus de Domarto's *Missa Spiritus almus*," 241 n. 14.

Table 5.1. Voice ranges of *Missa "Spiritus almus"*
and *Salve mundi gloria,* compared

	Mass	Motet	
Discantus	g–c″	a–a′	Discantus
Contratenor	c–f′	d–f′	Contratenor primus
Tenor primus	e–e′	d–f′	Contratenor secundus
Tenor secundus	A–a	♭ G–g	Tenor

1476.[30] The first part, in perfect time (○), has texting for discantus alone. It sets four stanzas, but leaves out the last two lines, "Nobis ut sis adjutrix / In valle laboris." The second part, in diminished imperfect time (₵), renders only the phrase *pietatis oculos* in the superius. Since the poem is known primarily from Central European sources, both separately and as an Alleluia verse, it appears not to be original.[31] Another phrase, *nos debiles,* appears in the *secunda pars* at the entrance of the tenor after a long upper-voice duo. It does not pertain to the poem as edited in *Analecta hymnica medii aevi,* and may represent a different continuation, or even the original text.[32]

Wegman writes of *Salve mundi gloria* that "In several ways this interesting piece seems to be a reflection of Domarto's Mass: it is in D Dorian, with generally low ranges, unusual ficta, slow harmonic movement, and little imitation in the full passages."[33] The low ranges in both Mass and motet reflect a requirement for men's voices (Table 5.1). In the Mass, both discantus and contratenor occasionally split at cadences, requiring at least two voices each. A minimal distribution would call for two singers each for the discantus and first contratenor and one singer for the tenor and low *tenor secundus,* for an ensemble of six men. In the motet, the lowest voice, labeled tenor, has an octave range, G–g, with a B♭ signature, as opposed to a range of A–a and no signature in the *tenor secundus* of the Mass. Since the Mass tenor carries the *cantus firmus,* its range is likewise restricted to an

[30] Munich, Bayerische Staatsbibliothek, MS Mus. 3154, fols. 67v–69r. On the dating and structure of the manuscript, see T. L. Noblitt, "Das Chorbuch des Nicolaus Leopold (München, Staatsbibliothek, Mus. Ms. 3154): Repertorium," *Archiv für Musikwissenschaft* 26 (1969): 170–71; T. L. Noblitt, ed., *Der Kodex des Magister Nicolaus Leopold: Staatsbibliothek München Mus. Ms. 3154,* 4 vols. (Kassel and New York: Bärenreiter, 1987–96), I, xi; II, 230–37.

[31] K.-H. Schlager, ed., *Alleluia-Melodien II ab 1100,* Monument monodica medii aevi 8 (Kassel and Basel: Bärenreiter, 1987), 777–79.

[32] G. M. Dreves *et al.,* eds., *Analecta hymnica medii aevi,* 55 vols. (Leipzig: O. R. Reisland, 1886–1920), vol. II, 151–52.

[33] Wegman, "Petrus de Domarto's *Missa Spiritus almus,*" 241 n. 14.

octave, e–e′, compared with a tenth, d–f′, in the *contratenor secundus* of the motet. The latter voice acts like a chanson contratenor in that it moves in irregular leaps, lacking a strong melodic flow. The *contratenor primus* of the motet has a similar range to the contratenor of the Mass, but the discantus is restricted to an octave, a–a′, as opposed to a full tenth or eleventh in the Mass, g–c″.

In the *Missa "Spiritus almus"*, the *tenor secundus* operates in counterpoint to the *cantus firmus*, in similar note values. The low tenor of the motet, moving primarily in breves, contributes to a sombre, majestic sound, very much like that of the Mass. Both works cultivate an octave, fifth, and third at the beginning of each *tempus* or measure. Further, a close examination of the motet tenor demonstrates that it is not based on chant. The first five notes are d-A-d-G-c, a combination of fourths and fifths unlike chant, but similar to the low *tenor secundus* of the Mass.

The end of *Salve mundi gloria* quotes the harmonies at the first full cadence of the Kyrie, coincident with the entrance of the *cantus firmus* on the word *Spiritus*.[34] In the Mass, the *tenor secundus* moves d-A-B♭-A, against f′-c′-d′-c♯′ in the discantus, a tenth above (Example 5.2A). The motet expands upon the opening of the Kyrie, utilizing the same melodic idea in the discantus (Example 5.2B). The downward leap in the tenor, d-A, arrives at A-B♭-A, this time harmonized c♯′-d′-c♯′ and marked by a fermata in all voices. This leads directly to the final sonority on D. In general, the motion from B♭ to A, the latter harmonized by either c′ or c♯′, characterizes the motet as a whole.

The beginning of the motet not only incorporates the headmotive of the *Missa "Spiritus almus"*; it specifically quotes the beginning of the Gloria, where the motive is heard in imitation between discantus and contratenor (Example 5.3). Mass and motet also share one important melodic motive. The start of the Qui tollis presents a falling fourth with a dotted semibreve, two semiminims, and a breve, sung at the third between the upper voices (Example 5.4A). The same idea, again doubled at the third, appears in the *secunda pars* of the motet, in the long duo that begins this section (Example 5.4B). If sung with a c♯′, followed immediately by the scribal b♭′ in the contratenor, the passage becomes still more striking.[35] The motive

---

[34]   Examples 5.2, 5.3, and 5.4 rely on two published editions: R. L. Gerber, ed., *Sacred Music from the Cathedral at Trent: Trent, Museo provinciale d'arte, Codex 1375 (olim 88)*, Monuments of Renaissance Music 12 (University of Chicago Press, 2007), 1155–80; T. L. Noblitt, ed., *Der Kodex des Magister Nicolaus Leopold*, vol. I, 230–37.

[35]   The opening duet of *Stella celi* in Trent 88, at the word *celi*, similarly quotes a two-voice passage near the end of the second Agnus Dei of the *Missa "So ys emprentid"* by Guillaume Le Rouge.

Example 5.2. (A) Domarto, *Missa "Spiritus almus"*, Kyrie, breves 4–6; (B) *Salve mundi gloria, secunda pars*, conclusion

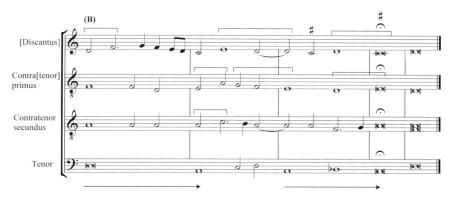

Example 5.3. (A) Domarto, *Missa "Spiritus almus"*, Et in terra, opening duo; (B) *Salve mundi gloria, prima pars*, opening duo

Example 5.4. (A) Domarto, *Missa "Spiritus almus"*, Qui tollis, beginning; (B) *Salve mundi gloria, secunda pars*, breves 6–9

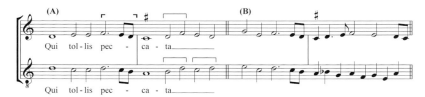

appears several times within the duo, including a passage in imitation. In contrast to contemporaneous English models, the duos that begin both sections of *Salve mundi gloria* share a restrained sense of surface rhythm with the two-voice passages in the Mass. Their construction shows the same masterful craftmanship as in the *Missa "Spiritus almus"*, with frequent voice crossing and memorable points of imitation.

The intertextuality and shared style of the *Missa "Spiritus almus"* and *Salve mundi gloria* argue for their coherence as a Mass-motet cycle. The quotation of the opening of the Mass at the end of the motet in effect brings the work full circle. The remarkable musical references invoking the Holy Spirit further support the potential identification of the cycle with the Burgundian foundation at the Church of Our Lady in Bruges. In addition, the proposed ascription of *Salve mundi gloria* to Petrus de Domarto serves to further our understanding of the widespread musical patronage of Philip the Good. The prominence of the foundation in turn helps explain the influence the Domarto exerted on Busnoys, who worked for Charles the Bold, despite the earlier composer's surviving output of only two Mass cycles and two chansons.

The practice of performing polyphony at the end of Mass goes back to the *Mass of Tournai* of the early fourteenth century, which concludes with the bilingual motet *Se grasse n'est/Cum venerint/Ite missa est*, and to the Guillaume de Machaut *La Messe de Nostre Dame*. These set both the versicle *Ite missa est* and the response *Deo gratias*, with which Mass concludes and from which it takes its name. Two motets in the Old Hall manuscript of the early fifteenth century incorporate the *Deo gratias* alone: *Are post*

Gerber, ed., *Sacred Music from the Cathedral at Trent*, 42, comments on the Mass-motet cycle that "Le Rouge uses the same mode, the same ranges of the upper three voices, and similar melodic patterns throughout the six movements." The two-voice quotation helps solidify the motet's attribution to Le Rouge, who worked for Charles, Duke of Orléans, from 1451–65. The famous poet had been in English captivity for twenty-five years following the Battle of Agincourt, and the text was a favorite of the English.

libamina/Nunc surgunt in populo, by the French composer Mayshuet, and the anonymous *Post missarum solennia*.[36] The triplum of the first begins, "At the altar, after the oblation, we will sing odes and songs with good intentions. It is best of all that we praise with careful movement of voice, as reason orders."[37] *Post missarum solennia*, modeled on Mayshuet's work, begins in a similar way:[38] "After the solemnity of Mass, after the divine eulogy, we will sing songs with sweetly fluent voice."[39] The latter two motets were also copied together in the "Royal English Choirbook," a now-fragmentary manuscript compiled in the Chapel Royal of Henry VI.[40] Two short motets from the second decade of the century appear with the acrostic "DEO GRATIAS" in the French-Cypriot manuscript Turin, Biblioteca nazionale universitaria, J.II.9.[41] The Lucca Choirbook transmits another English motet, *Deo gratias agamus* by John Stone.[42]

The Mass-motet cycles of the mid-fifteenth century continue in the same liturgical tradition, wherein the motet replaces or directly follows the *Deo gratias*. In relation to the other Mass-motet cycles at the end of Trent 88, the *Missa "O rosa bella" I* the *Missa "Esclave puist-il"*, Domarto's Mass differs in that it employs a chant tenor. The mensural transformation of that tenor is wholly original. Modeled on the anonymous English *Missa "Caput"*, it has a full, four-voice texture. While the motet lacks a *cantus firmus*, it employs two important techniques of unification: a common headmotive and internal quotation. Even though the text looks to be a later substitution, the original surely had a Marian subject. The symbolism of the *cantus firmus*, transformed in each successive statement to the words

---

36   London, British Library, MS Add. 57950, fols. 111v–112r and 112v, respectively.

37   *The Old Hall Manuscript*, ed. A. Hughes and M. Bent, Corpus mensurabilis musicae 46, 3 vols. (Rome: American Institute of Musicology, 1969–73), vol. I, 419–23: "Are post libamina / odas atque carmina / laudis iubilemus / Cui*us* finis bonus est / *ipsu*m bono*m* superest / totum ut laudemus / Vocis modulacio / sicut iubet racio / concinat cu*m* corde."

38   J. M. Allsen, "Style and Intertextuality in the Isorhythmic Motet, 1400–1440" (Ph.D. diss., University of Wisconsin-Madison, 1992), 260–68.

39   *The Old Hall Manuscript*, ed. Hughes and Bent, vol. I, 424–28: "Post missarum sollenia / divina post eulogia / voce cu*m* dulciflua / decantemus cantica."

40   Oxford, Bodleian Library, MS Don. b. 32. See M. Bent, "The Progeny of Old Hall: More Leaves from a Royal English Choirbook," in *Gordon Athol Anderson (1929–1981): In Memoriam von seinen Studenten, Freunden und Kollegen*, Musicological Studies 39, 2 vols. (Henryville, Ontario: Institute of Mediaeval Music, 1982), vol. I, 1–54.

41   The two motets, *De magne Pater rector Olimpi/Donis affatim perfluit orbis* and *Dignum summo Patri/Dulciter hymnos*, are copied at the top and bottom, respectively, of the same opening, fols. 91v–92r.

42   Lucca Choirbook, fol. 49v. Strohm, *Late Medieval Bruges*, 132, points to a second *Deo gratias* motet in the same source, *Agimus tibi gratias*, fol. 51v, which takes the textual form of a rondeau.

Illustration 5.1. J. van Meunincxhoven, *The Church of St. Donatian*, 1696, oil on canvas

"nourishing Spirit," gives way in the motet to an encomium of the heavenly Mother who nourished the growing flower on the branch, Christ.

Memorial motets at the Church of St. Donatian

Sacred music in fifteenth-century Bruges centered on the collegiate Church of St. Donatian (Illustration 5.1). As a collegiate church, it ministered not to the people, but to the clerks, chaplains, and thirty-one canons of the chapter, as well as to the inhabitants of the city *burg* ("citadel"), which included the court of Burgundy during its periods in residence. The responsibilities for polyphonic music devolved to the skilled singers among the *clerici installati* and chaplains, who also furnished the succentor and organist. The succentor taught music to the choirboys, whose number was fixed at four in a foundation of 1421. Foundations provided monies for additions to the liturgy of the church or for personnel, including chaplains, to carry out the liturgy. Each day following Matins, the succentor and choirboys were required to sing a polyphonic Mass in honor of the Virgin Mary, the *Missa de Salve*, in a chapel behind the main altar, the easternmost bay of the church.[43]

Evidence for motet performance at St. Donatian (Sint-Donaas) is contained in the fifteenth- and sixteenth-century obituary book of the church, called a *planarius*, which records numerous bequests for services made by both citizens and clergy. The manuscript Bruges, Bisschoppelijk Archief, Reeks A 141, takes the form of an extended calendar on which are recorded obits and foundations throughout the liturgical year.[44] An obit consisted of an anniversary Mass said or sung on a particular day of the year to speed the departed soul through Purgatory, often with prayers and the *Miserere mei* (Psalm 59) or *De profundis* (Psalm 129). Less frequent are the foundations, which add to or augment the liturgy of the church in specific ways. The larger foundations are recorded in a separate section at the back of the manuscript, which gives full details of the monetary payments that must be made and to whom. While obits rarely call for polyphonic music, several of the foundations for individual feast days provide for motets.

One such foundation at St. Donatian, dated April 22, 1417, was established by the gentlewoman Elisabeth Parols (see Appendix B1).[45] Parols was the widow of Robert de Capple, a councillor to Duke John the Fearless. The first section of the document creates an obit for her son, Henri de Capple, each year on September 3. The second section, however, establishes a foundation for the Octave of the feast of Corpus Christi:[46]

In addition, the said lady ordained that each year during Compline of the Octave of the feast of the Sacrament, the greater bell is to be rung from beginning to end. And Compline being finished, the curate . . . dressed in his alb and precious cap, begins the hymn *Veni Creator Spiritus* in the middle of the choir. Which finished, with the versicle and collect said, the chaplain cantor begins the antiphon *O sacrum convivium*; and a procession being made within the church, and the collect of the sacrament said in the choir, a motet is sung.

---

[43] Strohm, *Late Medieval Bruges*, 12–13, 22–23; P. Andriessen, *Die van Muziken gheerne horen: Muziek in Brugge 1200–1800* (Bruges: West-Vlaamse Gidsenkring, 2002), 129–30, 370–71. The *Missa de Salve* was so named because it began with the Introit *Salve sancta parens*.

[44] The manuscript was begun by 1415, with additions to the middle of the sixteenth century.

[45] P. Andriessen, *Muziek in Brugge*, 143 n. 77, citing Bruges, Bisschoppelijk Archief, MS Reeks A 50, *Acta capitulorum*, fol. 27v. While the foundation transcribed in Appendix B is in Latin, the entry in the *Acta capitulorum* appears in Flemish.

[46] The "Octave" occurs one week after the feast, or eight days later by medieval reckoning.

The elaborate memorial that follows Compline begins, unusually, with a hymn to the Holy Spirit. It continues with a procession through the church, to the familiar chant in honor of the sacrament, *O sacrum convivium*. The collect is said once the procession has returned to the choir, followed by a motet. As is typical for a *planarius*, however, the details have to be teased out of the payment records that follow. The procession, for example, consisted of the curate, two vicars, boys dressed and in attendance, boys to carry the torches, the chaplain cantor, the succentor, and the choirboys.

The succentor is paid specifically "for bringing together and teaching the singers of the motet," a rare reference to the rehearsal of music (see Appendix B1). Common sense suggests that the choirboys would not be able to sing a motet satisfactorily at sight. There is long precedence for regular practice: in the statutes of circa 1350 for the choirboys of the Sainte-Chapelle in Paris, the chapel of the French king, the choirboys were to rehearse three or four motets after Vespers each evening.[47] In 1420, the succentor of St. Donatian, Jacob Couterman, was commended for his diligence in instructing the boys in the singing of motets.[48] The reference in the Parols foundation to *cantores*, rather than simply *pueris*, indicates that the performance was joined by the succentor and at least one other adult singer, most likely the chaplain cantor. For a four-voice motet, the choirboys would sing the triplum and motetus, with one man each on the contratenor and tenor.

On July 12, 1447, Jacob Baderan, a canon and officer of St. Donatian, created a series of services for Lent (see Appendix B2). There are three parts to the foundation. First, each day from Ash Wednesday to Maundy Thursday, directly after Matins, a memorial to the Virgin Mary was said in the choir, beginning with the antiphon *Alma redemptoris mater*, sung "solemnly and slowly," followed by the versicle *Ave Maria*, *Post partum*, or *Ora pro nobis*, and the collect *Omnipotens sempiterne Deus qui gloriose*. Second, after the Morrow Mass ("called the Scellemesse") another Mass was read at a Marian altar in the nave of the church. The latter was celebrated

---

[47] M. A. Vidier, "Notes et documents sur le personnel, les biens et l'administration de la Sainte-Chapelle, du XIIIe au Xve siècle," *Mémoires de la Société de l'histoire de Paris et de l'Isle-de-France* 23 (1901): 345: "il ne doivent pas occuper le temps d'après disner en chanter, mais doivent entendre à faire leurs matieres ou à aprendre aucune autre chose de leur gramaire, et doit souffire ou cas dessus dit qu'il recordent chacun jour après vespres iij. ou iiij. mottez et des autres choses autant." The word *recordent* in this context means "they rehearse" or "they recite."

[48] A. C. de Schrevel, *Histoire du Séminaire de Bruges*, 2 vols. (Bruges: De Planck, 1895), II, 152, citing a capitular act of July 4, 1420: "DD. considerantes quod succentor Jac. Couterman sepissime etiam pueros in motetis erudiendo occupatus existit adeo, quod bene modo continuo choro vacare nequeat, concesserunt quod, sive presens, sive non, in choro lucrabitur [distributiones] cotidianas et hoc ab hinc usque festum natalis Domini proxime futurum."

by a chaplain of the choir, assisted by Baderan himself during his lifetime, and after his death, or in his absence, by the *tabularius* or keeper of records. The accounts paid for the lighting, bread, and wine necessary for the Mass. The church also distributed five *solidi* each day to the poor incarcerated by the city of Bruges, bringing sustenance to those who could not hear Mass. Third, on each Sunday of Lent, the succentor with his choirboys "sings before the said altar a motet of the Blessed Mary before the start of the said Mass, with a versicle and collect of the same saint." The succentor was paid three *solidi* on each occasion. In effect, Baderan created a second memorial to the Virgin Mary, this time before the Marian Mass at the altar in the nave of the church. Here, the motet took first position in the memorial, in the place of an antiphon. A copy of the foundation in the capitular acts makes the substitution plain, stating, "succentor cum pueris cantabit cum discantu *Salve Regina* vel aliam antiphonam vel motetum de Beata Maria ante principium dicte Misse" ("the succentor with the boys will sing the *Salve regina* or another antiphon or motet before the start of the said Mass").[49] The scribe of the *planarius* normalized the language to read simply, "a motet."

Following the memorial in the nave, according to the 1410 statutes of the choir, the choirboys would have left for the Marian chapel, where they performed the daily, polyphonic *Missa de Salve*. In performance of the motet, the succentor probably took the tenor part, while the four choirboys were divided into two equal parts in soprano range.[50] A single contratenor from the choir would have been required for a four-voice work, or a three-voice work with one discantus part. Since there are six Sundays in Lent, it is possible that six different motets were performed each year by the succentor and choirboys. Alternatively, they may have sung the same motet on six successive Sundays. The activity of the choirboys at this period appears in the accounts of 1452, when the succentor Johannes Roberti was paid to copy four septernions, or twenty-eight folios, into the *magno libro motetorum* ("great book of motets") at St. Donatian, which contained movements for the Mass as well.[51]

[49] Bruges, Bisschoppelijk Archief, MS Reeks A 51, fols. 185v–186r. The entry in the *Acta capitulorum* was kindly signaled by Andrew Brown.

[50] On the ranges of choirboys, see Table 7.2, below. See also D. Fallows, "Specific Information on the Ensembles for Composed Polyphony," in *Studies in the Performance of Late Mediaeval Music*, ed. S. Boorman (Cambridge University Press, 1983), 122–25.

[51] A. DeWitte, "Boek- en Bibliotheekwezen in de Brugse Donaaskerk," in *Sint-Donaas en de voormalige Brugse Kathedraal*, 2 vols. (Bruges: Jong Kristen Onthaal voor Toerisme, 1978–88), vol. I, 89.

The Vespers motet

At least two fifteenth-century foundations at the Church of St. Donatian provide for a Vespers motet, without further specification. The canon Jacob Baderan, in the final section of his foundation of July 1447, institutes an *Et in terra* at Mass on the feast day of St. Bavone, October 1. Whenever the feast day should fall on a Sunday, however, he ordains an *Et in terra* and *Patrem* at Mass, with a motet at second Vespers (see Appendix B2).[52] In this instance, the motet was sung by the men who also were responsible for the *Et in terra* and *Patrem*. The singer and chaplain Simon Coene, in a foundation of 1439, asks for an *Et in terra* and *Patrem* in discant at Mass on the feast of Sts. Simon and Jude, October 28, also with a motet at second Vespers sung by men.[53] Both these foundations employ polyphony in augmentation of the existing liturgy of the day.

The lack of further instruction suggests that motets, when required, held a standard position at St. Donatian in the Vespers liturgy for duplex and solemn feasts. An ordinal of the Cathedral of Tournai from the first half of the fifteenth century provides an initial response to the question. For solemn feasts, it dictates that following the Magnificat antiphon and collect, "The candlebearers before the lectern, without waiting for a sign, adjoin the *Benedicamus*, unless the cantor of the choirboys makes provision for a motet in place of the *Benedicamus*, declaiming it before the eagle."[54] The passage refers to the large lectern for the evangeliary, surmounted by an eagle, that even today stands in the middle of the choir in Flemish churches. (The eagle is the traditional symbol of St. John the Evangelist.) The motet thus was sung at the end of Vespers, in the middle of the choir, as the last item of the office.

Since Bruges belonged to the diocese of Tournai, a similar practice may have prevailed at St. Donatian.[55] A foundation of 1489, made by the canon

---

[52] In the dozen years following the establishment of the foundation, October 1 fell on a Sunday in 1447, 1452, and 1458.

[53] Bruges, Bisschoppelijk Archief, MS Reeks A 141, *Planarius*, fol. 108r: "Item succentori et sociis cantoribus die sanctorum symonis et Jude ut cantetur Et in terra et Patrem cum discantu ad missam et motetum in secundis Vesperis octo solidi paris."

[54] J. Pycke, *Sons, couleurs, odeurs dans la cathédrale de Tournai au 15e siècle*, Bibliothèque de la Revue d'histoire ecclésiastique 84, 2 vols. (Brussels: Nauwelaerts, 2004), vol. I, 37: "Et ceroferarii absque precepto ante lectrarium subiungant *Benedicamus*, nisi cantor scolarum provisis sit de moteto, loco de *Benedicamus* ante aquilam dicendo." Pycke, ibid., vol. I, 29–30, dates the principal source to 1420–50.

[55] A fifteenth-century copy of the Tournai ordinal, explicitly intended for reference outside the cathedral, still exists in the archives of St. Donatian. The manuscript, contained in Bruges, Bisschoppelijk Archief, Reeks A 122, comprises a single fascicle with the incipit "In omni festo

and composer Pierre Basin, confirms that a Vespers motet could take the place of the *Benedicamus Domino*. The passage, preserved in the *planarius* of St. Donatian, ordains that at first Vespers of St. Martin, November 10 (see Appendix B3):

a solemn procession shall be made by the community of the choir, as in the feast of Sts. Philip and James, leaving in procession with an antiphon of St. Martin, and afterwards the Magnificat with an antiphon and neuma, and moreover a collect of the saint in the Arbosio Chapel . . . Item, to the canon saying the collect at that time and place, vj d. p*ar*.[56] Item, to the companions in music, for singing the motet after the collect, and after the motet *Deo dicamus*, in the usual manner, vj S. p*ar*. Item, the procession returning to the choir, *Alma redemptoris* is sung, with a versicle and collect of the Blessed Virgin; and if there are suffrages of the saints, they will be sung in the accustomed manner.

Unusually, the procession begins in the choir directly after the hymn. The choir sings an antiphon in procession to the chapel of St. Martin in the nave of the church, founded by the Bishop of Tournai, Philip de Arbosio, in 1359. The choir sings the antiphon incipit and Magnificat, giving the antiphon in full at the end, with a textless neuma added for greater length. The versicle, collect, and motet follow in the Arbosio chapel. The motet, however, receives its own response, *Deo dicamus gratia*. We have already seen this text at the end of *Surexit Christus* by Johannes de Lymburgia, where it serves in place of the standard *Deo gratias*. Use of the versicle "R. Benedicamus Domino. V. Deo dicamus gratia" became widespread in the late Middle Ages.[57] Consequently, the reference to this versicle in Basin's foundation demonstrates that the motet takes the place of the *Benedicamus Domino*.[58] The phrase *more solito* ("in the usual manner") further suggests that the practice was not unique to this feast, as seen in the Tournai ordinal.[59]

cathedrali, scilicet Natalis Domini Pasche Dedicationis Ecclesie Pentechostes Eucharistie Assumptionis beate Virginis et Omnium Sanctorum, choro et altari pro more in ecclesia torn*acensis* observato ornatio et compositio."
[56] The form "vj S. p*ar*." employs "S." as an abbreviation for *solidi*; "p*ar*." or "*parisiensis*" refers to the coinage of Paris. There were twelve *denarii* (d.) in a *solidum*, and twenty *solidi* (S.) in a *libra* (L.). These abbreviations have been standardized throughout.
[57] J. Caldwell, review of *Le Magnus liber organi de Notre-Dame de Paris*, vol. I: *Les quadrupla et tripla de Paris*, ed. E. Roesner, *Music and Letters* 76 (1995): 643.
[58] Strohm, *Late Medieval Bruges*, 132, describes the motet in the Basin foundation rather as "an insertion."
[59] In the *Liber niger* of Lincoln Cathedral, compiled circa 1400–30, similar provision was made for polyphony (*organizacione*) of an unspecified nature in place of the *Benedicamus Domino* at Vespers on double feasts: "unde oracione finita eant aliqui bene cantantes cum premunicione magistri scolarum cantus et organizent ad lectrinam predictam . . . Set eos premunire non tenetur magister predictus nisi in maioribus duplicibus, quia in minoribus duplicibus

The foundations of Jacob Baderan and Simon Coene at St. Donatian may rely upon a similar practice.[60] The issue of the Vespers motet recurs at Cambrai Cathedral, where more direct evidence for its function survives (see Chapter 7).

The Three Saints

In the early 1470s, the financiers Colaert and Pieter de la Bye established yearly processions in Bruges in honor of Sts. Mary Magdalene, Katherine, and Barbara. The foundations occur severally in another *planarius*, pertaining to the collegiate Church of Our Lady.[61] The immediate motive for the foundations may have been the death of Colaert's wife, Magdalene, on May 29, 1473.[62] The processions were subsequently incorporated into the charter of the confraternity Drie Santinnen, dated December 18, 1474.[63] The Drie Santinnen, which counted the de la Bye brothers as principal founders, was a guild of the *Rederijkers*, or rhetoricians, dedicated to the performance of vernacular poetry and drama.[64] Moreover, the 1474 charter enters into agreement with the leaders of of three other confraternities – Our Lady of the Snow, the Ten Thousand Martyrs, and Our Lady of Grace – to participate in the yearly processions, as well as at the anniversary Masses of the founders, Colaert and Pieter de la Bye.

organizent pueri de choro et in superpellicijs. et hec organizacio erit in disposicione Succentoris. Cantu finito debent illi qua parte chorus est respondere cantando et stando *Deo dicamus.*" It is of interest that the choirboys participated only on minor doubles at this date. See H. Bradshaw, *Statutes of Lincoln Cathedral*, ed. C. Wordsworth, 3 vols. (Cambridge University Press, 1892–97), vol. I, 369. R. Bowers, "Lincoln Cathedral: Music and Worship to 1640," in *English Church Polyphony: Singers and Sources from the 14th to the 17th Century* (Brookfield: Ashgate, 1999), section VI, notes that "By 1407, there was a specialist to teach singing to the twelve choirboys, probably including discant."

[60] Bruges, Bisschoppelijk Archief, MS Reeks A 210 (unfoliated), a *planarius* from the first half of the sixteenth century, places the motet for St. Bavone specifically at the end of Vespers: "Soci*js* de musica ut cantent Kyrie in Missa, Et in terra et Patrem [si dominica sit] ac motetum post secundas Vesperas, x S." The entry for Sts. Simon and Jude reads similarly: "Soci*js* de musica cantantibus in Missa Kyrie, Et in terra, Patrem . . . et post secund*as* Vesper*as* motetum, viij S."

[61] Bruges, Archiv OCMW, Register 179, fols. 52r, 84v, 86v, respectively.

[62] P. A. Beaucourt de Noortvelde, *Description historique de l'eglise collegiale et paroissiale de Notre Dame a Bruges, avec une histoire chronologique de tous les prevots, suivie, d'un recueil des epitaphes anciennes & modernes de cette eglise* (Bruges: J. de Busscher, 1773), 248.

[63] Bruges, Stadsarchief, Oud Archief, MS Reeks 390, Cartularium Drie Santinnen, Inv. nr. 1, fols. 3r–4v, with specific reference to the *planarius* of the church. A copy of the charter is held at Bruges, Archief OMCW, Register 155, *Cartularium*, fols. 41r–42r. See also Bruges, Archief OCMW, Charter 305.

[64] See J. J. Gailliard, *Inscriptions funéraires & monumentales de la Flandre occidentale; avec des données historiques & généologiques*, 2 vols. (Bruges, 1861–67), II, 473.

The three processions took place after second Vespers on their respective feast days. They are virtually identical, except for the responsory sung upon leaving the choir. The procession for St. Mary Magdalene, July 22, serves to illustrate all three (see Appendix B4):

Nicolaus and Petrus de la Bye, brothers and notables of the parish, gave to the community of the choir of this church, for the procession to be conveyed around the choir on the day of Magdalene, upon completion of second Vespers, for going out with the responsory *O beata Maria Magdalena*, and for returning with the *Ave regina*...To the chaplains .xviij. S. par. To the cantor and his assistant, for beginning the said responsory, to each .vj. S. par. To the one who says the collect before Madgalene, and to his fellows, to each .vj. S. par. To the musician singers for singing the motet .iiij. S. par.

As in the memorial of Elisabeth Parols, plainchant was sung in procession: here, the responsory *O beata Maria Magdalena*. In the procession for St. Katherine, the responsory was *Virgo flagellatur*, and for St. Barbara, *Regnum mundi*. The cantor with his assistant sang the incipit and verse. In all three de la Bye memorials, the antiphon *Ave regina celorum* was sung in procession back to the choir. A collect was said *"coram Magdalena"*, which must refer to a painting or sculpture located behind the altar that served as the processional station. The wording of the foundation for St. Barbara, *coram Sancta Barbara*, confirms this. Such paintings or statues are typical for side chapels dedicated to individual saints; the confraternal charter indicates that the altar was already in place by December 1474. Further, a painting by the Master of the St. Lucy Legend was placed on the altarpiece by 1489, with the three saints in a central circle around the Madonna and Child.[65]

A motet in honor of the saint followed the collect. The wording of the foundation, *Cantoribus musicis*, suggests that it was sung entirely by men; the *pueri* in attendance need not have been choirboys. This would have been entirely possible at the Church of Our Lady, since after 1450 the church became an important center for sacred music in Bruges, thanks largely to the patronage of Philip the Good, Charles the Bold, and Charles' daughter, Marie of Burgundy.[66] As in the case of the painting, a commission for three motets would have been required, one for each of the saints.

---

[65] Master of the St. Lucy Legend, *Virgo inter virgines*, Brussels, Koninklijke Musea voor Schone Kunsten van België/Musées royaux des Beaux–Arts, inv. no. 2576. While the central circle consists of Sts. Katherine, Mary Magdalene, and Barbara, the outer group clusters four female saints on either side of the throne.

[66] Bloxam, "A Survey of Late Medieval Service Books," vol. I, 14.

The processional pattern followed by Colaert and Pieter de la Bye persisted through the last quarter of the fifteenth century and the first quarter of the sixteenth, in numerous foundations both at the Church of Our Lady and at the Church of St. Savior (Sint-Salvator).[67] The pattern corresponds to the standard Friday and Saturday procession after Vespers of Our Lady, but with the addition of a motet at the processional station:

Responsory – Versicle – Collect – Motet – Marian Antiphon[68]

A 1473 foundation of the curate Judocus Berthilde at the Church of St. Savior illustrates the standard liturgy.[69] Berthilde endowed a procession after first Vespers for St. Joseph, March 19:

Item dict*is* pr*imis* vesp*eris* portab*itur* process*io* in navi ecclesie canta*ndo* R. *Videte dignitatem* cum V*er*su *Gloria Patri* et coll*ecta* app*ropriante*, qua dicta, cantor cantabit motetu*m* cu*m* Juvenibus suis un*de* habebit ad cantor ii S p*ar*.

First Vespers being said, the procession shall be brought into the nave of the church with the singing of the responsory *Videte dignitatem*, with the verse *Gloria Patri*, and a suitable collect; which said, the cantor sings a motet with his children, whence the cantor retains ii S. par.[70]

Once again, the motet was performed by the choirboys and their master. Berthilde further directed that "during the said procession, the customary processional bell shall be sounded."[71]

A similar foundation at St. Savior's, established by Lodewyck Claes (Clays) in October 1473, requires a procession after first Vespers for St. Louis, August 25. The charter was but the first of a series underwritten by Claes at the Church of St. Savior in the 1470s.[72] The document is written in Flemish, denoting Claes as a layman. It dictates that the full choir of St. Savior exit the main choir after the collect, singing the antiphon *Magnificat*, with the cantor carrying his silver staff ("zelveren staven"). Arriving in the chapel of St. Agatha, the priest says another collect at the altar. A motet

---

[67]   D. Salokar, "*Ad augmentationem divini cultus*: Pious Foundations and Vespers Motets in the Church of Our Lady in Bruges," in *Musicologie en Archiefonderzoek*, ed. B. Haggh (Brussels: Archives et Bibliothèques de Belgique, 1994), 316–17; Strohm, *Late Medieval Bruges*, 53.

[68]   Salokar, "Pious Foundations," 314–15.

[69]   Brown, *Civic Ceremony and Religion*, 120, 313. Strohm, *Late Medieval Bruges*, 47, states that Berthilde, a bachelor of theology, created a number of similar foundations, together with his sister and brother-in-law, at the Church of Our Lady in 1474. See Bruges, Archief OCMW, Register 155, *Cartularium*, fols. 73v–75v.

[70]   Bruges, Rijksarchiev, MS Fonds découvertes 81 (*olim* 104), *Planarius Sint-Salvator*, fol. 11r.

[71]   Ibid.: "durante dicta process*io* pulsab*itur* ca*m*pana p*ro*cessionalis co*n*sueta."

[72]   Strohm, *Late Medieval Bruges*, 53.

follows, sung by the *cantere metten kindere*, a standard phrase in reference to the cantor and choirboys.[73] Claes, who names the processional bell as "Salvator," distinguishes the manner of bell-ringing from that at Mass. As in the Berthilde foundation, the entry serves as a reminder of the importance of the bells in enhancing the ceremony, particularly as the bellringers in both instances received as much as did the cantor.

The feast day of Sts. Cosmas and Damian

The trade guild of the barber-surgeons in Bruges, like the guild Drie Santinnen, had its own chapel, located at the parish church of St. James (Sint-Jacob). St. James lay in a wealthy parish that was home to many of the rich foreign merchants and financiers in Bruges, including Tomasso Portinari of Florence and Giovanni di Arrigo Arnolfini of Lucca. A charter of August 28, 1432, brought to light by Reinhard Strohm, details the feast of Sts. Cosmas and Damian, the patron saints of the guild (see Appendix B5).[74] The feast, celebrated on September 26, included first Vespers, Matins, all the little hours, High Mass, second Vespers, and Compline. The charter requires the use of the great organ at Mass, playing in alternation with plainchant at the Kyrie and sequence.

The charter, copied in Flemish on a single parchment bifolio, also calls for a procession at both first and second Vespers. The description is sufficiently detailed to allow a nearly complete reconstruction of the office. The first part of Vespers, through the hymn, took place in the church choir. The hymn was sung with the *groter orghele* in alternation with the choir. The procession began with the Magnificat, also sung *alternatim* with the organ as the choir moved through the church. At the guild chapel of Sts. Cosmas and Damian, the priest, dressed in his silk cap (*met eenre cappe*), censed the altar (*met wijroke*), behind which hung a painting of the two patron saints. The priest read the collect of the day to the guild gathered in the chapel.

[73] Bruges, Rijksarchief, Fonds Découvertes, MS 81, *Planarius*, ultimate folio verso: "Wel verstaende dat men naer der collecten vander eerster vesperen zal draghen processien metten vollen chore inde voorkerke ten outare van sinte aechte huut commend met eender antiphonem van sinte lodewyck *magnificat* zinghende ten zelven outare de antiphone volghende metter collecte daer ter dienende, ende een mottet aldaer zynghende naer de collecte de cantere metten kindere. / Waer voren de cantere hebben zal ij S. par. / De processien gheduerend men luden zal metter clocke gheherten *Salvator* waer voren de clocluders hebben zullen ij. S. par."
[74] Strohm, *Late Medieval Bruges*, 57.

Several of the choirboys and their master then sang a motet before the altar in honor of the saints, "according to custom." Its placement directly after the collect suggests that it replaced the *Benedicamus Domino*, as in the Basin foundation. The procession may have returned to the choir singing the Marian antiphon for the season, *Regina celi*.

The incorporation of the procession into the Vespers service itself also recalls the Basin foundation at St. Donatian. At St. James, the choir and organ brought the Magnificat into the nave of the church, while the motet, sung by the master and children, was heard by the assembled guildsmen in their chapel. The guildsmen would have donned their distinctive ceremonial clothing for the occasion. While High Mass took place in the church choir, the Vespers procession to the guild chapel lent the assembled congregation the most direct benefit of its heavenly praise.

The *lof* of Our Lady of the Snow

As elsewhere across Europe in the fifteenth century, Bruges had its share of religious confraternities; in Flanders, they were classified as *ghilden*, or free associations. Each of the guilds had its own patron saint, chapel, and meeting place, regardless of the differences in purpose. The guild of Our Lady of the Snow ("Onze Lieve Vrouw vander Snee") had an altar at the Church of Our Lady as early as 1450, although the earliest record book dates from 1467.[75] Its name refers to a vision of the Virgin Mary in Rome in the year 358, foretelling an August snowfall, which led to the foundation of the Basilica of Santa Maria Maggiore.[76] The feast day of Our Lady of the Snow was celebrated accordingly on August 5 each year.

The confraternity of Our Lady of the Snow was remarkable in several respects. First, it had an unusually large membership, with over 1,000 members between 1469 and 1491. Second, unlike many other religious confraternities, it counted women as just over half of its members. Third, Our Lady of the Snow represented "a good cross-section of urban society," ranging from the very wealthy to workmen; a wide variety of trades was also represented.[77] Such a range was possible because of the low yearly dues of

[75] A. Brown, "Bruges and the Burgundian 'Theatre-State': Charles the Bold and Our Lady of the Snow," *History* 84 (1999): 581.

[76] See R. Vicchi, *The Major Basilicas of Rome: Saint Peter's, San Giovanni in Laterano, San Paolo fuori le Mura, Santa Maria Maggiore* (Florence: Scala, 1999), 123–24.

[77] Brown, "Our Lady of the Snow," 581–84.

only two *denarii*; paupers on occasion had the dues paid for them out of charity. Unlike the more exclusive Dry Tree confraternity, to which a number of courtiers, artists, and foreign merchants belonged, the membership of Our Lady of the Snow remained overwhelmingly Flemish. At the same time, several aristocrats, beginning with Duke Charles the Bold in 1469, thought it worthwhile to join.[78] One of these, Louis of Gruuthuse, received permission to construct a small oratory in his house that connected to the church, where he and his family could overlook the confraternal chapel and main choir via a narrow window.[79]

The first polyphony underwritten by the confraternity of Our Lady of the Snow took on a characteristic Flemish form: the *lof,* from the Flemish word for "praise." A *lof* was an independent, extended service that surrounded the singing of the Marian antiphon *Salve regina.* As early as 1428, a daily *Salve regina* was endowed at the Church of Our Lady in Bruges.[80] In 1434, the layman Johannes Scateraers founded a polyphonic *Salve regina* at St. Donatian, to be performed in the nave each Saturday before an image of the Virgin Mary.[81] The gradual accretion during the fifteenth century of other chants, prayers, and music to the singing of the *Salve regina,* in towns throughout the Low Countries and northern France, took on a life of its own, and came to be called a *Salve* service or *lof.*

As in the case of Our Lady of the Snow, the *lof* often was underwritten by confraternities.[82] The record book of 1467 lists the names of 115 citizens who contributed to the foundation.[83] It began "op onser vrauwen dach in September" ("on Our Lady's day in September"), the vigil of the feast of the Nativity of the Virgin, which fell on Sunday, September 7 in 1466. Not surprisingly, Colaert and Pieter de la Bye, members of the confraternity, contributed four pounds to the subscription.[84] Fortunately, the book preserves a detailed description of the ceremony (see Appendix B6). The document, like that for the feast of Sts. Cosmas and Damian, is written in Flemish, rather than in Latin.

[78] Ibid., 574.
[79] The oratory and window still exist in the house, which now holds the Gruuthuse Museum.
[80] B. H. Haggh, "Music, Liturgy, and Ceremony in Brussels, 1350–1500" (Ph.D. diss., University of Illinois at Urbana-Champaign, 1988), 401.
[81] Andriessen, *Muziek in Brugge,* 144; Strohm, *Late Medieval Bruges,* 23.
[82] Haggh, "Music, Liturgy, and Ceremony," 417, observes that "individual donors introduced these services in many smaller churches and were responsible for their financial sustenance."
[83] Brown, "Our Lady of the Snow," 581, citing Bruges, Rijksarchief, Onze-Lieve-Vrouw MS 1501, *Cartularium en handboek,* 1467–1516, fols. 37r–40v.
[84] Bruges, Rijksarchief, Onze-Lieve-Vrouw MS 1501, *Cartularium en handboek,* 1467–1516, fol. 38r.

Table 5.2. Weekly *lof* of Our Lady of the Snow in Bruges (1466)

Item	Forces	Performance
Bells	Bellringers	Twelve and a half minutes
Hymn of Our Lady	Singers, organ	*Alternatim*
Salve regina. Virgo mater ecclesie	Singers, organ	*Alternatim* with soloist?
Ave Maria	Three boys	Improvised counterpoint over chant
Motet	Choirboys, tenor, contratenor	Written polyphony
De profundis	Succentor, choirboys	Reading
Liedekin – sacred song	Organ	Counterpoint?

In contrast to the practice of most foundations, which reserved the *Salve regina* for Saturdays, the *lof* of Our Lady of the Snow took place in the guild chapel at the stroke of four each Sunday evening, after Vespers. It began with the ringing of a church bell for "half a quarter of an hour." The *lof* was sung by the master and choirboys, a tenor, and a contratenor, sufficient for three- or four-part polyphony.[85] A "hymn of Our Lady" began the service, sung *alternatim*, with the choir taking the odd-numbered verses and the organ the even-numbered ones (Table 5.2). In a mixed choir, the boys necessarily sang an octave higher than the men. The *Salve regina* followed, elaborated and expanded with the common trope *Virgo mater ecclesie*. Since specific mention of the *Salve regina* occurs in the paragraph devoted to the duties of the organist, the antiphon may have been performed *alternatim* as well. Normal practice divided the antiphon into verses. Moreover, each of the three brief acclamations at the end of the antiphon was often prefaced by a longer verse, or trope, inserted into the chant, for a total of twelve verses (Figure 5.1). Typically, the organist took the odd-numbered verses, improvising over the plainchant, and the choir the even-numbered ones. There was no written tradition in which the organ participated in a troped *Salve regina*, however, which renders the exact disposition of forces uncertain. Nor was there a tradition of chant accompanied by organ.[86] The simplest solution would be to retain the customary division of the text, but to add

---

[85] Strohm, *Late Medieval Bruges*, 48, notes that the tenor and contratenor in 1472 came from the Church of St. Donatian. The charter specifies payment per service, which allowed maximum flexibility in securing skilled musicians.

[86] T. J. McGee, "Medieval Performance Practice," in *The Cambridge History of Medieval Music*, ed. M. Everist and T. F. Kelly (Cambridge University Press, forthcoming).

1. Salve regina misericordie.	Organ
2. Vita dulcedo et spes nostra salve.	Choir
3. Ad te clamamus, exules, filii heve.	Organ
4. Ad te suspiramus, gementes et flentes in hac lacrimarum valle.	Choir
5. Eia ergo, advocata nostra illos tuos misericordes oculos ad nos converte.	Organ
6. Et Jesum benedictum fructum ventris tui nobis post hoc exsilium ostende.	Choir
Trope	
7. Virgo mater ecclesie eterne porta glorie exaudi preces omnium ad te pie clamantium.	Soloist
8. O clemens.	Organ
Trope	
9. Virgo clemens virgo pia virgo dulcis o Maria esto nobis refugium aput Patrem et Filium.	Soloist
10. O pia.	Choir
Trope	
11. Gloriosa Dei mater cuius natus est ac pater ora pro nobis omnibus tui memoriam agimus.	Soloist
12. O dulcis virgo Maria.	Organ

Figure 5.1. Reconstruction of the *Salve regina* with trope *Virgo mater ecclesie*

a soloist for the trope, as was usual in both plainchant and polyphonic settings.[87] Since the children do not receive special mention here, one of the men likely had responsibility for the solo portions. The overall result is a richer variety of forces in performance, balancing three different sounds against each other during the second half of the antiphon.

In the *lof* of Our Lady of the Snow, the *Ave Maria* was next sung "in counterpoint" by three of the boys. The term suggests three-part, improvised counterpoint in close harmony, above and below the chant, with one of the choirboys taking the plainsong. A motet followed, sung solemnly, but as is typical for Bruges, the charter does not specify a text. The choice of motet would be left to the master of the children, meaning that any number of

---

[87] Haggh, "Music, Liturgy, and Ceremony," 414.

pieces could be performed. Certainly, the demand for motets at the weekly *lof* must have required a constant round of practice and rehearsal on the part of the master and choirboys at the Church of Our Lady. By the 1460s, numerous settings of Marian antiphons or antiphon texts from the Song of Songs were available, as witnessed in the Lucca Choirbook; many of these were English.

John Plummer's *Tota pulchra es I* from the Lucca Choirbook, setting an antiphon from the Song of Songs, gives an idea of the music available at the time. Plummer divides the anthem in three sections, changing from perfect (O) to imperfect time (C) and back again (O). The discantus occupies a range an octave higher than the tenor, with the contratenor in between: tenor c–f′, contratenor e–b♭′, discantus c′–d″. The top part would easily be addressed by choirboys, three or four in number, while one man each took the tenor and contratenor.[88] Plummer, who in 1444–55 was Master of the Choirboys in the Chapel Royal of Henry VI, plays on the contrast between the timbre of boys' voices and those of men, alternating on the same pitches (Example 5.5).[89] The composer is known especially for his euphonious sound and expressive use of imitation, in which all three voices achieve equal melodic activity and importance.

After the motet, the psalm *De profundis* ("Out of the deep") was read "over the souls of all the guild brothers and sisters" by the cantor and choirboys. The *lof* ended, surprisingly, with the organist playing *een liedekin* ("a little song"). The exact nature of the song is open to surmise, but the name most likely refers to the *gheestelijc liedekijn* that appears in later collections of devotional lyrics.[90] Such songs in the vernacular would have been well known to the brothers and sisters of Our Lady of the Snow.

The overall structure of the *lof*, repeated on a weekly basis, encompassed several different modes of musical performance (Table 5.2). A deliberate variety becomes especially evident in the weekly choice of a motet, sung in solemn adoration of the Virgin Mary. Variety itself, we learn from Johannes Tinctoris, is a virtue cultivated by the sophisticated composer within each

---

[88] Three choirboys were called for in the *Ave Maria*. The number of choirboys at the Church of Our Lady was set at four in October 1483, in a document establishing a daily Mass of St. Mary in memory of Duchess Marie of Burgundy; see Beaucourt de Noortvelde, *Description historique*, 199–202.

[89] R. Bowers, "Plummer, John," in *New Grove Dictionary of Music and Musicians*, 2nd edn. (London: Macmillan, 2000).

[90] A. M. J. van Buuren, "'Soe wie dit lietdkyn sinct of leest'. De Functie van de Laatmiddelnederlandse Geestelijke Lyriek," in *"Een zoet akkoord": Middeleeuwse lyriek in de Lage Landen*, ed. F. Willaert (Amsterdam: Prometheus, 1992), 234–54 at 247, quoting the heading of a song dated 1497.

Example 5.5. Plummer, *Tota pulchra es I*, beginning of second section

work, and it is here applied to the larger ceremony. The constant change from one medium of expression to the next clearly was meant to appeal to the common membership of the guild, as well as to townspeople gathered as auditors outside the chapel. In the guild of Our Lady of the Snow, as elsewhere in the Low Countries, the *lof* constituted an extended musical performance, without any officiant or liturgical action, other than the solemn memorial prayer and the offering of praise suggested by the name itself.

Motets in Bruges were thus performed in a remarkable variety of ceremonial situations during the fifteenth century. The foundation of Philip the Good in 1451 explicitly located the motet at the end of a polyphonic Mass Ordinary cycle. The parallel substitution of a motet for the *Benedicamus Domino* at the end of Vespers, as indicated in the Tournai ordinal, may have been more widespread than the bare annotations of the Jacob Baderan and Simon Coene foundations would suggest. At first Vespers of St. Martin, established by the singer Pierre Basin, a procession to the chapel took place within the Vespers office itself, concluding with a motet in place of the *Benedicamus Domino*. The processions at first and second Vespers to the guild chapel of Sts. Cosmas and Damian observed a similar liturgical structure.

The de la Bye foundations for the Drie Santinnen specify a procession to the saints' chapel directly following Vespers, where a memorial was said before the altar, solemnized with a motet. The traditional placement of memorials before Mass or after Compline likewise expanded to incorporate polyphony. On Sundays in Lent, Jacob Baderan dictated that a motet precede, rather than follow, the versicle and collect before Mass at the Marian altar in the nave of St. Donatian. In the foundation of Elisabeth Parols, a motet was sung in choir at the end of a procession after Compline. Finally, motets were incorporated into the weekly Sunday *lof* of the confraternity of Our Lady of the Snow, the only extra-liturgical usage that appears to have achieved broad currency in Flanders. It was a ceremony underwritten and attended not by the clerics of the church, but by the citizens of Bruges.

6 | Contemplation

Polyphonic music achieved an extraordinarily widespread sponsorship in Bruges during the fifteenth century. The *lof* of Our Lady of the Snow was underwritten by a long list of Flemish citizens from all walks of life.[1] The guild of barber-surgeons likewise drew directly from the burgher class. The daylong feast of Sts. Cosmas and Damian functioned as an advertisement of the guild's status and wealth and as an enactment of its corporate identity. The religious confraternity of the Dry Tree, to which many foreign merchants and members of the court of Burgundy belonged, sponsored lavish services at the Franciscan church in Bruges.[2] Among its members were the celebrated singer Jean Cordier and the painter Petrus Christus, whose *Madonna of the Dry Tree* may once have hung in the confraternal chapel.[3] The processions of the Drie Santinnen, although established on private initiative by Pieter and Colaert de la Bye, involved the leaders of four different confraternities at the Church of Our Lady.

Endowments by individuals contributed significantly to the proliferation of motets in Bruges. Jacob Baderan held a canonicate at St. Donatian, while Simon Coene held a chaplaincy. The curate Judocus Berthilde, who augmented the feast of St. Joseph at St. Savior's, also established several polyphonic Masses at the Church of Our Lady in May 1474, in conjunction with his sister, Barbara, and her husband.[4] Lodewyck Claes, a layman, undertook a series of foundations at St. Savior's, each requiring a motet, beginning with a procession at first Vespers on the feast of St. Louis in 1474. Besides the procession on the Octave of Corpus Christi at St. Donatian,

---

[1] Bruges, Rijksarchief, Onze-Lieve-Vrouw, MS 1501, *Cartularium en handboek*, 1467–1516, fol. 38r: "Hier naer volghen de name vanden personen / die haerlieden ducht ende Caritate ghegheven hebben ter fondacie vanden voir*seid* love."

[2] R. Strohm, *Music in Late Medieval Bruges*, 2nd edn. (Oxford: Clarendon Press, 1990), 70–73; R. Strohm, "Musikaal en Artistiek Beschermheerschap in het Brugse Ghilde vanden Droghen Boome," *Biekorf* 83 (1983): 5–18; A. de Schodt, "Confrérie de Notre-Dame de l'Arbre Sec," *Annales de la Société d'Emulation de Bruges/Handelingen van het Genootschap van Geschiedenis* 28 (1876–77): 41–87.

[3] Petrus Christus, *Madonna of the Dry Tree*, Museo Thyssen-Bornemisza, Madrid.

[4] Strohm, *Late Medieval Bruges*, 47; P. Andriessen, *Die van Muziken gheerne horen: Muziek in Brugge 1200–1800* (Bruges: West-Vlaamse Gidsenkring, 2002), 187.

the noblewoman Elisabeth Parols founded a chaplaincy in the chapel of the Holy Cross, later held by the composer Jacob Obrecht (1502).[5] Each of these services lacked an immediate audience outside the participants, the individuals themselves, and their families, yet was intended to augment the splendor of the liturgy at each church to the benefit of all.

All of these foundations and charters would have necessitated the commissioning of a motet for a particular moment of the liturgical year, specific to the required circumstances. The one clear exception to this pattern is the *lof* of Our Lady of the Snow, which required a steady supply of music to be rehearsed and performed on a weekly basis by the succentor and choirboys at the Church of Our Lady. Since the confraternal charter does not specify the nature of the motets, the choice would have been left to the succentor. As it turns out, only one of the motets documented in Bruges appears to have survived, *Salve mundi gloria*. In part, this is due to the wholesale loss of fifteenth-century books of polyphony from the territories of Burgundy. Such books are well documented in the records of St. Donatian in Bruges and at Cambrai Cathedral.[6] The loss results also from the very specificity of use, which meant that motets did not travel far from their point of origin.[7] Mass Ordinary cycles, on the other hand, given their shared texts, more easily migrated across political and ecclesiastical boundaries.

Still, at least four motets survive to represent the repertory that circulated in Bruges during the second and third quarters of the fifteenth century. The three-voice *O sanctissime presul/O Christi pietas*, written before 1435–37, is dedicated to St. Donatian, the patron saint of the city. *Salve mundi gloria*, attributable to Petrus de Domarto, may have been composed in 1451 in conjunction with his *Missa "Spiritus almus"*. Another three-voice work,

---

[5] Bruges, Bisschoppelijk Archief, MS Reeks G 8, 1502–03, fol. 23v: "Item Magistro Jacobo Hobrecht ad causam sue capellanie fundate per domicella de capple in capella sancte cruce xlj L. xij S." On the circumstances of Obrecht's appointment, see R. C. Wegman, *Born for the Muses: The Life and Masses of Jacob Obrecht* (Oxford: Clarendon Press, 1994), 306–08.

[6] On books at St. Donatian in Bruges, see A. DeWitte, "Boek- en Bibliotheekwezen in de Brugse Donaaskerk," in *Sint-Donaas en de voormalige Brugse Kathedraal*, 2 vols. (Bruges: Jong Kristen Onthaal voor Toerisme, 1978–88), vol. I, 61–98; Andriessen, *Muziek in Brugge 1200–1800*, 143–50, 208–12. On books at Cambrai Cathedral, see L. Curtis, "Music Manuscripts and Their Production in Fifteenth-Century Cambrai" (Ph.D. diss., University of North Carolina at Chapel Hill, 1991); L. Curtis, "Simon Mellet, Scribe of Cambrai Cathedral," *Plainsong and Medieval Music* 8 (1999): 133–66.

[7] One fascinating exception is the Battre fascicle of Trent, Castello del Buonconsiglio, MS 87, fols. 219–65, compiled by the composer Heinrich Battre, who apparently worked as a succentor in the Namur region. The fascicle has been little studied, but affords a clear window on musical practices in Burgundy during the early fifteenth century. See R. J. White, "The Battre Section of Trent Codex 87," 2 vols. (Ph.D. diss., Indiana University, 1975).

O pulcherrima mulierum, appears in the Lucca Choirbook and nine other sources, the earliest of which dates to circa 1450–52. Finally, the four-voice *Vidi speciosam* appears in the Lucca Choirbook, compiled by 1464, as well as in another Flemish source, Vatican City, Biblioteca apostolica Vaticana, MS Cappella Sistina 15.[8] The four works, three of them dedicated to the Virgin Mary, afford a representative picture of the diverse styles familiar in the churches and chapels of Bruges.

Formal considerations

To the extent that the sponsorship of motets in Bruges, both corporate and individual, cut across social and economic classes, the music sung in the city's churches perforce became more accessible to a lay audience. The four motets identified as current in Bruges all show formal and stylistic traits that allowed for more ready apprehension by the laity. Formal clarity frames the text and music in a direct way. The three-voice *O sanctissime presul/O Christi pietas* divides into three sections, the first and third in perfect time (○) with three voices, the middle section in imperfect time (C) with two voices. The outer sections begin with duets. *O pulcherrima mulierum,* attributable to the English composer John Plummer, maintains the same mensuration throughout (○), but divides the text into two parts via a strong cadence with fermata. The fermata splits the motet in an exact proportion of 3 : 4, the arithmetic ratio of a sounding perfect fourth. A duet between the discantus and contratenor begins the work, ten breves long, punctuated by another fermata to set off the acclamation *O* (Example 6.1). Both the four-voice motets, *Salve mundi gloria* and *Vidi speciosam,* are set in two sections in contrasting mensurations, ○ and ₵, demarcated with a full stop. *Salve mundi gloria* begins each part with a long duet for the discantus and first contratenor. The two sections divide in a proportion of 4 : 3.[9] As in *O pulcherrima mulierum,* the total represents seven, a Marian number. *Vidi speciosam* follows a different tack by stating the initial *cantus firmus* phrase twice at the beginning of each section, the first time with two trios,

[8] R. Strohm, ed., *The Lucca Choirbook: Lucca, Archivio di Stato, Ms 238; Lucca, Archivio arcivescovile, Ms 97; Pisa, Archivio arcivescovile, Biblioteca Maffi, cartella 11/III,* Late Medieval and Early Renaissance Music in Facsimile 2 (Chicago: University of Chicago Press, 2008), 32.

[9] The first section has a total of 180 semibreves in perfect time (○), including a long worth six semibreves at the medial cadence. The second section lasts 270 semibreves, which, if diminished by half under ₵, yields 135 equivalent semibreves.

Example 6.1. (?) Plummer, *O pulcherrima mulierum*, salutation

the second time with two duets.[10] These basic framing devices allow the audience to hear the text in discrete sections, amenable to memorization.

A high degree of plasticity in the melodic and polyphonic construction of the four motets heightens their aesthetic immediacy. The flowing melodies of the discantus in each work are supported and enhanced by a contratenor, singing in counterpoint at a lower range. The approach differs from that of works such as Johannes Brassart's *O flos fragrans*, composed circa 1430–31, with a single, finely sculpted melodic line supported by a slower-moving tenor and contratenor (Example 8.4). The practice differs still further from works such as Pietro Rosso's *Missus est Gabriel Angelus* or Antonio da Cividale's *O felix flos Florencia/Gaude felix Dominice*, which are more declamatory in their approach. Instead, the contrapuntal interest in these motets arises from the totality of the interaction between the two leading parts, in the continuous contrast or alternation of small-scale melodic figures. The use of choirboys, given the sharp juxtaposition in tone colors, would tend to focus attention on the interweaving of discantus and contratenor voices. In *Vidi speciosam*, the contratenor takes a leading role in numerous passages where the discantus rests (Example 6.2).

---

[10] J. E. Cumming, *The Motet in the Age of Du Fay* (Cambridge University Press, 1999), 274–76, with an edition of the *secunda pars*.

Example 6.2. Anonymous, *Vidi speciosam, prima pars*

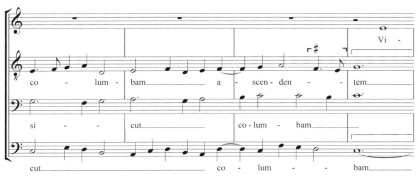

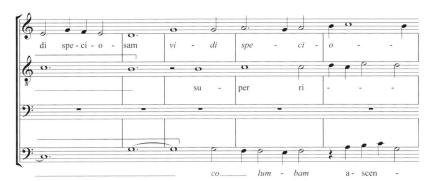

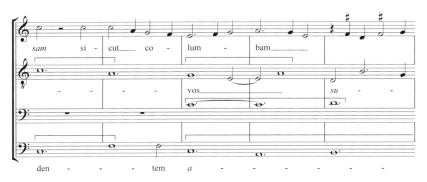

Example 6.2. (*cont.*)

Example 6.2. (*cont.*)

Example 6.2. (*cont.*)

O pulcherrima mulierum, which places a premium on melodic design, enhances the overall effect by the use of imitation at the beginnings of most phrases (Example 6.1). The process reaches an extreme in *Salve mundi gloria*, where even the cadences occur between the upper voices at the octave or unison (see Example 5.2B). Melodic phrases in these motets tend to be clearly defined but irregular in length. The lines themselves typically proceed with a high degree of syncopation and rhythmic variety, particularly in triple time (○). The more decorative, English style that prevails in *O sanctissime presul/O Christi pietas* and *O pulcherrima mulierum*, however, broadens out in the two four-voice works, balanced by a concomitant emphasis on harmony.

In terms of text delivery, the composers proceed in a similar way, assigning from two to four words to a single phrase. The text unfolds in discrete sense units, easily heard and absorbed by the listener. While the number of texted voices varies, even among manuscripts of the same work, the use of a single text supports an understanding of the words. Only *Salve mundi gloria* has a single texted voice, although probably not a setting of the original poem (see Example 5.3B). In the other motets, reiteration of the text unit in different voices underscores the verbal meaning, particularly when framed in imitation. Imitation, in fact, functions as a way to make the text phrase more memorable. At the same time, a characteristic verbal thinness shifts attention away from the text itself to the melodic lines that carry it, which spin out continuously without overt repetition. Artistic emphasis rests more on the beauty of contrapuntal and melodic design, especially given that the texts themselves, in contrast to those of secular songs, are not newly composed. *Vidi speciosam*, in particular, sustains the words over long stretches of melodic and contrapuntal invention, with continuously shifting textures (Example 6.2). Even *Salve mundi gloria*, which has by far the longest text of the four motets, focuses attention on the long, intricate duets that begin each section. When the full, four-voice texture enters, the sudden contrast forces an immediate aural re-evaluation upon the listeners.

Sight and sound

The foundations for motets in Bruges, despite disparate circumstances of location, liturgy, and audience, share a number of commonalities. To begin with, in every documented instance, the performance of a motet is paired with a collect, or common prayer.[11] In all but two cases, the prayer comes first. As a result, the motet necessarily takes on different functions from that of prayer. Collects were typically short, unadorned, and direct in their approach to the Deity. Unlike the personal, often rhymed prayers that appear in Books of Hours, which were familiar to many of the laity, collects are always in prose. The direct reading or chanting of the collect contrasts sharply with the soaring musical rhetoric, the harmony of word and sound, that characterize the motet. They are not just different in kind and function, but impart completely different experiences. Consequently, their several purposes must necessarily differ within the context of the larger ceremony.

Second, motets were performed within the spaces of a choir or chapel. These spaces held one or more altars, adorned with altarcloths, candlesticks, candles that were replenished for important days, and precious books. The spaces could be ornamented with tapestries or carpets, and often with paintings or statues of the saint or saints to whom the altar was dedicated. As in the chapel of the Drie Santinnen, such works of art decorated and visually informed a delimited space. Since every chapel had at least one chaplain to officiate at Mass and celebrate the offices, they were sanctified especially by prayer. By entering into a choir or chapel, one experienced a place made holy by the power of ritual and the ministry of those dedicated to the divinity.

Third, all four of the motets transmit single, pre-existent texts. This reflects a general tendency across Western Europe to move away from newly composed texts, particularly after 1440. As a result, these motets lack the referentiality of works with texts written especially for a particular ceremony, or those with two or more texts sung together. They are unable to address specific (earthly) audiences because of the common, shared quality of the words. Such motets do not function as ritual embassy, even though they are addressed to individual saints; they lack the undergirding of verbal rhetoric necessary to an embassy. Further, their essential nature in the harmonious conjunction of voices distinguishes them from prayer. The phenomenon corresponds to a distinction in Flemish painting of the fifteenth century between located and dislocated works of art.[12] Located works have specific physical settings that inform a defined space and with which the depicted

---

[11] *Salve mundi gloria* may have been sung in place of or directly following the *Deo gratias* at Mass, as discussed in Chapter 5. It thus would have followed the Postcommunion. According to A. Fortescue, "Postcommunion," in *The Catholic Encyclopedia* (New York: Robert Appleton, 1911), "The Postcommunion is said or chanted exactly like the Collect."

[12] B. L. Rothstein introduces the concept of located versus dislocated portraiture in *Sight and Spirituality in Early Netherlandish Painting* (Cambridge University Press, 2005), 96.

Illustration 6.1. Rogier van der Weyden, *Madonna in Red*, oil

figures interact. Dislocated works have minimal framing elements to shape the physical presence of the figures, which instead create their own sense of space through placement, modeling, color, and perspective.

The *Madonna in Red* by the Flemish painter Rogier van der Weyden, dated circa 1440, offers a fine example of a dislocated painting (Illustration 6.1). The simple Gothic frame is architectural in nature, as if the figures were a statue of the Madonna and Child come to life. The smooth frame is echoed by the curved figure of St. Mary, bending over the Christ Child in her lap. As she looks downward to her son, a simple white cloth sets off her serene features. Her red robe swirls around the unseen throne to the semicircular pedestal at her feet. Above, almost as an afterthought, an angel bears aloft the crown that the Madonna will wear in heaven. Van der Weyden portrays Christ not as an infant, but as a small child, reaching out to, and even crumpling, the parchment folios of the book – a breviary or Book of Hours – partially open in the Madonna's lap. His curiosity and realistic proportions make for an unusual image, an invitation to the viewer to delve further into the mysteries of faith. The book, in fact, lies at the center of the frame, symbolizing the centrality of the divine Word. The tactile sense conveyed in the painting, not just by the illustrated pages, but in the arresting, embroidered robes of St. Mary, also appeals to the viewer, who may have her own Book of Hours in hand.

During the late Middle Ages, the practice of divine contemplation became a powerful current in the religious experience of the Low Countries and across Western Europe. Systematic and practical teachings, originally directed to a monastic audience in the twelfth century, now circulated among the laity. One widely distributed guide is *The Ladder of Monks* by the twelfth-century Carthusian prior Guigo II. Guigo employs simple, plain language to distinguish four steps on the way to contemplation: *lectio, meditatio, oratio*, and *contemplatio*. He characterizes their relationship as follows:

> Reading comes first, and is, as it were, the foundation; it provides the subject matter we must use for meditation. Meditation considers more carefully what is to be sought after; it digs, as it were, for treasure which it finds and reveals, but since it is not in meditation's power to seize upon the treasure, it directs us to prayer. Prayer lifts itself up to God with all its strength, and begs for the treasure it longs for, which is the sweetness of contemplation. Contemplation when it comes rewards the labors of the other three; it inebriates the thirsting soul with the dew of heavenly sweetness.[13]

The reception of motets in the mid-fifteenth century shows distinct parallels with the guidelines for the practice of contemplation. Listening to the declamation of a motet parallels the experience of reading, since reading aloud was a common practice in the late medieval period. As Guigo states, "Listening is a kind of reading, and that is why we are accustomed to say that we have read not only those books which we have read to ourselves or aloud to others but those also which our teachers have read to us."[14] The slow

---

[13] Guigo II, *The Ladder of Monks: A Letter on the Contemplative Life and Twelve Meditations*, trans. E. Colledge and J. Walsh, Cistercian Studies Series 48 (Kalamazoo: Cistercian Publications, 1981), 79–80.

[14] Ibid., 80.

delivery of pre-existent texts, phrase by verbal phrase, allowed the listeners to ponder their inner meaning and connotations. Motets with pre-existent texts could thus be experienced as a form of meditation.

At the same time, the relationship between prayer and contemplation parallels the pairing of collect and motet as practiced in the churches of Bruges. While the collect expresses faith on behalf of all those present, uniting them in purpose, the nature of the motet allows for a more individual response. The potential for fifteenth- and sixteenth-century works of art to draw the individual into a state of contemplation has long been recognized by art historians. Sixten Ringbom writes that "The devotional image belongs to the domain of private piety where it is used as a recipient of prayer and benediction, or as an incentive and aid to meditation which is a preparatory stage for a higher level of contemplation, an image-less state of mind where external aids should no longer be needed."[15] The writer and cardinal Nicholas of Cusa describes in *The Vision of God* (1453) a painting of the *Salvator mundi* that he gave to a community of Benedictine monks for just such a purpose:

If now, while fixing his eye on the icon, [a brother] walk from west to east, he will find that its gaze continuously goeth along with him, and if he return from east to west, in like manner it will not leave him. Then will he marvel how, being motionless, it moveth, nor will his imagination be able to conceive that it should also move in like manner with one going in a contrary direction to himself.[16]

Like the *Mona Lisa* of Leonardo da Vinci, the eyes of the icon appear to follow the viewer around the room, establishing a point of personal contact. Cusa equates this with "the gaze of God." In the practice of contemplation, the viewer will be led to an experience beyond his imagination, a paradox that Bret L. Rothstein calls the "imagination of imagelessness."[17] Cusa himself acknowledges the paradox: "Thou, therefore, my invisible God, art seen of all and art seen in all seeing. Thou art seen by every person that seeth, in all that may be seen, and in every act of seeing... Therefore, Lord, it behoveth me to scale that wall of invisible vision beyond which thou art to be found."[18]

---

[15] S. Ringbom, *Icon to Narrative: The Rise of the Dramatic Close-up in Fifteenth-Century Devotional Painting* (Abo: Abo Akademy, 1965), 53.

[16] Nicholas of Cusa, *The Vision of God*, trans. E. G. Salter, 2nd edn. (New York: Frederick Ungar, 1960), 4–5.

[17] Rothstein, *Sight and Spirituality*, chapter 2, "The Imagination of Imagelessness."

[18] Nicholas of Cusa, *The Vision of God*, 54.

The icon becomes a starting-point, a place of embarkation for personal contemplation. Erwin Panofsky notes that devotional images arouse the viewer to a state of *Versenkung*, translated as "contemplative absorption."[19] Thus a sermon by Nicholas of Cusa, quoting from the writings of the Scottish monk Richard of St. Victor (d. 1173), describes three degrees of contemplation. The first degree is *mentis dilatatio* or expansion of the mind in turning to God, accomplished by prayer. The second degree is *mentis sublevatio* or the raising up of the mind, "and in this step diverse kinds of devotion are manifested, namely jubilation, spiritual inebriation, melting, and spiritual delight."[20] Cusa notes that the state is like the onset of sleep, but with the senses alert. The third step, *mentis alienatio* or the loss of reason, signifies also the loss of self in contemplation of the divine, "at one time through the greatest devotion, at another through the greatest admiration, at yet another through the greatest exultation; so that the mind of man may not grasp it, but elevated above itself, crosses over into alienation."[21]

Nicholas of Cusa in the *Vision of God*, Jean Gerson in *La montaigne de contemplation*, and other fifteenth-century writers share a preoccupation with the effects of external and internal stimuli on individual psychology.[22] Two writers on music, Gilles Carlier (ca. 1390–1472) and Johannes Tinctoris (ca. 1435–1511), take a similar tack when categorizing and defining the range of individual and social responses to vocal polyphony.[23] Carlier, a canon at Cambrai Cathedral and colleague of Guillaume Du Fay, writes specifically of church music in his *Tractatus de duplici ritu cantus ecclesiastici in divinis officiis* (*A Treatise on the Twofold Practice of Church Music in Divine Services*), contrasting plainchant and discant. Tinctoris, who studied at the University of Orléans and worked as succentor in the cathedral, ranks as the

[19] Cited in Ringbom, *Icon to Narrative*, 55.
[20] Nicholas of Cusa, "Signum magnum," in *Opera omnia*, vol. XVI, *Sermones I (1430–1431)*, part 2, *Sermones V–X* ed. R. Haubst *et al.* (Hamburg: Felix Meiner, 1973), 158–59: "Et hoc in gradu diversae species devotionis se manifestant, scilicet iubilus, ebrietas spiritus, liquefactio et spiritualis iucunditas."
[21] Ibid.: "modo prae magnitudine devotionis, modo prae magnitudine admirationis, modo prae magnitudine exsultationis, ut semet ipsam mens hominis non capiat, sed super semet ipsam in alienationem transeat." Cusa takes the passage directly from St. Bonaventure, "De perfectione vitae ad sorores" in *Opera omnia*, ed. A. C. Peltier, vol. XII (Paris: Ludovicus Vives, 1868), 218–21.
[22] J. Gerson, "The Mountain of Contemplation," in *Early Works*, trans. B. P. McGuire (New York: Paulist Press, 1998), 75–127.
[23] J. D. Cullington, ed. and trans., *"That liberal and virtuous art": Three Humanist Treatises on Music: Egidius Carlerius, Johannes Tinctoris, Carlo Valgulio* (Newtown Abbey: University of Ulster, 2001). For the *Complexus effectuum musices*, see also J. Tinctoris, *Opera theoretica*, ed. A. Seay, Corpus scriptorum de musica 22, 2 vols. ([Rome]: American Institute of Musicology, 1975), vol. II, 165–77.

most perspicacious music theorist of the fifteenth century. His *Complexus effectuum musices* (*A Compendium of Music's Effects*) was written at the Aragonese court in Naples, circa 1472–75.[24] While the treatise shows a clear indebtedness to the work of Carlier, Tinctoris undertakes a broader investigation, couched in almost aphoristic terms.

Both writers touch on the reception of sacred music in language that demonstrates its place in ecclesiastical devotion and the practice of contemplation. Carlier notes the commonality of plainchant and discant, in that "Both types of music, the plain and the jubilant, that is, draw the soul to godly contemplation, allowing for differences of rank, personality, time and place."[25] He acknowledges that social and personal circumstances necessarily alter the individual perception of music. Carlier devotes the second part of his treatise to the "special claims" of polyphony, however, both improvised and composed. He begins the fourth chapter by stating:

prima est quod est caelestium imago gaudiorum. Dulcis enim et bene composita musica typum gerit angelorum et sanctorum, qui non cessant laudare nomen Domini.

The first [special claim] is that it is a reflection of heavenly joys. Sweet and well-constructed music conveys an image of angels and saints continuously praising the name of the Lord.[26]

Angels were an important part of late medieval cosmology, and frequently serve as symbolic markers in fifteenth-century paintings. The word *typum* in Carlier's formulation recalls the neo-Platonic approach of *The Vision of God*, whereby earthly music aspires to the pure idea of angelic song, leading the listener from the here and now to the supernal. The more perfectly created the song, the more fully it embodies the type of angelic singing. Just as does the painted icon of Nicholas of Cusa, polyphony can draw one into an extended state of mental concentration.

But the statement also conveys a social reality concerning polyphonic choirs, namely, that the choirboys responsible for singing the great majority of motets in Bruges and Cambrai were trained to be angelic in character and demeanor.[27] In 1411, Jean Gerson, the Chancellor of the University of

[24] R. Strohm, introduction to Cullington, ed. and trans., *Three Humanist Treatises on Music*, 9.
[25] Cullington, ed. and trans., *Three Humanist Treatises*, 31, 48: "Uterque autem, cantus simplex, scilicet, et musicalis iubilatio, trahit animam ad divinam contemplationem, secundum diversitatem statuum, personarum, temporum et locorum."
[26] Ibid., 34, 50.
[27] A. E. Planchart, "Choirboys in Cambrai in the Fifteenth Century," in *Young Choristers: 650–1700*, ed. S. Boynton and E. Rice, Studies in Medieval and Renaissance Music 7

Paris, drew up a list of detailed statutes to govern their daily lives, education, and participation in divine services at the Cathedral of Notre Dame. The guidelines are extraordinarily restrictive; the choirboys were to be held apart from nearly all outside discourse, and could be punished for speaking French instead of Latin. Gerson adds:

Et maxime servent silentium, et gesta ordinatum circa Altare, dum celebrantur sacra missarum mysteria; sine risu, sine garritu, sine strepitu, sine dissoluto motu inter se et alios: sed assistant sicut Angeli Dei, ut omnis qui viderit eos dicat: huiusmodi sunt vere pueri Angelici, et tales quales habere debet Immaculata Virgo in Ecclesia sua totius orbis celeberrima.

And they should especially serve in silence and with appropriate decorum near the altar when the sacred mysteries of the Mass are celebrated without laughing, chattering, or making noise or indecent gestures among themselves or with others, but should serve just like angels of God so that all who might see them may say: "these are truly angelic boys and such as the Immaculate Virgin ought to have in her church, the most renowned in all the world."[28]

Carlier's phrase *caelestium imago gaudiorum* is thus meant to be taken quite literally. Not only were motets performed by choirboys, sanctified by their way of life and dressed in white, but the art, incense, and ecclesiastical vestments of the chapels and choirs intensified the experience of entering sacred space. Having been prepared through such means, the mind is free to receive further blessings. Indeed, Carlier writes, "The sixth special claim is that music earns the companionship of the angels."[29]

Carlier's introductory remarks likewise show an awareness of the usefulness of "euphonious music" for the practice of contemplation. He comments:

Ipsa suspiria et gemitus devotionis ex pectore parit, caelestem immittit amorem, terrena facit oblivisci, ut nisi fuerit animus gravibus peccatorum cathenis astrictus, gaudiis videatur interesse caelestibus, ubi praesertim cum voce modulata verba divina cor penetrant.

(Woodbridge: Boydell, 2008), 127, writes of Cambrai Cathedral that "The fifteenth-century regulations largely concern the need for the choristers to have the proper religious instruction, to observe decorum at all times, and to be taught the traditional plainsong."

[28] F. L. Chartier, *L'ancien chapitre de Notre-Dame de Paris et sa maîtrise: D'après les documents capitulaires (1326–1790)*, facsimile reprint (Paris: Perrin, 1897; Geneva: Minkoff, 1971), 70; trans. C. Wright, *Music and Ceremony at Notre Dame of Paris, 500–1500* (Cambridge University Press, 1989), 168.

[29] Cullington, ed. and trans., *Three Humanist Treatises*, 36, 52: "Sexta praerogativa quod meretur associationem angelorum."

This music wrings from the breast sighs and groans of devotion, instils heavenly love, and brings forgetfulness of earthly things, so that the mind – if not bound by the heavy chains of sin – seems to partake of heavenly joys, most of all when holy words combine with a tuneful voice to pierce the heart.[30]

Carlier alludes in passing to the necessity of repentance, in humility and an awareness of one's own human imperfection, as a precondition to the fullest experience of sacred music. His language encompasses two of the degrees of contemplation outlined by Richard of St. Victor. The experience of divine love and the longing of devotion pertain to the *mentis dilatatio*, while the experience of rejoicing and a forgetfulness of the mundane recall the *mentis sublevatio*. These are psychological states, well-defined in the literature of contemplation, and distinct from those occasioned by prayer. Moreover, the reference to *verba divina*, whether drawn from the liturgy or scripture, speaks to a preference for pre-existent texts, as increasingly occurs in the fifteenth-century motet.

Guigo II and other medieval writers place contemplation in direct relationship to prayer, from which it arises. They refer to intense, personal prayer, practiced in solitude.[31] As we have seen, a parallel relationship occurs in the pairing of prayer and motet in the Bruges foundations, whereby the motet is conjoined with a collect. Seen from this vantage point, Carlier's discussion of "the music of harmonious jubilation," distinct from the solemnity of plainchant, becomes not so much an aesthetic distinction as a functional one.[32] The performance changes the nature of the ceremony itself.[33] It allows the pairing of devout, collective prayer with the re-creation of angelic song via the motet.

The *Complexus effectuum musices* of Johannes Tinctoris outlines twenty different effects of music, covering a broad range of experience and activity. The brief chapters are arranged in a large cycle, beginning with the heavenly, descending to the terrestrial, and concluding with a message of salvation. Under the heading "Music enhances the joys of the blessed," Tinctoris points out that "painters, when wishing to depict the joys of the blessed, paint

---

[30] Ibid., 34, 50.

[31] The Franciscan preacher St. Bonaventure counsels, "Cum stas in oratione . . . omnium exteriorum oblivisci et toto corde, tota mente, toto affectu, toto desiderio, tota devotione debes te levare supra te" ("When you are motionless in prayer . . . you should forget all exterior things, and rise above yourself with your whole heart, whole spirit, your whole emotions, desire, and devotion"). See "De perfectione vitae ad sorores" in *Opera omnia*, vol. XII, 209–27.

[32] Cullington, ed. and trans., *Three Humanist Treatises*, 33, 50. The second part of the treatise is headed "De cantu iubilationis armonicae et utilitatae eius."

[33] I am grateful to the sociologist Sigmund Nosow for clarifying this distinction.

angels playing various musical instruments." As already noted, choirboys and their music were viewed as approaching an angelic state. Tinctoris describes a two-fold imitation, realized in the senses of vision and hearing, whereby "musical instruments symbolize the happiness of blissful hearts."[34]

In two consecutive chapters, Tinctoris explicates the utility of polyphonic music for the practice of contemplation. Chapter 11 pertains clearly to the stage of *mentis sublevatio*:

Undecimo: musica terrenam mentem elevat. Unde Bernardus *Super cantica*: Oculos cordis attollit iubilus laudis. Armoniae quidem dulcedine movetur mens ad contemplationem gaudiorum supernorum, quae summa pars est vitae melioris. Et hinc deficit a cogitatione terrenorum quae ad actionem vitae pertinens sollicitudinem ac turbationem inducit.

Eleventh: music uplifts the earthly mind. So Bernard in *Super cantica*: "The jubilation of praise exalts the eyes of the heart." Certainly the mind is led by the sweetness of concord to that contemplation of celestial joys which is the summit of a better life; and thus it forsakes that concentration on earthly things which, concerned as it is with practical living, causes anxiety and disturbance.[35]

Tinctoris plays here upon the contrast between the "active life" and the "contemplative life," which informs especially the discussions of Jean Gerson in *La montaigne de contemplation*. The underlying contrast speaks to the possibility of achieving divine contemplation even for those who, by choice or necessity, must dwell in the world and attend to its responsibilities and cares. Gerson included himself among this number, since his position as Chancellor of the University of Paris required him to engage fully with the requirements of his office. Tinctoris situates *armonia* within this dichotomy as leading to the *summa pars* of an active life, one that remains available to the layman as well as the cleric. As Gerson, writing in the vernacular, remarks, "Daily experience in lesser matters shows us that such a concentration of the soul's powers can take place."[36] One is able to leave behind, in the presence of divinely ordered harmony, the images and memories of daily life.

In the previous chapter, Tinctoris writes of a more extreme effect: *Musica extasim causat* ("Music causes ecstasy"). Tinctoris clarifies his statement by reference to Psalm 67:28, "There is the boy Benjamin in a trance," a central

---

[34] Cullington, ed. and trans., *Three Humanist Treatises*, 60, 77: "Hinc, quoniam felicitatem animorum beatorum instrumenta musica significant . . . pictores quando beatorum gaudia designare volunt, angelos diversa instrumenta musica concrepantes depingunt."

[35] Ibid., 62, 79.

[36] Gerson, "The Mountain of Contemplation," 105.

text in Richard of St. Victor's symbolic treatise *Benjamin major*.[37] He also quotes Aristotle: "Melodiae Olympi faciunt animas raptas" ("The melodies of Olympus enrapture the soul"). These characteristics relate to the *mentis alienatio*, in which the consciousness loses itself in contemplation. Music serves as an aid to climb the highest point of the mountain, which Gerson describes as fleeting and difficult to achieve. Nevertheless, the experience of ecstasy, or ecstatic love via music, certainly occurs in other aspects of religious life, well beyond the practice of contemplation.

The unfamiliar and abstract terms in which Tinctoris and Carlier express their arguments, with appeals to both classical and scriptural authorities, leave an impression of unreality, much like the fanciful descriptions of animals in a medieval bestiary. Yet the effects they describe concerning sacred music find historical confirmation in a variety of accounts, ranging from Italy to France and the Low Countries. Carlier himself, writing at Cambrai Cathedral, one of the great centers of polyphony in Western Europe, remarks of the church:

quae est sine macula et sine ruga; cuius laus est Deo gratissima et hominibus, quos nescio qua dulcedine cunctos tangit, et memores non sinit esse sui. Miro modo, ut auditur melodia, affluunt nedum de propinquis sed ex partibus remotis eam auribus suspensis et cordibus percepturi.

She is without blemish or wrinkle, and Her praise is most pleasing to God and to men, all of whom it touches with an unknown sweetness, making them forget their existence. It is amazing how, when melody is heard, they flock from near and far to listen to it with eager ears and hearts.[38]

Carlier confirms the broad currency of sacred music in the fifteenth century. Men and women, by implication from different walks of life, lose their memory of self in listening to vocal melody created by the clerical choir. The phrase "auribus suspensis et cordibus" suggests a kind of intuitive grasp or understanding of the sung text, recalling the phenomenon of "absorbed contemplation" in contemporary Netherlandish painting.

Two Italian writers, Giannozzo Manetti and Lapo da Castiglionchio, testify to the effects of the polyphony heard in the papal chapel of Eugenius IV. In his oration on the dedication of Santa Maria del Fiore in Florence on March 25, 1436, Manetti renders a detailed and personal account of the ceremonies that day (see Chapter 4). The music included at least one motet

---

[37] Cullington, ed. and trans., *Three Humanist Treatises*, 62, 79.
[38] Ibid., 37, 53, translation emended.

by Guillaume Du Fay, *Nuper rosarum flores*, performed by the papal choir. Manetti, writing to his brother, observes:

Interea tantis tamque variis canoris vocibus quandoque concinebatur, tantis etiam symphoniis ad celum usque elatis interdum cantabatur, ut angelici ac divini cantus nimirum audientibus apparerent adeoque audientium aures mira variarum vocum suavitate titillabantur ut multum admodum ceu de syrenum cantibus fabulantur obstupescere viderentur quod in celis etiam quotannis hac ipsa solemnissima die qua principium humane salutis apparuit ab angelis fieri non impie crediderim:

Meanwhile, from time to time so many and varied singing voices harmonized; in fact, so many symphonies were sung, reaching as far as the sky, that doubtless they seemed to the listeners like angelic and divine songs. The listeners' ears were titillated by the marvelous sweetness of the various voices to the extent that they appeared to be very much spellbound, as they say happens when the sirens sing. I would believe without being blasphemous that in heaven, too, the angels do this every year on this very solemn day in which the source of human salvation appeared.[39]

Once again, the image of angelic singing informs the listeners' understanding of the harmonic blending of voices. Manetti describes himself and others as "spellbound" or "astounded" by Du Fay's music. Moreover, he calls attention to the total environment of the consecration services, which create a verisimilitude of heavenly joys, "in part by hearing the most pleasant singing and most sweet playing; in part by smelling various aromatic fragrances; and finally in part by watching all sorts of marvelous decorations."[40] Manetti hears the music as an imitation of the feast day of the Annunciation as celebrated in heaven. The bringing together of terrestrial and celestial modes of praise helps to collapse the gap between subject and object, bringing the individual into the presence of angels singing and playing in praise of the Virgin Mary and the Trinity.

Manetti later returns to the same theme during the ceremony of High Mass. Not only does the pontiff consecrate the cathedral as a holy space, but the people of Florence participate in the sacred ritual through music:

[39] Quoted in S. Žak, "Die Quellenwert von Gianozzo Manettis Oratio über die Domweihe von Florenz 1436 für die Musikgeschichte," *Die Musikforschung* 40 (1987): 15 n. 70; trans. in M. Phelps, "A Repertory in Exile: Pope Eugenius IV and the MS Modena, Biblioteca Estense universitaria, α.X.1.11" (Ph.D. diss., New York University, 2008), 192, emended.

[40] Quoted in S. Žak, "Die Quellenwert von Gianozzo Manettis Oratio," 15 n. 70: "partim suavissimos cantus dulcissimosque sonos audientes, partim varios ac redolentes vapores olfacientes, partim denique admirabilia omnia ornamentorum genera conspicientes varie hilarescerent." Trans. in Phelps, "A Repertory in Exile," 192.

In cuius quidem sanctissimi corporis elevatione tantis armoniarum simphoniis, tantis insuper diversorum instrumentorum consonantionibus omnia basilicae loca resonabant, ut angelici ac prorsus divini paradisi sonitus cantusque demissi celitus ad nos in terris divinum nescio quid ob incredibilem suavitatem quandam in aures nostras insusurrare non inmerito viderentur. Quocirca eo tempore tantis equidem voluptatibus potitus sum ut beata vita frui hic videretur in terris; quod utrum ceteris astantibus acciderit non plane scio, de me ipse idoneus testis sum.

During the Elevation of the most sacred Body, all the places of the cathedral resounded with so many harmonic symphonies, and moreover with so many different instruments, that the angelic instrumental tones and the divine singing of paradise – sent from heaven to us on earth – seemed, because of their incredible sweetness, to whisper in our ears something divine. Therefore, during that time, I indeed enjoyed so many delights, that this man appeared to be favored on earth with the life of the blessed ones. If that happened also to other people who were present, I do not know for sure but can only speak for myself.[41]

Manetti reiterates still more strongly the intimation of the divine, even while the senses remain alert, an experience closely related to that of *mentis sublevatio.* The threshold between celestial and earthly perspectives narrows as the mind is raised up. The collapsing of those subject and object domains inherent in spoken language becomes possible via the "whispering" of angelic music. As Nicholas of Cusa explains in *The Vision of God,* "Thou, Lord, dost speak in me and say that there is no positive principle of otherness, and thus it existeth not."[42] At the same time, Manetti is unable to communicate what those around him have experienced; he can only note their visible reactions to the ceremony, which parallel his own.

Manetti's accounts are echoed in the writings of Lapo da Castiglionchio, a papal official at the time of the Council of Ferrara. His *De curiae commodis* (1438) reflects not only the experience of polyphony in the papal chapel, but the importance of its situation within the liturgy and the spaces of the church:

ac divini illi hymni ac psalmi disparibus variisque vocibus decantantur, quis est tam inhumanus, tam barbarus, tam agrestis, quis rursus tam immanis, tam Deo hostis, tam expers religionis, qui haec aspiciens audiensque non moveatur, cuius non mentem atque animum aliqua religione occupet et stupore perstringat et dulcedine quadam deliniat? Cuius non oculi mirifice aspectu ipso pascantur oblectenturque?

---

[41] Quoted in S. Žak, "Die Quellenwert von Gianozzo Manettis Oratio," 14 n. 68; trans. in Phelps, "A Repertory in Exile," 195–96, emended.

[42] Nicholas of Cusa, *The Vision of God,* 66.

Cuius non aures incredibili cantus suavitate et harmonia mulceantur? Quo quidem spectaculo quod in terris pulchrius, quod maius, quod divinius, quod admiratione, quod memoria ac literis dignius reperitur, ut non homines modo, qui intersunt et quibus hoc natura datum est, sed ipsius etiam parietes templi et exultare quodammodo et gestire laetitia videatur?

[when] those divine hymns and psalms are sung with different and diverse voices, who is so uncultured, so uncivilized, so boorish, who again is so savage, so inimical to God, so lacking in reverence, that he, seeing and hearing these things, may be unmoved, whose mind and soul shall not be seized with some feeling of reverence, and overcome by stupefaction, and captivated by a certain sweetness, whose eyes may not be marvelously nourished and delighted by the very sight, whose ears not be charmed by the incredible sweetness and harmony of the song? Indeed, what could be found in this world that is more beautiful, that is greater, that is more divine, that is more worthy of wonder, of remembrance and the historical record, than this sight – so that not just humans, who take part and to whom this is given by nature, but the very walls of the temple seem to be elated in some way, and to exult with happiness?[43]

In aesthetic terms, Castiglionchio praises the variety of voices in the papal choir for creating new and different tone colors. As in Manetti's oration, the descriptions presume a corresponding variety of performance practices, including plainchant and fauxbourdon, the latter employed especially for the Du Fay hymn cycle composed for the papal choir. Castiglionchio documents a pervasive appeal to the combined senses of sight and sound, which he describes in powerful terms, all in the subjunctive mood: *moveatur* ("shall be moved"), *occupet* ("seizes"), *perstringat* ("dazzles" or "overcomes"), *deliniat* ("charms"), *oblectentur* ("may be delighted"). The concomitant psychological effects, according to this witness, are well-nigh overwhelming. Castiglionchio testifies clearly to Tinctoris' laconic observation that "Music induces ecstasy." His interlocutor in the dialogue, Angelo, continues with further recollections that approach the state of *mentis alienatio*:

Vera narras, et, medius fidius, ipse praesens interdum ita afficior ut cogitatione abstrahar et non humana illa neque ab hominibus acta videre, sed sublimis raptus ad superos, ut de Ganimede veteres poetae fabulis prodidere, deorum mensis videar interesse.

43 C. S. Celenza, *Renaissance Humanism and the Papal Curia: Lapo da Castiglionchio the Younger's "De curiae commodis"* (Ann Arbor: University of Michigan Press, 2000), 130–33; trans. in R. C. Wegman, *The Crisis of Music in Early Modern Europe, 1470–1530* (New York and London: Routledge, 2005), 78–79, emended.

You describe true things, and when I am there, so help me God, I'm at times so affected that I am carried beyond rational thought, and seem to see neither those human things, nor deeds by humans, but rather to be present, being uplifted and seized to things on high, at the tables of the Gods, as the ancient poets reported about Ganymede.[44]

Angelo describes a religious state that leaves music and the operations of the rational mind behind. While the literature of contemplation may have provided a template for conceiving and expressing a variety of related psychological states, authors frequently try to convey their knowledge via metaphors. The reference to the myth of Ganymede invokes an image of being swept higher, as by an eagle: in abstract terms, collapsing and even reversing the divide between subject and object. The descriptions of Lapo da Castiglionchio, however, appear not to depend on any previous formulations concerning contemplation.

The experiences of Manetti and Castiglionchio seem far removed from the reading of scripture and the collective prayer that occupy so much of the office; for this very reason, they have left such exceptional, personal accounts. In general, they testify to sensory experiences designed to allow the devout to enter into a holy space and, through contemplation, to narrow the difference between subject and object, the parishioner and the saint. As did Netherlandish devotional painting, the polyphony sung in processions, at memorials, and at Vespers attempted to capture the immediacy of spiritual life for the layman.

At the end of the fifteenth century, a writer from Maastricht in the Low Countries, Mattheus Herbenus, testified directly to the use of motets in the practice of contemplation. Herbenus' *De natura cantus ac miraculis vocis* (*On the Nature of Song and the Wondrous Voice*), dated 1496, addresses the character of song in nature, in man, and in angels.[45] Herbenus, who was educated in Ferrara and Bologna, brings his humanist sensibilities to bear on the question of vocal polyphony, asserting the necessity for comprehension of the verbal content of any song. At the same time, he commends the motets of the contemporaneous Flemish composers Gaspar van Weerbecke and Jacob Obrecht, remarking:

Quamobrem ut mihi itidem et multis aliis credo placere tales cantus ac hymnos, quales Iaspar Cimber in divam parthenicen edidit plurimos et Jacobus Hoberti,

---

[44] Celenza, *Lapo da Castiglionchio the Younger's "De curiae commodis"*, 130–33; trans. in Wegman, *The Crisis of Music*, 79.

[45] K.-J. Sachs, "Herbenus, Mattheus," in *Die Musik in Geschichte und Gegenwart*, 2nd edn. (Kassel and New York: Bärenreiter, 1998–).

eius patriota, in honorem consecrationis templi atque salutiferae crucis, ceterique huiusmodi. Quibus singillatim comprehensis notulis, una cum verborum debite applicatis syllabis, mens ad altiorem contemplationem facile rapiter, dum pulchritudo cantus tam apte conservatur.

It is for this reason, I believe, that I myself and many others take pleasure in those songs and hymns of which Gaspar the Cimbrian wrote many for the Holy Virgin, and Jacob Hobrecht, his compatriot, in honor of the dedication of the church and of the salvific Cross, and more of this kind. The mind is easily carried off to a higher contemplation by those singly-understood notes, together with properly placed syllables, the beauty of the song being so aptly maintained.[46]

The relationship between reading, meditation, prayer, and contemplation, as set forth by Guigo II in the twelfth century, finds a new interpretation in the humanist emphasis on textual integrity. As Herbenus explains, the attainment of contemplation requires individual understanding of the text. He follows up by saying that "the senses need proper space for taking in the meanings: if that is not granted, how can reason judge about those imperfectly formed ideas?"[47] Motets current in Bruges in the mid-fifteenth century place a premium on deliberate delivery of the words, one phrase at a time. Yet Herbenus employs the word *rapiter* ("carried away") to describe the resultant experience, in language that echoes the traditional literature on contemplation. He makes it clear that the inherent quality of the music, created by reason, is responsible for its psychological effects.

The two Obrecht motets that Herbenus describes have been identified, and offer a means to assess his statements against the music itself: *Laudemus nunc Dominum/Non est hic aliud* and *Salve crux/O crux lignum*.[48] Both works are five-voice tenor motets with a texted *cantus firmus*. The tenor of *Laudemus nunc Dominum/Non est hic aliud* sets three consecutive Matins antiphons for the feast of the Dedication of a Church. The tenor of *Salve crux/O crux lignum* incorporates one stanza of the sequence *Laudes crucis attolamus*, for the Exaltation of the Holy Cross. The motet may well have been composed during Obrecht's first sojourn in Bruges, November 1485–January 1490, as succentor at the Church of St. Donatian;[49] the feast of the

---

[46] M. Herbenus, *De natura cantus ac miraculis vocis*, ed. J. S. van Waesberghe, Beiträge zur Rheinischen Musikgeschichte 22 (Cologne: Arno Volk, 1957), 58–59; trans. in Wegman, *The Crisis of Music*, 176.

[47] Herbenus, *De natura cantus*, 58–59; trans. in Wegman, *The Crisis of Music*, 176–77: "Requirit enim sensus spatium ad recipiendum intentiones conveniens; quod si non concedatur, quomodo de imaginationibus nondum bene formatis ratio iudicabit?"

[48] Wegman, *The Crisis of Music*, 227 n. 15.

[49] Wegman, *Born for the Muses*, 138, 158–59; M. J. Bloxam, "A Survey of Late Medieval Service Books from the Low Countries: Implications for Sacred Polyphony, 1460–1520," 2 vols. (Ph.D. diss., Yale University, 1987), vol. II, 335–44. Given the repeated references to war in the texts of

Exaltation of the Cross, September 14, was provided with motets sung by the succentor and choirboys in an elaborate foundation of 1415.[50]

Given Herbenus' comments on textual comprehension, it is surprising to find that both motets have double texts. In *Laudemus nunc Dominum*, Obrecht states the first antiphon twice in the tenor, spread across three phrases of the *prima pars*, primarily in larger note values. The second and third antiphons appear unornamented at the beginning and end of the *secunda pars*, respectively, sung almost entirely in strict breves. The tenor texts of the *secunda pars* have particular interest in that they invoke the composer's Biblical namesake:

Vidit Jacob scalam, summitas eius celos tangebat, et descendentes angelos, et dixit: Vere locus iste sanctus est.

Erexit Jacob lapidem in titulum, fundens oleum desuper.

Jacob saw a ladder, the top thereof touched heaven, and the angels were descending and he said: "Indeed, this place is holy."

Jacob set up a stone as a memorial pillar, pouring oil over it.[51]

The image of Jacob's ladder, often found at the entrance to churches, may have been interpreted as an invitation to contemplation, in its association with angelic visions. Against the *cantus firmus*, the other four voices sing a concatenation of Biblical texts bound together with new material, typical of the late fifteenth century. They begin in syllabic fashion, but with the entrance of the tenor broaden out into a more melismatic style. Like the *cantus firmus*, the text is self-referential in its invocation of the voices and sonorities of the choir: the *prima pars* begins "Laudemus nunc Dominum in canticis et modulationibus sonorum" ("Let us now praise the Lord with songs and melodious sounds"), while the *secunda pars* begins "Cantemus Domino canticum novum" ("Let us sing unto the Lord a new song").[52] Herbenus would appear to have had no difficulty in following this lengthy text, even when heard against a *cantus firmus*.

In *Salve crux/O crux lignum*, Obrecht makes it easy to follow the structure of the sequence text, *Salve crux*, by changing the forces for each of the nine

    Salve crux and *Per lignum crux*, the motet may have been composed for the feast of the Exaltation of the Cross in 1488 or 1489, when Bruges and Ghent revolted against Archduke Maximilian of Austria.

[50] The foundation by Johannes de Hagha does not precisely locate the motets within the liturgy. It is contained in the *planarius*, Bruges, Bisschoppelijk Archief, MS Reeks A 141, fols. 75v–76r. See R. Strohm, *Late Medieval Bruges*, 17–18.

[51] *New Obrecht Edition*, vol. XV, *Motets I*, ed. C. Maas (Utrecht: Koninklijke Vereniging voor Nederlandse Muziekgeschiedenis, 1995), 83.

[52] Ibid., 83.

Example 6.3. Obrecht, *Salve crux/O crux lignum*, first tenor entrance

stanzas, often reducing the texture to duos or trios. The first tenor enters with the *cantus firmus* at stanzas 3 and 6 in the *prima pars*, creating a double text (Example 6.3). The *secunda pars* begins with a third statement of *O crux lignum* in the first tenor, this time overlapping with the antiphon *Per lignum crucis* in the second tenor.[53] The last three stanzas of *Salve crux* follow in reduced textures. The end of the *secunda pars* moves the *cantus firmus* text to a canonic duet between superius and altus, in triple time, and concludes with a homorhythmic setting of the first line in all five voices: "O crux lignum triumphale." But Obrecht continues to surprise, continuing the text directly into the *tercia pars*, rounded off by a final *alleluia*. Despite

---

[53]   Bloxam, "A Survey of Late Medieval Service Books," vol. II, 338.

Example 6.3. (*cont.*)

the complex structure, only three of the five-voice passages have double text. As in *Laudemus nunc Dominum*, the texture alternates between melismatic and syllabic styles, or between free counterpoint and imitation. Herbenus countenances all of these features for the sake of the music's melodic and contrapuntal power, as well as for the aptness of the music to the words. At the same time, the subject of the Holy Cross is apposite for contemplation in sight and sound, insofar as the cross was commonly used as a means to focus one's attention on the divine.

Contemplation and community

Motets in Bruges were provided on feast days for purposes of celebration and adornment – "dulcis iubilatio armonicaque vocum concordio in divino resonat officio," in Carlier's words – which by their abstract quality, their very lack of referentiality, could lead one into a state of divine contemplation. The "dislocated" quality of these motets enabled them to mediate, not among social groups, but between the faithful and the saints. Motets with pre-existent texts are, in a sense, dislocated through the absence of referential elements, lacking in time and place. From our perspective, they have remained inscrutable because of the opaqueness of their verbal structures. While the liturgy endowed the ceremony with a common purpose, within that ritual, individuals could experience the divine Word in different ways, whether through meditation on scripture, the unscrolling of sung words, or through the harmony of the vocal *concentus*. Divine contemplation was conceived as an individual experience, which, as Manetti and Castiglionchio testify, could take place in just such ceremonial contexts.

The accessibility of the motets in form and style forms a necessary precondition for their employment in the process of aural and visual contemplation. One of the motets current in Bruges in the mid-fifteenth century addresses St. Donatian, while the other three are Marian in orientation: *O sanctissime presul/O Christi pietas, Salve mundi gloria, O pulcherrima mulierum*, and *Vidi speciosam*. Because the texts are pre-existent, their construction is not amenable to the rhetorical forms that underlie the creation of ritual embassy. Instead, their texts are more closely allied with the collective prayers with which motets are associated in the Bruges foundations.

The text of *O pulcherrima mulierum* more fully illustrates the differences in rhetorical approach from earlier works. The motet draws its Marian text from three familiar passages of the Song of Songs, with one interpolation:

5:9 O pulcherrima mulierum,

2:10 Surge propera amica mea, [columba mea,] formosa mea veni.

2:14 Ostende mihi faciem tuam, sonet vox tua in auribus meis, vox enim tua dulcis et facies tua decora.

O sweetest of women,

Arise, make haste, my love, my dove, my beautiful one, and come.

Show me thy face, let thy voice sound in my ears, for thy voice is sweet, and thy face comely.[54]

The resulting concatenation allows the composer to create both a two-voice introduction, on the acclamation *O*, and a dense, three-voice closing section on the word *decora* ("comely"). The reference to the face of the beloved, understood as the Virgin Mary, would be doubly appropriate under the gaze of a chapel painting such as the *Madonna in Red* (Illustration 6.1). By the same token, the heavenly voice is evoked by the sound of the choir, in imitation of the voices of angels. Indeed, the text consists merely of a series of praises of St. Mary, all the more powerful for her being unnamed. Like a Flemish painting with a simple visual frame, the motet is dislocated, focused on the call between choir and saint. Unlike a collect, the text speaks joyfully in the first person, on behalf of all the faithful present. The singers, indeed, sing also for themselves.[55] Even though the Virgin Mary was venerated as the great intercessor on behalf of humankind, the text makes no reference to her role in salvation.

At the same time, the text sources of *O pulcherrima mulierum* raise the question of genre, insofar as English anthems by definition set antiphon or other office texts. Reinhard Strohm very plausibly attributes the work to John Plummer, on the basis of its imitative style; in the Lucca Choirbook, it adjoins Plummer's *Tota pulchra es I*. Yet even if *O pulcherrima mulierum* were composed by Plummer, it necessarily transcends the boundaries of the anthem genre, as does Forest's *Ascendit Christus*. Given its presence in several song books, it may also have been intended as a through-composed Latin song.[56] The appearance of *O pulcherrima mulierum* in the Lucca Choirbook

54 Trans. in *Douay-Rheims Bible*: www.drbo.org (accessed April 11, 2011).
55 B. J. Blackburn, "For Whom Do the Singers Sing?" *Early Music* 25 (1997): 595.
56 D. Fallows, "Walter Frye's *Ave regina celorum* and the Latin Song Style," in *"Et facciam dolçi canti": Studi in onore di Agostino Ziino in occasione del suo 65 compleanno*, ed. B. Antolini, T. M. Gialdroni, and A. Pugliese, 2 vols. (Lucca: Libreria musicale italiana, 2003), vol. I, 331–45, discusses the difficulty of generic determination for Frye's *Ave regina celorum* and the anonymous *O pulcherrima mulierum*.

and three other Latin manuscripts points to its dual reception as a song and as a motet.[57] It is a rare and finely sculpted work, appropriate for both public ceremony and private devotion.

The multiple uses of Books of Hours, the most widely distributed category of book in the late Middle Ages, offer a further way to understand the paradox of public contemplation. Books of Hours were employed for private devotions, allowing the owner to say the hours of the day, especially the Hours of the Virgin, which parallel the course of the daily offices. They transmitted, among several items, calendars, psalms, and important prayers such as *Gaude Virgo mater Christi* and the *Obsecro te*.[58] Lay men and women brought them to the celebration of the Hours of the Virgin, to enable them to follow the words of the service, which often took place behind a choir screen, or to read their prayers in silence. Books of Hours are also important in that they indicate a wide familiarity with basic Latin texts among the merchant and aristocratic classes, so that at least important words or phrases within motets could be understood.[59] Even those who possessed little or no Latin had an alternative means of understanding via the visual aids of chapel paintings, such as the *Madonna of the Fountain*, painted at Bruges in the workshop of Jan van Eyck. The work clearly associates the Virgin Mary, the infant Christ, and the sacrament of baptism, represented by the fountain with its octagonal base (Illustration 6.2). Such a painting, with its variegated greenery and flowering trees in the background, would form a suitable analogue to motets based on the Song of Songs, including *O pulcherrima mulierum*, which convey the imagery of the garden of paradise.

The *Madonna of the Fountain* is based on a smaller oil painting by Jan van Eyck, appropriate for use in a private home, while the larger painting

---

[57] Trent, Castello del Buonconsiglio, MS 88, fols. 69v–70r; Trent, Archivio Diocesano, MS 93, fols. 368v–369r; New York City, Columbia University, Smith Western Add. MS 21, fol. 7v (fragment). In Trent 93, *O pulcherrima mulierum* is copied in gathering XXXII among Latin, German, French, and Italian songs. See D. Fallows, "Songs in the Trent Codices: An Optimistic Checklist," in *I codici musicali Trentini a cento anni dalla loro riscoperta: Atti del convegno Laurence Feininger, la musicologia come missione*, ed. N. Pirrotta and D. Curti (Trent: Provincia autonomo di Trento, Servizio di beni culturali, Museo provinciale d'arte, 1986), 174.

[58] On prayers in the Books of Hours, see V. Reinburg, "Popular Prayers in Late Medieval and Reformation France" (Ph.D. diss., Princeton University, 1985), chapter 2, "*Porta salutis*: Praying to the Virgin Mary and Saints." For translations of the "Obsecro te," "O intemerata," and other prayers, see *Time Sanctified: The Book of Hours in Medieval Art and Life*, ed. R. S. Wieck (New York: George Braziller, 1988), 163–66.

[59] V. Reinburg, "Prayer and the Book of Hours," in *Time Sanctified*, ed. R. S. Wieck, 40, observes of the literate classes that "a lifetime of immersion in the Church's liturgy and sacraments gave them a practical education in Latin that most twentieth-century observers would find alien."

Illustration 6.2. Workshop of Jan van Eyck, *Madonna of the Fountain*, oil on oak

was likely displayed in a chapel. The Virgin Mary clasps the infant Christ affectionately to her neck, while at her side rests a book, a breviary or Book of Hours, in open invitation to meditation on holy writ, to prayer, and to contemplation. She casts her eyes downward toward the fountain, half-closed, as if engaged in unknowing thought. More elaborate Books of Hours had their own miniatures that illustrated essential scenes of the Gospel and the lives of the saints, which could themselves serve as objects of contemplation, parallel to motets heard at the office of Vespers. As Bonnie J. Blackburn remarks, "Music adds one more dimension to praying before an image: vision and sound are fused, intensifying the experience of meditation."[60]

Just as Books of Hours made the liturgy of the church more open to the lay community, so did motets sung in Bruges bring a more accessible style to the celebration of important feasts, established and underwritten by citizens and clergy alike. Hence, the feasts could foster a sense of community even as they expressed the piety of the faithful. While the religious states described by the writers of the late Middle Ages cannot be fully known, writers such as Giannozzo Manetti articulate the quality and intensity of their personal experience. Both the Virgin Mary and the Holy Cross were considered as focal points for the practice of contemplation. In a sermon, Nicholas of Cusa declares that "Now [there is] a way of contemplation expedient to some: the contemplation of the Blessed Virgin Mary, surpassing all these modes; she appears ineffably visible to me, the sinner, because she treads with her feet upon all corruptibility and the moon itself."[61] While the gaze of Rogier van der Weyden's *Madonna in Red* (Illustration 6.1) invited the faithful into a state of redemption and innocence, so too did the aural intensification of ritual through the voices of the choir open a pathway to devotion. At the same time, by collapsing the distance between subject and object, motets enabled the listeners to lose themselves in the sounds of harmony, focused through ceremony on the world of the sacred.

---

[60] Blackburn, "For Whom Do the Singers Sing?," 599.
[61] Nicholas of Cusa, "Signum magnum," 159: "Nunc expedita aliquali via contemplationis: beatissimae virginis Mariae contemplatio hos omnes modos supergressa ineffabiliter exsistit mihi peccatori, quia omnia corruptabilia et ipsam lunam calcavit pedibus."

7 | The canons of Cambrai

In the early years of the fifteenth century, no city of the north supplied more singers to the Italian courts and cathedrals than Cambrai. Ruled by an archbishop in far northern France, it nevertheless fell under the sphere of influence of the Dukes of Burgundy. The archbishop's church, Cambrai Cathedral, was governed by a group of canons, who met on a regular basis and made decisions for the cathedral as a whole. Among these canons was the composer Guillaume Du Fay, who trained as a choirboy at the cathedral beginning in August 1409.[1] Thirty years later, in December 1439, Du Fay returned to Cambrai, where he took up the canonry that had been granted him by Pope Eugenius IV.[2] In the preceding two decades, he had created a strong network of patrons in Italy, in cities ranging from Ferrara and Florence to Rome. Du Fay appears to have spent several months with the Burgundian court in Lille and Bruges during the second half of 1439.[3] His return to Cambrai happened to coincide with the election of Jean de Bourgogne, natural son of Duke John the Fearless of Burgundy, as archbishop.[4] Thenceforth, Du Fay's ties to the court of Burgundy became particularly strong. In March–December 1450, Du Fay returned to Italy, accompanied by nine *religiosi*, possibly singers of Cambrai.[5] In 1452–58, he again absented himself from the cathedral, sojourning for a portion of the time in the alpine duchy of Savoy. The last sixteen years of his life, 1459–74, were spent exclusively at Cambrai. As the most famous composer in Europe, Du Fay received short or extended visits in Cambrai from musicians as diverse as Johannes Ockeghem and Johannes Tinctoris.[6]

---

[1] A. E. Planchart, "Guillaume Du Fay's Benefices and His Relationship to the Court of Burgundy," *Early Music History* 8 (1988): 119.

[2] D. Fallows, *Dufay* (London: J. M. Dent, 1982): 50–51.

[3] A. E. Planchart, "Connecting the Dots: Guillaume Du Fay and Savoy during the Schism," *Plainchant and Medieval Music* 18 (2009): 14.

[4] May 11, 1439–April 27, 1479. Jean de Bourgogne did not make his first entry into Cambrai until July 10, 1442.

[5] Fallows, *Dufay*, 66–67.

[6] C. Wright, "Dufay at Cambrai: Discoveries and Revisions," *Journal of the American Musicological Society* 28 (1975): 204–08, 220–21.

Remarkably, three other canons at Cambrai Cathedral had, like Du Fay, sung in the papal chapel: Gilles Flannel (1418–41), who served for several years as master of the chapel; Nicolas Grenon (1425–27), who arrived in Rome with four choirboys from Cambrai; and Jehan le Croix (1431–38).[7] Du Fay himself sang in the papal chapel in 1428–33 and 1435–37. Gilles Carlier, a theologian and the author of the *Tractatus de duplici ritu cantus ecclesiastici in divinis officiis*, served as dean of the chapter at Cambrai Cathedral in 1436–72. His term largely coincides with Du Fay's canonry at the cathedral. The composer Simon le Breton, who had long served in the Burgundian court chapel, became a canon of Cambrai in 1464. Another canon, Robert Auclou, Du Fay's longtime friend and colleague, represented the court of Burgundy in the papal curia in 1429–33.[8] Du Fay's motet *Rite majorem/Artibus summis/Ora pro nobis*, composed in Bologna in 1427–28, contains Auclou's name as an acrostic.[9]

Vespers motets for Cambrai Cathedral

The influence wielded by Du Fay and his colleagues appears in a long series of foundations for Vespers motets established by the cathedral canons beginning in 1449, as shown in Table 7.1. Details of the foundations occur in two separate fifteenth-century obituaries, comparable to the *planarius* manuscripts in Bruges: Cambrai, Médiathèque municipale, MS B 39, and Lille, Archives départementales du Nord, MS 4G 2009. The Cambrai manuscript belonged to the main choir of the cathedral, with a section at the end detailing specific foundations. The Lille manuscript contains two different calendars, the first pertaining to the chapel of St. Stephen.[10] At the end of the second calendar appears a section with complete foundations, for the most part duplicating those in Cambrai B 39, but with important additional entries.

---

[7] Fallows, *Dufay*, 248–50.

[8] Ibid., 244.

[9] Planchart, "Guillaume Du Fay's Benefices," 128–29; A. E. Planchart, "Four Motets of Guillaume Du Fay in Context," in *Sleuthing the Muse: Essays in Honor of William F. Prizer*, ed. K. Forney and J. L. Smith (Hillsdale: Pendragon, 2010).

[10] B. Haggh, "Guillaume Du Fay and the Evolution of the Liturgy at Cambrai Cathedral in the Fifteenth Century," *Cantus Planus: International Musicological Society Study Group: Papers Read at the Fourth Meeting, Pécs, Hungary, 3–8 September 1990*, ed. L. Dobszay and A. Papp (Budapest: Hungarian Academy of Sciences, Institute for Musicology, 1992), 562; B. Haggh, "Nonconformity in the Use of Cambrai Cathedral: Guillaume Du Fay's Foundations," in *The Divine Office in the Latin Middle Ages: Methodology and Source Studies, Regional Developments, Hagiography, Written in Honor of Professor Ruth Steiner*, ed. M. E. Fassler and R. Balzer (Oxford and New York: Oxford University Press, 2000), 373.

Table 7.1. Motet foundations at Cambrai Cathedral, 1449–76

Feast	First year[a]	Specifications
St. Gregory	1449/50	cum hymno et moteto per magistrum et pueros in utrisque vesperis
St. Egidius	1450/51	Magistro puerorum altaris pro motetto in utrisque vesperis . . . Ipsius pueris
Sts. Sebastian and Fabian	1454/55	hymno per pueros et moteto in utrisque vesperis ad instar fundacionis festi beati Gregorij
Visitation of the Virgin	1454/55	ad instar conceptionis et annunciationis eiusdem gloriosissime virginis / Magistro et pueris altaris pro hymno et moteto in utrisque vesperis
St. Jerome	1455/56	simili festo sancti gregorij / hymno et moteto a magistro et pueris in utrisque vesperis
St. Adrian	1465/66	Hympno et moteto per magistram et pueros in utrisque vesperis cantando / ad instar festi sancti Gregorij
Sts. Ambrose and Augustine	1470/71	aliis ceremoniis prout in festis sanctorum Gregorij et Jeronimi / Magister et pueri pro motetto
Dedication of the Church	July 1472	Magistro et pueris altaris pro hymno et moteto in utrisque vesperis
Octave of the Dedication	1471/72	In octavis dedicationis fit ad instar beati iheronimi duplum / Pro moteto
St. Quintin	1472/73	Magistro et pueris altaris pro decantatione hymni et moteti in primis vesperis
Sts. Simon and Jude	1473/74	unacum hymno et moteto in utrisque vesperis / magistro et pueris
St. Amato	1475/76	unacum hymno et moteto in utrisque vesperis / magistro et pueris

[a] Dates for the first year in which a foundation appears in the cathedral accounts are provided in Barbara Haggh, "Guillaume Du Fay and the Evolution of the Liturgy at Cambrai Cathedral in the Fifteenth Century," *Cantus Planus: International Musicological Society Study Group: Papers Read at the Fourth Meeting, Pécs, Hungary, 3–8 September 1990*, ed. L. Dobszay and A. Papp (Budapest: Hungarian Academy of Sciences, Institute for Musicology, 1992), 555–62, table 3.

By and large, the Vespers foundations take specific advantage of the considerable musical resources available at Cambrai Cathedral. Perhaps the most important one, which set a precedent for others to follow, was established by the canon Grégoire Nicolai for the feast of St. Gregory the Great, March 12 (see Appendix C1). The foundation, which first entered the cathedral accounts in 1449–50, elevated the saint's day to the rank of a double feast. Nicolai, who was a councillor to the Duke of Burgundy, revised the document in 1462, now raising the level to that of a major double feast.[11] The structure of the foundation is quite simple. It requires full illumination in the choir, in both lower and upper stalls. It further provides for two candles before the crucifix on the choir screen, one before the image of St. Mary at the high altar, and three before the image of St. Gregory in the chapel of St. Stephen. Finally, it mandates "solemn bell-ringing with a hymn and motet by the master and choirboys at both Vespers," to take place in the main choir.[12] The hymn may have been Du Fay's three-voice setting of *Iste confessor Domini*, for the Common of a Confessor. Du Fay had written a complete annual cycle of hymns for the papal chapel in the 1430s, a cycle copied at least in part at Cambrai.[13] The motet has not survived; in fact, none of the motets commissioned for the Vespers foundations appears to have survived, echoing the situation at the Church of St. Donatian in Bruges.

A second foundation by Grégoire Nicolai, for the feast of St. Jerome, explicitly builds on the earlier one ("similar to the feast of St. Gregory"). Sts. Gregory and Jerome were considered among the four great doctors of the church. The foundation was first carried out on September 30, 1455. It calls for "a ground covering of straw, a hymn and motet by the master and choirboys at both Vespers, and solemn bell-ringing" (see Appendix C2). The mention of sweet-smelling grasses strewn in the choir as decoration for the feast is an element often encountered in the Cambrai documents. In 1470–71, Nicolai elevated the feasts of the other two holy doctors of the church, St. Ambrose (April 4) and St. Augustine (August 28). The document mandates that the services for the four doctors of the church should be equal in all respects, as major double feasts (Table 7.1).

---

[11] Nicolai is best known for an incident in which he and Gilles Carlier were called to adjudicate a case of witchcraft in nearby Arras. They counseled "that if the accused were not relapsed and if they would recant they were not to be put to death, provided they had not committed murder and abused the Eucharist." Nevertheless, amid the hysteria in Arras, all four women were condemned. See H. C. Lea, *A History of the Inquisition of the Middle Ages*, 3 vols. (New York and London: Macmillan, 1922), vol. III, 521–23.

[12] From the elements cited in the foundation for St. Jerome, dated 1454, based on the first foundation for St. Gregory, it is clear that the original formulation also called for bell-ringing, with a hymn and motet sung by the succentor and choirboys.

[13] Haggh, "The Liturgy at Cambrai Cathedral," 567–68. On the hymn cycle, see M. Phelps, "A Repertory in Exile: Pope Eugenius IV and the MS Modena, Biblioteca Estense universitaria, α.X.1.11" (Ph.D. diss., New York University, 2008), 73–88, with a review of the literature; and A. E. Planchart, "Music for the Papal Chapel in the Early Fifteenth Century," in *Papal Music and Musicians in Late Medieval and Renaissance Rome*, ed. R. Sherr (Oxford: Clarendon Press; Washington, DC: The Library of Congress, 1998), 114–18. Phelps, "A Reperatory in Exile," 78–79, notes that Du Fay's polyphonic hymn cycle is the earliest to survive among the known manuscripts.

The hymn for all four saints may have been *Iste confessor* by Du Fay. In normal practice, the odd-numbered verses were sung in plainchant, with the even-numbered verses in polyphony. Du Fay's setting, in fauxbourdon, would require one man each on tenor and contratenor, while the choirboys sang the discantus line, paraphrasing the chant.

Two additional foundations, for Sts. Sebastian and Fabian (January 20) and St. Adrian (September 10), follow the established pattern. These appear in the church accounts for 1454–55 and 1465–66, respectively (see Appendix C3 and C4). The first, more detailed foundation was originally established in 1445 by Gilles Flannel, alias l'Enfant, longtime master of the papal chapel.[14] Given the reference to the feast of St. Gregory, it must have been revised in the intervening years. The foundation calls for three candles to be lit before a painting of the two saints. Flannel also possessed a statue of St. Sebastian that he donated to the church in his will, requesting that he be buried before the pillar on which it stood.[15]

The foundation specifies a payment of five *solidi* to the master and choirboys for the hymn and motet at first and second Vespers. The hymn may have been Du Fay's *Sanctorum meritis*, for the Common of Several Martyrs. It was standard practice for the Vespers hymn on the feast day of saints to originate with common, rather than proper use. Given Flannel's devotion to the saint and the collegial relationship between the two men, the motet could well have been Du Fay's *O beate Sebastiane*. The work appears in the third layer of Bologna, Museo internazionale e biblioteca della musica, MS Q15, dated to circa 1433–35, when both Flannel and Du Fay served in the papal chapel.[16] It is also copied among the Du Fay motets in Modena, Biblioteca Estense universitaria, MS α.X.1.11, compiled in the 1440s.[17] As in Du Fay's *Flos florum*, the discantus presents a finely crafted, melismatic line against a slower-moving, tenor-contratenor pair. The melody breaks into smaller fragments, separated by short rests, each fragment different from

---

[14] Haggh, "The Liturgy at Cambrai Cathedral," 557.

[15] J. Houdoy, *Histoire artistique de la Cathédrale de Cambrai, ancienne église métropolitaine Notre-Dame*, facsimile reprint (Lille, 1880; Geneva: Minkoff, 1972), 264; A. E. Planchart, "Notes on Guillaume Du Fay's Last Works," *Journal of Musicology* 13 (1995): 70–71. Planchart notes that the statue still survives "and is now in the Musée de Cambrai."

[16] No. 292, fols. 285v–86r. On the dating and compilation of the manuscript, see M. Bent, ed., *Bologna Q15: The Making and Remaking of a Musical Manuscript: Introductory Study and Facsimile Edition*, 2 vols. (Lucca: Libreria musicale italiana, 2009), vol. I, 19–23, 233.

[17] Fols. 58v–59r. K. Berger, "The Martyrdom of St. Sebastian: The Function of Accidental Inflections in Dufay's *O beate Sebastiane*," *Early Music* 17 (1989): 342–57, argues that the Modena version represents a recomposition of the work.

the one preceding. The line also generates a good deal of dissonance, both at the start of the *tempus* and in passing. The motet tenor and contratenor would have been sung by one man apiece, in support of the six choirboys;[18] because of its structural importance, the succentor most likely took the tenor. Moreover, since all but one of the foundations listed in Table 7.1 call for the *Magister et pueri*, the succentor must customarily have taken the tenor voice both in rehearsal and performance.

A more elaborate feast, that of the Visitation of the Virgin, was endowed by the canon Michael de Beringhen in 1454–55 (see Appendix C5). The feast, celebrated on July 2, commemorated St. Mary's visit to her cousin Elizabeth, as related in Luke 1:39–56. The services encompassed first and second Vespers, Matins, and High Mass. After Matins, the community repaired to the chapel of the Holy Trinity to say a memorial for the soul of the founder. Beringhen also dictated the singing of *Salve regina* after first Compline, the sequence *Inviolata* before Mass, and *Alma redemptoris mater* after second Compline. At Cambrai, each of these chants took place at a different, customary station of the church. *Alma redemptoris mater* was sung in the chapel of Notre Dame la Flamenghe, or La Flammande, named after an image of the Virgin Mary and child, with her visage surrounded by a halo of flames.[19] Beringhen requested that seven candles be lit before the image of Mary, "where is sung the *Alma*," as well as five each before the images of the Annunciation and Visitation. The bellringers, given the number of liturgical items, were compensated with twenty-eight *solidi*. In contrast, the master and choirboys, who sang the standard hymn and motet at both Vespers, received five *solidi*. Significantly, the entire feast is modeled on those of the Conception (December 8) and Annunciation (March 25) of the Virgin, signifying the presence of motets at these Marian feasts by mid-century.

An earlier, equally elaborate foundation at Cambrai, dated 1417–18, relates to the First Sunday in Advent, the beginning of the church year (see Appendix C6).[20] It calls for Matins, High Mass, and second Vespers,

---

[18] Fallows, *Dufay*, 12, places the number of cathedral choirboys in the early fifteenth century at six. The Johannes Martini foundation of August 1445, Appendix C9, specifically cites six choirboys. A. E. Planchart, "Choirboys in Cambrai in the Fifteenth Century," in *Young Choristers: 650–1700*, ed. S. Boynton and E. Rice, Studies in Medieval and Renaissance Music 7 (Woodbridge: Boydell, 2008), 129 n. 2, points out that "a 'seventh choirboy' is routinely mentioned in the accounts after 1407."

[19] For a manuscript illustration from 1446, depicting Notre Dame la Flamenghe, see P. Lacroix, *Military and Religious Life in the Middle Ages and the Renaissance* (London, Chapman and Hall, 1874), figure 235.

[20] Haggh, "The Liturgy at Cambrai Cathedral," 556.

with a memorial for the founder, Egidius de Bosco, after Mass. Among the services was a payment for the first responsory at Matins, *Aspiciens a longe*, sung by the greater and lesser vicars on both sides of the choir, possibly in counterpoint, and punctuated by the bell "Gloriosa." The placement and number of the motets, sung by the master and choirboys, is not specified. Rather, the importance of the de Bosco bequest lies in its testimony to the prominence of motets at major feasts by the second decade of the fifteenth century. In fact, the choirboys of the cathedral already possessed "livres des motez des enfans d'autel" ("books of motets for the boys of the altar") by 1417–18.[21]

Although most of Cambrai Cathedral was constructed in the twelfth and thirteenth centuries, the building was rededicated on July 5, 1472. The canon Jean du Rosut underwrote the feast, with illumination not only in the choir, but throughout the nave, to accommodate the laity (see Appendix C7). Bells accompanied each of the eight canonical hours, including the night office, Matins, for which the bellringer was paid the sum of fifty *solidi*. Since the Archbishop of Cambrai, Jean de Bourgogne, was indisposed with the gout, his place was taken by the aristocrat Jean de Ranchicourt, Bishop of Arras, some twenty miles to the northwest.[22] The feast for Ranchicourt and other distinguished visitors took place at Du Fay's house the day before, on July 4; the bishop, in fact, appears to have been a friend of the composer, having stayed there several times before.[23] While the majority of the services were probably performed in plainchant, including the *Te Deum* at Matins, the master and choirboys sang the customary hymn and motet at both first and second Vespers, receiving five *solidi* for each. The hymn would likely have been Du Fay's *Urbs beata Jerusalem*. A motet at second Vespers, but not a polyphonic hymn, was also sung at the Octave of the Feast of the Dedication, July 12. According to both custom and the articles of foundation, the cathedral observed the Dedication of the Church each subsequent year in the same manner.[24]

The Vespers foundations at Cambrai shared a number of elements in common. All called for full lighting in the choir of the cathedral. All but one also required candles lit before an image of the venerated saint, whether a painting or sculpture, located in the choir, a side chapel, or the nave. Vespers took place in the main choir, which was inaccessible to laymen of

---

[21] Planchart, "Choirboys in Cambrai," 131. [22] Houdoy, *Histoire artistique*, 376–77.

[23] Wright, "Dufay at Cambrai," 211–12; A. E. Planchart, "Du Fay's Last Works," 60–63; Fallows, *Dufay*, 79.

[24] The feast in future years was to fall on the first Sunday following the Translation of St. Thomas à Becket, July 3.

the town. In contrast to those at Bruges, none of the foundations called for a procession. Bell-ringing formed an invariable part of the day's ceremonies, and at times specific bells were required by name. Organs, on the other hand, were wholly lacking, and indeed seem not to have been present at Cambrai Cathedral in the fifteenth century.[25] Finally, in every case but one, the performance of a polyphonic hymn and motet fell to the master and choirboys.[26]

The consistent pairing of hymn and motet at Vespers leads to the presumption that, as at Tournai Cathedral, the motet held a standard position in the liturgy at Cambrai.[27] A foundation by the canon Johannes Martini, dated August 25, 1445, offers explicit evidence concerning the placement and performance of motets (see Appendix C9).[28] Martini endowed a shortened Vespers, to be celebrated each Saturday at the end of the liturgical day, following the *Salve regina*. The service tracks the order of the standard Vespers office, and is worth investigating in detail. It was performed by six *pueri altaris*, their master, and one contratenor. The participants were called together to the chapel of Notre Dame la Flamenghe by strokes of the bells "Aldegundis" and "Gloriosa," three times in alternation. A single choirboy began the service, singing the incipit of the Magnificat antiphon to the Virgin Mary, immediately followed by a second choirboy to intone the Magnificat itself. After completion of the Magnificat and *Gloria Patri*, everyone chanted the complete Magnificat antiphon together. Next came a versicle and collect, spoken by one of the choirboys, with the company in response. Finally, Martini directed that "a motet in place of the *Benedicamus Domino* will be sung by all those named above."

The document offers strong confirmation that Vespers motets at Cambrai were sung in place of the *Benedicamus Domino*, as described also in the Tournai ordinal. Further, the named personnel support the prior conclusion that motets were sung with six choirboys on discantus, the master on tenor, and one contratenor. If two discantus parts were required, the choirboys would have subdivided into groups of three plus three. The entire service was performed *a cappella*. These conclusions extend to the great feasts named in

---

[25] Houdoy, *Histoire artistique*, 58, 92; Wright, "Dufay at Cambrai," 199–201.

[26] See Table 7.1. In the foundation for St. Egidius, established by Gilles Carlier, the hymn was performed by four of the lesser vicars *cum jubilo*, rather than by the master and choirboys (Cambrai, Médiathèque municipale, fonds anciens MS B 39, fol. 52r).

[27] The manuscript Modena α.X.1.11, with its hymn cycle and motets by Du Fay, Magnificats by Du Fay and Binchois, and the great series of motets and anthems by Dunstable and other English composers, may reflect the direct importation of this polyphonic practice into Italy.

[28] Date courtesy of Barbara Haggh-Huglo.

the foundations at mid-century: the Conception of the Virgin, Christmas, and the Annunciation. By the mid-fifteenth century, placement of the motet had become standardized, though not exclusively so, to the end of Vespers on double feasts.

The practice of substituting motets for the *Benedicamus Domino* goes back to the third quarter of the fourteenth century. A 1367 foundation elaborates the Matins office on Wednesday of the Third Week in Advent, in commemoration of the Annunciation of the Virgin (see Appendix C13). The Cambrai document requires three different performing groups for the three great responsories of the office, essentially representing the cathedral community: two of the lesser vicars for the first, *Clama in fortitudine*; two of the chaplains for the second, *Orietur stella*; and two of the canons or greater vicars for the third, *Modo veniet*.[29] It continues, "In addition, at the end of Matins, five of the altar boys serving and their master are required to say a motet or at least a *Benedicamus* with discant; each one of these receives similarly for his labor two *denarii*." The wording makes clear that the motet is sung as the final item of the Office, in place of, rather than in addition to, the *Benedicamus*. Even at this early date, it was assigned to the master and the choirboys, who were five in number.

Two Christmas motets by Nicolas Grenon

According to the foundation for the Dedication of the Church (see Appendix C7), that day's ceremonies were modeled on those of Christmas. It follows that on Christmas Day the master and choirboys customarily performed a hymn and motet at first and second Vespers, particularly since the performance of motets at major feasts is documented as far back as 1417–18, for the First Sunday in Advent. Two Christmas motets by Nicolas Grenon were likely performed at Cambrai Cathedral: *Nova vobis gaudia* and *Ave virtus virtutum/Prophetarum/Infelix propera*. *Nova vobis gaudia* illustrates a tendency toward greater structural simplicity seen in certain motets of the early fifteenth century, while *Ave virtus virtutum/Prophetarum/Infelix propera* represents the opposite tendency toward greater complexity.[30]

[29] Cambrai, Médiathèque municipale, fonds ancien, MS 33, fol. 28r–v; Cambrai, Médiathèque municipale, fonds ancien, MS 38, fols. 21v–22r.

[30] J. M. Allsen, "Style and Intertextuality in the Isorhythmic Motet, 1400–1440" (Ph.D. diss., University of Wisconsin-Madison, 1992), 43–44, 77–81. Allsen notes that the great majority of the thirty-two Latin motets in the manuscript Turin, Biblioteca nazionale universitaria, J.II.9,

Grenon's first appearance at the cathedral dates to 1408–09, when he acted as *scholasticus*, responsible for teaching Latin to the boys in the grammar school associated with the cathedral.[31] He later became master of the choirboys in the Burgundian court chapel, circa 1412–19. Only slender documentation survives for Grenon's return to Cambrai Cathedral between June 1421 and January 1425, but he is securely recorded in 1423.[32] When he left for Rome in May 1425, Grenon brought four choristers from Cambrai along with him; since they remained under his care, he was paid separately from the rest of the papal chapel. Two additional choristers, also from Cambrai, arrived in Rome in early 1426, traveling under the care of the singer Toussaint de la Rouelle.[33] Since *Nova vobis gaudia* appears in the second layer of Bologna Q15, copied circa 1430–33, Grenon probably carried the piece with him to Italy.[34] Whether it was composed for Cambrai or for the Burgundian court, it would have been part of the repertory of the Cambrai choirboys; the text is particularly apt for first Vespers on Christmas Eve.

Nova vobis gaudia employs a clarified rhythmic structure that informs even the melodic details. Grenon lays out the tenor in two *colores*, each of which divides into two *taleae*. Each of the *taleae* corresponds to a single stanza of text. The mensuration remains in perfect time throughout (○), so that the four *taleae* project the same rhythms in all three voices, with a slight change in the tenor at the end of each *color*.[35] The individual *taleae*, in turn, are organized in three large phrases. The first begins with rhythmic imitation at the space of a breve, which at the start of the motet extends also to pitch, alerting the listener to the imitative texture. Rhythmic imitation dominates the second phrase, also at the space of a breve. The *talea* then ends with the *Noël* refrain traditional for the Christmas season in northern France. The two upper voices, which share the same range, call back and

---

of French-Cypriot origins, tend toward structural simplicity, with a single *color* divided into two or three *taleae*.

[31] On the grammar school, see Planchart, "Choirboys in Cambrai," 126–28.

[32] I am most grateful to Alejandro Enrique Planchart for providing documentation on the masters of the choirboys at Cambrai Cathedral in advance of publication. On Grenon's biography see D. Fallows, *A Catalogue of Polyphonic Songs, 1415–1480* (Oxford and New York: Oxford University Press, 1999), 696; C. Wright, "Grenon, Nicolas," in *The New Grove Dictionary of Music and Musicians*, 2nd edn. (London: Macmillan, 2000); J. M. Allsen, "Grenon, Nicolas," in *Die Musik in Geschichte und Gegenwart*, 2nd edn. (Kassel and New York: Bärenreiter, 1998–).

[33] Planchart, "Music for the Papal Chapel," 103; Planchart, "Guillaume Du Fay's Benefices," 127.

[34] Bologna Q15, no. 176, fols. 198v–199r. See also n. 16 above.

[35] Allsen, "Style and Intertextuality," 44–45.

Example 7.1. Grenon, *Nova vobis gaudia*, first refrain

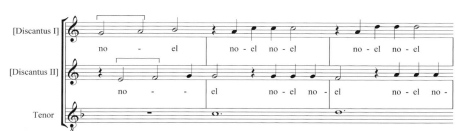

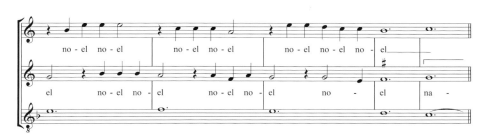

forth on the word *Noël*, with imitation now at the space of a semibreve, creating a hocket-like effect (Example 7.1). The rhythmic intensification leads to a strong cadence at the start of the next *talea*; at the conclusion, Grenon adds an *Amen* on two longs as final punctuation.

The rhythmic patterning and echoing refrain of *Nova vobis gaudia* lend it a charming, naïve quality appropriate to the Christmas season. In Bologna Q15, it is copied adjacent to Lymburgia's *Surexit Christus*, with its *Alleluya* refrain for Easter week. The tenor of *Nova vobis gaudia* moves in straightforward breves and longs, in contrast to the interlocking, breve-length melodic units of the two discantus parts, infusing the work with a vitality reminiscent of Johannes Ciconia. The tenor begins each *talea* on F or C, with a final on F, contributing to the tonal stability of the whole.[36] Moreover, the tenor melody derives from the Kyrie "de Angelis," for solemn feasts, resonating with the angelic greeting at Bethlehem:[37]

---

[36] Ibid., 44–45.

[37] Bent, ed., *Bologna Q15*, vol. I, 204. A close comparison between Grenon's tenor and the *cantus firmus* of Binchois' Kyrie "Angelorum," transmitted in Bologna Q15, no. 97, and eight concordant manuscripts, shows a clear but by no means identical relationship. Binchois, of course, composed for the court of Burgundy. Both melodies contrast with the simpler melody of the Roman use, found in the *Liber usualis* as Kyrie VIII, and represented by the plainchant Kyrie "Angelorum" in Bologna Q15, no. 11, fol. 11r.

Nova vobis gaudia refero
natus est rex virginis utero;
dum propero cursum considero
omnes de cetero talia dicite: Noël.

I announce new joys unto you:
A king is born from the virgin's womb.
While I hasten on the way, I ponder
such great tidings: now all you others, say "Noël."

The *Noël* refrain is well documented in France and Burgundy during the late Middle Ages, including one setting by Antoine Busnoys in Brussels, Royal Library, MS 5557, the "Burgundian Choirbook."[38] In performance, each of the two upper parts of *Nova vobis gaudia* showcased three of the six boys, with the master – Grenon himself – on the tenor. They sang either at their customary place, facing the altar in the middle of the choir, or from the rood-loft at the top of the choir screen, dressed in white as angels on high.[39]

A four-voice motet by Grenon, *Ave virtus virtutum/Prophetarum/Infelix propera*, likewise pertains to the Christmas season. The work appears in a single manuscript, Oxford, Bodleian Library, Canonici misc. 213, in a gathering that twice records the date 1423.[40] That year happens to coincide with Grenon's documented presence at Cambrai Cathedral as master of the choirboys. Both triplum and motetus expound on the prophecies of the coming of Christ, appropriate to Christmas. The fifth stanza of the triplum refers explicitly to the Book of Ezekiel:

---

[38] Fols. 69v–70r. The cry *Noël, noël*, was commonly sung at the processional entry of princes, including the Agincourt celebrations of Henry V.

[39] A chronicle from the Abbot of Saint-Gery in Cambrai, Jehan le Robert, describes the first entry of Bishop Jean de Bourgogne into Cambrai in 1442. At the end of the service at Saint-Gery, he writes, "pouis retourna & luy rassis se mittre sur son quief & en widant de l'Eglise les enfans d'autel canterent I mottet ou pulpitre tournez le visage vers l'autel" ("then he went back, and settled his mitre on his cap; and upon departure from the church, the altar boys sang a motet from the pulpitum, turning their faces towards the altar"). Cited in M. Dupont, *Histoire ecclésiastique et civile de la ville de Cambrai et du Cambresis*, 2 vols. (Cambrai: Samuel Berthoud, 1759–60), vol. II, ix.

[40] Fols. 120v–121r. See G. M. Boone, "Dufay's Early Chansons: Chronology and Style in the Manuscript Oxford, Bodleian Library, Canonici misc. 213" (Ph.D. diss., Harvard University, 1987), 99–105. The dated works in gathering 8 are Antonio da Cividale's *Strenua quem duxit/Gaudeat et tanti*, composed in 1412 (fols. 118v–119r), and Gaulthier Libert's *De tristesse* (fol. 121v). In addition, Du Fay's *Resveilliés vous* (fol. 126v) is securely dated to 1423.

Porta*m* clausa*m* pandit Ezechiel
cu*m* de Syon venit Hemanuel
cu*m* dubiu*m* solvit Ezechiel
cu*m* populus salvatur Israhel.

Ezekiel throws open the closed gate
when Emmanuel comes from Zion,
when Ezechiel dispels doubt,
when the people Israel are saved.

The first line alludes to the messianic prophecy in Ezekiel 44:2–3: "And the Lord said to me: This gate shall be shut, it shall not be opened, and no man shall pass through it . . . For the prince, the prince himself shall sit in it, to eat bread before the Lord: he shall enter in by the way of the porch of the gate, and shall go out by the same way."[41] The ninth stanza invokes Numbers 17:8, in which the rod of Aaron blossoms and bears almonds: "Aaron virga fructum dat hodie" ("Today the rod of Aaron gives forth fruit"). The motetus, on the other hand, alludes to the prophecy of Virgil's Fourth Eclogue, in which a heaven-sent child born among shepherds heralds a new Golden Age: "Cum de celo teste Virgilio / nova venit hec generatio" ("When from heaven, as Virgil attests / This new generation comes"). Virgil's poem was customarily interpreted in the Middle Ages as a pagan prophecy of the coming of Christ; the reference offers a reminder of Grenon's original position as a teacher of Latin grammar to the Cambrai choirboys.

Grenon organizes both triplum and motetus in four-line stanzas with ten-syllable lines. The triplum rhymes AAAA, BBBB, CCCC and so on across ten stanzas, while the motetus maintains the same rhyme in all eight stanzas. The second stanza of the triplum begins "Enixa est virgo puerpera" ("The virgin mother has given birth"), which echoes a verse of the hymn *A solis ortus cardine*, reading "Enixa est puerpera." That hymn was sung for both first and second Vespers at Christmas in Cambrai Cathedral. Another triplum verse, "tamquam sponsus de sua camera" ("just as the bridegroom from his chamber"), draws on the Matins antiphon "Tamquam sponsus Dominus procedens de thalamo suo," also heard as a versicle and response at first and second Vespers.[42] The tenor, in the meantime, sings the last double versicle

---

[41] Trans. in *Douay-Rheims Bible*: www.drbo.org (accessed April 11, 2011): "Et dixit Dominus ad me porta haec clausa erit non aperietur et vir non transiet . . . / Principi princeps ipse sedebit in ea ut comedat panem coram Domino per viam vestibuli portae ingredietur et per viam eius egredietur."

[42] Cambrai, Médiathèque municipale, fonds ancien, MS 33, fols. 43v–44r, 45r, 54v–55r.

of the sequence *Letabundus*, for the Christmas season, widely known in the Middle Ages (see Example 8.1). The text, fully underlaid in the tenor voice, is sung three times through, in six *colores*, the two halves of the melody being identical. In replacing the *Benedicamus Domino* and commenting on the relevant scriptures, with three simultaneous texts, the motet significantly added to the weight and meaning of the Christmas liturgy.

Further, the numerical structure of *Ave virtus virtutum/Prophetarum/ Infelix propera* ties it directly to *Nova vobis gaudia*. Grenon divides *Ave virtus virtutum* into four pairs of *taleae* with a postlude (Figure 7.1). The pairs last 144, 108, 72, and 36 ($\times$ 2) minims, a $4:3:2:1$ ratio.[43] With the addition of the postlude, the motet lasts 750 minims, or 125 breves in imperfect time, major prolation (c). In *Nova vobis gaudia*, on the other hand, all four of the *taleae* last 144 minims. The *cantus firmus* ends on two longs, worth 24 minims, bringing the total length to 600 minims, or 100 equivalent breves in perfect time, minor prolation ($\bigcirc$). The durations of the two motets thus relate in a $5:4$ ratio, or $125:100$ breves. The proportions are carefully chosen, for the total lengths of the *taleae* in each motet also relate in a $5:4$ ratio, or $720:576$ minims. For *Nova vobis gaudia*, 100 represents a perfect number in reference to the coming of Christ.[44] The square of 5 inherent in both works may represent the Incarnation, given that number's traditional associations with the five fingers and the five senses.[45] Grenon probably conceived the two works as a complementary pair, with *Nova vobis gaudia* performed at first Vespers on Christmas Eve, and *Ave virtus virtutum/Prophetarum/Infelix propera* at second Vespers on Christmas Day.

The procession of the Purification

The annual procession of the Purification, February 2, was an important civic occasion in Cambrai. The feast commemorates the forty-day period of purification that the Virgin Mary followed after the birth of Jesus. It

[43] Allsen, "Style and Intertextuality," 511–12.

[44] A. Schimmel, *The Mystery of Numbers* (New York: Oxford University Press, 1993), 21, points out that Dante's *Divina commedia* is organized in $1 + 33 + 33 + 33$ cantos. *Nova vobis gaudia* displays a similar sectional division into $24 + 24 + 24 + 24 + 4$ breves.

[45] V. F. Hopper, *Medieval Number Symbolism: Its Sources, Meaning, and Influence on Thought and Expression* (New York: Columbia University Press, 1938), 86. The total number of breves between the motets, 225, equals $5^2 \times 3^2$, symbolic of both the Incarnation and the Trinity.

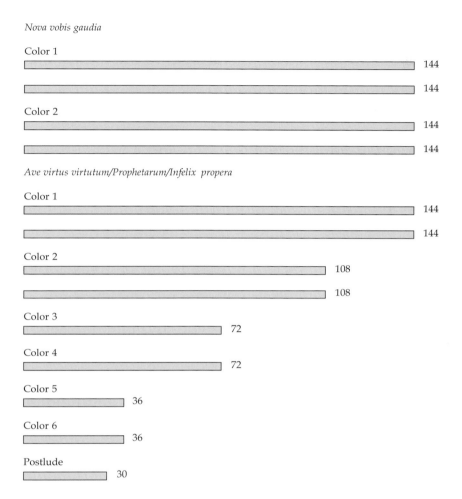

Figure 7.1. Nicolas Grenon, *Nova vobis gaudia* and *Ave virtus virtutum/Prophetarum/Infelix propera*, *talea* lengths in minims

coincides with the ritual presentation of Christ at the Temple of Jerusalem, where he was recognized as the Messiah by Simeon, as related in Luke 2:22–39. The feast thus brings together two threads of late medieval Christianity: the conception of Christ as "a light to the revelation of the Gentiles, and the glory of thy people Israel," and the virtue of the Virgin Mary in obedience to Mosaic law.

Accordingly, the central ceremonies of the feast of the Purification were two: the blessing of candles for the church year, and the procession of the faithful through the church, to commemorate the coming of Christ to the

Temple. The first portion of the ceremony, which followed Terce, culminated in the singing of the canticle of Simeon, *Nunc dimittis* (Luke 2:29–32) with the antiphon *Lumen ad revelationem*. The canticle retains the ancient form whereby the antiphon precedes and follows each of the four verses and *Gloria Patri*. The canticle accompanied the lighting of candles and their distribution to all the faithful present in the church. The second portion of the ceremony, with which we are concerned here, typically began with a priest intoning *Procedamus in pace* ("Let us proceed in peace") as a signal for the procession.

Du Fay's late motet *Fulgens iubar/Puerpera pura parens/Virgo post partum* was composed for the procession of the Purification at Cambrai Cathedral, probably in the years 1445–46. In the first place, the motetus text contains an acrostic that reads "PETRUS DE CASTELLO CANTA," taken from the initial letters of the first twenty-one lines, minus refrain. The acrostic refers to the master of the choirboys at Cambrai Cathedral, Pierre du Castel. As we have seen, the master and choirboys were responsible for the singing of motets at the cathedral during the fifteenth century. According to documents discovered by Alejandro Enrique Planchart, Pierre du Castel held this position between November 10, 1437 and December 1447.[46] In the second place, the motet appears as a late addition to Modena α.X.1.11, a central source for the hymns, Magnificats, and motets of Du Fay. *Fulgens iubar*, in fact, appears out of place in the manuscript, at the head of a series of six English motets (fols. 121v–123r). Third, Du Fay's triplum explicitly refers to the candles held by the participants in the procession of the Purification:

Quod purgari non indignaverit
Huius festo monstrat ecclesia
Per cereum, quem tunc quisque gerit;
Luce enim qua fulget candela
Persplendorum vite in Maria
Concorditer omnes ostendimus,
Ut per sua tandem precamina
Sublimemur sanctorum sedibus.

That she did not disdain to be cleansed
the Church makes manifest in her feast
by the taper which each worshipper then wields;
for by the light with which the candle shines

---

[46] Information provided courtesy of Alejandro Enrique Planchart.

we all signify in harmony the complete
splendor of life in Mary,
that at length by her prayers
we may be raised aloft in the dwelling of the saints.[47]

Laurenz Lütteken suggests that *Fulgens iubar* stems from the fiscal year 1445–46 or earlier, coincident with the repainting of the *civieres* ("pallets") for two silver reliquaries at the cathedral. The first reliquary, dedicated to the Virgin of the Assumption, represented the Queen of Heaven on her knees, crowned by God the Father. The second, dedicated to the Purification of the Virgin, displayed a painting of St. Mary in her childbed, St. Joseph bearing a staff, the baby Jesus on a cushion, and the words *Quem genuit adoravit.* The quotation, "She worshipped the one she bore," corresponds to the last three words of Du Fay's *cantus firmus.*[48] The opening words of the motetus may refer to the scene depicted: "Puerpera pura parens / Enixa regem seculi" ("O new mother, pure parent, / that didst bear the King of the world").[49] The reliquary, described in an inventory of March 1461, also represented God the Father holding a ball symbolic of the world and six angels, "two with censers and the others with melodious instruments." A third reliquary, explicitly dedicated to the Circumcision, had its pallet painted in silver gilt at the same period. The donor was the canon Toussaint le Mercier, who died in 1440, leaving the reliquary to the cathedral.[50]

The donor of the two silver reliquaries was Johannes Martini, the very same cleric who established the short Vespers for Saturdays at the chapel of Notre Dame la Flamenghe. A codicil to the Martini foundation, preserved in Lille, Archives départementales du Nord, MS 4G 2009, instituted a procession after Nones, or in Lent after the sermon, on each of the five Marian feasts of the year:[51] the Annunciation, Assumption, Nativity, Conception, and Purification of the Virgin. It must have been established between August 25, 1445, the date of the original foundation, and Martini's death in 1446. The codicil concerns the "ordo processionum in deportatione Reliquarij

[47] Edited and trans. in L. Holford-Strevens, "Du Fay the Poet? Problems in the Texts of His Motets," *Early Music History* 16 (1997): 146–47.

[48] L. Lütteken, *Guillaume Dufay und die isorhythmische Motette: Gattungstradition und Werkcharakter an der Schwelle zur Neuzeit*, Schriften zur Musikwissenschaft aus Münster 4 (Hamburg and Eisenach: K. D. Wagner, 1993), 300–01.

[49] Trans. after Holford-Strevens, "Du Fay the Poet?" 146–47.

[50] Houdoy, *Histoire artistique*, 188, 261, 350–51.

[51] Fol. 12r. The codicil is in the same hand as the foundation for the "Commemoration" of St. Mary, but represents a later addition, as evinced by the notably smaller script and closer-together lines.

Ad processionem
A. Adorna thalamum tuum Syon
A. Ave gratia plena Dei genetrix
R. Responsum accepit   V. Hodie beata Virgo Maria

In statione
R. Gaude Maria Virgo cunctas   V. Gabrielem archangelem
Prosa. Inviolata integra et casta
[Versicle and Response]
[Collect]

Ad ingressum chori
A. Homo erat in Iherusalem

Figure 7.2. The procession of the Purification at Cambrai Cathedral
A. = antiphon; R. = responsory; V. = responsory verse

Capillorum gloriose virginis Marie sumpt*ionis*" ("the order of the procession in transporting the reliquary of the lock of hair of the glorious Virgin
Mary of the Assumption"). The procession began in the choir, then moved
to the chapel of Notre Dame la Flamenghe. The coincidence of this foundation with the donation of the two silver reliquaries underscores Martini's
interest in the processional liturgy at Cambrai. Rather than the reparation
of the pallets, the proximate motivation for Du Fay's motet was likely the
gift of the second reliquary, first celebrated on the feast of the Purification
in the year 1445 or 1446.

The outlines of the procession in which Du Fay's motet was sung may be
reconstructed by reference to several sources. A winter processional from
Cambrai, dated before 1471, transmits the necessary chants for the ceremony, but precious few rubrics, as outlined in Figure 7.2.[52] The single
goal of the procession was a station dedicated to the Virgin Mary beneath
the bell tower at the front of the cathedral, where the prosa or sequence
Inviolata integra et casta was customarily sung. The first item is an elaborate processional antiphon, *Adorna thalamum*, originating with the Greek
church, which alludes to the figures of Mary, Christ, and Simeon. It was followed by two Marian chants, the antiphon *Ave gracia plena* and the respond
Responsum accepit. At the station, the lengthy responsory *Gaude Maria virgo
cunctas* was adjoined by its given prosa, the *Inviolata*. This was the only time
during the church year when the two chants were united; during the rest of
the year, the *Inviolata* stood on its own. In the Cambrai processional, every
verse of the *Inviolata* begins with a large initial, an indication of its relative

[52] M. Huglo, *Les manuscrits du processionnal*, 2 vols., RISM B IV (Munich: G. Henle, 1999), 34.

importance. No chant is given for the return through the nave of the church, but the antiphon *Homo erat in Iherusalem* accompanied the clergy at the entrance to the choir.

A Cambrai account book from 1501–02 records a payment for carrying the reliquaries on the feast of the Purification and other Marian feasts;[53] these followed the cross at the head of the procession. Both the silver reliquary of the Purification and the reliquary of Toussaint le Mercier would have been exposed; the latter, fashioned in the shape of an altar with candles, bore a painting of Simeon on one side, and St. Joseph with two turtledoves on the other. The twelve peers of the county of Cambrai, who owed their feudal allegiance to the archbishop, presented themselves to the church, each preceded by a herald with banner. The peers wore a helmet and coat of arms and bore a rapier made of wax. The swords would later be laid at the altar during the offertory at Mass.[54] The commoners of the town followed, men and women, all bearing candles.

Given the fullness of the Purification rituals, no obvious position presents itself for the performance of Du Fay's motet. The paired responsory *Gaude Maria virgo cunctas* and sequence *Inviolata* leave little time at the station in the narthex of the church, although the motet could have followed the subsequent versicle and collect (see Figure 7.2). The only place that remains is the traditional station before the rood, again following the versicle and collect, but preceding the antiphon *Homo erat in Iherusalem* at the entrance to the choir. In Cambrai, the arms of the crucifix on the choir screen had places for twelve or twenty-four candles that could be lit on major feasts.[55] On either side of the door were twin altars. A contemporaneous foundation by Egidius de Bosco, Sr., begun in 1445, called for a memorial before the crucifix in the nave "immediately after Compline on Easter Day and the six Sundays subsequent" (see Appendix C6).[56] It consisted of the *Regina celi*, sung in improvised or written discant, a versicle and response,

[53] Lille, Archives départementales du Nord, MS 4G 6793, fol. 3v, transcription courtesy of Craig Wright: "Item pro dup*lici Salve, Te deum* in matut*in*is, processione post mat*utinas, Inviolata* ante reliquar*um*, et *Alma* in festa purificat*ionis* beate Marie Virg*in*is iiij S. iiij d." Wright graciously made available his notebook of transcriptions from the Cambrai archives.

[54] E. Bouly, *Dictionnaire historique de la ville de Cambrai, des abbayes, des chateaux-forts et des antiquités du Cambresis*, facsimile reprint (Cambrai: Conseil municipal de Cambrai, 1854; Brussels: Editions Culture et Civilisation, 1979), 420–21.

[55] Cambrai B 39, fol. 42v: "O*bitus* mag*istri* petr*i* majoris can*onici* sub*di*aconi .x. L. xiii S. t*or*nacensis *cum* pulsat*ione* et ass*isie* et xxiiii cereis tam sup*er* trabem crucifixi *quod* coram duob*us* altarib*us in* introitu chori." See also Appendix C13.

[56] Haggh, "The Liturgy at Cambrai Cathedral," 557. The main section of the foundation, previously discussed, dates from 1417–18.

and the collect *Interveniat.* The foundation underscores the importance of the rood for the ceremonial life of the church. Pierre du Castel and Guillaume Du Fay on the first and second tenor, two contratenors on the motetus, and six choirboys on the triplum could have performed *Fulgens iubar* in the transept, facing outward to the long procession in the nave. Alternatively, one *petite vicaire* joined Pierre du Castel on the motetus, bearing his name in the acrostic, while two other *petites vicaires* sang the tenors.[57]

In many respects, *Fulgens iubar/Puerpera pura parens/Virgo post partum* has the character of a sermon addressed to the faithful.[58] The content and themes, though not the verbal phrasing, draw on the relevant chapter in Jacobus de Voragine's *The Golden Legend*, one of the most widely read of late medieval books. Johannes Martini specifically cites *The Golden Legend* in his foundation for a series of Marian processions, and Du Fay himself owned a copy. The motetus and triplum are both organized in four stanzas with a one-line refrain; though in Latin, they take the poetic form of a French ballade.[59] The triplum lines have ten syllables, while the motetus lines have eight, all in the same rhyme scheme: ababbcbC. The poetic structure is novel for a motet, yet appropriate in a work addressed to the twelve peers of the city, using a familiar form with repeated refrains. The stanzas, moreover, are delivered in tandem, parallel in subject as well as form. In the second stanza, the motetus addresses Mary, "Annuisti legi verens / Solvere legem" ("Thou consentedst to the law for fear / of undoing the law"). The triplum adds, "Illa tamen pro nobis omnibus / Legem tulit" ("But she for our sakes submitted to the law").[60] Both ideas stem from the *Golden Legend*, while the reliquary of Johannes Martini visually illustrated the process of ritual purification.

Fulgens iubar/Puerpera pura parens/Virgo post partum represents one of the last examples of the traditional French motet, yet one influenced by the late English motet style.[61] Its complex verbal, musical, and mathematical structures arise from a similar tendency as those of Grenon's *Ave virtus virtutum/Prophetarum/Infelix propera.* The *cantus firmus* comes from either of two Matins responsories, *Adorna thalamum* and *Senex puerum portabat,*

---

[57] Planchart, "Choirboys in Cambrai," 143. The motetus splits at the final cadence, thus requiring two singers. The greater weight accorded the motetus allows its text to be heard in counterbalance to the six choirboys on the triplum.

[58] On the motet as sermon, see M. J. Bloxam, "Obrecht as Exegete: Reading *Factor orbis* as a Christmas Sermon," in *Hearing the Motet*, ed. D. Pesce (Oxford and New York: Oxford University Press, 1997), 169–92.

[59] Holford-Strevens, "Du Fay the Poet?" 145–46.   [60] Ibid., 145–46.

[61] Allsen, "Style and Intertextuality," 191, 199.

which have the same text and music at the end: "Virgo post partum quem genuit adoravit" ("The Virgin after childbirth worshipped Him she bore").[62] The tenors have three *colores*, each divided into two *taleae*, in a proportional structure of $6:6:4:4:3:3$. The last two *taleae* are sung in diminution by half with respect to the first two. The measured time lengths of the individual *taleae* generate a series of golden sections; for the motet as a whole, the golden section occurs after the third *talea*.[63] Coinciding with the tenor *colores*, the upper voices repeat the same rhythms in each pair of *taleae* (1–2, 3–4, 5–6). Each *talea* also has an introductory duet between motetus and triplum, singing at a range a fifth apart, that takes up the first quarter of the section (Example 7.2). Both voices present fully formed, interlocking melodies, in the English manner. At the entrance of the two tenors, an abrupt change of melodic and harmonic motion results, whereby the triplum and motetus rhythms slow down to approximate more nearly the tenor voices. As a consequence, their melodic coherence is interrupted, sacrificed to the harmonic integration of four-voice polyphony. Overall, the double-texting and monumental character of the four-voice sections create a work fully in accordance with the civic and ecclesiastical splendor of the procession, with the church lit by the hands of the congregation.

The testament of Guillaume Du Fay

One of the most remarkable documents to originate at Cambrai Cathedral is the last will and testament of Guillaume Du Fay, dictated on July 7, 1474. Since the testament was published by Jules Houdoy in 1880, the musical items are well known and continue to attract scholarly interest.[64] Du Fay cites motets at two points in the document: in connection with the foundation for the feast of St. Anthony of Padua, June 13, and in connection with the composer's own last moments on earth. St. Anthony of Padua (1195–1230), a Portuguese follower of St. Francis in Italy, was renowned for his piety and eloquence. In his testament, Du Fay leaves a manuscript containing "the Mass of Saint Anthony of Padua" to the chapel of St. Stephen. Du Fay's

---

[62] Information courtesy of Barbara Haggh-Huglo, cited in Holford-Strevens, "Du Fay the Poet?" 145 n. 87. The *cantus firmus* does not entirely match the chants as transmitted in the thirteenth-century antiphonal, Cambrai, Médiathèque municipale, fonds ancien, MS 38, fols. 248v and 249v.

[63] R. Nosow, "Le proporzioni temporali in due messe di Dufay: *Se la face ay pale* e *Ecce ancilla Domini*," *Rivista italiana di musicologia* 28 (1993): 58–60. The golden section is a mathematical constant whereby for any quantity A, divided into two unequal sections, B and C, the ratio of A : B equals the ratio of B : C.

[64] Houdoy, *Histoire artistique*, 409–14.

Example 7.2. Du Fay, *Fulgens iubar*, third *talea*

instructions for the service require that the choirboys sing the Gloria, hence the manuscript contained an Ordinary setting. In fact, the calendar entry in Lille, Archives départmentales du Nord, MS 4G 2009 (fol. 6r) records the presence of the *pueris altaris*. The three-voice Mass Ordinary, one of the composer's most mensurally complex works, survives in the manuscript Trent 90 (fols. 72v–73r, 395v–406r). Du Fay's manuscript must also have contained a set of Propers for the saint, since this survives complete in Trent 88;[65] the Propers and Ordinary together formed a plenary Mass cycle,

65   See A. E. Planchart, "The Books that Guillaume Du Fay Left to the Chapel of Saint Stephen," in
     Sine musica nulla disciplina . . . Studi in onore di Giulio Cattin, ed. F. Bernabei and A. Lovato
     (Padua: Poligrafo, 2008), 188–90. Planchart argues strongly that the manuscript also contained
     a set of Propers for St. Francis of Assisi, which directly follow those for St. Anthony of Padua in
     Trent 88.

Example 7.2. (*cont.*)

rare in the fifteenth century. Moreover, the executors' account describes the manuscript as "Item pour j livre en grant volume en parchemin contenant les messes de St. Anthoine de Pade aveuc pluiseurs aultres anthiennes en noire note, xl S" ("Item, for one book of great size in parchment, containing the Masses of St. Anthony of Padua, with many other antiphons in black notes, xl *sous*").[66] Although the testament is silent on the subject, these antiphons belonged to a set of Vespers for St. Anthony of Padua. The passage in the testament that draws on the Vespers liturgy spells out the duties of the master and choirboys:

> volo tamen quod magister puerorum prefatus ultra dictam portionem habeat pro suo labore xx denarios, sex autem pueri qui post completorium in profesto ipsius sancti responsum *Si quereris miracula* cum versu et *Gloria*, necnon motetum, *O sydus Hispanie* de eodem sancto et in crastinum ad missam *Et in terra pax* decantabunt, percipient x solidos, unde cuilibet xx denarios que omnia simul sunt xli solidi viii denarii; volo insuper quod in fine hujus misse legatur *De profundis*, sicut in missa capelle Trinitatis, presbitero incipiente, aliis respondentibus, cum orationibus *Inclina* et *Fidelium*. Et post completorium veniant in dicta capella sancti Stephani socii qui fuerint in missa, cantaturi antiphona *O proles Hispanie* super cantu plano, deinde dicant pueri versum et presbiteri collectam, postea vero dicant pueri motetum *O lumen ecclesie* vel alium ad libitum magistri eorundem.

I wish nonetheless that the aforementioned master of the children should have for his efforts 20 *denarii* beyond the said portion; as for the six boys who will sing the responsory *Si quereris miracula* with its verse and *Gloria* after Compline on the eve of the feast of the same saint, as well as the motet *O sydus Hispanie* for the same saint, and on the morrow at Mass the *Et in terra pax*, they will receive 10 *solidi*, whence 20 *denarii* to each, so all together that makes 41 *solidi*, 8 *denarii*. In addition, I wish that at the end of this Mass the *De profundis* be read, just as in the Mass at the Trinity chapel, with the priest beginning and the others responding, together with the prayers *Inclina* and *Fidelium*. And after Compline the companions who were in the Mass shall come to the said chapel of St. Stephen, in order to sing the antiphon *O proles Hispanie* upon the plainchant, then the boys say the versicle and the priests the collect; and after that the boys will say the motet *O lumen ecclesie* or another at the discretion of their master.

All of the musical items cited here would have been available in Du Fay's parchment manuscript, bequeathed to the chapel of St. Stephen. The

---

[66] Wright, "Dufay at Cambrai," 228. Haggh, "Nonconformity," 394 n. 20, transcribes all three executors' accounts, two of which are couched in the plural and one in the singular, a circumstance explained by the presence of both the Ordinary and Proper Mass cycles for St. Anthony of Padua.

two works sung in the chapel after first Compline, the responsory *Si queris miracula* and motet *O proles Hyspanie/O sidus Hyspanie*, are copied adjacent to each other in Trent 87 (fols. 115v–117r and 113v–115r). They are among the last works copied by the main scribe, on paper dated to the years 1440–44.[67] Consequently, they were at least thirty years old when specified in Du Fay's will.

Si queris miracula is sung as a processional respond at Vespers in the Franciscan use. As David Fallows points out, the work sets both the verse and doxology, as prescribed in the testament.[68] The discantus ornaments the chant by Julian of Speyer, in mode 8 on G.[69] The four-voice motet *O proles Hyspanie/O sidus Hyspanie* sets two texts for St. Anthony of Padua, the first a Magnificat antiphon by Julian of Speyer, the second an antiphon attributed to Guy de Montfort. Montfort had the verses engraved on a silver reliquary that he donated on pilgrimage to the Basilica di Santo Antonio in Padua in 1350.[70] Similarly to *Fulgens iubar*, the motet incorporates the text inscribed on the reliquary that was carried in procession, on display to all the people; the circumstance lends further support to the claim of the Basilica di Santo Antonio as the original recipient of the polyphonic Vespers.[71] Du Fay identifies *O proles Hyspanie/O sidus Hyspanie* by its second text, to distinguish it from the antiphon sung on the feast day itself; the first contratenor voice, which carries the second text, functions as a motetus.[72] While *Si queris miracula* is an unicum, *O proles Hyspanie/O sidus Hyspanie* appears among the Du Fay motets in Modena α.X.1.11 (fols. 62v–64r), as well as in Trent 88 (fols. 205v–207r), the central source for Du Fay's music from the 1440s.

The pairing of a polyphonic responsory – a genre rare in itself – with a motet appears to be unique in the fifteenth century. The two works share a G final, but otherwise contrast markedly in form and style. *Si queris*

---

[67] S. E. Saunders, *The Dating of the Trent Codices from Their Watermarks* (New York: Garland, 1989), 56.

[68] Fallows, *Dufay*, 190–91.

[69] On the rhymed office by Julian of Speyer, see T. Scandaletti, "L'ufficio di Giuliano da Spira per S. Antonio: Problemi di ecdotica," in *Contributi per la storia della musica sacra a Padova*, ed. G. Cattin and A. Lovato (Padua: Istituto per la storia ecclesiastica padovana, 1993), 93–114; A. E. Planchart, "Guillaume Dufay's Masses: A View of the Manuscript Traditions," *Papers Read at the Dufay Quincentenary Conference, Brooklyn College, December 6–7, 1974*, ed. A. W. Atlas (New York: Dept. of Music, School of Performing Arts, Brooklyn College of the City University of New York, 1976), 33–37; Planchart, "The Books," 179–82, 185–89.

[70] L. de Chérancé, *Saint Antoine de Padoue* (Paris: Poussielgue, 1895), 39.

[71] Planchart, "The Books," 188–89.

[72] J. E. Cumming, *The Motet in the Age of Du Fay* (Cambridge University Press, 1999), 233–34; Planchart, "The Books," 182.

Table 7.2. Discantus ranges in works sung by the choirboys at
Cambrai Cathedral

Grenon, *Nova vobis gaudia*	c′–e″ / c′–e″
Grenon, *Ave virtus virtutum/Prophetarum/Infelix propera*	c′–d″
Du Fay, *O beate Sebastiane*	b–e♭″
Du Fay, *O proles Hyspanie/O sidus Hyspanie*	g–e″
Du Fay, *Si queris miracula* (responsory)	b–e″
Du Fay, *Fulgens iubar/Puerpera pura parens/Virgo post partum*	b–e″
Du Fay, *Ave regina celorum III*	b–f″
Du Fay, *Iste confessor* (hymn)	a–c″
Du Fay, *Sanctorum meritis* (hymn)	b–c″

miracula begins with an intonation and follows the sectional structure of the
chant, embedding the melody in the discantus. Du Fay not only repeats the
shortened respond (R₁) after the verse (V) and doxology (D), but provides
the second repeat (R₂) with new music, in the form R V R₁ D R₂. Both the
verse and doxology are set as duos, parallel to the practice of granting these
passages to soloists in the chant.

In *Si queris miracula*, the choirboys likely performed with the master on
tenor and a single contratenor, as specified in the Johannes Martini foundation. In fact, the vocal ranges for the works listed in Table 7.2 demonstrate
that the cathedral choirboys typically sang lines that covered an eleventh
to a thirteenth.[73] Du Fay constructs an intricate rhythmic counterpoint
in which the three voices are equally active, with a strong acceleration
toward major cadences. Because the discantus paraphrases the plainchant,
it remains almost entirely in the natural (C) and hard (G) hexachords,
across the range g–e″. The tenor and contratenor sing a fifth lower, with
a b♭ signature, employing the soft (F) and natural (C) hexachords in the
range d–a′. As a result, *Si queris miracula* creates a frequent and sometimes rapid alternation of b♮′ in the discantus with b♭ in the tenor and
contratenor. At the first major cadence, the discantus quotes thirteen notes
of the composer's *Magnificat sexti toni*, one step higher, in complex rhythms
(Example 7.3). Because of the cyclical nature of the latter setting, the same
cadence is heard twice, at the end of verses 2 and 10. The *Magnificat sexti*

---

[73] D. Fallows, "Specific Information on the Ensembles for Composed Polyphony, 1400–1475," in
Studies in the Performance of Late Mediaeval Music, ed. S. Boorman (Cambridge University
Press, 1983), 123, adduces the motet *Gaude virgo mater Christi* by Heinrich Battre, in which all
three of the voices marked *pueri* (d′–d″, a–b′, c′–c″) fall within the single range of the
discantus in *O proles Hypanie/O sidus Hyspanie* (g–e″).

Example 7.3. (A) Du Fay, *Si queris miracula*, end of first section; (B) Du Fay, *Magnificat sexti toni*, end of "Et exultavit"

toni, composed in the early 1430s, was widely distributed, appearing in seven sources. It likely formed part of first Vespers for St. Anthony of Padua, framed by Julian of Speyer's plainchant antiphon *O proles Hyspanie*, also in the sixth mode on F.

In *O proles Hyspanie/O sidus Hyspanie*, the choirboys and master would have taken the first text, while two contratenors presented the second.[74] The work incorporates the florid style of Du Fay's *O beate Sebastiane*, but with four voices and double-texting. The tenor and two contratenors all inhabit the same range, d–a′, over which the choirboys sing a marvelously flexible and eloquent line, set off as much by cross-rhythms as by speed. The texture harkens back to Hugo de Lantins' *Ave verum corpus*, written in the early 1420s, but with much lighter touch in the lower voices. Like de Lantins' work, *O proles Hyspanie/O sidus Hyspanie* presents an unstable melodic and harmonic surface. The tenor and contratenors frequently mutate to the B♭ hexachord, which requires e♭ or e♭′. Meanwhile, the discantus makes the corresponding change to b♭′, via the soft hexachord on F. It also moves to f♯′ at five cadences, implying the fictive hexachord on D. Overall, the motet creates a melodic and harmonic palette comparable to Du Fay's early chansons, but on a broader scale.

The long, opening *salutatio* allows for parallel declamation of the two incipits. The first section arrives at a series of *coronae*, with complementary, rhyming phrases, addressing the saint as "the light of Italy": "Fer, Antoni, gratie / Tu lumen Italie." In the middle section, the mensuration changes from perfect time, diminished (⊘), to the more deliberate perfect time, minor prolation (○), then back to diminished time (⊘) for the *Amen*. The central section features two brief passages in fauxbourdon texture, with three voices moving in parallel motion. The final *Amen* forms a purely musical *conclusio* on the single syllable *A*, beginning in four-part imitation. Tonal instability continues up to the final cadence as the discantus becomes increasingly complex, forcing the singers to modulate the precise contour of the melodic lines via the operations of *musica recta*.

For the music after second Compline, Du Fay's testament calls for a more traditional memorial: antiphon – versicle – collect – motet. The motet is simply added to the standard memorial structure. The testament requires the attendance at the chapel of St. Stephen of everyone who participated in the Mass for St. Anthony of Padua earlier that day (June 13). This included the master and choirboys and the nine men who sang the Mass, as well as the priest, deacon, and subdeacon from among the greater vicars who celebrated

---

[74] Only the redaction in Modena α.X.1.11, fols. 60v–62r, bears text in all four voices, with the first text, *O proles Hyspanie*, on the left-hand side of the opening and the second, *O sidus Hyspanie*, on the right-hand side. In Trent 87, fols. 113v–115r, the first contratenor is texted, but not the second. In Trent 88, fols. 207v–209r, only the discantus carries text, while the other three voices have the incipit *O proles yspanie*. Such variability in texting is fairly typical for motets of the period.

it.[75] According to the executors' accounts, during Du Fay's lifetime they all repaired afterwards to the composer's house for dinner, a total of twenty people including the composer; the executors continued to treat everyone to dinner for at least the first two years after his death.[76] The saint's feast in this case became a literal one, a cause for convivial celebration. The Mass itself continued to be performed as late as 1553.[77]

The documents thus show that the *Mass for St. Anthony of Padua* had been established during Du Fay's lifetime, even though the articles of foundation have not been located.[78] The same holds true for the Masses for St. Waudru and St. Guillaume, since the polyphonic manuscripts for those Masses were once in possession of the chapel of St. Stephen, and they are mentioned in the executors' accounts.[79] For the memorial after second Compline, the reunion of participants in the plenary *Mass for St. Anthony of Padua* afforded Du Fay the opportunity to specify a variety of performance modes, typical of Cambrai Cathedral. First came the antiphon *O proles Hyspanie*, sung by the men in counterpoint, in accordance with the codified rules governing such performance. Next came the versicle, chanted by the choirboys, with the response given by all, and the collect, spoken by the priests.

Lastly, the choirboys and master sang the motet *O lumen ecclesie*. The incipit is known from a Magnificat antiphon for St. Dominic, founder of the Dominican Order, but was also employed for other saints. The chant melody, however, was more familiar as *O quam suavis*, a Magnificat antiphon for Corpus Christi. Further, the antiphon text could be heard in reference to the brilliant preacher of the Franciscans:

O lumen ecclesie
Doctor veritatis,
Rosa patientie,
Ebur castitatis,

[75] D. Fallows, "Specific Information," 118–19. The will states that the adult singers are to receive a total of thirty *solidi*, but that each individually receives three *solidi*, four *denarii*. Since there were twelve *denarii* in one *solidus*, this works out to nine singers for the Mass.

[76] Planchart, "The Books," 187; Haggh, "Nonconformity," 393 n. 17.

[77] Planchart, "Du Fay's Last Works," 71.

[78] The calendar entry for the "missam de beato anthonio" in Lille, Archives départementales du Nord, MS 4G 2009, fol. 6r, promises complete details at the end of the book, which are lacking. See Planchart, "The Books," 177–78 n. 11.

[79] Lille, Archives départementales du Nord, MS 4G 2009, fol. 2r: St. Waudru, "habemus missam de ea fundatam per M. G. du fay in capella nostra // sub discantu sine revestitis et chorista"; St. Guillaume Confessor, "habemus missam de eo in capella nostra fundatam per M. G. du fay sub discantu sine revestitis et chorista ut supra." The executors' accounts, Lille, Archives départmentales du Nord, MS 4G 1313, p. 23, calls them "Item, iii haultes messes a discant a dire . . . le jour St. Anthoine de pade, St. guillaume, et Ste. Wautrud."

Aquam sapientie
Propinasti gratis;
Predicator gratie,
Nos junge beatis.
Alleluia.

Light of the Church,
Teacher of truth,
Rose of patience,
Ivory of chastity,
You passed on freely
The waters of wisdom.
Preacher of grace,
Unite us with the blessed.
Alleluia.[80]

Since all the other known musical items mentioned in Du Fay's will, aside from plainchant, are his own compositions, the likelihood remains that *O lumen ecclesie* represents a lost work. As in all the foundations at Bruges and Cambrai, without exception, no instruments were involved in performance of the motet.

Guillaume Du Fay's will provides for the ceremonies at his dying moments, a reflection of his characteristic attention to detail. He requests that "if time allows," eight men of the cathedral should sing the hymn *Magno salutis gaudio* "nearby, from my lectern," followed by the motet *Ave regina celorum*. The choice of hymn is interesting, in that *Magno salutis gaudio* was credited in the fifteenth century to St. Gregory, and was sung in the procession on Palm Sunday.[81] The men are instructed to perform *submissa voce*, a term that appears frequently in the late Middle Ages with the meaning "in a soft voice."[82] They were paid five *solidi* apiece, a considerable sum that suggests contrapuntal performance. If the hymn were composed, it must have been Du Fay's own work, now lost.[83]

---

[80]   Trans. by the Dominican Central Province at www.domcentral.org/life/olumen.htm (accessed April 12, 2011).

[81]   G. M. Dreves *et al.*, eds., *Analecta hymnica medii aevi*, 55 vols. (Leipzig: O. R. Reisland, 1886–1922), vol. LI, 73–74.

[82]   Planchart, "Choirboys in Cambrai," 135.

[83]   Du Fay continued to create hymns late in his career, since a lost setting of *O quam glorifica* by the composer was copied at Cambrai in 1464; see L. Curtis, "Simon Mellet, Scribe of Cambrai Cathedral," *Plainsong and Medieval Music* 8 (1999): 162. *Magno salutis gaudio* appears in the anonymous hymn cycle in Cambrai, Médiathèque municipale, fonds ancien, MS 17. This

The performance forces for the motet *Ave regina celorum III* are once again very specific: six choirboys, the succentor, and two of the adult singers present. Assuming that the master sang tenor, the other two men would have taken the contratenors, in clefs a fifth apart. The wide range of the discantus part, b–f″, is comparable to that of *O proles Hyspanie/O sidus Hyspanie*, as shown in Table 7.2. The singers and choirboys each received three *solidi*, four *denarii*, the same amount the boys were to receive to attend the exequies the following day.

If *Magno salutis gaudio* tells the story of Jesus of Nazareth and his entrance into Jerusalem, then the four-voice *Ave regina celorum III* salutes his mother as Queen of the Heavens. Du Fay planned the music to usher his soul through the dangerous phase of the *transito* ("transition"), when the soul left the body and was taken to Purgatory, where it would undergo a time of purification, according to church doctrine. If a person's mind were not focused on the holy, and if the dying soul were not contrite in the face of a lifetime of sins, then the possibility arose that the servants of the devil would snatch it to perdition. Du Fay wished to die a good death, as prescribed in the treatises of the *ars moriendi*: the hymn and motet were designed to ensure his concentration on sacred music and words, even at the last breath.[84]

Ave regina celorum III was probably copied at Cambrai in 1464–65, and is the composer's last motet, composed some twenty years after *Fulgens iubar*.[85] It represents a newer style, one that forges connections with the generation of Johannes Ockeghem and Antoine Busnoys. Du Fay divides the motet into two parts, in triple time (○) and duple time (C). As shown in Table 7.3, the tenor carries the *cantus firmus*, paraphrased and often extended. The overall procedures recall those of the anonymous *Vidi speciosam* in the Lucca Choirbook.[86] The discantus carries a personal trope on the antiphon, pleading mercy for Du Fay himself. It also incorporates the chant to a high degree. Of the eight melodic phrases, the discantus states phrases 1 and 4 in full, and the beginnings of phrases 3, 5, and 7. In addition, the first contratenor elaborates phrase 2. Each of these chant phrases is then taken up by the tenor, either varied, when stated in full in the discantus, or in imitation, when shortened. Because the first two phrases of the chant are musically identical, the beginning of the motet states the same melody four times in a row, each time expressed differently. The four phrases all cadence

---

setting for four, five, and six voices testifies to the presence of *Magno salutis gaudio* in the polyphonic tradition at Cambrai during the early sixteenth century.

[84] R. Nosow, "Song and the Art of Dying," *The Musical Quarterly* 82 (1998): 537–50.

[85] L. Curtis, "Simon Mellet," 162.

[86] Cumming, *The Motet in the Age of Du Fay*, 278.

Table 7.3. *Cantus firmus* phrases and counterpoint in Guillaume Du Fay, *Ave regina celorum III*

Measures	Superius	Contra 1	Tenor	Contra 2	Trope
1–10	no. 1	*			
11–16		no. 2		*	
17–20		free extension		*	
21–29	*	*	no. 1, imitation	*	1
30–40	*	*	no. 2, varied	*	1
41–44 /	*	*	free extension	*	1
45–47	no. 3, start	*			
47–53	*	*	no. 3, imitation	imitation	
54–64	no. 4	*		*	2
65–73	*	*	no. 4, varied	*	2
74–76 //	*	*	free extension	*	2
77–79	no. 5, start			*	
79–85	*		no. 5, imitation	*	
86–96	*	*		*	3
97–108 /	*	*	no. 6	*	3
109–12	no. 7, start			*	
112–15	*		no. 7, start, imitation	*	
115–18	*			*	
118–25	*	*			
126–33	*	*	no. 7, end	*	4
134–49/	*	*		*	4
150–54	*		no. 8, start	*	4
155–59	*	*	no. 8, end	*	4
159–70//	*	*	free extension	*	4

no. 1 = first phrase of the *cantus firmus*
* = free counterpoint; / = fermata; // = bar line

on C, including a free extension and fermata. The chant structure helps to account for an unusually strong emphasis on the C final at the beginning, which continues throughout the motet. To vary the tonal profile, Du Fay sets the two fermatas in the *secunda pars* to cadences on G and A. He also abruptly begins the first and third tropes with an e♭″ in the discantus, at the word *Miserere*, the second time in imitation with the contratenor, effectively transforming the mode in accordance with the text (Example 7.4).

In terms of texture, the first contratenor has the same clef as the tenor, but its range is two notes wider. The discantus lies a fifth above the tenor, with the second contratenor, a contratenor bassus, nearly an octave below it. Since the discantus and tenor carry the chant, they also serve as the lead melodic voices. Nevertheless, all four parts project a similar rhythmic

Example 7.4. Du Fay, *Ave regina celorum III*, first tenor entrance with trope

profile. Contrasts result largely from the introduction of duets and trios, particularly in the *secunda pars* (Table 7.3). Perhaps the most striking textural contrast occurs at the beginning of the *secunda pars*, in which the change of mensuration to duple time (C) coincides with a vastly simplified rhythmic structure. Not until the lengthy trio following the second fermata (measure 149) does the same degree of rhythmic and contrapuntal complexity return, only to be interrupted by a *tripla* section in fast triple time (**3**). At the return of duple time, all four voices resume with the same intensity as before, pushing to the final cadence. Throughout the motet, Du Fay exerts a breathtaking control of rhythmic pacing and the plasticity of individual melodic lines.

Du Fay died at his house in Cambrai on November 27, 1474, the First Sunday of Advent. Because of "the shortness of time," neither *Magno salutis gaudio* nor *Ave regina celorum III* was sung.[87] Instead, they were performed in the chapel of St. Stephen at the end of the polyphonic Requiem Mass

---

[87] Wright, "Dufay at Cambrai," 219; Lille, Archives départementales du Nord, MS 4G 1313, p. 19.

composed by Du Fay on the following day, Monday.[88] The hymn and motet were appended at the end, performed as specified in the will. The circumstances are of interest not only for the placement of the hymn and motet, but because the large congregation in attendance, given as "ninety-one clerics from the cathedral and 126 priests from without," was in a position to understand fully the implications of the motet and its personal tropes.[89] The ceremony thus ended with a plea to the Virgin Mary, the patron saint of Cambrai Cathedral, on behalf of its most renowned musician.

[88] Lille, Archives départementales du Nord, MS 4G 1313, p. 19: "les exequies faites pour ledit deffunct / . . . vigiles, commendisses, et le messe *de Requiem* en descant que ledit deffunct avoit faite / et en le fin dicette messe ledit hymne *Magno salutis gaudio* / et *Ave Regina celorum.*" Du Fay's polyphonic Requiem was sung again on Tuesday, November 29, 1474, the third day of Advent, as called for in the testament and noted in MS 4G 1313, p. 22: "que disent landemain les exequies en le capelle St. estienne le messe *de Requiem* que fist ledit deffunct en son vivant . . . anthiennes / *de profundis* et les colectes *Inclina* et *Fidelium* comme il avoit ordine per son testament." The testament did not mandate the polyphonic *Requiem* for the exequies, but the executors' accounts show that it was sung regardless.

[89] Wright, "Dufay at Cambrai," 219.

8 | Choir and community

Fifteenth-century motets were deeply embedded in their ritual situations, which affected their potential meanings. As motets developed within the multiple relations of a complex society, they in turn bestowed greater depth on the ceremonies in which they were performed. The heterogeneous verbal and musical content of the fifteenth-century motet developed in response to diverse, and potentially conflicting, social requirements. The clerical choir stood at the center of this process, invested with authority to address different actors, both earthly and divine, in a process of mediation. The choir, as representative of the church, applied its language, knowledge, and authority in ways that bestowed legitimacy in the exercise of power, and eloquence in the exercise of prayer. Motets, while dynamic in performance, represented a point of rest within the ceremony that allowed the formation of shared values. As artworks both intense and brief, they proved useful in a variety of ritual types.

Heterogeneity in the motet

The fifteenth-century motet displays a high degree of heterogeneity that appears in terms of both verbal and musical materials. This heterogeneity stems in part from the history of the genre. Already by the late thirteenth century in France, it had became common to combine two or even three simultaneous texts, of sacred or secular import, in the contrasting languages of Latin and French. The interaction – symbolic, aural, and poetic – of these texts has been the subject of considerable and continuing study. In *Li doz maus m'ocit/Trop ai lonc/Ma loiautés/In seculum* from the Montpellier Codex, the quadruplum represents a conventional encomium of the power and physical attributes of the beloved. The duplum, in opposition, asks for vengeance against the lady as it bewails her pitilessness and the pains of love. Meanwhile, the triplum addresses the Virgin Mary as if the saint were the object of courtly love. Underneath, the *In seculum* tenor, with its repeated, five-note rhythmic cell, quotes from the Easter Gradual *Hec dies quam fecit Dominus* ("This is the day the Lord hath made"). In *Li doz*

201

maus m'ocit/Trop ai lonc/Ma loiautés/In seculum, the layering of different texts redolent of spring and its theological symbolism, in combination with a Latin tenor, does not obviate the clash of disparate subjects and points of view, which clearly was relished by thirteenth-century composers.[1] The borrowing or superimposition of entire voices from one motet to the next, so characteristic of the thirteenth century, arises from a similar impulse.

The tradition of double-texted works was taken up by the *Ars nova* and continued throughout the fourteenth century. All but one of Guillaume de Machaut's first seventeen motets, the *locus classicus* of the genre, combine a French motetus and triplum. Machaut composed the French poems so as to articulate complex points of interaction with the Latin tenor, taken from chant. As Anne Walters Robertson explains, "these poems are transformed from solely lyrical pieces into narrative/didactic works under the influence of the tenors."[2] Machaut made an exception for *Fons tocius/O livoris feris/Fera pessima*, for allegorical purposes.[3] By the early fifteenth century, however, motets were sung almost exclusively in Latin. In double motets, both texts were often newly composed: each addresses a different topic or audience. It was also possible to combine a new text with a pre-existent one, or to combine two pre-existent texts, in which case their disparate origins and aural juxtaposition preserve the effect of verbal heterogeneity.

A particularly arresting example is John Dunstaple's *Veni Sancte Spiritus/Veni Sancte Spiritus et infunde/Veni Creator Spiritus/Mentes tuorum*. The triplum sets the sequence *Veni Sancte Spiritus*, known as the "Golden Sequence," for Mass on Pentecost Sunday. The contratenor sets the hymn *Veni Creator Spiritus*, sung at Terce on Pentecost in the Sarum rite. *Veni Creator Spiritus* was also sung at the coronation of English kings in Westminster Abbey, being intoned by the Archbishop of Canterbury at the moment when the sovereign kneelet before the high altar; in consequence, it had direct royal associations. The tenor presents the melody for the second and third verses of *Veni Creator Spiritus*, singing a text which the contratenor presents in full. Heterogeneity in this instance also arises from the image of diverse tongues that descended upon the apostles at Pentecost, to which the hymn refers.[4] In contrast, the motetus is newly composed; while *Veni Sancte Spiritus et infunde* begins with the same words as the triplum, its tone is penitential rather than celebratory. Where the contratenor sings of

[1] D. J. Rothenberg, "The Marian Symbolism of Spring, ca. 1200–ca. 1500: Two Case Studies," *Journal of the American Musicological Society* 59 (2006): 345–50.
[2] A. W. Robertson, *Guillaume de Machaut and Reims: Context and Meaning in His Musical Works* (Cambridge University Press, 2002), 178.
[3] Ibid., 137–51.   [4] Acts 2:1–12. I am grateful to James Haar for this suggestion.

"the living fountain," and the triplum sings of light, the motetus speaks of expurgation, of human weakness in need of grace poured out by the Holy Spirit. Its language appears out of keeping with the joyous tone of Pentecost, but befits the motet's station as a memorial for the English Chapel Royal (see Chapter 1). Dunstaple enfolds these diverse verbal meanings and associations within the careful mathematical and musical structure of the motet.

A more typical work is Johannes Ciconia's *Petrum Marcello Venetum/O Petre antistes inclite*, composed for the first entry of the Venetian Bishop of Padua, Pietro Marcello, in July 1409 (see Chapter 3). The two texts match in length, each with four quatrains in octosyllabic lines. Even though they are composed by the same hand, their simultaneous delivery prevents the adoption of a unitary poetic tone.[5] While the first discantus addresses the city of Padua, the Marcello family, and the cathedral choir, the second speaks directly to the new bishop, Pietro Marcello. Moreover, the two texts simultaneously speak with two contrasting tones of voice:

Exultet urbs Euganee	O pater amantissime
adventu tanti presulis	nos oves tuas dirige
exultet plausu jubilis	et aberrantes corrige
voces sonent etheree.	judex cunctis justissime.
Let the Euganean city rejoice	O most loving father,
at the arrival of such a leader.	direct us, thy sheep;
Let it rejoice with applause and	and set the erring straight,
shouts of joy;	
let the heavenly voices resound.	most righteous judge over all.[6]

The juxtaposition is deliberate, as Ciconia avoids opportunities to stagger the vocal delivery or to highlight individual words and phrases. Instead, the most significant places of clarity and unity occur at the beginning of the motet (see Example 3.2), with the overlapping phrases *Petrum Marcello* and *O Petre*, and at the end, where the second discantus continues alone with the composer's own name, *Cyconie*. Furthermore, the poems have been modeled on the Ciconia motet for Marcello's predecessor, *Albane misse celitus/Albane doctor maxime* (see Figure 3.1). While the bishop, Pietro

---

5 On text–music relations in this motet, see J. Alden, "Text/Music Design in Ciconia's Ceremonial Motets," in *Johannes Ciconia: Musicien de la transition*, ed. P. Vendrix (Turnhout: Brepols, 2003), 46–48, 57–64.

6 Trans. M. J. Connolly in *The Works of Johannes Ciconia*, ed. M. Bent and A. Hallmark, Polyphonic Music of the Fourteenth Century 24 (Monaco: L'Oiseau-Lyre, 1985), 224.

Marcello, may not have realized the intertextuality of the two works, performed at the same location in the installation ceremony, the choir would have understood it, as would Ciconia's patron, Francesco Zabarella, archpriest of the cathedral. The cultivation of such multiple perspectives was important to the ritual presentation of the motet.[7]

Verbal heterogeneity of a different kind appears in Du Fay's late *Ave regina celorum III*, dated to 1464–65. The discantus and contratenor interweave the antiphon text with four personal tropes on behalf of the composer himself.[8] While the antiphon and trope address the Virgin Mary in the second person, the trope refers to Du Fay in the third, beginning with the words "Miserere, tui labentis du Fay / Peccatorum *ne* ruat in ignem fervorum" ("Have pity on thy du Fay as he slippeth / Lest he fall into the fire where sinners burn").[9] The stark, supplicatory tone of the trope contrasts with the antiphon text sung simultaneously in the tenor, which carries the paraphrased *cantus firmus* (see Example 7.4). The antiphon begins "Ave regina celorum / Ave domina angelorum" ("Hail, Queen of the Heavens / Hail, O mistress of the angels"). The distance – symbolic, verbal, musical – between the antiphon and its trope leads to a kind of bifurcation played out within the structure of the motet.[10] These irreducible contrasts draw on the cosmology of Marian piety, in which nine layers of crystalline spheres separated man from the reign of the blessed angels.

Du Fay's *Ave regina celorum III* further provides a cogent instance of the musical heterogeneity that informs the fifteenth-century motet. As related in Chapter 7, the first two phrases of the plainsong antiphon *Ave regina celorum* present the same pitches to parallel words. In the motet, the discantus and contratenor ornament these two phrases, and then the tenor does so twice in succession, producing four different versions of the same melodic line (see Table 7.3). The motet invokes the ghost of the original plainchant, hovering behind the melodic surface, a chant that nevertheless represents a different musical dialect from Du Fay's intricate mensural polyphony. The process continues through the balance of the motet, as each new statement glosses

---

[7] E. W. Rothenbuhler, *Ritual Communication: From Everday Conversation to Mediated Ceremony* (Thousand Oaks: Sage, 2000), 18, comments that "symbols can work in different ways for different people simultaneously, depending on their sensitivity to different valences."

[8] The contratenor has only partial text for the antiphon, but its structure shows that it should sing the same text as the discantus throughout. See the edition in G. Dufay, *Opera omnia*, ed. H. Besseler, Corpus mensurabilis musicae 1, 6 vols. (Rome: American Institute of Musicology, 1951–66), vol. V, 124–30.

[9] Trans. L. Holford-Strevens in the notes to New London Chamber Choir, *The Brightest Heaven of Invention: Flemish Polyphony of the High Renaissance*, CD sound recording (Amon Ra Records, CD, SAR-52, 1992), 19–20.

[10] R. Nosow, "Song and the Art of Dying," *The Musical Quarterly* 82 (1998): 543–45.

the original antiphon. When the statements occur in the tenor, they recede into a complex web of three- or four-voice polyphony (see Example 7.4).

In Du Fay's *Nuper rosarum flores* (1436) the two tenors take up the same segment of chant, *Terribilis est locus iste* ("Awesome is this place"), the words that begin the Mass for the Dedication of a Church. Du Fay transmutes the pitches of the original plainsong into mensural notation at the level of longs and breves. His use of number symbolism in constructing the work leads to a saturation with the numbers 4, 7, and 28, a kind of language familiar in the late medieval period, but difficult to interpret now. The two tenors present discontinuous, interlocking rhythms, whereby the second tenor sings the same fourteen pitches, a fifth higher.[11] Each of the four *cantus firmus* statements takes on a different mensuration; in the original, the signs were arrayed vertically at the start.[12] Yet the tenors occupy only the second half of the four *taleae*, all of which begin with a duet of twenty-eight breves between the upper voices. The motet in effect balances two different types of discourse, one in a free-flowing melodic style, the other with a doubled version of *cantus firmus* technique. The tension between these two dialects helps build the dramatic power of the work.

In general, the motet in the first three-quarters of the fifteenth century is characterized by a musical heterogeneity in which the composer fuses two or more dialects within the same composition. As the two Du Fay motets demonstrate, the work may employ rhythmicized or paraphrased *cantus firmus* technique. Such internal contrasts arise with *any* use of *cantus firmus* in the motet, when contrapuntal melodic lines are woven against it. They are implicit in the genre from the earliest developments in the thirteenth century. Rather than considering the *cantus firmus* as foundational, as the term implies, we may view it as introducing an exogenous musical element, which the composer then transforms in the service of his polyphonic art.[13]

---

[11] It is plausible that Du Fay intended a symbolic reference to the Brunelleschi dome of the new cathedral, with its double shell construction, as set forth in V. S. Ramalingam, "*Nuper rosarum flores*, Brunelleschi's Dome, and the Iconography of Mary," unpublished paper delivered at the Annual Meeting of the Renaissance Society of America, Florence, Italy, March 23, 2000.

[12] In Modena, Biblioteca Estense universitaria, MS. α.X.1.11, fols. 67v–68v, the first three signs are so disposed, with the last sign after the page turn. In Trent, Castello del Buonconsiglio, MS 92, fols. 21v–23r, the scribe was copying from an exemplar with all four signs arranged vertically, but erased the bottom two signs in the first tenor and placed them before the statement on the second opening.

[13] E. H. Sparks, *Cantus Firmus in Mass and Motet, 1420–1520* (Berkeley and Los Angeles: University of California Press, 1963), 52–53, makes a similar point concerning the *cantus firmus* in an Agnus Dei by Binchois: "By putting the free tones all in one place he does not ornament the melody at all in the sense of florid variation. What he actually does is *transform* it, and he transforms it so that it becomes remarkably like one of his freely composed chanson melodies."

Nicolas Grenon's *Ave virtus virtutum/Prophetarum/Infelix propera*, a tenor motet in the French tradition, presents an extreme instance of musical heterogeneity. The work likely was composed for second Vespers on Christmas Day at Cambrai Cathedral (see Chapter 7). Grenon draws the *cantus firmus* from the last double versicle of the Christmas sequence *Letabundus exultet fidelis chorus*:

Infelix propera, crede vel vetera.
Cur damnaberis, gens misera?
Quem docet littera natum considera
Ipsum quem genuit puerpera.

Unhappy people, make haste, believe the ancients;
miserable nation, why should you be damned?
Consider this child of whom scripture tells us;
a maiden gave him birth.[14]

These verses are affixed to the tenor, two per statement, as seen in the unique manuscript source, Oxford, Bodleian Library, Canonici misc. 213 (fols. 120v–121r). As a consequence, the *cantus firmus* appears to have been texted throughout. Directly beneath the tenor, Grenon places a canon in Latin, directing the singers how to realize the *cantus firmus*. This in itself would be typical procedure for the period, except that the *cantus firmus* appears in its final state, in imperfect time, major prolation (C), rather than in its initial guise. The tenor sings the *cantus firmus* once in augmentation by a factor of eight, once by a factor of six, twice by a factor of two, and twice at the notated rhythm (see Figure 7.1). At duple augmentation, the notation moves to the level of *modus* and *tempus*, while at sextuple augmentation, the notation is read at the level of *maximodus* and *modus*, with the note values of the maxima and long. As J. Michael Allsen points out, however, to conceive the notation in octuple augmentation would indicate "a level above *maximodus*," which in itself is rare.[15] But there is no note value larger than the maxima in the mensural system. In effect, Grenon places the performance of the tenor into the realm of *musica speculativa*, with its scholastic underpinnings betokened by the elegant Latin of the canon. In this respect, the motet accords with the tradition of music-theoretical writings that hark back to the *Ars nova* of early fourteenth-century France.

---

[14] Trans. in J. E. Stevens, *Words and Music in the Middle Ages: Song, Narrative, Dance, and Drama, 1050–1350* (Cambridge University Press, 1986), 91–92.
[15] J. M. Allsen, "Style and Intertextualityin the Isorhythmic Motet, 1400–1440" (Ph.D. diss., University of Wisconsin-Madison, 1992), 511–12.

In rhythmic contrast to the tenor, the triplum – so named – and motetus share the same four mensurations. Each of these four sections divides into two halves, during which the rhythms are repeated, creating two *taleae* apiece.[16] Moreover, the paired *taleae* in the upper voices fit with statements 1, 2, 3–4, and 5–6 of the tenor melody (see Figure 7.1). In the last statement, the motetus and triplum are noted in augmentation (**2**), with breves and semibreves, requiring diminution by half to mesh with the semibreves and minims of the tenor and contratenor. Such procedures typify the more complex representatives of the tenor motet in early fifteenth-century France and Italy, taking the *Ars nova* techniques of *color* and *talea* to new levels of mathematical and notational control.

But this is not the whole story. The motet ends with a postlude, during which the tenor takes up a new melodic phrase. When one puts the entire tenor melody together, it becomes apparent that Grenon has created a literal quotation of the *cantus firmus* (Example 8.1). The sequence *Letabundus*, sung after the *Alleluia* in the first Mass on Christmas Day, was so well known in the late Middle Ages that it gained popular currency. Already by the thirteenth century, it had been translated into French.[17] Johannes de Grocheo, in his *De musica* of circa 1300, compares the performance of sequences like *Letabundus* to the *ductia*. He adds, "The *ductia* is a cantilena, light and swift in ascent and descent, which is sung in chorus by youths and girls."[18] When finally sung at tempo at the end of the motet, the *Letabundus* tune sounds very much like a French popular song, naïve in its effect. In this respect, the tenor approaches the ethos of Grenon's *Nova vobis gaudia* and its *Noël* refrain, also sung at Christmas in Cambrai Cathedral (see Chapter 7). In fact, the melody is very close to the *cantus firmus* of an anonymous three-voice *Letabundus* setting in Trent, Castello del Buonconsiglio, MS 92 (Example 8.2).[19] The long–short, trochaic patterns of the tune recall the Easter sequence *Surexit Christus* set by Johannes de Lymburgia. Far from twisting the notes into abstract rhythmic figures, Grenon observes the straightforward rhythms and phrase structure of the original, with a minim pickup at the beginning of each phrase and a minim rest at the end. The untexted postlude may duplicate the *Alleluia* or *Amen* melody that

---

[16] The contratenor shares the same mensuration as the upper voices in sections 1–3, then joins the tenor in the seventh and eighth *taleae*.

[17] P. Aubrey, *Le plus anciens monuments de la musique française*, Mélanges de musicologie critique 3 (Paris: Welter, 1905), plate VI.

[18] B. Gillingham, *The Polyphonic Sequences in Codex Wolfenbuettel 667*, Musicological Studies 35 (Henryville and Ottawa: Institute of Mediaeval Music, 1982), 16–17.

[19] Fols. 68v–69r. A setting of *Letabundus* by Du Fay, copied nearby in Trent 92, fols. 66v–67r, presents similar rhythms for the last double versicle. Du Fay's *cantus firmus* reads a step higher in pitch, F to G, which necessarily changes the mode.

Example 8.1. Grenon, *Ave virtus virtutum/Prophetarum/Infelix propera*, sixth *color* with postlude

frequently concludes the sequence in liturgical books. At the beginning of the motet, the extremely long notes of the *cantus firmus* remain abstract, but by the last four statements they come into sharper focus, dominating the texture. Even the upper voices seem to be affected. Whereas the beginning of the motet is heavily harmonic in effect, with declamatory text delivery and liberal passing dissonance, by the end the repeated notes of the triplum and motetus remind one of the patter song in Du Fay's setting of the folk tune *La belle se siet* (Example 8.1). The stark contrast between

Example 8.2. Anonymous, *Letabundus exultet fidelis chorus*, final tenor phrase

the folk-like *cantus firmus* and the complexity of the motet's organization takes on an almost revelatory dimension, reflective of the prophecies of incarnation expounded in the texts.

Johannes de Lymburgia's *Surexit Christus* represents the opposite pole from *Ave virtus virtutum/Prophetarum/Infelix propera*, despite the literal use of a *cantus firmus* (see Chapter 3). The first stanza quotes the entire sequence tune in the tenor, with counterpoint in the two discantus voices. Like the *Letabundus* melody, the sequence gained wide currency in cultures across Western Europe. The tenor rhythms undoubtedly stem from the performance practice of Vicenza Cathedral, complete with one- or two-semibreve rests in all voices at the end of each poetic line (see Example 3.3). In the second stanza, the tenor still predominates, but Lymburgia lends it an entirely new melody, almost as a free extension of the *cantus firmus* (see Figure 3.3). The monophonic *Alleluya* refrain follows with the first half of the original tenor melody. The surprising and unique refrain, heard four times altogether, serves as an aural reminder of the diverse musical dialects that coexist in the fifteenth-century motet. Moreover, the simplified rhythms and counterpoint in *Surexit Christus* recall the north Italian *lauda*, or song of praise. The *lauda*, in turn, draws from the tradition of Italian secular song, both written and unwritten, which is evident above all in the duo passages between the two upper voices. The admixture of two different styles in *Surexit Christus*, to the point of blurring generic boundaries, exemplifies the way in which the fifteenth-century motet communicated with its diverse audiences and heightened the symbolic density of the ritual moment.

Style transference

The manifold stylistic developments, or subgenres, of the motet during the fifteenth century may be explained in large part by reference to a process of style transference, which was enhanced by the increasing movement of musicians across geographic boundaries. Recent studies of the motet have mapped the extent and complexity of these stylistic changes.[20] The motet as a genre seems to have invited the incorporation or contrast of diverse musical dialects. Composers such as Du Fay, Grenon, and Lymburgia utilized the historical receptivity of the genre to verbal and musical heterogeneity to fashion their works for different and varied ceremonial circumstances. Conversely, the development of different motet styles in the fifteenth century stemmed as much from the variety of social environments that gave rise to complex polyphony as from the restless creativity of the composers.

A significant body of motets from the fifteenth century betrays the direct or indirect influence of secular song, whether Italian, French, or English. These works can be identified by the basic contrapuntal framework of discantus and tenor voices, with a contratenor that helps fill in the rhythms and harmonies. Scholars have called such works "song motets," "discantus-tenor motets," or simply "cantilenas." They are distinguished from sacred contrafacta – a common feature in manuscripts at mid-century – by through-composition, lacking the internal markers or repetitions of stanzaic song forms. One of the most widely disseminated song motets is Johannes Touront's *O gloriosa regina*, which appears in no fewer than fourteen sources from the second half of the century or later. Most of the manuscripts are song books, causing David Fallows to label this and six other Touront works as "Latin songs."[21] On the other hand, works such as the anonymous *O pulcherrima mulierum* in the Lucca Choirbook also appear at the beginning or end of song books, just as people of the time customarily began or ended a journey with a prayer.[22]

Johannes Touront probably came from Torhout in Flanders, to the south of Bruges; his style has been compared to that of Antoine Busnoys and Firminus Caron.[23] A papal document of July 3, 1460 describes him as a

[20] Allsen, "*Style and Intertextuality*"; J. E. Cumming, *The Motet in the Age of Du Fay* (Cambridge University Press, 1999); R. M. Nosow, "The Florid and Equal-Discantus Motet Styles of Fifteenth-Century Italy" (Ph.D. diss., University of North Carolina at Chapel Hill, 1992); T. Schmidt-Beste, *Textdeklamation in der Motette des 15. Jahrhunderts* (Turnhout: Brepols, 2003).

[21] D. Fallows, *A Catalogue of Polyphonic Songs, 1415–1480* (Oxford and New York: Oxford University Press, 1999), 589.

[22] B. J. Blackburn, "For Whom Do the Singers Sing?" *Early Music* 25 (1997): 595.

[23] P. Gancarczyk, "The Links between the Strahov Codex and Austria and the Imperial Court of Frederick III," *Muzyka* 49 (2004): 79–88; M. Staehelin, "Petrus Wilhelmi de Grudencz: Notes on the Coherence of His Biography, His Work, and Its Transmission," *Muzyka* 49 (2004): 16–17; C. A. Reynolds, *Papal Patronage and the Music of St. Peter's, 1380–1513* (Berkeley and Los Angeles: University of California Press, 1995), 278 n. 25.

singer and familiar in the chapel of Emperor Frederick III, granting him a benefice at the Church of Our Lady in Antwerp. His continued activity in central Europe in the 1460s and 1470s would help to account for the unstable text transmission of his motets, given the Bohemian and Austrian propensity for contrafact music in Latin. *O gloriosa regina* does present a stable text tradition, however. A strong framework of discantus and tenor garners the principal melodic and contrapuntal interest, with the low contratenor relegated to a subsidiary harmonic and rhythmic role. The motet begins with a long series of imitations between the main voices, first one starting and then another, in an almost playful manner. Like other mid-century works, it delivers the prose text in a leisurely fashion, one verbal phrase at a time. The mensuration, diminished imperfect time (₵), lends itself to uncomplicated rhythms and strong cadences. Just before the midpoint, the main voices branch out with freer ideas, staggered at the start of phrases, then at times joining together in parallel motion. The climax, at the words *Ave virgo pulcherrima* ("Hail, sweetest of virgins"), brings the top voice up a seventh from d′ to c″, then leaps to high f″ in mid-phrase, while the tenor climbs to the top of its range in support (see Example 8.3). The final phrase returns to imitation, varying the same music heard a quarter of the way through, a gesture to the chanson that does not precisely replicate any formal structures of secular song. These stylistic markers contribute to the effect of musical heterogeneity, of a work wavering between secular and sacred registers.

In Johannes Brassart's *O flos fragrans*, a single discantus part dominates the texture, giving voice to an elongated, polished melodic line in praise of the Virgin Mary. The text delivery owes a great deal to Italian secular song, with rapidly moving, untexted passages at the end of every verse or two (see Example 8.4), or with a melisma stretching out the penultimate syllable. Conversely, the beginnings of lines are syllabic or lightly melismatic, on occasion even declamatory. The three manuscript sources for the motet show a remarkable agreement in the text underlay for the discantus voice.[24] The tenor and contratenor work together as a pair, with a b♭ signature in a range one fifth below the discantus, creating a plain backdrop for the highly figured discantus melody.

A native of Liège, Brassart served in the papal chapel with Guillaume Du Fay from late 1430 to October 1431. While the melodic style recalls Italian

---

[24] Bologna, Museo internazionale e biblioteca della musica, MS Q15, no. 264, fols. 264v–265r; Oxford, Bodleian Library, Canonici misc. 213, fols. 7v–8r; Trent, Castello del Buonconsiglio, MS 87, fols. 143v–144r.

Example 8.3. Touront, *O gloriosa regina*, interior phrases with imitation

song, Brassart clearly models his motet on Du Fay's *Flos florum*. Both the
verbal and musical incipits call attention to the relationship between the
two motets (Example 8.5).[25] The openings share not only alliteration but a
common poetic imagery:

Flos florum,	O flos fragrans iam vernalis
fons ortorum	cuius ortus est regalis
regina polorum	virgo plena gratia
Flower of flowers,	O sweetly smelling flower, now vernal,
Fountain of gardens,	Whose garden is royal,
Queen of the skies.	Virgin full in grace.[26]

[25] Nosow, "Motet Styles," 216–21; P. Wright, "Johannes Brassart and Johannes de Sarto,"
Plainsong and Medieval Music 1 (1992): 47–49; Cumming, *The Motet in the Age of Du Fay*,
112–13.

[26] Nosow, "Motet Styles," 155, 220.

Example 8.4. Brassart, *O flos fragrans*, interior phrase

Example 8.5. (A) Du Fay, *Flos florum* and (B) Brassart, *O flos fragrans*, incipits

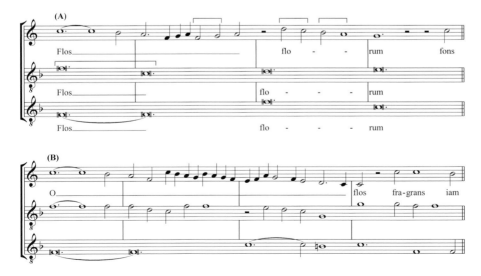

As does Du Fay in *Flos florum*, Brassart inserts a passage marked by *coronae* or fermatas, with the line *Pia virgo Maria* ("O kindly Virgin Mary") marking the end of a stanza. In *O flos fragrans* it occurs midway through rather than at the end, reserving the *conclusio* for a passage in imitation between discantus and tenor. That passage begins with the final text phrase, *paradisi gaudia* ("the delights of paradise"), then continues untexted. Up to this point, however, the tenor remains in the background, lacking any real melodic interest.

O flos fragrans forms part of a closely related group of eleven motets from the 1420s and 1430s in the style of *Flos florum*, all of which exploit the same swift, expansive melodic writing for the discantus voice.[27] The motets include Du Fay's *O beate Sebastiane* and *O proles Hyspanie/O sidus Hyspanie*, Arnold de Lantins' *O pulcherrima mulierum*, and three by Bertran Ferragut, a composer from Avignon active in northern Italy.[28] One of the motets, *O quam mirabilis* by Johannes de Sarto, is in turn modeled on *O flos fragrans*, to the point of incorporating similar melodic figures.[29] Another, the astonishingly florid *Salve cara Deo* by Ludovicus de Arimino, sets a verse letter by Francesco Petrarch in praise of Italy, and is one of the very few settings of Petrarch made in the fifteenth century. One can perceive the voice of Du Fay even while listening to the extravagant melodies and refined Latin hexameters of *Salve cara Deo*. The motet represents the only work in the group written by an Italian, a Franciscan friar active in his native Rimini.[30] The interdependency of these works further demonstrates

27 Nosow, "Motet Styles," chapter 6, "*Flos florum* and the Florid Motet Style," 216–58; Schmidt-Beste, *Textdeklamation*, 124–28. Cumming, *The Motet in the Age of Du Fay*, Chapter 5, "A New Hybrid Sub-Genre: The Cut-Circle Motet," 99–124, subsumes these works within a larger category, designated by the characteristic mensuration of diminished perfect time (𝇋).

28 R. Nosow, "Ferragut, Bertran," in *Die Musik in Geschichte und Gegenwart*, 2nd edn. (Kassel and New York: Bärenreiter, 1998–).

29 Wright, "Johannes Brassart and Johannes de Sarto," 41–61.

30 Nosow, "Motet Styles," 274–79; Schmidt-Beste, *Textdeklamation*, 131–32. Only three works of the composer survive, all in the fourteenth gathering of Trent 87, fols. 155–166, with a watermark dated to 1433–36. A document from the Augustinian monastery in Pesaro, dated September 21, 1435, recounts how a young Augustinian friar from Tolentino was sent to Rimini to learn singing and organ playing from Ludovico: "An. 1435, septemb. 21. – Arimini. – Missimus fri. Petro de Rechaneto, Priori conventus Pensauri, quod visa ratione satisfactum sit Ven. Bachalario fri. Ludovico, Ordinis Minorum, qui docuit et cantare et pulsare in organis frem. Iacob conventus nostri Tolentini, in duobus ducatis, de bonis suis, si que reperiantur, scilicet, fris. Iacob, et hoc in meritum obedientie precipientes etc." See "De conventu S. Augustini Pisaurensi notitiae," *Analecta Augustiniana* 17 (1940): 559–60. Besides placing the composer in Rimini, where Du Fay was active at the start of his career, the entry is informative in two respects. First, it represents a rare reference to the private teaching of music. Second, Ludovicus is described as possessing a baccalaureate, which would accord with his setting of Petrarch and status as a teacher.

the receptivity of the genre to different forms of heterogeneity, even in the fashioning of new stylistic paradigms.

English anthems were copied among the motets in numerous continental manuscripts of the fifteenth century, sometimes in well-defined sections or fascicles, but often without attribution. In part because so few insular manuscripts survive, and those that do are often fragmentary, much work remains to be done in understanding the chronology and outlines of their development.[31] But they must have been enormously influential. Julie E. Cumming finds that the earliest imitators of the anthem, the "continental cantilenas," by and large incorporate chant paraphrase in the discantus voice.[32] At the same time, English composers created anthems without *cantus firmus* paraphrase, which also were taken as models across Western Europe.

Forest's *Ascendit Christus* presents an interesting case of heterogeneity within the English anthem or cantilena itself. As discussed in Chapter 2, the contratenor sings only the first six notes of the plainchant antiphon. This extends into a luxurious duet between discantus and contratenor, thirty-two breves long; another duet of twenty-four breves begins the second half. When the tenor enters, however, it paraphrases the antiphon *Alma redemptoris mater*, even while singing the words of *Ascendit Christus*. The mismatch of words and chant paraphrase belies the euphonious effect of the music.[33] During the course of the work, the paraphrase becomes less literal, setting up a final duet of six breves' duration between the discantus and tenor. Forest's technique of placing the chant paraphrase in the tenor voice, rather than in the triplum, recurs in the anonymous *O sanctissime presul/O Christi pietas*, written for Bruges.[34] The procedure later paved the way for such mid-century tenor motets as the anonymous *Vidi speciosam* in the Lucca Choirbook.

---

[31] For a recent study of the anthem and its texts in the second half of the fifteenth century, see N. Bisson, "English Polyphony for the Virgin Mary: The Votive Antiphon, 1430–1500" (Ph.D. diss., Harvard University, 1998).

[32] Cumming, *The Motet in the Age of Du Fay*, 195–99.

[33] Seen from this perspective, Forest's *Alma redemptoris mater/Anima mea liquefacta es*, as transmitted in Modena, Biblioteca Estense universitaria, MS α.X.1.11, fols. 94v–95r, was intended to have double text, with the contratenor singing *Anima mea liquefacta es* against *Alma redemptoris mater* in the discantus and tenor, another instance of heterogeneity within the insular anthem genre. None of the voices carries a *cantus firmus*. The other three redactions of the work, all anonymous, have the text only for *Alma redemptoris mater*: Aosta, Biblioteca del Seminario Maggiore, Codice 15, fols. 196v–197r, no. 147; Bologna Q15, fol. 186v, no. 164 (discantus only); Trent 90, fols. 341v–342r.

[34] Cumming, *The Motet in the Age of Du Fay*, 216.

Motets in the fifteenth century were multi-dimensional artworks, saturated with verbal and musical symbolism. The prevalence of verbal and musical heterogeneity in the motet broadened its frames of reference, enabling it to function in diverse ceremonial circumstances. The delivery of two or even three texts simultaneously contributed to this expanded dimensionality, like a statue that can be viewed from several angles at the same time. *Cantus firmus* treatment, whether through strict treatment via *color*, *talea*, and verbal canon, or via the more supple technique of *cantus firmus* paraphrase, created different layers of musical and liturgical reference. The processes of style transference and hybridization, as in the song motet or through the widespread adoption of the techniques of the English anthem, had the effect of widening the angles of approach, further expanding the social reach of the motet during the period. At the same time, the presence of different musical and verbal dialects caused internal tensions within the motet itself, for that very multi-dimensionality added to its artistic vibrancy and its capacity to communicate ritual meaning.

Choir and community

The reception of a motet by the larger community was modulated by the structure of the ceremony in which the choir participated: sponsoring institutions, individual or corporate actors, their ritual movements in time and space. Even the physical placement of the ceremony within the urban or ecclesiastical landscape could shape auditory and social perceptions. As Thomas A. Boogaart remarks of the annual Holy Blood procession in Bruges, "Specific landmarks provided a stage for the recitation of individual segments of the ritual, while the landscape served as a permanent backdrop for the ritual performance as a whole."[35] The polyphonic choir, which belonged to a church or chapel, stood at the center of any motet performance. Its members included priests, clerics in minor orders, monks or friars, and, in certain institutions, choirboys. The church's position of sacred trust within the polity allowed the choir to address different audiences in turn. In its customary role, the choir sought divine aid and guidance on behalf of all present; such prayers, however brief, are incorporated in

---

[35] T. A. Boogaart II, "Our Saviour's Blood: Procession and Community in Late Medieval Bruges," in *Moving Subjects: Processional Performance in the Middle Ages and the Renaissance*, ed. K. Ashley and W. Hüsken (Amsterdam and Atlanta: Rodopi, 2001), 90. On the Holy Blood procession of May 3, see also A. Brown, *Civic Ceremony and Religion in Medieval Bruges c. 1300–1520* (Cambridge University Press, 2011), chapter 1, "The Holy Blood Procession."

the great majority of motets. Philip Weller observes that "The splendour and harmony of the well-made work provided a fitting reflection of divine orderliness and 'luminosity' (*claritas*)."[36] The motet, as voiced by the choir, addresses one or more distinct audiences, setting them in relation to one another and to the divine realm via mediation.[37] Although the quality of motet texts varies widely, in all cases the performance was heightened by virtue of the composer's and singers' skill. The audiences are acknowledged overtly and via the shape of the language itself.

The use of Latin in motets of the early fifteenth century underscores their message as ritual instruments. Latin represents the language of the university, the language of the judicial and notarial systems, the language of foreign embassy, and, above all, the language of the church. The wide variety of verse forms in the motet, both strophic and freely rhymed, as well as prose forms such as the antiphon, gave composers and their poets a great deal of flexibility in responding to the needs and exigencies of the particular ceremony.[38] The message and the rhetorical shape of the motet, whether with single text or double text, drew on the Latin culture of the church and, in some cases, of an emerging humanism.

The authority of the choir lies also in its separateness from the other ceremonial actors. In a sense, the choir has license to comment on events, speaking to different quarters of the community, just as the chorus in a Greek tragedy addresses its comments on events or characters directly to the audience. Andrew Kirkman and Philip Weller note, quite rightly, that authority for the ceremony is shared not just by the actors but by the institutions that sponsor the event.[39] The preceding chapters have shown the wide array of individuals and institutions that supported polyphony in the fifteenth century, whether laymen, canons, cathedrals, or religious confraternities. It is in the context of just such shared authority, however, that the choir can speak to different aspects of the community, to place them in relation to each other and in relation to divine power. Ritual thereby

[36]   P. Weller, "Rites of Passage: *Nove cantum melodie*, the Burgundian Court, and Binchois's Early Career," in *Binchois Studies*, ed. A. Kirkman and D. Slavin (Oxford and New York: Oxford University Press, 2000), 74.

[37]   Compare A. Kirkman and P. Weller, "Review: Binchois's Texts," *Music and Letters* 77 (1996): 590–91. The authors note that "In the context of religious observance and mediation any artifact necessarily had a two-way focus. While inhabiting the sublunary world where things were by nature unstable and transient, it was also directed towards the divine region where things were eternal and immutable."

[38]   Schmidte-Beste, *Textdeklamation*, offers an excellent study of the text forms and their delivery as they were employed in different kinds of motets.

[39]   Kirkman and Weller, "Binchois's Texts," 589–91.

functions in such a way as to mediate among these different interests and audiences, creating in the process a nexus of shared identities and values.

We have seen that motet texts tend to fall into two broad categories: pre-existent and newly composed. The first category created shared values by virtue of common knowledge and associations. These necessarily changed by location, but certain texts, such as the antiphon *Alma redemptoris mater*, were universally known. Others, including the sequence *Gaude virgo mater Christi*, set by Guillaume Du Fay and Heinrich Battre, were commonly found in Books of Hours.[40] The increased use of pre-existent texts toward mid-century drew on just such shared cultural values and associations. At the same time, even slight changes in the text, as in Lymburgia's *Veni dilecte my*, discussed below, had the potential to alter its reception. Further, the clothing of a known text in three- or four-voice polyphony radically alters its meaning: a prose antiphon becomes high poetry, or a rhymed sequence takes the listener on a symbolic procession. The motet could be used for purposes of divine contemplation, with the listener intent on the individual phrases and word-sounds voiced in harmony (see Chapter 6). Ritual itself had the potential to change the familiar associations of a known text, or to develop new, multi-dimensional meanings. Such transformations are inherent in the power of ritual.

Newly composed texts allow the creation of ritual embassy in the performance of the work (see Chapter 4). *Excelsa civitas Vincencia* by Bertran Ferragut belongs to the group of florid motets from the 1420s and 1430s connected to Du Fay's *Flos florum*. Its text is constructed in long lines disposed in four rhyming couplets (Figure 8.1).[41] Daniela Rando, noting the marriage trope that describes the union of city and bishop, concludes that it was composed for the first entry of Bishop Francesco Malipiero into Vicenza Cathedral in May 1433.[42] As such, it parallels Ciconia's *Albane misse celitus/Albane doctor maxime* and *Petrum Marcello Venetum/O Petre antistes inclite*, written for the city of Padua. Since Venice had taken control of

---

[40] R. Nosow, "Du Fay and the Cultures of Renaissance Florence," in *Hearing the Motet*, ed. D. Pesce (New York and Oxford: Oxford University Press, 1997), 104–21, contrasts Du Fay's *Gaude virgo mater Christi* and *Mirandas parit*, the latter with a newly composed text in dactylic hexameters.

[41] Schmidt-Beste, *Textdeklamation*, 124. Figure 8.1 draws on a translation summary by Benito Rivera, generously made available to the author.

[42] D. Rando, "Ceremonial Episcopal Entrances in Fifteenth-Century North-Central Italy: Images, Symbols, Allegories," in *Religious Ceremonials and Images: Power and Social Meaning (1400–1750)*, ed. J. P. Paiva (Coimbra: Palimage Editores, 2002), 41–42. Although the papal bull granting Malipiero's translation to Vicenza is dated May 11, 1433, the exact date of the entry is unknown.

Excelsa civitas Vincencia, gaude et letare
tanto sponsata sponso decorata decore,
quem virtutum sublimitas tibi destinavit,
Francescum Malimpetrum pro te adornavit
sciencia, dulcedine, concordia et pace vera.
Exultet celum laudibus aer ponthus et terra,
musicorum nobilium societas preclara
psallentes: Eya, eya, beata nobis gaudia.

Exalted city of Vicenza, rejoice and be glad;
you are fittingly honored, betrothed to such a groom:
Francesco Malipietro, whom loftiness of virtue
destined for you, and adorned for you
with knowledge, sweetness, concord, and true peace.
Let the heavens ring with praises, sky, sea, and earth,
as the illustrious company of renowned musicians
sings, "Huzzah! Huzzah! Blessed our happiness!"

Figure 8.1. Bertran Ferragut, *Excelsa civitas Vincencia*, text and translation

Vicenza in 1404, Malipiero, a Benedictine monk and doctor of canon laws, represented Venetian interests.[43] *Excelsa civitas Vincencia* fulfills the function of ritual embassy, but in undertaking this mission places the name of the city first.[44] The motet shows its communal orientation in that, like Du Fay's *Nuper rosarum flores*, it speaks directly to the people of the city, with praise of the ecclesiastical dignitary couched in the third person. The motet sets three spheres of power in relation to each other, as shown in Figure 8.2: the city, the Venetian bishop, and the church. In its sacral role, distinct from the daily commerce of the city, the choir fulfills the task of mediating between citizens and bishop and, though barely alluded to here, between Vicenza and its dominant neighbor, Venice: "concordia e pace vera." The conventional reference to the virtues of the bishop highlights the Venetian interest in moral conduct for officers within its dominions.[45] The word *destinavit* is also suggestive, since it can mean either "destined" or "appointed."

---

[43] G. Mantese, *Memorie storiche della chiesa vicentina*, 5 vols. (Vicenza: Istituto S. Gaetano, 1952), vol. III, part 2, 119–20.

[44] *Excelsa civitas Vincencia* was long cited as having been composed for the induction of Pietro Emiliani as bishop in 1409, since the original name was obliterated, then twice replaced. M. Bent, "A Contemporary Perception of Early Fifteenth-Century Style: Bologna Q15 as a Document of Scribal Editorial Initiative," *Musica Disciplina* 41 (1987): 187–88, shows that this date is untenable, that the original name was *franciscum maripitro*, and that the work was copied in 1433 or shortly thereafter.

[45] J. S. Grubb, *First-Born of Venice* (Baltimore: Johns Hopkins University Press, 1988), 128–30. Grubb cautions that bishops did not function as a direct branch of Venetian secular authority.

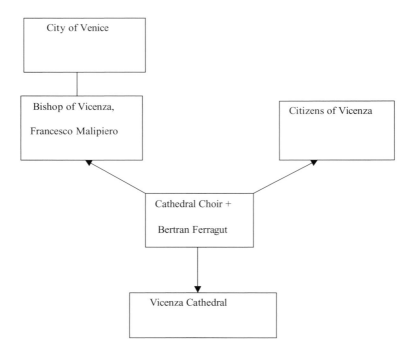

Figure 8.2. Spheres of interest in Bertran Ferragut, *Excelsa civitas Vincencia*

Finally, the motet turns to the "illustrious company of renowned musicians singing" as the voice of the church, reflexively invoking the power of music (Example 8.6). The verb *psallo* is found specifically in ecclesiastical use to denote singing of the psalms of David. Such repeated references to singers in fifteenth-century motets from the Veneto, reinforced by the records of Santa Maria dei Battuti in Treviso, once again point to the purely vocal nature of the genre. The *a cappella* performance of motets is confirmed by numerous, unambiguous foundations and charters from Bruges and Cambrai. Musical instruments, moreover, bore completely different cultural associations, which they would bring to the performance of any work, changing its ritual significance. Instruments were the province of social groups within the urban sphere quite separate from the polyphonic choir. With the exception of organs, they were normally prohibited from churches. In the present instance, Ferragut, an Augustinian friar, would have joined Vicenza Cathedral's own musicians for the rehearsal and performance of the motet.[46] Since *Excelsa civitas Vincencia* requires two contratenors, either

---

[46] Ferragut may have been summoned specifically on commission to write this one motet; so far as we know, he had no official connection to Vicenza itself. Despite a slender documentary trail, he appears to have been active in Ferrara in the early 1430s: see Nosow, "Ferragut, Bertran."

Example 8.6. Ferragut, *Excelsa civitas Vincencia*, conclusion

Ferragut or Johannes de Lymburgia, who were both *tenoriste*, could have sung tenor, with the three cathedral choirboys under Lymburgia's direction on discantus, for a minimal ensemble of six musicians.[47] Despite the absence of any direct prayers, the motet's language clearly reflects the vocabulary of ecclesiastical ceremony, as in the final acclamation "Eya, eya, beata nobis gaudia," set in *coronae* (Example 8.6).

John Dunstaple's most widely circulated anthem, *Quam pulcra es*, apparently served as a model for Johannes de Lymburgia's *Veni dilecte my*.[48] Both works are marked by brevity and a deceptive simplicity. The homorhythmic delivery of the text in *Quam pulcra es* finds a counterpart in Lymburgia's discantus and tenor (Examples 8.7 and 8.8). *Quam pulcra es* draws on the English tradition of near-homophonic settings written in score, which

---

[47] The final notes for the contratenor are c and g′, a twelfth apart. The discantus has a range of b – f″, within the boundaries for choirboys as shown in Table 7.2.

[48] Cumming, *The Motet in the Age of Du Fay*, 126, 394.

Example 8.6. (*cont.*)

in turn derive from the native practice of improvised counterpoint. Both works share a kind of quiet eloquence, with subtly varied rhythms distributed among the voices, that contributes to the flow of words. Lymburgia adjusts the placid, consonant sound of *Quam pulcra es* to his own melodic style and three-part counterpoint. *Veni dilecte my* was liked well enough to be copied in three manuscript collections, making it the most widely distributed of the composer's motets.[49]

Veni dilecte my belongs to a series of five motets by Johannes de Lymburgia taken from the Song of Songs, one with an antiphon text and four with

---

[49] Aosta, Biblioteca del Seminario Maggiore, Codice 15, fol. 206v, no. 148; Bologna Q15, No. 279, fols. 275v–276r; Trent 87, fol. 125v. In both Aosta and Trent 87, the motet is attributed to Du Fay. Very little of the music of Johannes de Lymburgia survives outside of Bologna Q15, marking him as a composer of local reputation.

Example 8.7. Dunstaple, *Quam pulcra es*, salutation

Biblical texts: *Surge propera amica mea* and *Tota pulcra es amica mea* in four voices, and *Descendi in ortum meum*, *Pulcra es amica mea*, and *Veni dilecte my* in three.[50] The antiphon setting, *Descendi in ortum meum*, employs chant

50 J. H. Etheridge, "The Works of Johannes de Lymburgia," 2 vols. (Ph.D. diss., Indiana University, 1972), vol. I, 198; J. de Lymburgia, *Four Motets: The Song of Songs*, ed. A. Lewis (Newton Abbot, Devon: Antico, 1985), 1. Cumming, *The Motet in the Age of Du Fay*, 145, lists all the

Example 8.8. Lymburgia, *Veni dilecte my*, salutation

paraphrase in the top voice, but the other motets are freely composed.[51] In the first four motets, the Bridegroom speaks to the beloved, indicating a

motets in Bologna Q15 based on the Song of Songs. See also S. Burstyn, "Early 15th-Century Polyphonic Settings of Song of Songs Antiphons," *Acta musicologica* 49 (1977): 200–77.
[51] Lymburgia, *Four Motets*, 1.

traditional Marian interpretation of the words. In *Veni dilecte my*, on the other hand, the Bride speaks, which raises the question of who is being addressed. Moreover, the brief text of *Veni dilecte my* has been altered from the Biblical reading, as italicized below:

Veni dilecte my, apprehendam te,
et inducam te in domum *patris* mei;
et in cubiculum genitricis mee,
ibi me docebis *precepta Domini.*

Come, my beloved, I will take hold of thee,
And bring thee into the house of *my Father,*
And into the bedchamber of my mother;
There you will teach me *the precepts of the Lord.*[52]

The Vulgate Bible gives *matris* for *patris*, while the phrase *precepta Domini* is lacking altogether in the Song of Songs, forcing a reconsideration of the motet. "The house of my Father" would likely be understood as a reference to the edifice of the church, where "the precepts of the Lord" are taught to the faithful.[53] The speaker of the poem would then be the church, often equated, like St. Mary, with the Bride of the Song of Songs. She addresses the Bridegroom, inviting him into her halls. The phrase "the bedchamber of my mother," however, points in a different direction. It evokes the *thalamum*, or bridal chamber, to symbolize the city, a traditional image in the late medieval entry ceremony.[54] In fact, the entire motet could be read as an allegory for the reception of the Bishop of Vicenza, Francesco Malipiero, in May 1433. In this interpretation, the citizens first meet the bishop and take the bridle of his horse. The second and third lines, with the word *cubiculum*, describe the procession through the holy city to the cathedral. The last line, "There you will teach me the precepts of the Lord," invokes the messianic attributes of the new pontiff.

Several descriptions of the first entry of the bishops of Vicenza survive from the fifteenth and sixteenth centuries. An eyewitness account of the reception of Cardinal Pietro Barbo as bishop on October 10, 1451 describes the participants, the bishop's vestments, and the route of the procession:

---

[52] Song of Songs 7:11 and 8:2.

[53] The phrase appears, for instance, in Deuteronomy 6:17: "Keep the precepts of the Lord thy God, and the testimonies and ceremonies which he hath commanded thee."

[54] G. Kipling, *Enter the King: Theatre, Liturgy, and Ritual in the Medieval Civic Triumph* (Oxford: Clarendon Press, 1998), 16–17, 237–64. Kipling, ibid., 237, writes that, "In the most common staging of this idea, the medieval civic triumph represents the city as the sovereign's beloved."

quando il Vescovo [fu] giunto a S. Giuliano vi vennero tutte le Fraglie con l'arti, e li suoi confaloni con tutta la Chieresia di Vicenza in processione. Il Vescovo se vestì d'un piovale di panno d'oro con una mitra in testa di prezzo di tre milla Ducati, si vestì a modo di Vescovo non come Cardinale, e montò a cavallo, e si fermò, e vide passar le Fraglie con tutta la Chieresia. Vide a passar il Duca con tutta la sua Famiglia, similmente il Conte con la sua Famiglia, ed il Marchese fece il Comun di Vicenza per il Vescovo, per dimostrar, che il Vescovato di Vicenza ha quei titoli, poi seguitò il Vescovo sotto il Baldachino, entrò per la Porta detta da Padova ... fece gettar via denari dall'Isola [degli Nodari] fino al Duomo, fece la strada sino al Castel vecchio, e gionto al Duomo il Baldacchino fu squarciato conforme al solito.

When the bishop [had] arrived at St. Giuliano, all the confraternities and guilds with their flags, and all the clergy of Vicenza, came there in procession. The bishop was dressed in a cope of cloth of gold, with a mitre on his head worth three thousand ducats; he was dressed in the manner of a bishop, not a cardinal. Mounted on a horse, he stopped and saw the confraternities and all the clergy pass by. He saw pass the duke with all his familiars, likewise the count with his familiars, and the marquis, all of whom the Commune of Vicenza created to demonstrate that the Bishop of Vicenza held those titles. Then the bishop followed under the baldachin. He entered through the Paduan gate ... and threw coins in the street from the House of Notaries to the cathedral; he followed the street toward the old Castle, and arriving at the *duomo*, the baldachin was ripped open in accordance with custom.[55]

The first major rite occurred outside the Paduan Gate, on the eastern side of Vicenza, when all the religious brotherhoods, trade guilds, and clergy passed before the mounted bishop (see Illustration 3.1). The palfrey and white bridle were furnished by the chronicler Mattio Bissaro, a right held by his family for generations. Given the brevity of *Veni dilecte my* and its incisive imagery, it was appropriate to be heard before the gates of Vicenza for the welcome to the learned bishop, Francesco Malipiero.[56] Like

---

55 A. di Santa Maria, *Biblioteca e storia di quei scrittori così della città come di territorio di Vicenza*, 6 vols. (Vicenza: Giovanni Battista Vendramini Mosca, 1772–82), vol. II, 104. On the entrance of Bishop Niccolò Ridolfi in 1543, see G. Milanesi, "Alcune lettere di Donato Giannotti novamente trovate nell'Archivio Centrale di Stato," *Giornali storico degli archivi toscani* 7 (1863): 158–61. On the entrance of Bishop Matteo Priuli in 1565, see S. Castellini, *Storia della città di Vicenza: Ove si vedono i fatti e le guerre de' Vicentini così esterne come civili, dall'origine di essa città sino all'anno 1630*, 14 vols. (Vicenza: Parise, 1821), vol. XIV, 95–98.

56 In the entry procession of 1565 for Matteo Priuli, when the bishop approached the Paduan gate: "montato a cavallo venne ad un altare eretto fuori della Porta, dove giunto smontò, ed inginocchiatosi, l'Archidiacono, ch'era Simon Porto, col piviale indosso gli lesse certi Sermoni, terminati i quali s'intuonarono alcuni Cantici" ("mounted on a horse, he came to an altar erected outside the gate, where he dismounted, and kneeling, the Archdeacon, who was Simon Porto, dressed in a pluvial, read to him certain speeches, which finished they struck up some songs"). See Castellini, *Storia della città di Vicenza*, vol. XIV, 97. The bishop's horse and mantle

Excelsa civitas Vincencia, the motet would have been performed by a small ensemble of musicians. Lymburgia's appropriation of the declamatory style of Dunstaple's *Quam pulcra es* served the allegorical purpose of the Biblical words. Ferragut's motet, addressed directly to the citizens and clergy of the town rather than to Francesco Malipiero himself, was more suited to singing at the *duomo,* perhaps within the choir of the cathedral (see Illustration 3.2). Moreover, the motets could be performed for the bishop each year, in commemoration of his installation to the episcopal see of Vicenza.

In all such ritual situations, the clerical choir had special authority to speak to all participants in a ceremony through the vehicle of the motet, to realize its multifaceted meanings and "interpretive potential."[57] But to what extent did the choir convey those meanings to the diverse participants in the ceremony? Certainly the townspeople of Florence, upon hearing Du Fay's *Nuper rosarum flores* for the first time in March 1436, would not have absorbed the full import of the Latin poetry; their understanding might be limited to such key words as *flores, Eugenius,* and *consecrare,* given their cognation to Italian (see Figure 4.5). Nor would the alliterative texts in Dunstaple's *Preco preheminencie/Precursor premittitur/Inter natos* be intelligible at first hearing, even to the educated ear. Instead, the most important factor would be that the language, and the music that carries it, should be both sonorous and decorous.[58] As Christopher Page observes, "Of all the musical genres known to the Middle Ages, it is the motet which most candidly acknowledges the importance of verbal sound over verbal sense by placing two or even three texts together, minimizing their intelligibility but maximizing their phonic contrast."[59] Such a disposition was appropriate for a culture in which oral learning and transmission predominated.

were still furnished by four brothers of the Bissaro family, of whom the eldest held the bridle, while the architectural monuments along the processional route were designed by Andrea Palladio.

[57] R. C. Wegman, "*Miserere supplicanti Dufay*: The Creation and Transmission of Guillaume Dufay's *Missa Ave regina celorum,*" *Journal of Musicology* 13 (1995): 52–53. Wegman remarks on "historical periods in which not the fixity of the texts but their interpretive potential was central, where interpretive authority resided in performance traditions not the composer, and where the distinctions between authorial and scribal revisions or recompositions were consequently irrelevant." See also Kirkman and Weller, "Binchois's Texts," 590–91.

[58] I wish to thank Paul F. Gehl for this observation.

[59] C. Page, *Discarding Images: Reflections on Music and Culture in Medieval France* (Oxford: Clarendon Press, 1993), 85–86. P. Weller, "Rites of Passage," 72, remarks that "despite the very real importance of the verbal text, which by its explicitness was intimately tied to the ritual purpose and significance of the occasion, there is no compelling reason to assume that the words of a polytextual motet for a ceremonial occasion should have been fully intelligible to the human sense of hearing. From a ritual perspective, it is enough that they should have been properly uttered."

Full understanding of a newly created text was available only to those who had access to the written note and word. Here we run up against the circumstance that motet texts of the fifteenth century very seldom appear in separate copies. Rather, it was the complete motet that was copied and read as an artistic whole. For instance, a motet was composed for the birth of Marie of Burgundy, daughter of Charles of Charolais and future Duchess of Burgundy, on February 14, 1456. Binchois had written just such a work, *Nove cantum melodie,* on the baptism of a son and heir to Philip the Good on January 18, 1431.[60] To mark the occasion, the Count of Charolais ordered a special copy of the motet (now lost) to be prepared:

Item pour avoir fait d'enluminure ung grand rolle de parchemin d'un motet qui fu fait à la nativité de mademoiselle de Bourgoigne, IIII escus d'or valent LXXII S.

Item, for having illuminated a great roll of parchment with a motet that was made upon the birth of the Mademoiselle of Burgundy, four *ecus* of gold, worth seventy-two *sous.*[61]

The pay entry confirms that presentation copies of motets were a feature of musical life at the time.[62] Moreover, the court ordered a presentation copy of a motet in honor of the Virgin Mary that same year:

Et pour ung leut fait en parchemin d'enluminure et de musique à ung motet de Nostre Dame, IIII l[ivres].

And for having illuminated a lute on parchment with the music of a motet of Our Lady, four *livres.*[63]

The entry immediately recalls the famous *La harpe de melodie* of Jacob Senleches in the theory manuscript Chicago, Newberry Library, 54.1 (fol. 10r), where the chanson takes the shape of a beautiful harp, while its strings become the lines of the musical staff. In the case of the motet for St. Mary, the lute does not appear to be integral to the conception of the work, but rather a way to present it in ornamental form. Moreover, at least

---

[60] D. Fallows, "Binchois, Gilles de Bins dit," in *The New Grove Dictionary of Music and Musicians,* 2nd edn. (London: Macmillan, 2000).

[61] L. Marquis de Laborde, *Les ducs de Bourgogne: Études sur les lettres, les arts et l'industrie pendant le XVe siècle et plus particulièrement dans les Pays-Bas et le duché de Bourgogne,* 2 parts (Paris: Plon Frères, 1849–52), part 2, vol. I, 467.

[62] According to Andrew Hughes, such a copy, on one large piece of parchment or paper, appears to have been the exemplar for Du Fay's five-voice *Ecclesie militantis/Sanctorum arbitiro/Bella canunt gentes/Gabriel/Ecce nomen Domini* in Trent 92; see J. E. Cumming, "Music for the Doge in Early Renaissance Venice," *Speculum* 67 (1992): 360 n. 109.

[63] Laborde, *Les ducs de Bourgogne,* part 2, vol. I, 467.

two presentation copies survive of motets from the late fifteenth century. Arnoldo Giliardi's *Sena vetus que diceris urbs O virginis alme* occupies a large parchment sheet inscribed with gold initials and the arms of the city of Siena.[64] Written in classical hexameters in the early 1480s, the motet praises Siena, its virtues, liberty, and women; it was long held in a Sienese family archive. As in *Excelsa civitas Vincencia*, the final words are sung in *coronae*. Another motet, *Celsa cumque*, preserved on an ornate parchment leaf dated 1494, decorated with the arms of Jost von Silenen, Bishop of Sion in Switzerland, confirms that the practice continued through the end of the century.[65] In the same manner, Walter Frye's *Ave regina celorum*, perhaps the most widely distributed motet of the fifteenth century, survives in three recognizable painted copies.[66] These instances of motets as graphic art demonstrate that they were available in written form outside the immediate bounds of the polyphonic choir. They were conceived and understood as complete works, not with text and music separated.

The transmission of motets in written form presents an ongoing paradox, in that study of the notated version allowed for a fuller appreciation of the content and subtleties of a work, which then were realized only in performance. The closer to the center of the performance, the greater the comprehension of the musico-textual matrix.[67] When Charles of Charolais visited Cambrai on October 23, 1460, a motet of his own composition "fu chantè en se pre*s*ence ap*re*s messe en le venerable ecclesie de Cambrai p*er* le maist*re* et les enfants" ("was sung in his presence after Mass in the venerable Cathedral of Cambrai by the master and boys").[68] The note states that Charles "fist ung mottet et tout le chant," meaning perhaps that he wrote both words and music.[69] In this instance, the count did not sing (he was reputed to have had a bad voice) but merely listened to the performance;

---

[64] Siena, Archivio di Stato, Frammenti musicali no. 155. On this motet, including a facsimile, see F. D'Accone, *The Civic Muse: Music and Musicians in Siena during the Middle Ages and the Renaissance* (University of Chicago Press, 1997), 243–46.

[65] Cumming, "Music for the Doge," 360. On the attribution of the motet to Bartholomäus Frank, see M. Staehelin, "Neues zu Bartholomäus Frank," in *Festschrift Arnold Geering zum 70. Geburtstag: Beiträge zur Zeit und zum Begriff des Humanismus vorwiegend aus dem Bereich der Musik*, ed. V. Ravizza (Berne and Stuttgart: Paul Haupt, 1972), 119–21.

[66] S. Kenney, *Walter Frye and the "contenance angloise"* (New Haven: Yale University Press, 1964), 78, 153–54.

[67] I am indebted to Andrew Kirkman for proposing this conceptual model.

[68] Cambrai, Médiathèque municipale, fonds ancien, MS B 28, fol. 74v.

[69] My thanks go to Sean Gallagher for this suggestion. Two three-voice songs are attributed to Charles: *Ma dame helas* and *Ma dame trop vous m'esprenés*. See R. Nosow, "Karl der Kühne," in *Die Musik in Geschichte und Gegenwart*, 2nd edn. (Kassel and New York: Bärenreiter, 1998–).

the courtiers in his immediate circle would no doubt have seen the piece in advance.

The initial performance of Du Fay's *Fulgens iubar/Puerpera pura parens/Virgo post partum* in 1445 or 1446 represents a singular event in the history of Cambrai Cathedral. Only the singers in the cathedral nave would see the acrostic "PETRUS DE CASTELLO CANTA" in the motetus, inaudible to the townspeople (see Chapter 7). The texts they rehearse and sing, with the assistance of the composer, are clearly laid out on the page of the choirbook or fascicle before them. Other clergy of the cathedral – Johannes Martini, Gilles Carlier, Nicolas Grenon, or Gilles Flannel – would know in advance the motetus and triplum texts that are performed in simultaneity. They are privy to the "inside joke" contained in the acrostic, for Pierre du Castel does indeed sing. Further, they may recognize the elegant mathematical structure of the work and appreciate its splendid harmonies.[70] The assembled clergy of the cathedral and city would recognize the tenor melody, sung twice at Matins that morning. Moreover, the last words of the tenor, *Quem genuit adoravit* ("She worshipped the one she bore"), are inscribed on the silver reliquary of the Purification carried in procession through the cathedral. Because the motetus rhythms are slower than those of the triplum, they occupy a different place within the overall sound, allowing these longer articulations to be picked out within the choral texture. A distinction in the speed of declamation between motetus and triplum allows the listener to concentrate on and apprehend one or the other voice. The contrast between boys' and men's voices contributes to this distinction. Thus, the twelve peers of Cambrai in the procession may at least come to recognize the double refrains at the end of the four stanzas in the triplum and motetus. The remainder of the townspeople, however, would understand little of the complexities of the work, concentrating their attention on the word-sounds evoked in continuous, heightened contrast. Their comprehension, instead, is enhanced primarily by the images painted on the two reliquaries at the head of the procession.

The Vespers hymns and motets instituted by the canons of Cambrai Cathedral were sung exclusively in the choir (see Appendix C). As a consequence, the musicians sang primarily for themselves and the other clergy in attendance, according to the foundation. The motets often addressed an image of the saint or saints, which figured their virtues and divine, intercessory power (see Illustrations 6.1 and 6.2). The mathematical bases of

---

[70] R. Nosow, "Le proporzioni temporali in due messe di Dufay: *Se la face ay pale* e *Ecce ancilla Domini*," *Rivista italiana di musicologia* 28 (1993): 58–60.

harmony further served to connect the human with the divine, whereby the perfect ratios of the fifth, octave, and twelfth resonate with the cosmos. Such motets could be used by the singers to enter into a contemplative state (see Chapter 6). As Bonnie J. Blackburn explains, "To sing these prayers with devotion requires attention not just to the music and the declamation of the text, but entry into the most heightened state of belief, contemplating unfathomable divine mystery."[71] The foundations were thus created by the canons and priests for the benefit of the cathedral as a whole, a closed social system that discouraged outside influences. The hermeticism of cathedral life accounts for the relative uniformity of the Vespers foundations over time.

By contrast, foundations for polyphony in Bruges were open to the citizenry at large, taking on a bewildering variety of forms (see Chapter 5). The three estates – clergy, aristocracy, and commoners – all contributed their support. Reinhard Strohm notes that "It is characteristic of Bruges that the instrumental music and the polyphonic singing at church festivals were rooted in popular faith, and also supported by the munificence of rich citizens and merchants."[72] This openness had two related effects: first, it encouraged dialectical contrasts, and second, it led to greater accessibility for the finished work. The anonymous motet *O sanctissime presul/O Christi pietas* illustrates both attributes. The discantus and contratenor set the responsory text *O sanctissime presul Christi Donatiane* for the feast of St. Donatian, October 14. Meanwhile, the tenor borrows the first section of the Magnificat antiphon *O Christi pietas*, for Vespers of the same feast, creating a musical contrast with the freely composed voices.[73] The tenor lacks text so that the verbal contrasts remain unvoiced.[74] The motet lies in three sections, with the central portion a duet for discantus and contratenor in imperfect time (C), and the outer portions in perfect time (O). The *salutatio*, "O sanctissime presul Christi Donatiane," appears as a duet between discantus and contratenor in the English manner, but slightly less polished than its insular counterparts (Example 8.9). Although the tenor closely follows the chant, it becomes elongated at the three major cadences. Since the responsory *O sanctissime presul* appears in a Bruges processional book copied in 1600, it is very possible that the chant was sung in civic processions on the feast

---

[71] Blackburn, "For Whom Do the Singers Sing?," 603.

[72] R. Strohm, *Music in Late Medieval Bruges*, 2nd edn. (Oxford: Clarendon Press, 1990), 16.

[73] Ibid., 118–20, with an edition at 185–89.

[74] The antiphon phrase is "O Christi pietas omni prosequenda laude." The tenor retains only the antiphon incipit, but could in practice have been sung with complete text.

Example 8.9. Anonymous, *O sanctissime presul/O Christi pietas*, salutation

day of the city's patron saint.[75] The central section of the motet solicits aid "Ab hostili animarum et corporum impugnatione" ("From the assaults of enemies on body and soul"). In this light, it is particularly interesting to hear the strong English influence on the structure, vocal ranges, and decorative melodic style.[76] The euphonious counterpoint would have appealed to the Flemish townspeople, as also to the many English and Italian merchants resident in the city, who would have recognized the distinctive English style. The motet thus served to broaden the approaches to learned counterpoint for the benefit of a diverse audience in one of Europe's most cosmopolitan cities.

Ritual types

The case studies of motets from the years 1400–75 cover four areas of their most intense cultivation in Western Europe: England, the Veneto, Bruges,

[75] Bruges, Bibliotheek Grootseminarie, MS 75-37, fols. 13r–14r.
[76] Strohm, *Late Medieval Bruges*, 118–20.

Table 8.1. Works associated with ritual types, 1400–75

Ritual type	City	Motet or anthem
Civic processions	Florence	Du Fay, *Nuper rosarum flores*
	London	*Ave rex Anglorum/Flos mundi/Miles Christi* (lost)
	Padua	Ciconia, *Albane misse celitus/Albane doctor maxime*
	Padua	Ciconia, *Petrum Marcello Venetum/O Petre antistes inclite*
	Treviso	Rosso, *Missus est Gabriel Angelus*
	Vicenza	Ferragut, *Excelsa civitas Vincencia*
Ecclesiastical processions	Cambrai	Du Fay, *Fulgens iubar/Puerpera pura parens/Virgo post partum*
	Unknown	Dunstaple, *Beata Dei genetrix* (anthem)
	Unknown	Dunstaple, *O crux gloriosa/O crux splendidior* (anthem)
	Vicenza	Lymburgia, *Surexit Christus*
	Westminster	Cooke, *Alma proles/Christi miles/Ab inimicis nostris*
Mass-motet cycles	Bruges?	*Salve mundi gloria*
	Orléans?	Le Rouge, *Stella celi/So ys emprentid*
	Unknown	*O pater eterne/O rosa bella*
	Unknown	*Gaude Maria Virgo/Esclave puist-il*
Memorials	Cambrai	Du Fay, *O proles Hispanie/O sidus Hispanie*
	Cambrai	Du Fay, *Si queris miracula* (responsory)
	Cambrai	*O lumen ecclesie* (lost)
	Westminster	Dunstaple, *Preco preheminencie/Precursor premittitur/Inter natos*
	Westminster	Dunstaple, *Veni Sancte Spiritus/Veni Sancte Spiritus et infunde/ Veni Creator Spiritus/Mentes tuorum*
	Westminster	Forest, *Ascendit Christus* (anthem)
Vespers	Cambrai	Du Fay, *O beate Sebastiane*
	Cambrai	Grenon, *Nova vobis gaudia*
	Cambrai	Grenon, *Ave virtus virtutum/Prophetarum/Infelix propera*

and Cambrai. In every instance, the motet was performed as part of a ceremony, making possible an interplay of documentary evidence – whether chronicles, account books, liturgical books, charters, or church calendars – with interpretive readings of the individual work. Yet a limited number of ritual categories characterize the motet in the fifteenth century. Motets were sung in civic and ecclesiastical processions, at the end of Mass, in memorials, or in place of the *Benedicamus Domino* at Matins and Vespers. Civic processions traversed the urban landscape, while ecclesiastical processions remained within the confines of a single church. Specific works that reasonably fall into these categories are summarized in Table 8.1. In addition, motets were heard within the Flemish *lof*, a distinctive institution that grew in importance after 1450, known elsewhere as the *Salve* service. All of these ritual types continued into the late fifteenth century and beyond, even as the motet and anthem changed markedly in structure and style.

The specificity of use for the fifteenth-century motet meant that each was fashioned and voiced with particular ends in mind, to meet the exigencies of the moment. Concrete details of Cooke's *Alma proles/Christi miles/Ab inimicis nostris* – the unusual choice of *cantus firmus*, the numerical construction of texts and music, the poems that invoke divine favor on behalf of the sovereign – all are calibrated to the requirements of a particular ceremony, the daily procession before Mass in the Chapel Royal of Henry V. Indeed, the importance of processional motets and anthems has been little recognized heretofore. Processions count among the most dynamic and pervasive ritual forms of the late Middle Ages, to which motets contributed a distinctive voice. Johannes de Lymburgia's *Surexit Christus*, for the Easter week procession at Vicenza Cathedral, integrates a partial *cantus firmus* with the attributes of the Italian *lauda* (see Example 3.3). Two- and three-voice polyphony decorated the station at the baptismal font, in alternation with a monophonic *Alleluya* refrain. The composer fitted this hybrid style to the traditional Vespers procession through the cathedral.

The foundation of Philip the Good at the Church of Our Lady in Bruges serves as a reminder that polyphonic Mass cycles could also be created with specific conditions in mind, conditions that are fulfilled by the *Missa "Spiritus almus"* of Petrus de Domarto (see Chapter 5). The phrase "cum moteto post missam" in the church *planarius* indicates that a motet either took the place of the *Deo gratias* or directly followed it. Mass-motet cycles flourished chiefly in the years around 1450, just at the time when the cyclic Mass began to take hold across Western Europe. In three of the Mass-motet cycles listed in Table 8.1, the motet presents the same *cantus firmus* as the movements of the Mass Ordinary. That the motet need not carry a *cantus firmus*, however, is suggested by the *Missa "Spiritus almus"* and anonymous motet *Salve mundi gloria*.[77]

Memorials or suffrages were short, self-enclosed liturgical items situated in time and space at the instigation of the founder, to whom spiritual benefits also accrued.[78] Memorial motets could be sung in the choir, in side chapels, or in the nave. Movement away from the enclosed space of the choir made

[77] Reinhard Strohm, *The Rise of European Music, 1380–1500* (Cambridge University Press, 1993), 428–29, similarly notes the link of the *Missa "Sine nomine"* and motet *Flos de spina* by Johannes Puyllois, despite the lack of a shared *cantus firmus*.

[78] A. Kirkman, *The Cultural Life of the Early Polyphonic Mass: Medieval Context to Modern Revival* (Cambridge University Press, 2010), 40, explains that "spiritual advantages accrued not only to the endower of devotions but also to those performing and participating in them. This collective emphasis served actively to reinforce the social bond that linked endowed devotions with the giving of alms."

polyphony more accessible to the laity. Memorial motets at times were sung within processions, as in the foundation for the Drie Santinnen at the Church of Our Lady in Bruges. The Jacob Baderan foundation placed a memorial at the Marian altar in the nave each Sunday morning in Lent, when the people were likely to gather at the Church of St. Donatian. Motets with a single, pre-existent text addressed to the Virgin Mary or other saints were apt for ecclesiastical feasts. Such works inevitably contrasted in function with the versicle and collect that preceded or followed. They offered praise or pled for intercession, and could lead men and women on the steps to divine contemplation.

The variability of memorial motets distinguishes them from motets that replaced the *Benedicamus Domino* at the conclusion of Vespers in Tournai, Bruges, and Cambrai. Nicolas Grenon's *Nova vobis gaudia* and *Ave virtus virtutum/Prophetarum/Infelix propera* constitute a complementary pair for first and second Vespers at Cambrai Cathedral. The divergent attributes of these two motets – single versus triple texting, simple versus complex structure, three voices against four – accord with the changes in festive atmosphere from Christmas Eve to Christmas Day. *Ave virtus virtutum/Prophetarum/Infelix propera*, with its explication of the prophecies of the coming of Christ, functions almost as a learned sermon for the canons, chaplains, and choirboys of the cathedral community.

In a fundamental sense, the interest of a motet, created in collaboration between the composer and ecclesiastical choir, resides in the way the polyphonic voices respond to each other within the limits of refined counterpoint. The control of time via mensural notation is a feature as fundamental to the work as the harmonic interaction of individual voices. As Laurenz Lütteken notes, the ceremonial moment retards time, bringing different interests to a focus within the work and performance itself.[79] As time slows down, ritual meanings resonate in the matrix of singing voices. As a result, the shape of the Latin texts and musical language anticipated and responded to the ceremonial situation in a dialectical fashion. The verbal and musical heterogeneity characteristic of the fifteenth-century motet furthered the relationship between choir and community in multiple ways, amplifying the symbolic content of the work. Heterogeneity allowed the composer and

---

[79] L. Lütteken, *Guillaume Dufay und die isorhythmische Motette: Gattungstradition und Werkcharakter an der Schwelle zur Neuzeit*, Schriften zur Musikwissenschaft aus Münster 4 (Hamburg and Eisenach: K. D. Wagner, 1993), 331: "Die Motetten sind gleichsam ein retardierendes Moment: Im Augenblick ihrer 'Aufführung' kommt die feierliche Handlung zu einem Stillstand."

choir to fashion the multiple perspectives necessary to that moment of controlled time, suspended between heaven and earth. The singers deliberately cultivated a diversity of tone and topic, their voices reaching outward to the ceremonial participants. The motet thus served to bring the listeners into the circle of the ceremony and offer, as Giannozzo Manetti writes, the succor of "angelic and divine songs."

Appendix A | Accounts of Santa Maria dei Battuti

Treviso, Archivio di stato, Ospedale di Santa Maria dei Battuti

1443: Busta 2, fol. 435v

30 Marzo dito *contadi* a p*re* iacomo da ma*n*toa p*re*b*en*da in domo insegno ai garzonj i canti del agnol e dela maria in luogo del m*agister* scolar*um* duc*ati* 3 a *peso* 114 ut s*up*ra l*i*re xvij s*oldi* ij

dito dj [30 Marzo] contadi a Menogny merzer p*er* para 16 guanti di Camoza fornidi di seda un[o] p*er* m*esser* lo veschovo . m*esser* lo podestà . 4 gastaldi .1. qua*ttor*vice / 1. Sindico .2. chavalcanti / l'agnol e la maria / el thesauriere i*n* domo el Magister Scholarum e l'archidiachono paro .1. p*er* cadaun / et a m*esser* p*re* piero rosso fé el canto se ca*n*ta in + di via / missus est ang*elus* gabriel etc. paro .1. a lira 2 soldi 10 el paro / E p*er* dozene .2. di guanti p*er* l'angoleti . . . .. l*i*re xlviiij s*oldi*

dito di [5 Aprile] a i trombeti sonò ala dita festa sego*n*do uxa*n*za *contadi* a s*er* Zanus uno di deti trombeti i*n* s*er* martin dito l*i*re ij

28 Zugno fo p*er* una dozena di guanti de capreto dopli s*e*chuti dati a Cantadorj e officiadorj i*n* domo / ala dita festa . . . .. l*i*re x s*oldi* vj

30 zugno 1445 . . . e p*er* malvaxio e brazedelli lui comprò p*er* la colatio*ne* a i sagrestanj et officiadorj l*i*re 1 s*oldi* 4//come disse s*er* marti*n* da comuda fo sindico

1444: Busta 2, fol. 517v

14 April p*er* malvaxii fate 4 p*er* far colatio*ne* a ma*n*sion*ari* ca*n*tadori e puti . . . .. s*oldi* xviiij

dito di [14 April] *com*eza guanti p*er* cantadorj e mansionarj . . . da Ja*copo* dal gallo . . . .. s*oldi* xviij

6 dito [Mazo] – *contadi* a ser Zanusso et .1. *compagno* trombeti / sonò ala dita festa . . . .. l*i*re ij

ditto di [27 Zugno] p*er* menogni merzaro p*er* para 17 guanti di camoza fornidi di seda / par .1. p*er* m*esser* lo podestà / para 4 / p*er* 4 gastaldi / par .1. p*er* il quatt*or*vice / par .1. p*er* il sindico / para 2 p*er* 2 cavalcanti / par al thesauriere par .1. al m*agister* scolar*um* / par .1. a m*esser* prè piero rosso fexe el ca*n*to .missus est gabriel ecc. / par .1. al Archidiacono

237

para 2 per l'agnol e la maria / par .1. a ser Altimer chavalcante vechio / e par .1. a messer prè Nicolò baberin conzolò l'agnol e la maria / fo di conto di signor[i] gastaldi / a soldi 55 per el paro . . . E per 4 dozene de guanti pizoli per l'Agnoleti a lire 4 soldi 10 . . . E per dozene 2 de guanti di capreto dople per li mansionarij e altri officialj . . . . . lire lxxvj soldi viij

27 Octobre 1444 / per messer pre parentin Magister scolarum in domo per haver insigna aj garzonj e zagi el Canto del angol e de la Maria per la dita festa ducati 3 oro a peso 114 per ducato . . . . . lira xvij soldi ij

1445: Busta 2, fol. 599v

4 dito [April] per malvaxia e brasedelli per i sagrestanj e quelli conzò le mane

dito di [13 April] per messer prè Parentin magister scolarum per haver insegnato a garzonj e zagi el canto del Agnol ed la maria l'ano pasante segondo uxanza ducati .3. oro a peso val 114 per ducato val . . . . . lire xvij soldi ij

21 dito [April] contadi a ser Zanusso trombeta per lui e per. 1. compagno per sonò ala [dita] festa . . . . . lira ij soldi

1447: Busta 3, fol. 168r

16 dito [Marzo] dato per una docena di guanti per dar a i mansionarj cantdorj et altrj officalj / comprandi da Messer Zuan merzer [et] per para 4 guanti comprandi dal dito per i zanchanarj e cavalj marianj lire viiij soldi iiij

22 dito [Marzo] per naranze 60 . . . per far par 19 di guanti / per le tutte persone videlicet / messer lo vescho[vo] / messer lo podestà / 4 gastaldi / un quattorvice / 1. sindico / 1 coaiutor / 2 cavalcanti / el thesaurier del domo / el magister scolarum / l'archidiacono / messer pre piero rosso fexe el canto missus est angelus gabriel / messer pre Nicolò Patavini el qual apparechia l'agnol e la maria / l'agnol e la maria / . . . . . lire xx soldi xviiij

24 dito [Marzo] per malvaxia e brazadeli fate per far colatione al'agnol [e] la maria cantadorj . . . . . lire 1 soldi vij

3 April contadi a piero macharon e compagni piffari e zaramelle et trombeta / per haver sona ala dita festa . . . . . [lira] iij

dito di [Mazo 15] per messer prè Parentin magister scolarum in domo per insegnar a i zagi e garzonj fo agnol e maria / et ali altri ando a imparar al domo canto fo agnol e la maria ala dita festa et ali altri garzonj andò a imparar al dom canto segondo uxanza / ducati 3 . . . . . lire xvij soldi ij

Appendix B | Foundations and charters in Bruges

Abbreviations: L. = libre; S. = solidi; d. = denarii

1. Bruges, Bisschoppelijk Archief, Reeks A 141, *Planarius*, fol. 104v

Foundations of Elizabeth Parols, wife of Robert de Capple, Church of St. Donatian (April 22, 1417)

Insuper ordinavit dicta damicella quod tempore officij completorij octavarum festi sacramenti singulis annis a primo ad finem major campana pulsetur. Et Completorio finito . . . eius alba et cappa preciosa indutus in medio chori incipiet hymnum Veni creator spi[ritus]. Quo finito, et versu, et collecta dictis cantor capellanus incipiet Antiphonam .O sacrum convivium. et facta processione infra ecclesiam, et collecta de sacramento in choro dicta cantabitur motetus. Pro qua ordinacione distribuentur .tres. L. parisienses. videlicet in choro equa porcione quadraginta .S. parisienses. Item curato .tres. S. Item duobus vicariis .ii. S. Item hostiario chori .xi. d. Item custodi sanctuarij .xii. d. Item pulsatoribus .viij. S. Item succentori ad congregandum et monendum cantores moteti .xij. d. Item pueris indutis et vestitis .xij. d. Item pueris torcheas tenentibus .xij. d. Item capellano cantoriam tenenti .xij. d. Item distributori .xij. d.

2. Bruges, Bisschoppelijk Archief, Reeks A 141, *Planarius*, fol. 96r–v

Diverse foundations of Jacob Baderan, canon, Church of St. Donatian (July 12, 1447)

Dominus Jacob Baderan presbyter, Canonicus huius ecclesie donavit officio obediencie . . . Primo quidem ordinavit, instituit et voluit idem dominus Jacobus quod singulis diebus quadragesime incipiendo die cinerum, videlicet Feria .iiii. in capite jeiunij usque ad feriam quartam post dominicam In Ramis palmarum inclusive finitis matutinis ad statim cantetur sollemniter et tractim Antiphona Alma redemptoris, cum versu Ave maria, vel Post partum, sive Ora pro nobis, et collecta Omnipotens sempiterne deus qui gloriose et cetera, Concludendo, Per eiusdem christianum. Et interessentibus dicte antiphone a principio usque ad finem voluit distribui in pitancia .decem. S.

parisienses quolibet die in quibus decem .S. lucrabuntur, dumtaxat illi qui
in matutinis .x. S. consueverunt lucrari et sine diminucione dictorum .x. S.
qui in huiusmodi matutinis distribui consueverunt. Item finitis matutinis et
prima missa qua dicitur Scellemesse unus sacerdotum de gremio chori per
ipsum dominum Jacobum quoad viverit et prius fuerit, et post eius obitum,
vel in eius absencia per tabularium communitatis, ad hoc ordinandum
accedet ad altare beate marie virginis situm in navi ecclesie, et ibi cele-
brabit qualibet die quadragesime usque ad feriam quartam post dominicam
palmarum inclusive unam missam legendo, Cui dictum officium solvet pro
qualibet missa quatuor .S. parisienses. Custodi vero pro suo labore qualibet
missa .ii. d. Et fabrice qui providebit de ornamentis, Luminari, Pane, Vino,
ad huiusmodi missam qualibet die quatuordecim denarios parisienses. Inde
dabit fabrica molieri pro pane et vino duos denarios parisienses monete
predicte. Singulis autem diebus dominicis quadragesime succentor cum
pueris suis cantabit ante dictum altare unum motetum de beata maria ante
inchoacionem dicte misse cum versu et collecta de eadem. Cui succentori
obediencia solvet qualibet vice tres solidos parisienses. Item officium obediencie predictum distribuet, vel distribui faciet per tabularium predictum
singulis diebus quadragesime incipiendo ipso die cinerum, et continuando
usque ad vigiliam pasche inclusive pauperibus captivis in camera obscura
brugis quinque solidos parisienses, Cui distributori obediencia solvet pro suo
labore viginti solidos parisienses. Que quidem onera ascendunt in universo ad
quadraginta sex. libras. septem solidos .iiij. d. parisienses monete predicte. Et
quod superfuerit de principali summa recepte remanebit obediencie contra
casus fortuitos salva moderacione supradicta si casus occurrat ...

Item idem dominus Jacobus singulari devotione erga sanctum bavonem
confessorem motus ... Et dicetur ad suffragium antiphona Confessorem
domini vel propria de ipso sancto[.] Ad matutinas xxx S. Et ad suffragium
de sancto bavone cum antiphona Justum longius vel propria x S. Et post
matutinas ad prosam Inviolata x S. Ad missam xxxiiij S. Ad sequentiam
propriam vel mundi etate octava, que habetur feria vj in penthecostalibus
x S. In secundis vesperis xx S. Et ad suffragium de sancto cum antiphona
Iste homo vel propria x S. Et cantoribus musicis ut cantent ad missam Et
in terra[.] Et si dominica fuerit Patrem solemniter Et motetum in secundis
vesperis x S. Duobus capellanis cantoriam tenentibus .ii. S. Canonico ebdo-
madario pro horis tenendis ij S. Clerico turris cum suis pro pulsu sub
duplici festo et tenebitur in profesto et in ipso die festo pulsare de sero
campaniam que dicitur bernaerd. et in fine bayardare sicut in festo sancti
leonardi xx S. Et fabrice pro luminari videlicet octo cereis ante feretra iiij[or] ad

magnum altare iiij^{or} horis et duobus magnis cereis accendendis sicut in festis duplicibus est consuetum xx S. Tabulario pro suo labore ij S. Quequidem onera ascendunt simul ad x. L. parisienses annuatim, pro quibus prefatus dominus Jacobus legavit obediencie predicte xii. L. grossorum et fructus anni sui post mortem, quos executores sui testamenti fecerunt valentes viij L. grossorum sunt simul xx L. grossorum hoc est xxiiij^{or} denario pro denario[.] Et hijs mediantibus dicta obediencia solvet annis singulis perpetuo onera predicta

3. Bruges, Bisschoppelijk Archief, Reeks A 141, *Planarius,* fol. 123r

Processional and other foundations of Pierre Basin, canon, Church of St. Donatian (1489)

In festo sancti martini fiet solemnis processio per communitatem chori sicut in festo philippi et jacobi cum antiphona de sancto martino in exitu processionis et postea magnificat cum antiphona et neuma ac collecta de sancto martino in capella de arbosio et distribuet dicta obedientia communitati chori ad dictam processionem equa portione xx S. parisienses. Item Canonico dicenti collectam tunc ibidem vj d. parisienses. Item socijs de musica decantantibus post collectam motetum et post motetum deo dicamus more solito vj S. parisienses. Item in reditu processionis in choro cantabitur alma redemptoris cum verso et collecta de beata vergine et si sint suffragia de sanctis illa decantabuntur more solito.

4. Bruges, Archief OCMW, Register 179, *Planarius,* fol. 52r

Foundation of Colaert and Pieter de la Bye, Church of Our Lady (1474)

Nicolaus et petrus de labye fratres et notabiles parrochiani dederunt communitati chori huius ecclesie pro processione portanda in ambitu chori ipso die magdalene finitis secundis vesperis exeundo cum Responsorio O beata maria magdalena et redeundo cum Ave regina In annuis et perpetuis redditibus xxviij S. parisiensis. Inde in huius communitatis communi choro .xx. S. parisiensis. Capellanis .xviij. d. parisiensis. pueris vj d. parisiensis. Cantori et coadiutori dictum Responsorium inchoanti cuilibet .vj. d. parisiensis. Dicenti collectam coram magdalena et suo consortio cuilibet .vj. d. parisiensis. Cantoribus musicis pro moteto cantando .iiij S. parisiensis.

5. Bruges, Stadsarchief, Charter blauw no. 8128

Charter of the guild of barber-surgeons, Church of St. James
(August 28, 1432)

op der vors*eid* maertelaers avond / die alle jare es den zesse en*de* twintichsten
dach van Septembre in Sint Jacobs kerke vors*eid* / daer die vande*n* vors*eid*
ambochte haerlied Capelle hebben staende / ant westhende vander zuudzide
vander vors*eid* kerke / Ende tsander daghes / ende de andre daghen / die hier
naer verclaerst staen / den dienst vande*n* vors*eid* helighe*n* maertelaers, inder
maniere*n* hier naer volghende / Eerst datmen alle Jare ewelike gheduerende
up den vors*eid* zesse en*de* twintichsten dach van Septembre luden zal noene
mette*n* groten lude der vors*eid* kerke also men oyt gheploghen heeft. / Item
datmen sacht[h]oens zal luden vesperen mette*n* grote*n* lude vors*eid* / ende
die zinghen inden choor naer costume der vors*eid* kerke metten ghemeene*n*
choore ende orghelen de hympne ende Magnificat mette*n* groter orghele
/ en*de* dat de choor binnen den eersten en*de* den andre*n* vesperen met
p*r*ocessien uten vors*eid* choore com*m*en zal te Magnificat also men binnen
der kerke vorseid ghecostumeerd es in die vorkerke / ende zal voort de
prieste*n* die de vespere*n* houden zal / com*m*en met eenre cappe ende met
wijroke / In svors*eid* ambochts capelle voor de beelden vanden vors*eid*
Sancten en*de* daer up den outaer lezen der vors*eid* Sancte*n* collecte / Ende
de kindre*n* up daer eenighe zijn daer zinghen een motet zo alst costume est. /
Item vander daghes zal men luden mattmen ende zinghen also men ghewone
es up zulke ghelike daghen / Ende voord luden en*de* zinghen inden choor
Prime Tierce Hoofdmesse orghelende Kyrie en*de* Sequentie al mette*n* vors*eid*
groter orghele middach noene vesperen ende Complie / ghelike oft ware up
een cleene principael/. Item men zal stellen op den vors*eid* avond / ende den
vors*eid* dach / der vors*eid* Sancten tsavens te vesperen / ende sander daghes
te hooghmesse ende te vesperen inden choor vors*eid* boven den hoghen
outaer / viere wassinne kersen / up den vors*eid* hooghe outaer drie wassinne
kersen up drie candelaers / ende up de keese dertiene wassinne kersen / Ende
up de grote candelaers twee groote wassinne scallichten also men ghewone
es maer ten tweeden vesperen up den dach / ne zal de vors*eid* Keese met
bernen om*m*e dat gheeve costume es / Ende men zal den vors*eid* choor
danne behanghen / als of het ware up een cleene principael. Item zal men
doen de zevene ghetiden vanden / daghen die hier naer volghen / Te wetene
den achtentwintichsten / den neghenentwintichsten / den dertichsten van
Septembre / den tweeden en*de* den derden van octobre / binne*n* den choore
der vors*eid* kerke / naer costumen van daer / ende also de ordenance van
des*er* tyd inhoudt.

6. Bruges, Rijksarchief, Onze-Lieve-Vrouw, 1501, *Cartularium en handboek*, fol. 37r–v

Charter of the *lof* of Our Lady of the Snow, Church of Our Lady
(September 1466)

Ten love heere waerdichede van gode van hemelrike. Ende van zijnder ghebenedider moeder ende maghet maria. Ter zalichede / troost / ende lavenesse van alle kerstmen zielen. Ende principalicke van onsen ghilde-broeders ende ghildezusters van deser weerelt verscheeden zijnde. ooc mede ter ghesticticheyt ende devocien van allen goeden ghetrauwen diennaers vander keynder maghet maria/. Omme bij unddel van haer ghenade te / vererighenne voor haren ghebenediden zone ihesum *christu*m. Zo was int Jaer ons heeren. M.CCCC.lxvj. gheordineirt / ende begonnen / up onser vrauwen dach in September. bij tween ghildebroeders vander voir*seid* ghilde. / Een lof. twelke men es singhende alle zondaghe ten. iiij. hueren naer vesperen. ten houtare vander voir*seid* ghilde / in der manieren hier naer up tcorte verclaerst.

Eerst datmen stappans naerden. iiij. hueren ghesleghen zijnde. men lude*n* sal een scoone clocke / gheduerende een half vierendeel van eender huere. Daer toe dat gheordinert ende over een ghedreghen was bijden clocluders / ende consente vanden kercmeesters dat zij hebben zouden over haerlieder arbeit alle Jare vander voir*seid* clocke te ludenne / de somme van. vj. S g.

Item de clocke ghehent zijnde / men sal beghinnen Een lof. met een ympne van onser vrauwe. metten orghele / ooc mede tsalve /.+ Ende int hende / al ghesonghen ziinde. Een liedekin spelen metter voir*seid* orghele.+ Daer voren dat gheordinert was voor den arbeyt vanden voir*seid* orghelare/. tsiaers de somme van. v. S g. Ende voor zijn diennare. xij [d.] g.

Item was al doe gheordineirt dat de cantre met zijnen kindren./ mets-gaders een tonneur/. ende een contre tvor*seid* lof. // te wetenne/. een ympne van on*ser* vrauwen. Salve regina / metten versekins daer toe diennende. / Te wetenne. Virgo mater ecclesie. etc. Ende naer tvor*seid* salve. Een / ave maria. in conterpointe met.iij. voysen vanden kindren / daer naer een motet sollempnelitke / singhen sullen. Ende naer tvor*seid* motet / de cantere met zinen voor*seid* kindren / lezen zal / een de profundis. over de ziele van allen ghildebroeders ende ghildesusters vander voir*seid* ghilde / waer of de voir*seid* canter hebben sal voor siin salaris alle Jare de somme van. x. S g. / de voir*seid* ton*n*eur ende contre van elcker reyse / elc eenen nieuwen grooten.

Appendix C | Foundations at Cambrai Cathedral

Abbreviations: L. = libre; S. = solidi; d. = denarii; tur. = turonenses (coinage of Tours)

1. Cambrai, Médiathèque municipale, fonds ancien, B 39, fol. 52r

Feast of St. Gregory, augmented by Grégoire Nicolai, canon

Festum sancti Gregorij augmentatum est per magistrum Gregorium Nicolai canonicum subdyaconum. de novem libris et quinque solidis accipiendis in triginta duabus libris per dictum Gregorium in emptione cense de Wastina de suis et certorum aliorum canonicorum pecunijs facta acquisitis prout in fundatione obitus ipsius magistri Gregorij latius continetur. Ita quod fiet duplum solenne cum assizia circa chorum ac in inferiori et superiori viis, duobus eciam cereis ante crucifixum et uno ante ymaginem beate marie supra hostium chori. Necnon tribus similibus ante ymaginem sancti Gregorij erga capellam sancti stephani, et pulsatione solenni cum hymno et moteto per magistrum et pueros in utrisque vesperis.

Inde fabrice lx. S. pulsatori .viii. S. magistro et pueris .vi. S. socijs ultra tres denarios alborum ab olim fundatos .iiij. d. tur. et clerico revestiarij pro accensione cereorum, hac et certis alijs in revestiario, declaratis quinque S. residuum dominis. Item super aquesta .xxx. S. super geraldimontem clerico revestiarij ut tabulam sancti gregorij aperiat candelabrum mundet et cereos in ibi ac ante ymaginem sancti Jeronimi statutis temporibus accendat ultra dictos .v. S. in hoc festo .xx. d.

2. Cambrai, Médiathèque municipale, fonds ancien B 39, fol. 52r

Feast of St. Jerome, augmented by Grégoire Nicolai

Festum sancti Jeromini augmentatum est per magistrum Gregorium Nicolai in utroque iure licentiatum canonicum subdiaconum de .ix. L. x. S. accipiendis in .xvj. L. super maioria seu feudo de oudeghem de suis et certorum aliorum canonicorum bonis aquisita vel aquisito. Ita quod fiet duplum solenne cum plena assizia simili festo sancti gregorij, et accensione trium ante ipsius beati Jeronimi et trium cereorum ante sancti gregorij ymagines, stratura herbar*um* hy*m*no et moteto a mag*ist*ro et pueris in utrisq*ue* vesperis, et pulsatione sole*n*ni.

Inde fabrice .lx. S. pulsatori .viij. S. pro herbis .v. S. mag*ist*ro et p*uer*is .vj. S. soc*iis* ultra .iij. d. albor*um* olim fundatos .iiij. d. t*ur*. cl*er*ico revestiarij .v. S. residuu*m* do*mi*nis. Et ultra hoc ex aquesta .xxx. S. *pro*pe geraldimonte*m* h*abe*bit idem cl*er*icus revestiarij in hoc festo pro certis c*er*eis acce*n*dend*is*, et tabula *sancti* gregorij diebus in revestiario declaratis aperienda, et candelabro mundando .xx. d.

3. Cambrai, Médiathèque municipale, fonds ancien B 39, fol. 53v

Feast of Sts. Sebastian and Fabian, founded by Gilles Flannel dit l'Enfant, canon

Festum s*ancto*r*um* m*artyrum* Sebastiani et Fabiani q*uo*d prius sub officio .ix. l*ec*tio celebratur ex fundac*i*one d*omi*ni Egidij Fla*n*nel al*ia*s l'enfant can*on*ici sacerdotis fieri habebit ut festum celebre et magnu*m* duplu*m* videlicet cu*m* pulsatione sole*n*ni, Assizia plenaria cu*m* tribus cereis ante ymagine*m* d*ict*i *sancti*, hymn*o* per pueros et moteto in utrisq*ue* vesperis ad instar funda*cio*n*is* festi beati gregorij et c*etera*. Pro quibus distribue*nt*ur .xij^{c*im*}. libre modo sequen*ti*:

Primo fabrice pro hui*usmo*d*i* plenaria assiz*i*a .lx. S. Sociis .vj. d. Cloq*ue*ma*n*no .viij. S. Mag*ist*ro et pueris altaris .v. S. Quatuor cappella-nis revestit*is* .ij. S. Pro revestitis .iiij^{or}. vicariorum .xvj. d. Cantori pro .iiij^{or}. choris .ij. S. albor*um* val*ent* .ij. S. x. d. Pro hui*usmo*di tribus c*er*eis accen-dend*is* diebus et festivitatibus seque*ntibus*, videlicet: Nativitatis d*omi*ni, Pasche, penthecostes, o*mn*ium s*ancto*rum, [omnium] a*nim*arum, Ascen-scio*n*is, trinitatis, sacramenti, Sex gl*or*iosissime virg*in*is, nativitatis b*e*ati Joh*ann*is baptiste et b*e*ate barbare .xl. S. Clerico revestiarij .iiij. S. Residuum dominis.

Pro q*uib*us aquisivit d*ic*tus d*omi*n*us* Egidius sup*er* d*omi*nio de Audeghe*m* empto erga Rener*um* bocart .xvj. L. de redditu, unde penes officiu*m* pro supportandis onerib*us* quarta pars sc*i*l*ice*t .viij. L. manebit. residuu*m* quod est .xij. L. distribuetur ut supra.

4. Cambrai, Médiathèque municipale, fonds ancien B 39, fol. 54v

Feast of St. Adrian, founded by Bussardus Balduini, canon

Festum *sancti* Adriani m*arty*ris decima die septembr*is* *per*petuo cele-brand*um* fundatu*m* est per d*omi*nu*m* Bussardu*m* balduini canonicu*m*

cameracens*em*, magnu*m* duplex ad instar festi *sancti* Gregorij. Itaq*ue* fiat
duplex sole*n*ne, cu*m* plena assizia circa choru*m*, ac in inferiori et sup*er*iori
vijs, duobus etiam cereis ante crucifixu*m*, et uno ante ymagine*m* be*a*te marie
supra ostiu*m* chori, necnon trib*us* similib*us* ante ymagine*m* sanc*ti* Adriani,
cum pulsatione sole*n*ni, hympno et moteto per m*agistr*um et pueros in
utrisq*ue* vesperis cantand*is*.

5. Cambrai, Médiathèque municipale, fonds ancien B 39, fol. 54r

Feast of the Visitation of the Virgin, founded by Michael de
Beringhen, canon

Festum visitac*io*nis gloriosissime virg*in*is q*uo*d celebrat*ur* die secunda Julij
fundatu*m* per m*agistr*um michaelem de beringhen cano*n*icum p*res*byt*er*um
ad instar festor*um* concepc*io*nis et annuntiac*io*nis euisde*m* gloriosissi*me*
virg*in*is. Videlicet cu*m* pulsac*io*ne assizia q*uin*q*ue* c*er*eis ante ymagines
annu*n*tiac*io*nis et visitac*io*nis ips*i*us, et septe*m* ante ymagine*m* be*a*te marie
le flamenghe du*m* d*i*citur Alma, Stratura, hy*m*no, moteto, Salve, Inviolata
et Alma, cu*m* mem*o*r*ia* in fine matuti*n*ar*um* in capella sanc*ti*ssime trinit*atis*
p*er* certu*m* R*esponsoriu*m a*ut* v*er*sum et coll*ectam* in ordinario designat*ur*
de .xxiiij. L. t*ur*.

    Inde fabrice .C. vj. S. cuil*ibet* socior*um* ad p*ri*mas vesp*er*is .ij. d. Ad salve
.iiij. d. Ad mat*utinis* ij. d. In me*moria* post mat*utinis* .ij. d. Ad inviolata .iiij.
d. In missa .ij. d. Ad sec*und*is vesp*er*is totide*m* et Alma .vj. d. Mag*ist*ro et
pueris alt*ar*is p*ro* hy*m*no et moteto in utrisq*ue* vesp*er*is .v. S. [pro] herb*is* .v. S.
Cloq*ue*ma*n*no xxviij. S. Cap*ell*ano et cl*er*ico revestiarij p*ro* p*re*par*ando* alt*are*
et capas seric*as* .iiij. S. eide*m* cl*er*ico revest*iarij* p*ro* accensione c*er*eor*um* .ij. S.
duob*us* chorist*es* pro viij choris .v. S. viij. d. pro .iiij^{or}. cap*ell*anis ad missa*m*
revestit*is* .ij. S. p*ro* revestita*ndo* puerorum vicarior*um* .xvj. d. Residuu*m*
dom*in*is.

    Pro quibus acquisivit ide*m* m*agiste*r michael sup*er* censa de Criecourt
iuxta latuyd xxxij. L. t*ur*. de redditu. Unde penes officiu*m* p*ro* supporta*ndis*
onerib*us* quarta pars sc*ilicit* .viij. L. manebit, et sic solu*m* distribue*n*tur ut
s*upra*. xxiiij. L. t*ur*.

6. Cambrai, Médiathèque municipale, fonds ancien B 39, fol. 51v

First Sunday in Advent, founded by Egidius de Bosco, Senior, canon

Dom*i*nica p*ri*ma in adventu d*o*mini fit magnum duplu*m* fundatum per
d*o*min*um* Egidium de Bosco can*on*icum sacerd*o*te*m* oriundu*m* de sanc*t*o

Amando in pabula. Cuius fundatio est de .xix. cor*onis* francie pro quib*us* distribuuntur .xxv. L. xiii. S.

Inde reserva*n*tur p*ro Alma* .lxxv. S. Restant pro augmentatione Salve et pro duplo .xxi. L. xviii. S. qui sic distribuuntur: P*resbytero* celebra*n*ti magnam missam pro memoria .xii. d. Quatuor p*arvis* vicariis revest*itis* cuil*ibet* .iiii. d. Cantori ebd*omario* pro .iiii*or*. choris ii. S. x. d. § Sociis chori cuil*ibet* .vi. d. trip*art*ite, Matut*inis*, missa *et vesp*eris. Vicariis magnis et parvis Cantantib*us* responsu*m* Aspiciens pro dext*ra* parte chori .vj. sol. equal*iter* dividendos. Item pro sinistra parte [similiter] .vj. S. Pue*ris* et mag*istro* p*ro* motetis .iiii. S. Pro missa ad altare crucifixi .iiii. S. § Clerico eiusd*em* .vj. d. § Clericis pro accensione lu*minaru*m iii S. Videlic*et* revestiarij .ii. S. et altri .xii. d. § Pro salve d*omi*nis .vi. d. cum antiqua fundatione § Sociis et aliis cuil*ibet* .ii. d. si*m*ilit*er* § Item pro de profundis qual*ibet* d*omi*nica p*er* annu*m* presbytero .viii. d. Et si per decanu*m* p*ra*bendatum .xvj. d. Et parvo vicar*io* .iiii. d. Fabrice .C.ij. S. Cloquema*n*n[o] qui tenetur pulsare gloriosam ad antiph*onas* Salve et Alma, et ad responsum Aspiciens et totu*m* festu*m* solenniter .xviii. S. residuum d*o*minis § Sequitur pro Alma .lxxv. S. Inde d*omi*nis cuil*ibet* .xij. d. & Sociis et aliis .vj. d. Residuu*m* officio assizie.

Item fundavit idem d*omi*nu*s* Egidius de Bosco senior decantati*on*em .Regina celi letare. cum versu et coll*ecta* Interveniat, fiendam perpetuo in navi ec*cles*ie ante ymagine*m* crucifixi post completorium i*m*mediate die sancto pasche et sex diebus d*om*inicis subsequentibus[.] Que fundacio est .xxj. librarum turon*ensium*.

7. Cambrai, Médiathèque municipale, fonds ancien B 39, fol. 58r

Dedication of the Cathedral of Cambrai, founded by Jean du Rosut, canon

Dedicatio huius maioris ec*cles*ie Cameracen*sis* que fuit consecrata Anno d*omi*ni millesimo quadringentesimo .lxxii°. die d*omi*nica quinta Jullij. Celebratur dominica prima post translationem sancti thome apostoli. Et fiunt distributiones prout sequitur.

Festum dedicati*on*is huius ec*cles*ie Cameracen*sis* quod celebrat*ur* prima d*omi*nica post t*ra*nslatione*m* sanc*ti* thome fundatu*m* per Joha*n*nem du Rosut cano*n*icum p*resbyter*um Ad instar festi natal*is* d*omi*ni, videl*ic*et cu*m* pulsati*on*e sole*n*ni et ante matut*in*um totu*m* classicum, plenissima assizia, tam in q*uin*que coronis ferreis q*uam* in navi et circa, ac infra chor*um* stratura hy*m*no et moteto cu*m* Elemosina .xxx*ta*. panu*m* albor*um* in fine misse. xxx. paup*eribus* erogand*orum*, de .xlj. L. x. S. t*uro*nensibus.

Inde fabrice xvj. L. Cerario vel eidem fabrice pro factura cereorum quinque coronarum .xviij. S. Cloquemanno pro pulsando de nocte totum classicum et omnes horas .l. S. Et pro ponendo coronas ferreas et removendo et accendendo cereos dictarum coronarum .viij. S. iiij. d. Cuilibet sociorum quadripartite .viij. d. Item ad salve .ii. d. ac ad Te deum totidem, et ad processionem .iiij. d. Cuilibet dominorum ad salve ultra solitum .vj. d. Item ad Te deum .vj. d. et pro Inviolata et processione ultra antiquam fundationem .x. d. Magistro et pueris altaris pro hymno et moteto in utrisque vesperis .v. S. pro herbis .v. S. duobus choristis pro .viij. choris pro quolibet .x. d. [sunt] vj. S. viij. d. Dominis dyacono et subdyacono ultra .ii. S. vj. d. ab antiquo fundationis .iiij. S. ii. d. Quatuor capellanis ad missam revestitis .ij. S. Et pro revestitura puerorum vicariorum .xvj. d. Capellano et clerico revestiarij pro parando altare et capas sericas .iiij. S. Eidem clerico pro accensione cereorum .ii. S. Et officio elemosine pro dictis .xxx. panibus dictis miches gallice .xxxᵃ. pauperibus erogandis inclusis .xii. d. pro distributoribus .x. S. Item pro qualibet missa privata accidente eadem die et per octavas .xv. d. turonenses. et pro quolibet choro per dictas octavas .vj. d. alborum. Residuum dominis.

8. Cambrai, Médiathèque municipale, fonds ancien B 39, fol. 58v

Octave of the Dedication of the Cathedral of Cambrai, founded by
Jean du Rosut, canon

In octavis dedicationis fit ad instar beati Iheronimi duplum, fundatum per venerabilem dominum Johannem du Rosut canonicum sacerdotem, eiusdem dedicationis institutorem et fundatorem de xv L. turonensibus.

Inde fabrice lx S. Sociis chori quadripartite .viii. d. Choristis v S. viiii d. Quatuor capellanis revestitis .ij. S. parvis etiam vicariis pro revestitis xvi d. Pro moteto vi S. pro herbis v S. Clocquemanno viii S. Clerico revestiarij ii S. ac officio elemosine pro xxx panibus prebendalibus x S. Residuum dominis.

9. Cambrai, Médiathèque municipale, fonds ancien B 39, fol. 12r

Saturday commemoration of the Blessed Virgin, founded by Johannes
Martini, canon

[N]os decanus et capellani cameracensis ecclesie ad preces confratris nostri magistri Johannis martini acceptavimus institucionem cuiusdam commemorationis beate virginis marie fiende singulis diebus sabbati post salve circa solis occasum ante altare feretrorum in ecclesia nostra per magistrum cum sex pueris altaris suo regimini commissis assistente sibi uno contratenente[.] In qua anthiphona de beata maria inchoata per unum pueror*um* predictor*um* alter intonabit ps*almus* Mag*nificat* quo dicto decantabitur ant*iphona*. et postea *versus* et coll*ecta* per unum ex pueris dicetur deinde loco Benedicamus motetum decantab*itur* per omnes supra memoratos quib*us* fiet distributio singulis ebdomadis per officiu*m* assizie hoc modo[:] quil*ibet* sex pueror*um* ipsor*um* percipiet .iiii*or*. d. mag*iste*r .x. d. soci*us* contratenens .vj. d. pulsator qui trib*us* vicib*us* separatim tanget vel tintinabit campanas no*m*inat*as* aldegundis et gloriosa ad convocationem prenominator*um* et p*op*uli singulis annis in festis nativitatis d*om*ini et b*e*ati Jo*h*annis bapt*iste* percipiet mediatim .xxiiii. S. pro quib*us* omnib*us* sic faciendis[.]idem mag*iste*r Jo*h*annes martini acquisivit nobis in villa n*os*tra de Bery n*os*tre d*om*ine .liii. mencaldit*as* terre ad mensuram illi*us* loci qua*m* co*m*memorationem fieri volum*us* et promisim*us* q*uam* diu pignus dura-bit[.]

10. Cambrai, Médiathèque municipale, fonds ancien B 39, fol. 42v

Feast of Sts. Simon and Jude, augmented by Reginaldus de Leonibus, canon

Symon*is* et iude ap*ostolor*um* duplu*m*. d*om*inis .ii. S. Soc*iis* .iii. d. Quod quidem duplu*m* augmentatu*m* est per mag*istr*um* Reginaldu*m* de leonib*us* canonicum sacerdote*m* de .ix. L. tur*onensibus*. et fit solenne cu*m* pulsatione et assizia circa choru*m* ac in inferiori et superiori viis, duob*us* etiam cereis ante crucifixu*m* et uno ante ymagine*m* b*e*ate marie supra ostium chori, una cu*m* hymno et moteto in utrisq*ue* Vesp*er*is.

   Inde fabrice .lx. S. pulsatori .viii. S. mag*ist*ro et pueris .vi. S. Sociis ultra d*ictos* iii. d. albor*um* ab olim fundatos .iiii. d. tur. clerico revestiarii .ii. S. et residuu*m* dom*in*is.

11. Cambrai, Médiathèque municipale, fonds ancien B 39, fol. 42v

Feast of St. Quentin, augmented by Nicolas Ploncet, canon

Quintini martiris. D*om*inis xii d. Soc*iis* ii. d. Magnu*m* duplu*m* cu*m* plena assisia et pulsatione sole*n*ni, ex fundatione facta per executores venerabilis d*om*ini nicolai ploncet canonici et scolastici cameracen*sis* p*r*out in suo testa-mento ordinav*er*at de .xii. L. tur*onensibus* ultra fundatione*m* facta*m* d*om*inis et sociis[.]

   Inde fabrice. lx. S. pulsatori .viij. S. cuil*ibet* quatuor capellanor*um* assistentiu*m* sacerdoti in missa maiori .vj. d. cuil*ibet* quatuor parvor*um* vicario*rum* qui antiquitus assistebant .iiij. d. viii choriste in primis vesperis matutinis et missa .ij. S. albo*rum*. Sociis cu*m* duobus denarijs olim fundatis in toto .viii. d. Magistro et pueris altaris p*ro* decantatione hymni et moteti in primis vesp*er*is .vj. S. hec omnia habentur sup*er* antiquitade qua . . . finem huius libri et in ordinatio.

12. Cambrai, Médiathèque municipale, fonds ancien B 39, fol. 47v

Feast of St. Eligius, augmented by Jean Rodolphi dit Flamingi, canon

Eligii conf*essori* epi*scopi* ¶Dom*i*nis ii S. iii. d. Quodquide*m* festu*m* augmen-tatu*m* est per magistru*m* ioha*n*nem Rodolphi al*ias* flamingi utriusq*ue* Juris doctore*m* cantore*m* et canonicu*m* hui*us* eccle*s*ie, et fit duplu*m* sole*n*ne de .ix. L. tur*onensibus*.

   Inde fabrice .lx. S. cloq*ue*manno .viij. S. pro moteto .vj. S. c*ler*ico revestiarij .ii. S. Capellanis et vicar*iis* revestitis .iij. S. iiij. d. Soc*iis* .iiij. d. et Residuu*m* dom*i*nis. Pro quib*us* acquisit*is* su*n*t in patria .iiij^or. officioru*m* flandrie .xii. L. t*ur*. Et pro chor*is* iii. S. x. d.

13. Lille, Archives départementales du Nord, 4G 2009, fol. 63v

Wednesday in the Third Week of Advent, founded by Nico[laus] de Sancto Vedasto, greater vicar

Anno dom*i*ni m°. ccc°. lxvij°. dom*i*nica t*er*c*ia* in adve*n*tu ordinatu*m* fuit p*er* dom*i*nos de cap[itolo] q*uod* singu*l*is a*n*nis feria iiij^ta . . . acce*n*du*n*t[ur] xii. ca*n*dele q*ui* sunt sup*er* trabem crucifixi et arde*n*t usq*ue* ad finem magn*orum* matut*inorum*. Et dyaco*nus* et s*ub*dy*aconus* induti alb*is* vestib*us* sicut in missis B*eate* mar*ie* cu*m* m[agna] cruce, duob*us* cereis et thur-ribu*lo* asce*n*du*n*t sup*er*ius in pulpitu*m* incepta loco benedictio*n*is ca*n*tatu*r* in choro anth*iphona* .Salve regina. Et du*m* incipitur Sa[lve] pulsa*n*tur due magne ca*m*pane, vel un*us* sole*n*nis ict*us* pluriu*m* campana*rum* in finem p*ri*me lectio*n*is. Finito Salve leg*itur* p*ri*ma lectio. P*ri*mum R*esponsorium* a duobus p*ar*v[is] vicar*iis* ad modu*m* semidupl*um* quoru*m* qu*i*libet ii. d. alb. recipiet pro labore. S*ecund*um [R*esponsorium*] a duob*us* cap*ellanis* quor*um* quil*ibet* s*imiliter* ii. d. recipiet. Tertiu*m* vero R*esponsorium* a duobus dom*i*nis v[el] magnis vicar*iis* quor*um* quil*ibet* iiij°. d. recipiat. Veru*m*tamen qui s*ecund*u*m* leget L[ectionem] iiij^or di co*n*similes recipiet, *similiter* et t*er*ciam. Sacerdos aut*em* matut*inos* celebra*n*s et f[aciens] iiij^or. d. co*n*similes h*abe*at. In sup*er* quinq*ue* pueri altar*is* servie*n*tes et m*agister* eor*um* in fi[ne] mat*utinorum* unu*m* motetu*m* vel saltem unu*m* be*n*edica*mus* cu*m* disca*n*tu dic*ere* tenea*n*tur pro labore *similiter* ii. d. hor*um* quil*ibet* merea*tur*.

Bibliography

Primary sources

I. Music manuscripts and prints

Aosta, Biblioteca del Seminario Maggiore, Codice 15, "Aosta Codex"

Bologna, Biblioteca universitaria, 2216

Bologna, Museo internazionale e biblioteca della musica, Q15

Bruges, Bibliotheek Grootseminarie, 75-37

Brussels, Bibliothèque royale de Belgique/Koninklijke Bibliotheek van België, 5557, "Burgundian Choirbook"

Cambrai, Médiathèque municipale, fonds ancien, B 28

Cambrai, Médiathèque municipale, fonds ancien, 17

Cambrai, Médiathèque municipale, fonds ancien, 33 (37)

Cambrai, Médiathèque municipale, fonds ancien, 38 (40)

Cambrai, Médiathèque municipale, fonds ancien, 72 (73)

Cambridge, Magdalene College, Pepys 1236

Cambridge, University Library, Add. 4435, "Royal English Choirbook"

Canterbury, Cathedral Library, 128/13

Chicago, Newberry Library, 54.1

Ghent, Rijksuniversiteit Bibliotheek, 15 (1)

Ghent, Rijksuniversiteit Bibliotheek, 15 (2)

's-Hertogenbosch, Rijksarchief in Noord-Brabant, Archief van de Illustre Lieve Vrouwe Broederschap, Codex Smijers

Liber selectarum cantionum quas vulgo Mutetas appellant 6, 5 et 4 vocum. Augsburg: S. Grimm and M. Wirsing, 1520

London, British Library, Add. 57950, "Old Hall"

Lucca, Archivio archivescovile 97, "Lucca Choirbook"

Lucca, Archivio di stato, 234, "Lucca Choirbook"

Modena, Biblioteca Estense universitaria, α.X.1.11, "Modena B"

Montpellier, Faculté de Médecine, H 196, "Montpellier Codex"

Munich, Bayerische Staatsbibliothek, Mus. 3154, "Chorbuch des Nicolaus Leopold"

Munich, Bayerische Staatsbibliothek, Mus. 3725, "Buxheimer Orgelbuch"

New York City, Columbia University, Smith Western Add. 21

Oxford, Bodleian Library, Canonici misc. 213

Oxford, Bodleian Library, Don. b. 32, "Royal English Choirbook"

Paris, Bibliothèque nationale, fonds lat. 15182

Pisa, Archivio arcivescovile e Biblioteca "Cardinale Pietro Maffii," Cartella 11/III, "Lucca Choirbook"

Prague, Památník Národního Písemnictví, Strahovská Knihovna, D.G.IV.47, "Strahov Codex"

Processionale ad usum Sarum. Edited by Richard Pynson. Facsimile reprint. London, 1502; Clarabricken, Clifden, County Kilkenny: Boethius Press, 1980

Siena, Archivio di stato, Frammenti musicali no. 155

Trent, Archivio diocesano, 93 (*olim* BL)

Trent, Museo provinciale d'arte, Castello del Buonconsiglio, 1374 (Trent 87)

Trent, Museo provinciale d'arte, Castello del Buonconsiglio, 1375 (Trent 88)

Trent, Museo provinciale d'arte, Castello del Buonconsiglio, 1377 (Trent 90)

Trent, Museo provinciale d'arte, Castello del Buonconsiglio, 1377 (Trent 91)

Trent, Museo provinciale d'arte, Castello del Buonconsiglio,1379 (Trent 92)

Turin, Biblioteca nazionale universitaria, J.II.9

Vatican City, Biblioteca apostolica Vaticana, Cappella Sistina 15

Vatican City, Biblioteca apostolica Vaticana, San Pietro B80

Vicenza, Seminario vescovile, U.VIII.11

II. Documents and chronicles

Adam of Usk. *The Chronicle of Adam of Usk.* Edited and trans. Chris Given-Wilson. Oxford: Clarendon Press, 1997.

Belcari, Feo. "The Consecration of the Cathedral of Florence." In *Images of Quattrocento Florence*, trans. Stefano Ugo Baldassarri and Arielle Saiber, 239–40. New Haven: Yale University Press, 2000.

Bisticci, Vespasiano da. *Le vite.* Edited by Aulo Greco. Florence: Istituto Nazionale di Studi sul Rinascimento, 1970–76.

Bradshaw, Henry. *Statutes of Lincoln Cathedral.* Edited by Christopher Wordsworth. 3 vols. Cambridge University Press, 1892–97.

Bruges, Archief OCMW, Charter 305.

Bruges, Archief OCMW, Register 155, *Cartularium.*

Bruges, Archief OCMW, Register 179, *Planarius.*

Bruges, Bisschoppelijk Archief, Reeks A 50, *Acta capitulorum.*

Bruges, Bisschoppelijk Archief, Reeks A 51, *Acta capitulorum.*

Bruges, Bisschoppelijk Archief, Reeks A 55, *Acta capitulorum.*

Bruges, Bisschoppelijk Archief, Reeks A 141, *Planarius.*

Bruges, Bisschoppelijk Archief, Reeks A 122, ordinal of Tournai.

Bruges, Bisschoppelijk Archief, Reeks A 210, *Planarius.*

Bruges, Bisschoppelijk Archief, Reeks G 8, 1502–03.

Bruges, Bisschoppelijk Archief, Reeks G 131[1], 1481–82, 1503–04.

Bruges, Rijksarchiev, Fonds découvertes 81 (*olim* 104), *Planarius Sint-Salvator.*

Bruges, Rijksarchief, Onze-Lieve-Vrouwe, 735.

Bruges, Rijksarchief, Onze-Lieve-Vrouw, 1501, *Cartularium en handboek*, 1467–1516.

Bruges, Stadsarchief, Charter blauw no. 8128.

Bruges, Stadsarchief, Oud Archief, Reeks 390, *Cartularium Drie Santinnen*, Inv. nr. 1.

Bruni, Leonardo. *History of the Florentine People*. Edited and trans. James Hankins. 3 vols. I Tatti Renaissance Library 27. Cambridge, Mass.: Harvard University Press, 2001.

Brussels, Archives générales du royaume, Trésor de Flandre, 1er série, Charter 1698.

The Brut or The Chronicles of England. Edited by Friedrich W. D. Brie. 2 vols. London: Kegan Paul, Trench, Trübner, 1908.

Caeremoniale episcoporum iussu Clementis VIII, Pont. Max. novissimè reformatum: omnibus ecclesiis, praecipue autem metropolitanis cathedralibus & collegiatis perutile ac necessarium. Rome: Typographia linguarum externarum, 1600.

Calzaiuolo, Giovanni. "Nel tempo che Firenze era contenta." In *Lirici toscani del Quattrocento*, edited by Antonio Lanza. 2 vols., vol. II, 683–87. Rome: Bulzone, 1973–75.

Cambi, Giovanni. *Istorie di Giovanni Cambi cittadino fiorentino*. Vols. XX–XXIII of *Delizie degli eruditi toscani*. Edited by Ildefonso di San Luigi. 25 vols. Florence: Gaetano Cambiagi, 1770–89.

Cambrai, Médiathèque municipale, fonds ancien, B 39.

A Chronicle of London from 1089 to 1483; Written in the Fifteenth Century. Facsimile reprint. London: Longman, Rees, Orme, Brown and Green, 1827; Felinfach: Llanerch, 1995.

Cole, Charles Augustus, ed. *Memorials of Henry the Fifth, King of England*. Rerum Britannicarum medii aevi scriptores, or Chronicles and Memorials of Great Britain and Ireland during the Middle Ages 11. London: Longman, Brown, Green, Longmans and Roberts, 1858.

Dondi Orologio, Francesco Scipione. *Dissertazione nona sopra l'istoria ecclesiastica padovana*. 2 vols. Padua: Tipografia del Seminario, 1817.

   Dissertazione ottava sopra l'istoria ecclesiastica padovana. 2 vols. Padua: Tipografia del Seminario, 1815.

Foro-Juliensis, Titus Livius de. *Vita Henrici Quinti*. Oxford: Theatro Sheldoniano, 1716.

Gesta Henrici Quinti: The Deeds of Henry V. Edited and trans. by Frank Taylor and John S. Roskell. Oxford: Clarendon Press, 1975.

Kingsford, Charles L., ed. *English Historical Literature in the Fifteenth Century*. Oxford: Clarendon Press, 1913.

Liber regie capelle: A Manuscript in the Biblioteca publica, Evora. Edited by Walter Ullmann. Henry Bradshaw Society 92. London: Henry Bradshaw Society, 1961.

Liber sacerdotalis nuperrime ex libris sancte Romane ecclesie. Venice: Victor a Rabanis, 1537.

Lille, Archives départementales du Nord, 4G 1313.

Lille, Archives départementales du Nord, 4G 2009.

Lille, Archives départementales du Nord, 4G 6793.

London, British Library, Cotton Julius E. IV.

London, British Library, Cotton Vespasian D. XIII.

London, British Library, Harley 861.

London, British Library, Royal 13A XVI.

Manetti, Giannozzo. "Oratio," edited by Eugenio Battisti. *Archivio di filosofia* 105 (1960): 310–20.

Milanesi, Gaetano. "Alcune lettere di Donato Giannotti novamente trovate nell'Archivio Centrale di Stato." *Giornali storico degli archivi toscani* 7 (1863): 155–73.

Ordinale Exon.: Exeter Chapter Ms. 3502 Collated with Parker Ms. 93: With Two Appendices from Trinity College, Cambridge Ms. B.XI.16 and Exeter Chapter Ms. 3625. Edited by John Neale Dalton. 4 vols. Henry Bradshaw Society 37, 38, 63, 79. London: Henry Bradshaw Society, 1909–40.

Oxford, Bodleian Library, Rawlinson liturg. e. 46.

Padua, Archivio capitolare del Duomo, *Acta capitulorum* III.

Pontificale noviter impressum: Pro pulchrisque characteribus diligentissime annnotatum. Lyons, 1511.

Pontificale Romanum. Rome: Stephan Plannck, 1497.

Raine, James. "The Statutes Ordained by Richard Duke of Gloucester for the College of Middleham, Dated July 4, 18 Edw. IV. [1478]." *Archaeological Journal* 14 (1857): 160–70.

Strozzi, Alessandra Macinghi. *Lettere di una gentildonna fiorentina.* Edited by Cesare Guasti. Florence: G. C. Sansoni, 1877.

Thomae de Elmham Vita & Gesta Henrici Quinti, Anglorum regis. Edited by Thomas Hearne. Oxford: Theatro Sheldoniano, 1727.

Treviso, Archivio di stato, Ospedale di Santa Maria dei Battuti, Busta 1.

Treviso, Archivio di stato, Ospedale di Santa Maria dei Battuti, Busta 2.

Treviso, Archivio di stato, Ospedale di Santa Maria dei Battuti, Busta 3.

Walsingham, Thomas. *The St. Albans Chronicle, 1406–1420, Edited from Bodley MS. 462.* Edited by Vivian Hunter Galbraith. Oxford: Clarendon Press, 1937.

Secondary sources

Alden, Jane. "Text/Music Design in Ciconia's Ceremonial Motets." In *Johannes Ciconia: Musicien de la transition,* edited by Philippe Vendrix, 39–64. Turnhout: Brepols, 2003.

Allen, Michael J. B. *Nuptial Arithmetic: Marsilio Ficino's Commentary on the Fatal Number in Book VIII of Plato's "Republic."* Berkeley and Los Angeles: University of California Press, 1994.

Allsen, J. Michael. "Forest, John (?)," "Grenon, Nicholas." In *Die Musik in Geschichte und Gegenwart*. 2nd edn. Kassel and New York: Bärenreiter, 1998–.

"Style and Intertextuality in the Isorhythmic Motet, 1400–1440." Ph.D. dissertation, University of Wisconsin-Madison, 1992.

Andriessen, Pieter. *Die van Muziken gheerne horen: Muziek in Brugge 1200–1800*. Bruges: West-Vlaamse Gidsenkring, 2002.

Anonymous of Bologna. "The Principles of Letter Writing." In *Three Medieval Rhetorical Arts*, edited by James Jerome Murphy, 1–26. Facsimile reprint. Medieval and Renaissance Texts and Studies 228. Berkeley: University of California Press, 1974; Tempe: Arizona Center for Medieval and Renaissance Studies, 2001.

Ashley, Kathleen. "Introduction: The Moving Subjects of Processional Performance." In *Moving Subjects: Processional Performance in the Middle Ages and Renaissance*, edited by Kathleen Ashley and Wim Hüsken, 7–34. Amsterdam and Atlanta: Rodopi, 2001.

Aubrey, Pierre. *Le plus anciens monuments de la musique française*. Mélanges de musicologie critique 3. Paris: Welter, 1905.

Bailey, Terence. *The Processions of Sarum and the Western Church*. Studies and Texts 21. Toronto: Pontifical Institute of Mediaeval Studies, 1971.

Bakhtin, Mikhail M. *The Dialogic Imagination: Four Essays*. Edited by Michael Holquist. Trans. by Caryl Emerson and Michael Holquist. Austin: University of Texas Press, 1981.

Beaucourt de Noortvelde, Patrice A. *Description historique de l'eglise collegiale et paroissiale de Notre Dame a Bruges, avec une histoire chronologique de tous les prevots, suivie, d'un recueil des epitaphes anciennes & modernes de cette eglise*. Bruges: J. de Busscher, 1773.

Bell, Catherine M. *Ritual: Perspectives and Dimensions*. New York and Oxford: Oxford University Press, 1997.

Belvederi, Giulio. "Cerimonie nel solenne ingresso dei Vescovi in Bologna durante il Medio Evo." *Rassegna Gregoriana* 2 (1913): cols. 169–86.

Bent, Margaret. "A Contemporary Perception of Early Fifteenth-Century Style: Bologna Q15 as a Document of Scribal Editorial Initiative." *Musica Disciplina* 41 (1987): 183–201.

"Cooke, John," "Forest," "Johannes de Lymburgia," "Old Hall Manuscript." In *The New Grove Dictionary of Music and Musicians*. 2nd edn. London: Macmillan, 2000.

Dunstaple. London and New York: Oxford University Press, 1981.

"The Fourteenth-Century Italian Motet." In *L'Ars nova italiana del Trecento VI: Atti del congresso internazionale "L'Europa e la musica del Trecento," Certaldo, Palazzo Pretorio, 19–21 luglio 1984*, edited by Giulio Cattin, 85–125. Certaldo: Polis, 1990.

"Pietro Emiliani's Chaplain Bartolomeo Rossi da Carpi and the Lamentations of Johannes de Quadris in Vicenza." *Il saggiatore musicale* 2 (1995): 5–15.

"The Progeny of Old Hall: More Leaves from a Royal English Choirbook." In *Gordon Athol Anderson (1929–1981): In Memoriam von seinen Studenten, Freunden und Kollegen.* 2 vols. Musicological Studies 39, vol. I, 1–54. Henryville, Ontario: Institute of Mediaeval Music, 1982.

"*Resfacta* and *Cantare super librum.*" In *Counterpoint, Composition, and Musica Ficta*, 301–19. New York and London: Routledge, 2002.

"Sources of the Old Hall Music." *Proceedings of the Royal Musical Association* 94 (1967–68): 19–35.

Bent, Margaret, ed. *Bologna Q15: The Making and Remaking of a Musical Manuscript: Introductory Study and Facsimile Edition.* 2 vols. Lucca: Libreria musicale italiana, 2009.

Berger, Karol. "The Martyrdom of St. Sebastian: The Function of Accidental Inflections in Dufay's *O beate Sebastiane.*" *Early Music* 17 (1989): 342–57.

Bisson, Noël. "English Polyphony for the Virgin Mary: The Votive Antiphon, 1430–1500." Ph.D. dissertation, Harvard University, 1998.

Blackburn, Bonnie J. "For Whom Do the Singers Sing?" *Early Music* 25 (1997): 593–609.

Bloxam, M. Jennifer. "Obrecht as Exegete: Reading *Factor orbis* as a Christmas Sermon." In *Hearing the Motet*, edited by Dolores Pesce, 169–92. Oxford and New York: Oxford University Press, 1997.

"A Survey of Late Medieval Service Books from the Low Countries: Implications for Sacred Polyphony, 1460–1520." 2 vols. Ph.D. dissertation, Yale University, 1987.

Bonaventure, Saint. "De perfectione vitae ad sorores." In *Opera omnia*, vol. XII, 209–27. Paris: Ludovicus Vives, 1868.

Boogaart, Thomas A. II. "Our Saviour's Blood: Procession and Community in Late Medieval Bruges." In *Moving Subjects: Processional Performance in the Middle Ages and Renaissance*, edited by Kathleen Ashley and Wim Hüsken, 69–116. Amsterdam and Atlanta: Rodopi, 2001.

Boone, Graeme MacDonald. "Dufay's Early Chansons: Chronology and Style in the Manuscript Oxford, Bodleian Library, Canonici Misc. 213." Ph.D. dissertation, Harvard University, 1987.

Borgerding, Todd. "Imagining the Sacred Body: Choirboys, Their Voices, and Corpus Christi in Early Modern Seville." In *Musical Childhoods and the Cultures of Youth*, edited by Susan Boynton and Roe-Min Kok, 25–48. Middletown: Wesleyan University Press, 2006.

Bouly, Eugène. *Dictionnaire historique de la ville de Cambrai, des abbayes, des chateaux-forts et des antiquités du Cambresis.* Facsimile reprint. Cambrai: Conseil Municipal de Cambrai, 1854; Brussels: Editions Culture et Civilisation, 1979.

Bowers, Roger. "Cooke, John." In *Die Musik in Geschichte und Gegenwart*. 2nd edn. Kassel and New York: Bärenreiter, 1998–.

"Lincoln Cathedral: Music and Worship to 1640." In *English Church Polyphony: Singers and Sources from the 14th to the 17th Century*, section VI. Brookfield: Ashgate, 1999.

"Plummer, John." In *The New Grove Dictionary of Music and Musicians*. 2nd edn. London: Macmillan, 2000.

Brewer, Charles E. "The Introduction of the Ars Nova into East Central Europe: A Study of Late Medieval Polish Sources." Ph.D. dissertation, City University of New York, 1984.

Brown, Andrew. "Bruges and the Burgundian 'Theatre-State': Charles the Bold and Our Lady of the Snow." *History* 84 (1999): 573–89.

Civic Ceremony and Religion in Medieval Bruges c. 1300–1520. Cambridge: Cambridge University Press, 2011.

Brown, Carleton. "Lydgate's Verses on Queen Margaret's Entry into London." *The Modern Language Review* 7 (1912): 225–34.

Bryant, David, and Michele Pozzobon, *Musica, devozione, città: La Scuola di Santa Maria dei Battuti (e uno suo manoscritto musicale) nella Treviso del Rinascimento*. Treviso: Fondazione Benetton and Editrice Canova, 1995.

Bryant, Lawrence M. *The King and the City in the Parisian Royal Entry Ceremony: Politics, Ritual, and Art in the Renaissance*. Geneva: Droz, 1986.

Bukofzer, Manuel. *Studies in Medieval & Renaissance Music*. New York: Norton, 1950.

Burstyn, Shai. "Early 15th-Century Polyphonic Settings of Song of Songs Antiphons." *Acta musicologica* 49 (1977): 200–77.

Buuren, A. M. J. van. "'Soe wie dit lietdkyn sinct of leest': De functie van de Laatmiddelnederlandse Geestelijke Lyriek." In *"Een zoet akkoord": Middeleeuwse Lyriek in de Lage Landen*, edited by Frank Willaert, 234–540. Amsterdam: Prometheus, 1992.

Caldwell, John. "Plainsong and Polyphony 1250–1550." In *Plainsong in the Age of Polyphony*, edited by Thomas Forrest Kelly, 6–31. Cambridge: Cambridge University Press, 1992.

Review of *Le Magnus liber organi de Notre-Dame de Paris*, vol. I: *Les quadrupla et tripla de Paris*, edited by Edward Roesner. *Music and Letters* 76 (1995): 641–46.

Castellini, Silvestro. *Storia della città di Vicenza: Ove si vedono i fatti e le guerre de' Vicentini così esterne come civili, dall'origine di essa città sino all'anno 1630*. 14 vols. Vicenza: Parise, 1821.

Cattin, Giulio. "Uno sconosciuto codice quattrocentesco dell'Archivio capitolare di Vicenza e le Lamentazioni di Johannes de Quadris." In *L'Ars nova italiana del Trecento: Secondo convegno internazionale, 17–22 luglio 1969*, edited by

F. Alberto Gallo, 281–304. Certaldo: Centro di Studi sull'Ars Nova Italiana del Trecento, 1970.

Celenza, Christopher S. *Renaissance Humanism and the Papal Curia: Lapo da Castiglionchio the Younger's "De curiae commodis"*. Ann Arbor: University of Michigan Press, 2000.

Charles, Sydney Robinson. "The Provenance and Date of the Pepys Ms 1236." *Musica Disciplina* 16 (1962): 57–71.

Chartier, François Léon. *L'ancien chapitre de Notre-Dame de Paris et sa maîtrise: D'après les documents capitulaires (1326–1790)*. Facsimile reprint. Paris: Perrin, 1897; Geneva: Minkoff, 1971.

Chérancé, Léopold de. *Saint Antoine de Padoue*. Paris: Poussielgue, 1895.

Ciconia, Johannes. *The Works of Johannes Ciconia*. Edited by Margaret Bent and Anne Hallmark. Polyphonic Music of the Fourteenth Century 24. Monaco: L'Oiseau-Lyre, 1985.

Clercx, Suzanne. *Johannes Ciconia: Un musicien liégeois et son temps*. 2 vols. Brussels: Académie Royale de Belgique, 1960.

Cox, Bobby Wayne. "The Motets of MS Bologna, Civico Museo Bibliografico Musicale, *Q 15*." 2 vols. Ph.D. dissertation, North Texas State University, 1977.

Cullington, J. Donald, ed. and trans. *"That liberal and virtuous art": Three Humanist Treatises on Music: Egidius Carlerius, Johannes Tinctoris, Carlo Valgulio*. With an introduction by Reinhard Strohm. Newtown Abbey: University of Ulster, 2001.

Cumming, Julie Emelyn. "Concord out of Discord: Occasional Motets of the Early Quattrocento." Ph.D. dissertation, University of California, Berkeley, 1987.

The Motet in the Age of Du Fay. Cambridge: Cambridge University Press, 1999.

"Music for the Doge in Early Renaissance Venice." *Speculum* 67 (1992): 324–64.

Cummings, Anthony M. *The Politicized Muse: Music for the Medici Festivals, 1512–1537*. Princeton: Princeton University Press, 1992.

Curtis, Gareth, and Andrew Wathey. "Fifteenth-Century English Liturgical Music: A List of the Surviving Repertory." *Royal Musical Association Research Chronicle* 27 (1994): 1–69.

Curtis, Liane. "Music Manuscripts and Their Production in Fifteenth-Century Cambrai." Ph.D. dissertation, University of North Carolina at Chapel Hill, 1991.

"Simon Mellet, Scribe of Cambrai Cathedral." *Plainsong and Medieval Music* 8 (1999): 133–66.

D'Accone, Frank A. *The Civic Muse: Music and Musicians in Siena during the Middle Ages and the Renaissance*. University of Chicago Press, 1997.

D'Andrea, David M. *Civic Christianity in Renaissance Italy: The Hospital of Treviso, 1400–1530*. Rochester: University of Rochester Press, 2007.

"De conventu S. Augustini Pisaurensi notitiae." *Analecta Augustiniana* 17 (1940): 554–61.

Destombes, Cyrille Jean. *Notre Dame de Grace et le culte de la Sainte Vierge à Cambrai et dans le Cambrésis*. Cambrai: Carion, 1871.

DeWitte, Alphons. "Boek- en Bibliotheekwezen in de Brugse Donaaskerk." In *Sint-Donaas en de voormalige Brugse Kathedraal*. 2 vols., vol. I, pp. 61–98. Bruges: Jong Kristen Onthaal voor Toerisme, 1978–88.

"Gegevens betreffende het muziekleven in de voormalige Sint-Donaaskerk te Brugge, 1251–1600." *Annales de la Société d'émulation de Bruges/Handelingen van het Genootschap van Geschiedenis* 111 (1974): 129–74.

Di Bacco, Giuliano, and John Nádas. "Papal Chapels and Italian Sources of Polyphony during the Great Schism." In *Papal Music and Musicians in Late Medieval and Renaissance Rome*, edited by Richard Sherr, 50–56. Oxford: Clarendon Press; Washington, DC: The Library of Congress, 1998.

"Verso uno 'stile internazionale' della musica nelle cappelle papale e cardinalizie durante il Grande Scisma (1378–1417): Il caso di Johannes Ciconia da Liège." In *Collectanea I*, edited by Adalbert Roth, 7–74. Città di Vaticano: Biblioteca Apostolica Vaticana, 1994.

Dreves, Guido Maria *et al.*, eds. *Analecta hymnica medii aevi*. 55 vols. Leipzig: O. R. Reisland, 1886–1922.

Dufay, Guillaume. *Opera omnia*. Edited by Heinrich Besseler. Corpus mensurabilis musicae 1. 6 vols. Rome: American Institute of Musicology, 1951–66.

Dunstaple, John. *John Dunstaple: Complete Works*. Edited by Manuel Bukofzer. 2nd edn. Revised by Margaret Bent, Ian Bent, and Brian Trowell. Musica Britannica 8. London: Stainer & Bell, 1970.

Dupont, M. *Histoire ecclésiastique et civile de la ville de Cambrai et du Cambresis*. 2 vols. Cambrai: Samuel Berthoud, 1759–60.

Etheridge, Jerry Haller. "The Works of Johannes de Lymburgia." 2 vols. Ph.D. dissertation, Indiana University, 1972.

Falcioni, Anna. "Malatesta, Carlo." In *Dizionario biografico degli italiani*. Rome: Istituto della Enciclopedia italiana, 1960–.

Fallows, David. "Binchois, Gilles de Bins dit," "Fedé, Johannes." In *The New Grove Dictionary of Music and Musicians*. 2nd edn. London: Macmillan, 2000.

A Catalogue of Polyphonic Songs, 1415–1480. Oxford and New York: Oxford University Press, 1999.

Dufay. London: J. M. Dent, 1982.

"Songs in the Trent Codices: An Optimistic Checklist." In *I codici musicali Trentini a cento anni dalla loro riscoperta: Atti del Convegno Laurence Feininger, la musicologia come missione*, edited by Nino Pirrotta and Danilo Curti, 170–79. Trent: Provincia autonomo di Trento, Servizio di beni culturali, Museo provinciale d'arte, 1986.

"Specific Information on the Ensembles for Composed Polyphony." In *Studies in the Performance of Late Mediaeval Music*, edited by Stanley Boorman, 109–59. Cambridge: Cambridge University Press, 1983.

"Walter Frye's *Ave regina celorum* and the Latin Song Style." In *"Et facciam dolçi canti": Studi in onore di Agostino Ziino in occasione del suo 65 compleanno,* edited by Bianca Maria Antolini, Teresa M. Gialdroni, and Annunziato Pugliese. 2 vols., vol. I, 331–45. Lucca: Libreria musicale italiana, 2003.

Finot, Jules, ed. *Inventaire sommaire des Archives départementales antérieures à 1790, Nord. Archives civiles. Série B.* Vol. VIII. Lille: L. Daniel, 1895.

Fischer, Kurt von. "Zur Anwendung der musikethnologischen Begriffe von 'Use' und 'Function' auf die historische Musikwissenschaft und Musikgeschichts-schreibung." *Die Musikforschung* 30 (1977): 148–51.

Ford, Wyn K. "Some Wills of English Musicians of the Fifteenth and Sixteenth Centuries." *RMA Research Chronicle* 5 (1965): 80–84.

Fortescue, A. "Postcommunion." In *The Catholic Encyclopedia.* New York: Robert Appleton, 1911.

Gailliard, Jean Jacques. *Inscriptions funéraires & monumentales de la Flandre occidentale; avec des données historiques & généologiques.* 2 vols. Bruges: Gailliard, 1861–67.

Gallo, F. Alberto, and Giovanni Mantese. *Ricerche sulle origini della cappella musicale del duomo di Vicenza.* Venice and Rome: Istituto per la collaborazione culturale, 1964.

Gancarczyk, Pawel. "The Links between the Strahov Codex and Austria and the Imperial Court of Frederick III." *Muzyka* 49 (2004): 79–88.

Gennep, Arnold van. *The Rites of Passage.* Trans. Monika B. Vizedom and Gabrielle L. Caffee. Chicago: University of Chicago Press, 1960.

Gerber, Rebecca L., ed. *Sacred Music from the Cathedral at Trent: Trent, Museo provinciale d'arte, codex 1375 (olim 88).* Monuments of Renaissance Music 12. Chicago: University of Chicago Press, 2007.

Gerson, Jean. "The Mountain of Contemplation." In *Early Works,* 75–127. Trans. Brian Patrick McGuire. New York: Paulist Press, 1998.

Gillingham, Bryan. *The Polyphonic Sequences in Codex Wolfenbuettel 667.* Musicological Studies 35. Henryville and Ottawa: Institute of Mediaeval Music, 1982.

Grubb, John S. *First-Born of Venice.* Baltimore: Johns Hopkins University Press, 1988.

Gülke, Peter. *Guillaume Du Fay: Musik des 15. Jahrhunderts.* Stuttgart: Metzler; Kassel: Bärenreiter, 2003.

Guigo II. *The Ladder of Monks: A Letter on the Contemplative Life and Twelve Meditations.* Trans. Edmund Colledge and James Walsh. Cistercian Studies Series 48. Kalamazoo: Cistercian Publications, 1981.

Haggh, Barbara. "Guillaume Du Fay and the Evolution of the Liturgy at Cambrai Cathedral in the Fifteenth Century." In *Cantus Planus: International Musicological Society Study Group: Papers Read at the Fourth Meeting, Pécs, Hungary, 3–8 September 1990,* edited by László Dobszay and A. Papp, 549–69. Budapest: Hungarian Academy of Sciences Institute for Musicology, 1992.

"Music, Liturgy, and Ceremony in Brussels, 1350–1500." Ph.D. dissertation, University of Illinois at Urbana-Champaign, 1988.

"Nonconformity in the Use of Cambrai Cathedral: Guillaume Du Fay's Foundations." In *The Divine Office in the Latin Middle Ages: Methodology and Source Studies, Regional Developments, Hagiography, Written in Honor of Professor Ruth Steiner*, edited by Margot E. Fassler and Rebecca Balzer, 372–97. Oxford and New York: Oxford University Press, 2000.

Hallmark, Anne. "Gratiosus, Ciconia, and Other Musicians at Padua Cathedral: Some Footnotes to Present Knowledge." In *L'Ars nova italiana del Trecento VI: Atti del Congresso internazionale "L'Europa e la musica del Trecento," Certaldo, Palazzo Pretorio, 19–21 luglio 1984*, edited by Giulio Cattin, 69–84. Certaldo: Polis, 1990.

Hamm, Charles, and Ann Besser Scott. "A Study and Inventory of the Manuscript Modena, Biblioteca Estense, α.X.1.11 (ModB)." *Musica Disciplina* 26 (1972): 101–43.

Harper, John. *The Forms and Orders of Western Liturgy from the Tenth to the Eighteenth Century*. Oxford: Clarendon Press, 1991.

Harrison, Frank Ll. *Music in Medieval Britain*, 4th edn. Buren, the Netherlands: Frits Knuf, 1980.

Harriss, G. L. *Cardinal Beaufort: A Study of Lancastrian Ascendancy and Decline*. Oxford: Clarendon Press, 1988.

Hazlitt, William Carew. *The Venetian Republic: Its Rise, Its Growth, and Its Fall*. 2 vols. London: Adam and Charles Black, 1900.

Herbenus, Mattheus. *De natura cantus ac miraculis vocis*. Edited by Joseph Smits van Waesberghe. Beiträge zur Rheinischen Musikgeschichte 22. Cologne: Arno Volk, 1957.

Holford-Strevens, Leofranc. "Du Fay the Poet? Problems in the Texts of his Motets." *Early Music History* 16 (1997): 97–165.

Translations for New London Chamber Choir, *The Brightest Heaven of Invention: Flemish Polyphony of the High Renaissance*. CD sound recording. Amon Ra Records, CD SAR-52, 1992.

Hopper, Vincent F. *Medieval Number Symbolism: Its Sources, Meaning, and Influence on Thought and Expression*. New York: Columbia University Press, 1938.

Houdoy, Jules. *Histoire artistique de la Cathédrale de Cambrai, ancienne église métropolitaine Notre-Dame*. Facsimile reprint. Lille, 1880; Geneva: Minkoff, 1972.

Howlett, David. Notes to Orlando Consort, *Dunstaple*. CD sound recording. Metronome MET CD 1009, 1995.

Hughes, Andrew, and Margaret Bent. "The Old Hall Manuscript." *Musica Disciplina* 21 (1967): 97–147.

Huglo, Michel. *Les manuscrits du processionnal*. 2 vols. RISM B IV. Munich: G. Henle, 1999.

Huot, Sylvia. *Allegorical Play in the Old French Motet: The Sacred and the Profane in Thirteenth-Century Polyphony.* Stanford: Stanford University Press, 1997.

Kanazawa, Masakata. "Polyphonic Music for Vespers in the Fifteenth Century." 2 vols. Ph.D. dissertation, Harvard University, 1966.

Kantorowicz, Ernst H. "The 'King's Advent' and the Enigmatic Panels in the Doors of Santa Sabina." *Art Bulletin* 26 (1944): 201–31.

Kenney, Sylvia. *Walter Frye and the "contenance angloise".* New Haven: Yale University Press, 1964.

Kipling, Gordon. *Enter the King: Theatre, Liturgy, and Ritual in the Medieval Civic Triumph.* Oxford: Clarendon Press, 1998.

Kirkman, Andrew. *The Cultural Life of the Early Polyphonic Mass: Medieval Context to Modern Revival.* Cambridge: Cambridge University Press, 2010.

   "The Invention of the Cyclic Mass." *Journal of the American Musicological Society* 54 (2001): 1–47.

Kirkman, Andrew, and Philip Weller. "Review: Binchois's Texts." *Music and Letters* 77 (1996): 566–96.

Kohl, Benjamin G. "Government and Society in Renaissance Padua." *Journal of Medieval and Renaissance Studies* 2 (1972): 205–21.

   Padua under the Carrara, 1318–140. Baltimore and London: Johns Hopkins Press, 1998.

Laborde, Léon Marquis de. *Les ducs de Bourgogne: Études sur les letters, les arts et l'industrie pendant le XVe siècle et plus particulièrement dans les Pays-Bas et le duché de Bourgogne.* 2 parts. Paris: Plon Frères, 1849–52.

Lacroix, Paul. *Military and Religious Life in the Middle Ages and the Renaissance.* London: Chapman and Hall, 1874.

Lea, Henry Charles. *A History of the Inquisition of the Middle Ages.* 3 vols. New York and London: Macmillan, 1922.

Lefferts, Peter M. "Dunstaple." In *Die Musik in Geschichte und Gegenwart.* 2nd edn. Kassel and New York: Bärenreiter, 1998–.

Liber usualis: Missae et officii. Tournai: Desclée, 1953.

Linden, Herman vander. *Itinéraires de Philippe le Bon, duc de Bourgogne (1419–1467) et de Charles, comte de Charolais (1433–1467).* Brussels: Palais des Académies, 1940.

The Lucca Choirbook: Lucca Archivio di Stato Ms 238, Lucca Archivio arcivescovile Ms 97, Pisa Archivio arcivescovile Biblioteca Maffi cartella 11/III. Edited by Reinhard Strohm. Late Medieval and Early Renaissance Music in Facsimile 2. Chicago: University of Chicago Press, 2008.

Lütteken, Laurenz. *Guillaume Dufay und die isorhythmische Motette: Gattungstradition und Werkcharakter an der Schwelle zur Neuzeit.* Schriften zur Musikwissenschaft aus Münster 4. Hamburg and Eisenach: K. D. Wagner, 1993.

Lymburgia, Johannes de. *Four Motets: The Song of Songs.* Edited by Ann Lewis. Newton Abbot, Devon: Antico, 1985.

MacMillan, Sharon L. *Episcopal Ordination and Ecclesial Consensus*. Collegeville: Liturgical Press, 2005.

Mantese, Giovanni. *Memorie storiche della chiesa vicentina*. 5 vols. Vicenza: Istituto S. Gaetano, 1952.

Movimento di riforma ecclesiastica pretridentina nel Quattrocento Vicentino. Vicenza: Istituto S. Gaetano, 1990.

Miller, Maureen C. "The Florentine Bishop's Ritual Entry and the Origins of the Medieval Episcopal Adventus." *Revue d'histoire ecclésiastique* 96 (2002): 5–28.

"Why the Bishop of Florence Had to Get Married." *Speculum* 81 (October 2006): 1055–91.

Morrissey, Thomas E. "*Ecce sacerdos magnus*: On Welcoming a New Bishop. Three Addresses for Bishops of Padua by Franciscus Zabarella." In *Nicholas of Cusa on Christ and the Church: Essays in Memory of Chandler McCuskey Brooks*, edited by Gerald Christianson and Thomas M. Izbicki, 57–70. Leiden and New York: Brill, 1996.

Muir, Edward. *Ritual in Early Modern Europe*. 2nd edn. Cambridge: Cambridge University Press, 2005.

Murphy, James Jerome. *Rhetoric in the Middle Ages: A History of the Rhetorical Theory from Saint Augustine to the Renaissance*. Facsimile reprint. Medieval and Renaissance Texts and Studies 227. Berkeley: University of California Press, 1974; Tempe: Arizona Center for Medieval and Renaissance Studies, 2001.

Nicholas of Cusa. "Sigmum Magnum." In *Opera omnia*, vol. XVI, *Sermones I (1430–1441)*, part 2, *Sermones V–X*. Edited by Rudolf Haubst *et al.*, 144–74. Hamburg: Felix Meiner, 1973.

The Vision of God. Trans. Emma Gurney Salter. 2nd edn. New York: Frederick Ungar, 1960.

Noblitt, Thomas L. "Das Chorbuch des Nicolaus Leopold (München, Staatsbibliothek, Mus. Ms. 3154): Repertorium." *Archiv für Musikwissenschaft* 26 (1969): 169–208.

Noblitt, Thomas L., ed. *Der Kodex des Magister Nicolaus Leopold: Staatsbibliothek München Mus. MS. 3154*. 4 vols. Kassel and New York: Bärenreiter, 1987–96.

Nosow, Robert. "Du Fay and the Cultures of Renaissance Florence." In *Hearing the Motet*, edited by Dolores Pesce, 104–21. New York and Oxford: Oxford University Press, 1997.

"The Equal-Discantus Motet Style after Ciconia." *Musica Disciplina* 40 (1991): 221–75.

"Ferragut, Bertran," "Karl der Kühne." In *Die Musik in Geschichte und Gegenwart*. 2nd edn. Kassel and New York: Bärenreiter, 1998–.

"The Florid and Equal-Discantus Motet Styles of Fifteenth-Century Italy." Ph.D. dissertation, University of North Carolina at Chapel Hill, 1992.

"Le proporzioni temporali in due messe di Dufay: *Se la face ay pale* e *Ecce ancilla Domini*." *Rivista italiana di musicologia* 28 (1993): 53–77.

"Rubeus, Petrus." In *The New Grove Dictionary of Music and Musicians*. 2nd edn. London: Macmillan, 2000.

"Song and the Art of Dying." *The Musical Quarterly* 82 (1998): 537–50.

Obrecht, Jacob. *New Obrecht Edition*, vol. XV, *Motets I*. Edited by Chris Maas. Utrecht: Koninklijke Vereniging voor Nederlandse Muziekgeschiedenis, 1995.

The Old Hall Manuscript. Edited by Andrew Hughes and Margaret Bent. 3 vols. Corpus mensurabilis musicae 46. Rome: American Institute of Musicology, 1969–73.

Page, Christopher. *Discarding Images: Reflections on Music and Culture in Medieval France*. Oxford: Clarendon Press, 1993.

Pesce, Luigi. *La chiesa di Treviso nel primo Quattrocento*. 3 vols. Italia sacra 37–39. Rome: Herder, 1987.

Ludovico Barbo, vescovo di Treviso (1447–1443). 2 vols. Padua: Antenore, 1969.

Phelps, Michael. "A Repertory in Exile: Pope Eugenius IV and the MS Modena, Biblioteca Estense universitaria, α.X.1.1." Ph.D. dissertation, New York University, 2008.

Pirrotta, Nino. "Il codice di Lucca, III. Il repertorio musicale," *Musica Disciplina* 5 (1951): 115–42.

Planchart, Alejandro Enrique. "The Books that Guillaume Du Fay Left to the Chapel of Saint Stephen." In *Sine musica nulla disciplina . . . Studi in onore di Giulio Cattin*, edited by Franco Bernabei and Antonio Lovato, 175–212. Padua: Poligrafo, 2008.

"Choirboys in Cambrai in the Fifteenth Century." In *Young Choristers: 650–1700*, edited by Susan Boynton and Eric Rice, 123–45. Studies in Medieval and Renaissance Music 7. Woodbridge: Boydell, 2008.

"Connecting the Dots: Guillaume Du Fay and Savoy during the Schism." *Plainchant and Medieval Music* 18 (2009): 11–32.

"Four Motets of Guillaume Du Fay in Context." In *Sleuthing the Muse: Essays in Honor of William F. Prizer*, edited by Kristine Forney and Jeremy L. Smith. Hillsdale: Pendragon, 2010.

"Guillaume Du Fay's Benefices and His Relationship to the Court of Burgundy." *Early Music History* 8 (1988): 117–71.

"Guillaume Dufay's Masses: A View of the Manuscript Traditions." In *Papers Read at the Dufay Quincentenary Conference, Brooklyn College, December 6–7, 1974*, edited by Allan W. Atlas, 26–60. New York: Dept. of Music, School of Performing Arts, Brooklyn College of the City University of New York, 1976.

"Music for the Papal Chapel in the Early Fifteenth Century." In *Papal Music and Musicians in Late Medieval and Renaissance Rome*, edited by Richard Sherr, 93–124. Oxford: Clarendon Press; Washington, DC: The Library of Congress, 1998.

"Notes on Guillaume Du Fay's Last Works." *Journal of Musicology* 13 (1995): 55–72.

Polak, Emil J. "Dictamen." In *Dictionary of the Middle Ages*, edited by Joseph R. Strayer. New York: Scribner's, 1989.

Processionale ad usum insignis ac praeclarae ecclesiae Sarum. Edited by William G. Henderson. Facsimile reprint. Leeds: M'Corquodale, 1882; Farnborough, Hants.: Gregg International, 1969.

Pycke, Jacques. *Sons, couleurs, odeurs dans la cathédrale de Tournai au 15e siècle.* 2 vols. Bibliothèque de la Revue d'histoire ecclésiastique 84. Brussels: Nauwelaerts, 2004.

Quatuor principalia. In *Scriptorum de musica medii aevi nova series a Gerbertina altera.* 4 vols. Edited by Edmund de Coussemaker, vol. IV, 200–06. Paris: Durand, 1864–76.

Ramalingam, Vivian S. "*Nuper rosarum flores*, Brunelleschi's Dome, and the Iconography of Mary." Unpublished paper delivered at the Annual Meeting of the Renaissance Society of America, Florence, Italy, 2000.

Rando, Daniela. "Ceremonial Episcopal Entrances in Fifteenth-Century North-Central Italy: Images, Symbols, Allegories." In *Religious Ceremonials and Images: Power and Social Meaning (1400–1750)*, edited by José Pedro Paiva, 27–46. Coimbra: Palimage Editores, 2002.

Reaney, Gilbert, ed. *Early Fifteenth-Century Music.* Corpus mensurabilis musicae 11. 7 vols. Neuhausen-Stuttgart: American Institute of Musicology, 1955–83.

Reinburg, Virginia. "Popular Prayers in Late Medieval and Reformation France." Ph.D. dissertation, Princeton University, 1985.

"Prayer and the Book of Hours." In *Time Sanctified: The Book of Hours in Medieval Art and Life*, edited by Roger S. Wieck, 39–43. New York: George Braziller, 1988.

Rendle, William. *Old Southwark and Its People.* London: Drewett, 1878.

Reynolds, Christopher A. *Papal Patronage and the Music of St. Peter's, 1380–1513.* Berkeley and Los Angeles: University of California Press, 1995.

Ringbom, Sixten. *Icon to Narrative: The Rise of the Dramatic Close-up in Fifteenth-Century Devotional Painting.* Abo: Abo Akademy, 1965.

Robertson, Anne Walters. *Guillaume de Machaut and Reims: Context and Meaning in His Musical Works.* Cambridge: Cambridge University Press, 2002.

Rothenberg, David J. "Marian Feasts, Seasons, and Songs in Medieval Polyphony: Studies in Musical Symbolism." Ph.D. dissertation, Yale University, 2004.

"The Marian Symbolism of Spring, ca. 1200–ca. 1500: Two Case Studies." *Journal of the American Musicological Society* 59 (2006): 319–98.

Rothenbuhler, Eric W. *Ritual Communication: From Everyday Conversation to Mediated Ceremony.* Thousand Oaks: Sage, 2000.

Rothstein, Bret Louis. *Sight and Spirituality in Early Netherlandish Painting.* Cambridge: Cambridge University Press, 2005.

Rubin, Miri. *Corpus Christi: The Eucharist in Late Medieval Culture.* Cambridge: Cambridge University Press, 1991.

Sachs, Klaus-Jürgen. "Herbenus, Mattheus." In *Die Musik in Geschichte und Gegenwart*. 2nd edn. Kassel and New York: Bärenreiter, 1998–.

Salokar, Douglas. "*Ad augmentationem divini cultus*: Pious Foundations and Vespers Motets in the Church of Our Lady in Bruges." In *Musicologie en Archiefonderzoek*, edited by Barbara Haggh, 306–25. Brussels: Archives et Bibliothèques de Belgique, 1994.

Sandon, Nick. "Fragments of Medieval Polyphony at Canterbury Cathedral." *Musica Disciplina* 30 (1976): 37–53.

Santa Maria, Angiolgabriello. *Biblioteca e storia di quei scrittori così della città come di territorio di Vicenza*. 6 vols. Vicenza: Giovanni Battista Vendramini Mosca, 1772–82.

Saucier, Catherine. "Acclaiming Advent and *Adventus* in Johannes Brassart's Motet for Frederick III." *Early Music History* 27 (2008): 137–80.

Saunders, Suparmi Elizabeth. *The Dating of the Trent Codices from Their Watermarks*. New York: Garland, 1989.

Saviolo, Pietro. *Thesaurus urbis Paduanae*. Padua: Frombotti, 1682.

Scandaletti, Tiziana. "L'ufficio di Giuliano da Spira per S. Antonio: Problemi di ecdotica." In *Contributi per la storia della musica sacra a Padova*, edited by Giulio Cattin and Antonio Lovato, 93–114. Padua: Istituto per la storia ecclesiastica padovana, 1993.

Schimmel, Annemarie. *The Mystery of Numbers*. New York: Oxford University Press, 1993.

Schlager, Karl-Heinz, ed. *Alleluia-Melodien II ab 1100*. Monument monodica medii aevi 8. Kassel and Basel: Bärenreiter, 1987.

Schmidt-Beste, Thomas. *Textdeklamation in der Motette des 15. Jahrhunderts*. Turnhout: Brepols, 2003.

Schnith, Karl. "Musik, Liturgie, Prozession als Ausdrucksmittel der Politik Heinrichs V. von England." In *Festschrift Rudolf Bockholdt zum 60. Geburtstag*, edited by Norbert Dubowy and Sören Meyer-Eller, 41–52. Pfaffenhofen: Ludwig, 1990.

Schodt, Alphonse de. "Confrérie de Notre-Dame de l'Arbre Sec." *Annales de la Société d'Emulation de Bruges/Handelingen van het Genootschap van Geschiedenis* 28 (1876–77): 41–87.

Schrevel, Arthur C. de. *Histoire du Séminaire de Bruges*. 2 vols. Bruges: De Planck, 1895.

Sherr, Richard. "The Performance of Chant in the Renaissance and Its Interactions with Polyphony." In *Plainsong in the Age of Polyphony*, edited by Thomas Forrest Kelly, 178–208. Cambridge: Cambridge University Press, 1992.

Shevtsova, Maria. "Dialogism in the Novel and Bakhtin's Theory of Culture." *New Literary History* 23 (1992): 747–63.

Snow, Robert. "The Mass-Motet Cycle: A Mid-Fifteenth-Century Experiment." In *Essays in Musicology in Honor of Dragan Plamenac on His 70th Birthday*, edited by Robert Snow, 301–20. Pittsburgh University Press, 1969.

Sommé, Monique. *Isabelle de Portugal, duchesse de Bourgogne: Une femme au pouvoir au XVe siècle*. Villeneuve d'Ascq: Presses Universitaires du Septentrion, 1998.

Sparks, Edgar H. *Cantus Firmus in Mass and Motet, 1420–1520*. Berkeley and Los Angeles: University of California Press, 1963.

Staehelin, Martin. "Neues zu Bartholomäus Frank." In *Festschrift Arnold Geering zum 70. Geburtstag: Beiträge zur Zeit und zum Begriff des Humanismus vorwiegend aus dem Bereich der Musik*, edited by Victor Ravizza, 119–28. Berne and Stuttgart: Paul Haupt, 1972.

"Petrus Wilhelmi de Grudencz: Notes on the Coherence of His Biography, His Work, and Its Transmission." *Muzyka* 49 (2004): 9–19.

Staley, Lynn. *Languages of Power in the Age of Richard II*. University Park: Pennsylvania State University Press, 2005.

Stevens, John E. *Words and Music in the Middle Ages: Song, Narrative, Dance, and Drama, 1050–1350*. Cambridge: Cambridge University Press, 1986.

Strohm, Reinhard. "Alte Fragen und Neue Überlegungen zum Chorbuch Lucca (Lucca, Archivio di Stato, Biblioteca Manoscritti 238 =I-Las 238)." In *Musikalische Quellen – Quellen zur Musikgeschichte: Festschrift für Martin Staehelin zum 65. Geburtstag*, edited by Ulrich Konrad, 51–64. Göttingen: Vandenhoeck & Ruprecht, 2002.

Music in Late Medieval Bruges. 2nd edn. Oxford: Clarendon Press, 1990.

"Musikaal en Artistiek Beschermheerschap in het Brugse Ghilde vanden Droghen Boome." *Biekorf* 83 (1983): 5–18.

The Rise of European Music, 1380–1500. Cambridge: Cambridge University Press, 1993.

Tacconi, Marica. *Cathedral and Civic Ritual in Late Medieval and Renaissance Florence: The Service Books of Santa Maria del Fiore*. Cambridge: Cambridge University Press, 2005.

Tinctoris, Johannes. *Opera theoretica*. Edited by Albert Seay. 2 vols. Corpus scriptorum de musica 22. [Rome]: American Institute of Musicology, 1975.

Tolmie, Sarah. "*Quia hic homo multa signa facet*: Henry V's Royal Entry into London, November 23, 1415." In *The Propagation of Power in the Medieval West: Selected Proceedings of the International Conference, Groningen 20–23 November 1996*, edited by Martin Gosman, Arjo Vanderjagt, and Jan Veenstra, 363–79. Groningen: Egbert Forsten, 1997.

Trachtenberg, Marvin. "Architecture and Music Reunited: A New Reading of Dufay's *Nuper rosarum flores* and the Cathedral of Florence." *Renaissance Quarterly* 54 (2001): 740–75.

Trexler, Richard C. *Public Life in Renaissance Florence*. New York: Academic Press, 1980.

Twemlow, J. A., ed. *Calendar of Entries in the Papal Registers Relating to Great Britain and Ireland*, vol. IX, *1431–1447*. London: Public Records Office, 1912.

Calendar of Entries in the Papal Registers Relating to Great Britain and Ireland, vol. X, *1447–1455*. London: Public Records Office, 1896.

Tyler, J. Jeffery. *Lord of the Sacred City: The "Episcopus exclusus" in Late Medieval and Early Modern Germany*. Studies in Medieval and Reformation Thought, 72. Leiden and Boston: Brill, 1999.

Vicchi, Roberta. *The Major Basilicas of Rome: Saint Peter's, San Giovanni in Laterano, San Paolo fuori le Mura, Santa Maria Maggiore*. Florence: Scala, 1999.

Vidier, M. A. "Notes et documents sur le personnel, les biens et l'administration de la Sainte-Chapelle, du XIIIe au Xve siècle." *Mémoires de la Société de l'histoire de Paris et de l'Isle-de-France* 23 (1901): 213–383.

Viti, Paolo. "Dati, Leonardo." In *Dizionario biografico degli italiani*. Rome: Istituto della Enciclopedia Italiana, 1960–.

Warren, Charles W. "Brunelleschi's Dome and Dufay's Motet." *The Musical Quarterly* 44 (1973): 92–105.

Wathey, Andrew. "Dunstaple in France." *Music and Letters* 67 (1986): 1–36.

Music in the Royal and Noble Households in Late Medieval England: Studies of Sources and Patronage. New York and London: Garland, 1989.

Wegman, Rob C. *Born for the Muses: The Life and Masses of Jacob Obrecht*. Oxford: Clarendon Press, 1994.

The Crisis of Music in Early Modern Europe, 1470–1530. New York and London: Routledge, 2005.

"For Whom the Bell Tolls: Reading and Hearing in Busnoy's *Anthoni usque limina*." In *Hearing the Motet*, edited by Dolores Pesce, 122–41. Oxford and New York: Oxford University Press, 1997.

"From Maker to Composer: Improvisation and Musical Authorship in the Low Countries, 1450–1500." *Journal of the American Musicological Society* 49 (1996): 409–79.

"Mensural Intertextuality in the Sacred Music of Antoine Busnoys." In *Antoine Busnoys: Method, Meaning, and Context in Late Medieval Music*, edited by Paula Higgins, 175–214. Oxford: Clarendon Press, 1999.

"*Miserere supplicanti Dufay*: The Creation and Transmission of Guillaume Dufay's *Missa Ave regina celorum*." *Journal of Musicology* 13 (1995): 18–54.

"Musical Offerings in the Renaissance." *Early Music* 33 (2005): 425–38.

"Petrus de Domarto's *Missa Spiritus almus* and the Early History of the Four-Voice Mass in the Fifteenth Century." *Early Music History* 10 (1991): 235–303.

Weller, Philip. "Rites of Passage: *Nove cantum melodie*, the Burgundian Court, and Binchois's Early Career." In *Binchois Studies*, edited by Andrew Kirkman and Dennis Slavin, 49–83. Oxford and New York: Oxford University Press, 2000.

White, Richard James. "The Battre Section of Trent Codex 87." 2 vols. Ph.D. dissertation, Indiana University, 1975.

Wieck, Roger S., ed. *Time Sanctified: The Book of Hours in Medieval Art and Life*. New York: George Braziller, 1988.

Williams, Ethel Carleton. *My Lord of Bedford, 1389–1435*. London: Longmans, 1963.

Williamson, Magnus. "Royal Image-Making and Textual Interplay in Gilbert Banaster's *O Maria et Elizabeth.*" *Early Music History* 19 (2000): 237–78.

Wilson, Blake. "Heinrich Isaac among the Florentines." *Journal of Musicology* 23 (2006): 97–152.

Witt, Ronald. "Medieval 'ars dictaminis' and the Beginnings of Humanism: A New Construction of the Problem." *Renaissance Quarterly* 35 (1982): 1–35.

Wright, Craig. "Dufay at Cambrai: Discoveries and Revisions." *Journal of the American Musicological Society* 28 (1975): 175–229.

"Dufay's *Nuper rosarum flores*, King Solomon's Temple, and the Veneration of the Virgin." *Journal of the American Musicological Society* 47 (1994): 395–441.

"Grenon, Nicolas." *The New Grove Dictionary of Music and Musicians.* 2nd edn. London: Macmillan, 2000.

Music and Ceremony at Notre Dame of Paris, 500–1500. Cambridge: Cambridge University Press, 1989.

"The Palm Sunday Procession in Medieval Chartres." In *The Divine Office in the Latin Middle Ages: Methodology and Source Studies, Regional Developments, Hagiography, Written in Honor of Professor Ruth Steiner*, edited by Margot E. Fassler and Rebecca Balzer, 344–72. Oxford and New York: Oxford University Press, 2000.

"Performance Practices at the Cathedral of Cambrai 1475–1550." *The Musical Quarterly* 64 (1978): 295–328.

Wright, Peter. "Johannes Brassart and Johannes de Sarto." *Plainsong and Medieval Music* 1 (1992): 41–61.

Žak, Sabine. "Die Quellenwert von Gianozzo Manettis Oratio über die Domweihe von Florenz 1436 für die Musikgeschichte." *Die Musikforschung* 40 (1987): 2–32.

Zarotti, G. "Codici e corali della cattedrale di Parma." *Archivio storico per le province parmensi*, series IV, 20 (1968): 181–216.

Index